THINK!
DIVERGENT CONCEPTS ON THEORY AND PRACTICE IN EDUCATIONAL PSYCHOLOGY

THINK!
DIVERGENT CONCEPTS ON THEORY AND PRACTICE IN EDUCATIONAL PSYCHOLOGY

EDITORS

DOV LIBERMAN
ASSOCIATE PROFESSOR OF EDUCATIONAL PSYCHOLOGY
UNIVERSITY OF HOUSTON

HELEN M. GORE-LAIRD
CLINICAL THERAPIST
DePELCHIN CHILDREN'S CENTER
HOUSTON, TEXAS

SURVEY
PUBLICATIONS

NEW HAVEN

Printed in the United States of America
by Survey Publications
P.O. Box 1345
Cheshire, CT 06410

For Fax Orders only 1-888-339-3434

TABLE OF CONTENTS

PART I
Science, Theory, and Education

PART II
What Is the Teacher's Role?

PART III
Psychological Theories and
Their Applications

A. LEARNING THEORIES

B. COGNITIVE DEVELOPMENT

PART IV
Comparison of Theories

PART V
Intelligence Testing, Standardized Testing and Assessment:
The Labeling Game

The following article was reprinted with the kind and generous special permission of the *Moral Education Forum*.

Binfet, J. T., "Creating a Positive Moral Climate Within the Public School Classroom: An Application of Moral Reasoning Theory to Practice." *Moral Education Forum*, 1995, vol. 20, no. 1, 18–24.

The following article was reprinted with the kind and generous special permission of the Journal of Adult Education.

Carroll, Jan B., "Theory to Practice: Self-Efficacy Related to Transfer of Learning as an Example of Theory-Based Instructional Design." *Journal of Adult Education*, Fall 1993, vol. 22, no. 1, 37–43.

The following article was reprinted with the kind and generous special permission of the *Journal on Excellence in College Teaching*. The journal is located at Miami University in Oxford, Ohio.

Edwards, Harriet C., "Mistakes and Other Classroom Techniques: An Application of Social Learning Theory." *Journal on Excellence in College Teaching,* 1993, vol. 4, 49–60.

The following article was reprinted with the kind and generous special permission of the International Society for Technology in Education (I.S.T.E.) and the Special Interest Group for Teacher Educators (S.I.G.T.E.), both located at 1787 Agate Street, in Eugene, Oregon.

Friedman, Batya, "Social and Moral Development Through Computer Use: A Constructivist Approach." *Journal of Research on Computing in Education*, Summer 1991, vol. 23, no. 4, 560–567.

The following three articles were reprinted with the kind and generous special permission of Dr. Thomas Karger, of S. Karger Publishers, Inc., in Switzerland.

Kahn, Peter H., Jr., "Bounding the Controversies, Foundational Issues in the Study of Moral Development." *Human Development*, 1991, vol. 34, 325–341.

The following article was reprinted with the kind and generous special permission of *The Alberta Journal of Educational Research*. The journal is published by the Education Faculty of the University of Alberta in Edmonton, Alberta, Canada.

> Wangler, David G., "Is the Bell Curve a Ringer?" *The Alberta Journal of Educational Research,* September 1995, vol. 61, no. 3, 360–366.

The following articles were reprinted with the special permission from the authors/editors and/or publishers of the articles/journals indicated in the citation.

> Bell, Margaret E., "A Systematic Instructional Design Strategy Derived from Information-Processing Theory." *Educational Technology*, 1981, vol. 21, no. 3, 32–35.

> Berk, Laura E., "Vygotsky's Theory: The Importance of Make-Believe Play." *Young Children*, November 1994, vol. 50, no. 1, 30–39.

> Calfee, Robert C., "Cognitive Assessment of Classroom Learning." *Education and Urban Society*, August 1994, vol. 26, no. 4, 340–351.

> Cooper, Eric J., "Toward a New Mainstream of Instruction for American Schools." *Journal of Negro Education*, vol. 58, no. 1, 102–116.

> Daly, Norene F., *Andragogy: Implications for Secondary and Adult Education Programs*. ERIC, ED186 627.

> Durica, Karen Morrow, "The Labeled Child." *Reading Teacher*, 1995, 503.

> Goodman, Gay, and Mary Jo Poillion, "ADD: Acronym for Any Dysfunction or Difficulty." *Journal of Special Education*, 1992, vol. 26, no. 1, 37–56.

> Gore-Laird, Helen M., "The Development of the Ego: Implications for Educational Settings."

> Hilliard, Asa G., "What Good is This Thing Called Intelligence and Why Bother to Measure It?" *Journal of Black Psychology*, November 1994, vol. 20, no. 4, 430–444.

Howard-Hamilton, Mary F., "A Just and Democratic Community Approach to Moral Education: Developing Voices of Reason and Responsibility." *Elementary School Guidance and Counseling*, December 1995, vol. 30, 118–130.

Kamii, Constance, *The Scientific Foundation of Education.* Paper presented at a celebration in Honor of Jean Piaget, sponsored by the Erikson Institute of Loyola University and The University of Chicago Press, Chicago, Illinois, 5 December 1980, ERIC, ED 198 948.

Piaget, Jean, and Elizabeth Duckworth, "Piaget Takes a Teacher's Look." *Learning*, 1974, vol. 2, no. 2, 22–27.

Rogers, Carl B., "Questions I Would Ask Myself If I Were a Teacher." *Education*, 1974, vol. 95, no. 2, 134–139.

Strauss, Sidney, "Theories of Learning and Development for Academics and Educators." *Education Psychologist*, 1993, vol. 28, no. 3, 191–203.

Taylor, George R., *Integrating Social Learning Theory with Educating the Deprived.* ERIC, ED 349 260.

Taylor, Ron, "Intellectual Assessment Tips." *Diagnostique*, 1990, vol. 16, 52–54. Copyright by The Council for Exceptional Children.

Van Ryn, Michelle and Catherine A. Heaney, "What's the Use of Theory?" *Health Education Quarterly*, Fall 1992, vol. 19, no. 3, 315–330.

Warner, Allen R., *Maslow and Field Experiences in Competency-based Teacher Education.* Paper presented at the 1975 annual conference of the Association of Teacher Educators, New Orleans, Louisiana, 6 February 1975, ERIC, ED 132 152.

Wilgenbusch, Nancy, *Maslow's Concept of Peak Experience Education: Impossible Myth or Possible Mission?* ERIC, ED 199–250.

Zachary, G. Pascal, "Male Order: Boys Used to Be Boys, But Do Some Now See Boyhood as a Malady?" *The Wall Street Journal*, 2 May 1997, A1, A6.

The editors and publisher wish to note that rather than attempt to alter the style used by the original authors of the articles for this text, the works were copied as initially published, including errors, if any. Each of the original authors used his or her own style in capitalizing. They often did not follow a standardized method regarding the use of hyphens when referring to ethnic groups such as Mexican-Americans, or possessive forms such as Piagetian or Piagetan. The same applied to punctuation marks such as a tilde or accent, as in Onate/Oñate or Jose/José, or to periods falling before or after a parenthetical reference. All of the grammatical choices and spellings are the initial authors' own as well. Any choice of name for an ethnic group such as Indians, American Indians, Native Americans, or Amerindians are the original authors' own decision. We sought to accurately portray the original published work of fellow academicians, whether such references might be deemed by others as proper or improper. Despite numerous efforts at proofing, mistakes will inevitably occur. Therefore, the editors and publisher apologize in advance for any copying errors in this text.

PREFACE

*It ain't what you don't know that hurts you. Its what you do know
that just ain't so. . . .*

Artemis Ward

Teacher training courses that focus on teaching techniques and methods of
classroom management constitute the bulk of most teacher education programs. They are largely concerned with answering the question, "How do
I do this?" While there can be no doubt that such courses are an essential
part of teacher training, this book is dedicated to the proposition that to be
effective educators, teachers and other educational practitioners must have
an understanding of the theories that underlie educational practices. The
techniques one implements, the materials one uses, indeed the very purpose
of education itself, should all be the direct result of one's understanding of
human development and learning. Educators who are uninformed by theory
have little rationale to justify what they are doing in the classroom or in
other educational settings. Neither do they have a basis upon which to evaluate practice or program.

This reader was constructed with several purposes in mind. It is intended to present educators with an overview of various psychological theories and how they influence educational goals and methods. It is our hope
that it will be a tool that readers can use to construct their own philosophy
of learning, development and education. We have also included articles
which critically examine current educational practices. Teachers who understand psychological theory, and practice that is informed by theory, can
become critical consumers of educational programs and methods rather
than passive recipients of whatever new idea or curriculum that comes
along. Teachers who are aware of the logical and theoretical problems with
current school routines can help implement effective change rather than
participate in ineffective or even harmful undertakings.

We admit to our own philosophy of education. We believe that the
primary purpose of schools should be to help children reason, understand,

and analyze critically and effectively training them rather than (while building their self-esteem), to give predetermined correct answers. It is our goal to provide educators with information that can help them turn children into better thinkers. But perhaps an even more important purpose of this book is to stimulate educators to become thinkers themselves.

We hope that this book will lead to the asking of questions other than the overused . . . "How?"

Instead, it is our hope that it will stimulate educators to ask these important questions:

1. Why is this being taught?
2. What is the theory of human learning and development reflected by this program?
3. Do I agree with that theory?
4. How do you know that is true?
5. Does that make sense?
6. Is this practice in the best interests of the child?

Those who do not ask these questions, who do not consider theory before acting, will find themselves operating on the basis of myth, conjecture, guesswork, and incorrect information. Critical thinking is the building block to knowledge and accurate understanding. This reader is presented in the hope that it will help educators and future educators gain some of that understanding.

Dov Liberman and Helen M. Gore-Laird

PART I

SCIENCE, THEORY, AND EDUCATION

TEN MYTHS OF SCIENCE: REEXAMINING WHAT WE THINK WE KNOW ABOUT THE NATURE OF SCIENCE

by William F. McComas
University of Southern California

This article addresses and attempts to refute several of the most wide-spread and enduring misconceptions held by students regarding the enterprise of science. The ten myths discussed include the common notions that theories become law, that hypotheses are best characterized as educated guesses, and that there is a commonly-applied scientific method. In addition, the article includes discussion of other incorrect ideas such as the view that evidence leads to sure knowledge, that science and its methods provide absolute proof, and that science is not a creative endeavor. Finally, the myths that scientists are objective, that experiments are the sole route to scientific knowledge and that scientific conclusions are continually reviewed conclude this presentation. The paper ends with a plea that instruction in and opportunities to experience the nature of science are vital in preservice and inservice teacher education programs to help unseat the myths of science.

Myths are typically defined as traditional views, fables, legends or stories. As such, myths can be entertaining and even educational since they help people make sense of the world. In fact, the explanatory role of myths most likely accounts for their development, spread and persistence. However, when fact and fiction blur, myths lose their entertainment value and serve only to block full understanding. Such is the case with the myths of science.

Scholar Joseph Campbell (1968) has proposed that the similarity among many folk myths worldwide is due to a subconscious link between

3

all peoples, but no such link can explain the myths of science. Misconceptions about science are most likely due to the lack of philosophy of science content in teacher education programs, the failure of such programs to provide and require authentic science experiences for preservice teachers and the generally shallow treatment of the nature of science in the precollege textbooks to which teachers might turn for guidance.

As Steven Jay Gould points out in *The Case of the Creeping Fox Terrier Clone* (1988), science textbook writers are among the most egregious purveyors of myth and inaccuracy. The fox terrier mentioned in the title refers to the classic comparison used to express the size of the dawn horse, the tiny precursor to the modern horse. This comparison is unfortunate for two reasons. Not only was this horse ancestor much bigger than a fox terrier, but the fox terrier breed of dog is virtually unknown to American students. The major criticism leveled by Gould is that once this comparison took hold, no one bothered to check its validity or utility. Through time, one author after another simply repeated the inept comparison and continued a tradition that has made many science texts virtual clones of each other on this and countless other points.

In an attempt to provide a more realistic view of science and point out issues on which science teachers should focus, this article presents and discusses 10 widely-held, yet incorrect ideas about the nature of science. There is no implication that all students, or most teachers for that matter, hold all of these views to be true, nor is the list meant to be the definitive catalog. Cole (1986) and Rothman (1992) have suggested additional misconceptions worthy of consideration. However, years of science teaching and the review of countless texts has substantiated the validity of the inventory presented here.

MYTH 1: HYPOTHESES BECOME THEORIES WHICH BECOME LAWS

This myth deals with the general belief that with increased evidence there is a developmental sequence through which scientific ideas pass on their way to final acceptance. Many believe that scientific ideas pass through the hypothesis and theory stages and finally mature as laws. A former U.S. president showed his misunderstanding of science by saying that he was not troubled by the idea of evolution because it was "just a theory." The president's misstatement is the essence of this myth; that an idea is not worthy of consideration until "lawness" has been bestowed upon it.

The problem created by the false hierarchical nature inherent in this myth is that theories and laws are very different kinds of knowledge. Of course there is a relationship between laws and theories, but one simply does not become the other—no matter how much empirical evidence is amassed. Laws are generalizations, principles or patterns in nature and theories are the explanations of those generalizations (Rhodes & Schaible, 1989; Homer & Rubba, 1979; Campbell, 1953).

For instance, Newton described the relationship of mass and distance to gravitational attraction between objects with such precision that we can use the law of gravity to plan spaceflights. During the Apollo 8 mission, astronaut Bill Anders responded to the question of who was flying the spacecraft by saying, "I think Isaac Newton is doing most of the driving right now" (Chaikin, 1994). His response was understood by all to mean that the capsule was simply following the basic laws of physics described by Isaac Newton centuries earlier.

The more thorny, and many would say more interesting, issue with respect to gravity is the explanation for why the law operates as it does. At this point, there is no well-accepted theory of gravity. Some physicists suggest that gravity waves are the correct explanation for the law of gravity, but with clear confirmation and consensus lacking, most feel that the theory of gravity still eludes science. Interestingly, Newton addressed the distinction between law and theory with respect to gravity. Although he had discovered the law of gravity, he refrained from speculating publicly about its cause. In *Principial*, Newton states ". . . I have not been able to discover the cause of these properties of gravity from phenomena, and I frame no hypothesis . . ." ". . . it is enough that gravity does really exist, and acts according to the laws which we have explained . . ." (Newton, 1720/1946).

MYTH 2: A HYPOTHESIS IS AN EDUCATED GUESS

The definition of the term hypothesis has taken on an almost mantra-like life of its own in science classes. If a hypothesis is always an educated guess as students typically assert, the question remains, "an educated guess about what?" The best answer for this question must be, that without a clear view of the context in which the term is used, it is impossible to tell.

The term hypothesis has at least three definitions, and for that reason, should be abandoned, or at least used with caution. For instance, when Newton said that he framed no hypothesis as to the cause of gravity he was saying that he had no speculation about an explanation of why the law of gravity operates as it does. In this case, Newton used the term hypothesis to represent an immature theory.

As a solution to the hypothesis problem, Sonleitner (1989) suggested that tentative or trial laws be called generalizing hypotheses with provisional theories referred to as explanatory hypotheses. Another approach would be to abandon the word hypothesis altogether in favor of terms such as speculative law or speculative theory. With evidence, generalizing hypotheses may become laws and speculative theories become theories, but under no circumstances do theories become laws. Finally, when students are asked to propose a hypothesis during a laboratory experience, the term now means a prediction. As for those hypotheses that are really forecasts, perhaps they should simply be called what they are, predictions.

MYTH 3: A GENERAL AND UNIVERSAL SCIENTIFIC METHOD EXISTS

The notion that a common series of steps is followed by all research scientists must be among the most pervasive myths of science given the appearance of such a list in the introductory chapters of many precollege texts. This myth has been part of the folklore of school science ever since its proposal by statistician Karl Pearson (1937). The steps listed for the scientific method vary from text to text but usually include . . .

1) define the problem,
2) gather background information,
3) form a hypothesis,
4) make observations,
5) test the hypothesis, and
6) draw conclusions.

Some texts conclude their list of the steps of the scientific method by listing communication of results as the final ingredient.

One of the reasons for the widespread belief in a general scientific method may be the way in which results are presented for publication in research journals. The standardized style makes it appear that scientists follow a standard research plan. Medawar (1990) reacted to the common style exhibited by research papers by calling the scientific paper a fraud since the final journal report rarely outlines the actual way in which the problem was investigated.

Philosophers of science who have studied scientists at work have shown that no research method is applied universally (Carey, 1994; Gibbs & Lawson, 1992; Chalmers, 1990; Gjertsen, 1989). The notion of a single scientific method is so pervasive it seems certain that many students must be disappointed when they discover that scientists do not have a framed copy of the steps of the scientific method posted high above each laboratory workbench.

Close inspection will reveal that scientists approach and solve problems with imagination, creativity, prior knowledge and perseverance. These, of course, are the same methods used by all problem-solvers. The lesson to be learned is that science is no different from other human endeavors when puzzles are investigated. Fortunately, this is one myth that may eventually be displaced since many newer texts are abandoning or augmenting the list in favor of discussions of methods of science.

MYTH 4: EVIDENCE ACCUMULATED CAREFULLY WILL RESULT IN SURE KNOWLEDGE

All investigators, including scientists, collect and interpret empirical evidence through the process called induction. This is a technique by which individual pieces of evidence are collected and examined until a law is discovered or a theory is invented. Useful as this technique is, even a preponderance of evidence does not guarantee the production of valid knowledge because of what is called the problem of induction.

Induction was first formalized by Frances Bacon in the 17th century. In his book, *Novum Organum* (1620/1952), Bacon advised that facts be assimilated without bias to reach a conclusion. The method of induction he suggested is the principal way in which humans traditionally have produced generalizations that permit predictions. What then is the problem with induction?

It is both impossible to make all observations pertaining to a given situation and illogical to secure all relevant facts for all time, past, present and future. However, only by making all relevant observations throughout all time, could one say that a final valid conclusion had been made. This is the problem of induction. On a personal level, this problem is of little consequence, but in science the problem is significant. Scientists formulate laws and theories that are supposed to hold true in all places and for all time but the problem of induction makes such a guarantee impossible.

The proposal of a new law begins through induction as facts are heaped upon other relevant facts. Deduction is useful in checking the validity of a law. For example, if we postulate that all swans are white, we can evaluate the law by predicting that the next swan found will also be white. If it is, the law is supported, but not proved as will be seen in the discussion of another science myth. Locating even a single black swan will cause the law to be called into question.

The nature of induction itself is another interesting aspect associated with this myth. If we set aside the problem of induction momentarily, there is still the issue of how scientists make the final leap from the mass of evidence to the conclusion. In an idealized view of induction, the accumulated evidence will simply result in the production of a new law or theory in a procedural or mechanical fashion. In reality, there is no such method. The issue is far more complex—and interesting—than that. The final creative leap from evidence to scientific knowledge is the focus of another myth of science.

MYTH 5: SCIENCE AND ITS METHODS PROVIDE ABSOLUTE PROOF

The general success of the scientific endeavor suggests that its products must be valid. However, a hallmark of scientific knowledge is that it is subject to revision when new information is presented. Tentativeness is one of the points that differentiates science from other forms of knowledge. Accumulated evidence can provide support, validation and substantiation for a law or theory, but will never prove those laws and theories to be true. This idea has been addressed by Home and Rubba (1978) and Lopushinsky (1993).

The problem of induction argues against proof in science, but there is another element of this myth worth exploring. In actuality, the only truly conclusive knowledge produced by science results when a notion is falsified. What this means is that no matter what scientific idea is considered, once evidence begins to accumulate, at least we know that the notion is untrue. Consider the example of the white swans discussed earlier. One could search the world and see only white swans, and arrive at the generalization that "all swans are white." However, the discovery of one black swan has the potential to overturn, or at least result in modifications of, this proposed law of nature. However, whether scientists routinely try to falsify their notions and how much contrary evidence it takes for a scientist's mind to change are issues worth exploring.

MYTH 6: SCIENCE IS PROCEDURAL MORE THAN CREATIVE

We accept that no single guaranteed method of science can account for the success of science, but realize that induction, the collection and interpretation of individual facts providing the raw materials for laws and theories, is at the foundation of most scientific endeavors. This awareness brings with it a paradox. If induction itself is not a guaranteed method for arriving at conclusions, how do scientists develop useful laws and theories?

Induction makes use of individual facts that are collected, analyzed and examined. Some observers may perceive a pattern in these data and propose a law in response, but there is no logical or procedural method by which the pattern is suggested. With a theory, the issue is much the same. Only the creativity of the individual scientist permits the discovery of laws and the invention of theories. If there truly was a single scientific method, two individuals with the same expertise could review the same facts and reach identical conclusions. There is no guarantee of this because the range and nature of creativity is a personal attribute.

Unfortunately, many common science teaching orientations and methods serve to work against the creative element in science. The majority of laboratory exercises, for instance, are verification activities. The teacher discusses what will happen in the laboratory, the manual provides step-by-step directions, and the student is expected to arrive at a particular answer. Not only is this approach the antithesis of the way in which science actually operates, but such a portrayal must seem dry, clinical and uninteresting to many students. In her book, *They're Not Dumb, They're Different* (1990) Sheila Tobias argues that many capable and clever students reject science as a career because they are not given an opportunity to see it as an exciting and creative pursuit. The moral in Tobias' thesis is that science itself may be impoverished when students who feel a need for a creative outlet eliminate it as a potential career because of the way it is taught.

MYTH 7: SCIENCE AND ITS METHODS CAN ANSWER ALL QUESTIONS

Philosophers of science have found it useful to refer to the work of Karl Popper (1968) and his principle of falsifiability to provide an operational definition of science. Popper believed that only those ideas that are potentially falsifiable are scientific ideas.

For instance, the law of gravity states that more massive objects exert a stronger gravitational attraction than do objects with less mass when distance is held constant. This is a scientific law because it could be falsified if newly-discovered objects operate differently with respect to gravitational attraction. In contrast, the core idea among creationists is that species were placed on earth fully-formed by some supernatural entity. Obviously, there is no scientific method by which such a belief could be shown to be false. Since this special creation view is impossible to falsify, it is not science at all and the term creation science is an oxymoron. Creation science is a religious belief and as such, does not require that it be falsifiable. Hundreds of years ago thoughtful theologians and scientists carved out their sphere of influence and have since coexisted with little acrimony. Today, only those who fail to understand the distinction between science and religion confuse the rules, roles, and limitations of these two important world views.

It should now be clear that some questions simply must not be asked of scientists. During a recent creation science trial for instance, Nobel laureates were asked to sign a statement about the nature of science to provide some guidance to the court. These famous scientists responded resoundingly to support such a statement; after all, they were experts in the realm of science (Klayman, Slocombe, Lehman, & Kaufman, 1986). Later, those interested in citing expert opinion in the abortion debate asked scientists to issue a statement regarding their feelings on this issue.

Wisely, few participated. Science cannot answer the moral and ethical questions engendered by the matter of abortion. Of course, scientists as individuals have personal opinions about many issues, but as a group they must remain silent if those issues are outside the realm of scientific inquiry. Science simply cannot address moral, ethical, aesthetic, social and metaphysical questions.

MYTH 8: SCIENTISTS ARE PARTICULARLY OBJECTIVE

Scientists are no different in their level of objectivity than are other professionals. They are careful in the analysis of evidence and in the procedures applied to arrive at conclusions. With this admission, it may seem that this myth is valid, but contributions from both the philosophy of science and psychology reveal that there are at least three major reasons that make complete objectivity impossible.

Many philosophers of science support Popper's (1963) view that science can advance only through a string of what he called conjectures and refutations. In other words, scientists should propose laws and theories as conjectures and then actively work to disprove or refute those ideas. Popper suggests that the absence of contrary evidence, demonstrated through an active program of refutation, will provide the best support available. It may seem like a strange way of thinking about verification, but the absence of disproof is considered support. There is one major problem with the idea of conjecture and refutation. Popper seems to have proposed it as a recommendation for scientists not as a description of what scientists do. From a philosophical perspective the idea is sound, but there are no indications that scientists actively practice programs to search for disconfirming evidence.

Another aspect of the inability of scientists to be objective is found in theory-laden observation, a psychological notion (Hodson, 1986). Scientists, like all observers, hold a myriad of preconceptions and biases about the way the world operates. These notions, held in the subconscious, affect everyone's ability to make observations. It is impossible to collect and interpret facts without any bias. There have been countless cases in the history of science in which scientists have failed to include particular observations in their final analyses of phenomena. This occurs, not because of fraud or deceit, but because of the prior knowledge possessed by the individual. Certain facts either were not seen at all or were deemed unimportant based on the scientist's prior knowledge. In earlier discussions of induction, we postulated that two individuals reviewing the same data would not be expected to reach the same conclusions. Not only does individual creativity play a role, but the issue of personal theory-laden observation further complicates the situation.

This lesson has clear implications for science teaching. Teachers typically provide learning experiences for students without considering their prior knowledge. In the laboratory, for instance, students are asked to perform activities, make observations and then form conclusions. There is an expectation that the conclusions formed will be both self-evident and uniform. In other words, teachers anticipate that the data will lead all pupils to the same conclusion. This could only happen if each student had the same exact prior conceptions and made and evaluated observations using identical schemes. This does not happen in science nor does it occur in the science classroom.

Related to the issue of theory-based observations is the allegiance to the paradigm. Thomas Kuhn (1970), in his ground-breaking analysis of the history of science, shows that scientists work within a research tradition called a paradigm. This research tradition, shared by those working in a given discipline, provides clues to the questions worth investigating, dictates what evidence is admissible and prescribes the tests and techniques that are reasonable. Although the paradigm provides direction to the research it may also stifle or limit investigation. Anything that confines the research endeavor necessarily limits objectivity. While there is no conscious desire on the part of scientists to limit discussion, it is likely that some new ideas in science are rejected because of the paradigm issue. When research reports are submitted for publication they are reviewed by other members of the discipline. Ideas from outside the paradigm are liable to be eliminated from consideration as crackpot or poor science and thus do not appear in print.

Examples of scientific ideas that were originally rejected because they fell outside the accepted paradigm include the sun-centered solar system, warm-bloodedness in dinosaurs, the germ-theory of disease, and continental drift. When first proposed early in this century by Alfred Wegener, the idea of moving continents, for example, was vigorously rejected. Scientists were not ready to embrace a notion so contrary to the traditional teaching of their discipline. Continental drift was finally accepted in the 1960s with the proposal of a mechanism or theory to explain how continental plates move (Hallam, 1975 and Menard, 1986). This fundamental change in the earth sciences, called a revolution by Kuhn, might have occurred decades earlier had it not been for the strength of the paradigm.

It would be unwise to conclude a discussion of scientific paradigms on a negative note. Although the examples provided do show the contrary aspects associated with paradigm-fixity, Kuhn would argue that the blinders created by allegiance to the paradigm help keep scientists on track. His review of the history of science demonstrates that paradigms are responsible for more successes in science than delays.

MYTH 9: EXPERIMENTS ARE THE PRINCIPLE ROUTE TO SCIENTIFIC KNOWLEDGE

Throughout their school science careers, students are encouraged to associate science with experimentation. Virtually all hands-on experiences that students have in science class are called experiments even if it would be more accurate to refer to these exercises as technical procedures, explorations or activities. True experiments involve carefully orchestrated procedures along with control and test groups usually with the goal of establishing a cause and effect relationship. Of course, true experimentation is a useful tool in science, but is not the sole route to knowledge.

Many note-worthy scientists have used non-experimental techniques to advance knowledge. In fact, in a number of science disciplines, true experimentation is not possible because of the inability to control variables. Many fundamental discoveries in astronomy are based on extensive observations rather than experiments. Copernicus and Kepler changed our view of the solar system using observational evidence derived from lengthy and detailed observations frequently contributed by other scientists, but neither performed experiments.

Charles Darwin punctuated his career with an investigatory regime more similar to qualitative techniques used in the social sciences than the experimental techniques commonly associated with the natural sciences. For his most revolutionary discoveries, Darwin recorded his extensive observations in notebooks annotated by speculations and thoughts about those observations. Although Darwin supported the inductive method proposed by Bacon, he was aware that observation without speculation or prior understanding was both ineffective and impossible. The techniques advanced by Darwin have been widely used by scientists Goodall and Fossey in their primate studies. Scientific knowledge is gained in a variety of ways including observation, analysis, speculation, library investigation and experimentation.

MYTH 10: ALL WORK IN SCIENCE IS REVIEWED TO KEEP THE PROCESS HONEST

Frequently, the final step in the traditional scientific method is that researchers communicate their results so that others may learn from and evaluate their research. When completing laboratory reports, students are frequently told to present their methods section so clearly that others could repeat the activity. The conclusion that students will likely draw from this request is that professional scientists are also constantly reviewing each other's experiments to check up on each other. Unfortunately, while such a check and balance system would be useful, the number of findings from one scientist checked by others is vanishingly small. In reality, most scientists are simply too busy and research funds too limited for this type of review.

The result of the lack of oversight has recently put science itself under suspicion. With the pressures of academic tenure, personal competition and funding, it is not surprising that instances of outright scientific fraud do occur. However, even without fraud, the enormous amount of original scientific research published, and the pressure to produce new information rather than reproduce others' work dramatically increases the chance that errors will go unnoticed.

An interesting corollary to this myth is that scientists rarely report valid, but negative results. While this is understandable given the space limitations in scientific journals, the failure to report what did not work is a problem. Only when those working in a particular scientific discipline have access to all of the information regarding a phenomenon—both positive and negative—can the discipline progress.

CONCLUSIONS

If, in fact, students and many of their teachers hold these myths to be true, we have strong support for a renewed focus on science itself rather than just its facts and principles in science teaching and science teacher education. This is one of the central messages in both of the new science education projects. Benchmarks for Science Literacy (AAAS, 1993) and the National Science Education Standards (National Research Council, 1994) project both strongly suggest that school science must give students an opportunity to experience science authentically, free of the legends, misconceptions and idealizations inherent in the myths about the nature of the scientific enterprise. There must be increased opportunity for both preservice and inservice teachers to learn about and apply the real rules of the game of science accompanied by careful review of textbooks to remove the "creeping fox terriers" that have helped provide an inaccurate view of the nature of science. Only by clearing away the mist of half-truths and revealing science in its full light, with knowledge of both its strengths and limitations, will learners become enamored of the true pageant of science and be able fairly to judge its processes and products.

WHAT'S THE USE OF THEORY?

by Michelle van Ryn, PhD, MPH
and Catherine A. Heaney, PhD, MPH

The barriers to the use of theory in health education practices are addressed by exposing common misperceptions of the nature and usefulness of theory. First, the mystique of theory is addressed through a discussion of theory development and the roots of theory in everyday experience. Two characteristics of theory, generalizability across settings or situations and test ability, are described and linked to benefits for practice. Second, a guide for practitioners in applying theory to each stage of the intervention process is provided. A case example illustrates how theory can guide practice as well as the benefits to be gained by applying theory to program development. Finally, the bases for common negative misperceptions of theory are identified and clarified, and the beneficial nature of theory reviewed.

INTRODUCTION

This paper addresses some of the barriers to the use of theory in health education practice created by common misperceptions of the nature and usefulness of theory. First, the nature of theory is explored through a discussion of theory development and the roots of theory in everyday experience. Then, the section entitled "Uses of Theory" will provided a guide for practitioners in applying theory to each stage of the intervention process. A case example illustrates both how theory can guide practice and the benefits to be gained by applying theory to program development. Finally, the bases for common negative misperceptions of theory are identified and clarified.

WHAT IS THEORY?

Dictionary definitions of the term theory generally reflect our confusion and ambivalence about the role and usefulness of theory in our lives and work. For example, Webster's II New Riverside University Dictionary defines theory as:

 1a. Systematically organized knowledge applicable in a relatively wide variety of circumstances . . . devised to analyze, predict, or otherwise explain the nature or behavior of a specific set of phenomena.
 1b. Such knowledge or such a system distinguished from experiment or practice.
  2. Abstract reasoning: speculation.
  3. An assumption or guess based on limited knowledge or information.

Rogets II: The New Thesaurus provides a slightly different twist in defining theory as:

 1. A belief used as the basis for action.
 2. Something taken to be true without proof.
 3. Abstract reasoning.

In addition to documenting the confusion present in common usage of the term theory, these definitions clearly illustrate a central problem involved in discussing theory. When academics, researchers, and theoreticians talk about theory to their practitioner colleagues, are they heard to be discussing something that is commendable and useful ("systematically organized knowledge"), unapproachable and out of reach ("abstract knowledge"), or pitiful and unusable ("an assumption or guess based on limited knowledge or information")? This is a crucial question. After all, what health educator would not welcome and cherish something that is "organized knowledge applicable in a relatively wide variety of circumstances," that could be ". . . used as the basis for action," and energetically avoid something that is "speculation," "taken to be true without proof"? The very need for this special issue suggests that formal education has failed to convincingly portray theory as the former welcome and desirable guide to intervention development.

THE LINK BETWEEN EVERYDAY EXPERIENCE AND THEORY

The dictionary definition that most closely corresponds to a formal scientific definition of theory is Webster's first. According to this definition, a theory is an impressive thing:

Systematically organized knowledge applicable in a relatively wide variety of circumstances . . . devised to analyze, predict, or otherwise explain the nature or behavior of a specific set of phenomena.

Where does such a lofty entity come from? Are theories sprung fully formed from the mind of a god, like Athena from the head of Zeus? Quite the contrary! Most social and behavioral science theories are rooted in the same fertile ground that engenders most of human creative endeavors: common everyday experience. For example, Piaget's theory of child development was rooted in his observations of his own children, and social learning theory was rooted in observations about the way people learn. Even as important a discovery as the theory of gravity may have been precipitated by Newton's observation of a falling apple.

Most of us, guided by our own personal observations, have developed incipient or partial theories about our day-to-day experiences. These particular theories are systems of beliefs which help us make sense of how things work or why things happen. For example, health educators may believe that the likelihood that their new projects will be accepted by their employing organizations depends on certain factors. These factors might include:

1. Management's perceptions of the level of success of their last project.
2. The number of problems or issues management is currently facing.
3. The amount of money needed for implementation of their ideas.
4. The perceived likelihood that their ideas will generate revenues.

They may have a fairly complex set of beliefs or hypotheses about the relationship between these factors. Some examples might be:

1. If management thinks the project is likely to generate revenues, they will be more receptive to it.
2. If management is currently dealing with many problems, they will be more likely to reject the project because they are overwhelmed and cannot cope with anything else, unless the new project is perceived to address one of the problems.
3. If the last project was successful, management will be more likely to accept the new idea, unless:
   (a) They are currently overwhelmed with problems, or
   (b) the project costs a lot of money.

Personal belief systems, such as the one described, provide a basis for action. The health educator with this explanatory belief system is likely to have developed related strategies for enhancing the likelihood that her idea will be accepted. For example, she might decide to present her new idea during a slow period or highlight the success of her last program before presenting her new idea.

This example of a personal belief system for explaining a phenomenon of interest has many of the elements of a formal scientific theory. However, there are some useful distinctions between belief systems and formal theories that, as we will describe below, make theory especially valuable to practice. A completely developed theory contains three major elements:

1. The major explanatory factors that influence the phenomena of interest (e.g., a well-developed theory of individual behavior in crowds will specify the factors that affect the way a person behaves in a crowd).
2. The relationship among these factors.
3. The conditions under which these relationships do or do not occur.

Some theories also address strategies for modifying explanatory factors. These theories are often the most useful in guiding program development.

The above example of a personal belief system has the elements of formal scientific theory: it identifies the major explanatory factors and how these factors are related to the outcome of interest. It provides a basis for predicting events and for deciding on courses of action. However, it differs from a formal theory in that it may not be generalized across a wide variety of settings, and may not be testable or disprovable.

Generalizability

The belief system described above is specific to this particular health educator's organization, and is not intended to generalize to all or most organizations. A belief system which is very useful in one setting may be entirely useless in another. Thus, what is learned through "common sense" with one population may make no sense with another. In contrast, a theory must be applicable in a wide variety of circumstances. It must generalize across settings and populations. Any relationships between factors that are suggested by a well-developed theory must hold true in most cases, and exceptions should be specified. It is exactly this generalizability that is so useful to practitioners who often deal with many types of clients in many settings.

Testability

In addition to sharing many of the elements of formal theory, the health educator's belief system shares another characteristic of any given theory: it is testable. This is a very important quality. Consider, for example, the possibility that this health educator is wrong about the factors that influence organizational receptivity to her ideas; perhaps this receptivity is entirely governed by what color outfit she is wearing the day she presents her ideas (as some enterprising marketers would have us believe). Perhaps she is assuming that management is overwhelmed with problems, when in fact management is overwhelmed by the color of her shirt—a glowing shade of orange. It is likely that over time the health educator would notice that her hypothesized relationships between her explanatory factors and outcomes were NOT occurring. For example, she might notice that an idea presented during a slow period was still not accepted.

By way of contrast, a belief that the behavior of one's boss is affected by invisible and unmeasurable rays from the planet Mars is untestable. Since there is no way to measure the ostensible rays, we cannot prove or disprove this belief. A system of beliefs (whether involving rays from outer space or any other unmeasurable factors) does not have to be testable; a theory does. It is this element of theory that distinguishes it from a system of beliefs. Please note that this has nothing to do with ultimate truth, merely our ability to determine veracity. The testable nature of theory gives it a practical advantage over personal belief systems or common sense. Once theories have been tested, they can be applied to practice with more confidence, assurance, and likelihood of success than the most widely held or personally appreciated common sense idea.

USES OF THEORY

The second section of this paper seeks to demystify the process of applying theory to health education practice by providing specific descriptions of the use of theory in all aspects of the program development and implementation process. Just as "incipient theories" can guide an individual's actions and responses, "full-blown" theories can guide a health educator through the four stages of the program development process: planning, implementation, evaluation, and reformulation and generalization. We will describe how theories can aid in each of these stages and illustrate our points with a case example. Rather than starting with a theory and finding a problem to apply it to, we have chosen to more exactly duplicate a practitioner's position. We will begin with a problem, choose a theory to apply to the problem, and develop a program based on hypotheses derived from the theory. The problem that we have chosen to address is the rationale for this special issue of *Health Education Quarterly*: the inadequate use of theory by health education practitioners. Thus, our case example will focus on using theory to guide an intervention intended to increase the number of theory-based programs developed by health educators.

Choosing a Theory

Scholars who are engaged in basic research often start with a theory and search for problems to which the theory can be applied. Practitioners, on the other hand, are faced with public health problems and must look for a theory that will help them develop solutions. Clearly, there are many theories from which the practitioner must choose. How does a health educator go about this process of choosing a theory? We will present several guidelines to aid in this process.

The first step in choosing an appropriate theory is clarifying the purpose or goals of the proposed program. The explicit goals of the program provide the marker for identifying classes of theories which may be applicable. Theories are often specific to targets of intervention or units of practice. For example, some theories address individual behavior change and others organizational change processes. Even within a unit of practice, there are distinctions to be made. For instance, within the class of behavior change theories, some explain and predict solely volitional behavior, while others generalize to addictive behaviors. If a program needs to address an addictive behavior, it should not be based on a theory that only addresses voluntary behavior. Likewise, a program that has the goal of behavior maintenance should not be based on a theory that explains only initial behavior change. Identifying the specific target and goals of the program will narrow the field of applicable theories. However, even once this guideline has been followed, there are often many theories from which to choose.

The next step is to identify the relevant theories and evaluate the evidence for each of them. What reason is there to believe that a particular theory represents an accurate assessment of the way the world works? Has the theory been applied to a problem similar to the one currently being address? Has the theory been tested with people who are similar to those who will participate in the program? Finding the answers to these questions can sometimes take more time than a busy health educator has available. For this reason, it may be useful to enlist the aid of a health behavior or health education specialist. It is part of the responsibility and mission of health behavior specialists in academic settings to provide this type of consultation. Such a person should have a working knowledge of the potentially relevant theories and should have the resources to help evaluate their applicability. If such a person is not available, there are health education tests that review the evidence for theories and give examples of health education applications.

Lastly, health educators should choose a theory that makes sense to them, given their experience and what they know and believe about the world. Theories reflect general views about the world and the nature of people. For example, some theories about behavior change emphasize psychological influences on behavior. Other theories stress the importance of environmental and social influences on behavior. Naturally, health educators will choose theories that complement or are in concert with their world views. We are not suggesting that health educators become complacent and stop challenging some of their basic assumptions about people. It is only through such challenging that a profession progresses and new approaches are developed. However, at the same time, it does not make sense to base a program on theoretical ideas that are at odds with one's own philosophy or belief system.

For our case example, the goal of the program will be to increase the use of theory in health educators' program development processes. Thus, we need to choose a theory that addresses the acquisition and maintenance of complex, ongoing behaviors. Individual behavior change theories that best explain one-shot behaviors such as getting immunized or behaviors that do not necessitate the learning and practicing of new skills will be inadequate for our purpose. In addition, we prefer a theory that has been rigorously tested in a number of different contexts. Lastly, we prefer a theory that fits with our ecological view of individual behavior. We believe that individuals are influenced by their physical and social environments and that programs should not target individual persons isolated from the context within which they live and work.

With these criteria in mind, we chose social learning theory (SLT) as the basis for our program. (The reader should note that SLT was not chosen because it is endorsed over all other behavior change theories, but rather because of the value of this theory for our case example.) SLT states that behavior change is mediated through cognitive processes (e.g., thinking, perceiving, believing), and that cognitions (attitudes and beliefs) about a behavior are altered most easily through actual performance or observed performance of the behavior. Tests of this theory have been very supportive of its ability to represent how people learn and adopt a wide variety of new behaviors. Figure 1 depicts the explanatory factors of SLT and how these explanatory factors can be modified. The three important explanatory factors can be defined as follows:

1. Behavioral capacity: having the skills necessary for the performance of the desired behavior. For our case example, this would involve skills related to the translation of theory into practice, such as identifying and evaluating theories.
2. Efficacy expectations: beliefs regarding one's ability to successfully carry out a course of action or perform a behavior. For our case example, the relevant efficacy expectations would involve the degree to which health educators believe they have the skills and abilities needed to apply theory to the program development process, and the strength of their confidence in these abilities.
3. Outcome expectations: beliefs that the performance of a behavior will have desired effects or consequences. For our case example, this refers to the degree to which health educators expect that applying theory to the program development process will result in an effective program. Outcome expectations might also include expectations regarding personal satisfaction when a program has been successful, or expectations of other kinds of rewards, such as professional recognition.

These are the three factors that must be modified in order for the new behavior to be acquired, performed, and maintained.

SLT is useful to program development because, in addition to de-

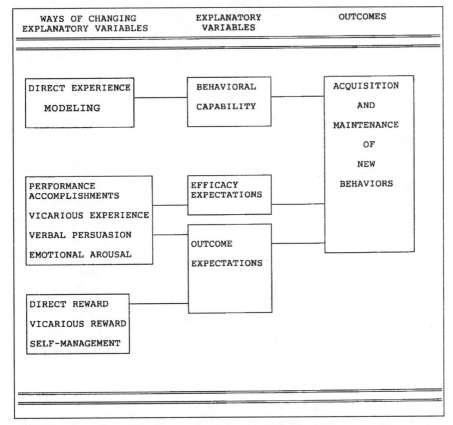

FIGURE 1. SOCIAL LEARNING THEORY: COMPONENTS AND PROCESSES

scribing the important influences on behavior change, it describes the processes through which these influences can be modified. Thus, as indicated in Figure 1, behavioral capacity or skill level can be modified through both direct experience or practice and through observing someone else model the desired behavior. Both outcome and efficacy expectations can be modified by four different processes. Performance accomplishments refer to performing the behavior or close approximations of the behavior. Successful performance can increase a person's sense of confidence (self-efficacy) in being able to perform the behavior again. If the behavior leads to a desirable outcome, then that person's outcome expectations become more positive as well. A second important influence on expectations is observational learning or vicarious experience. Through seeing others who are similar to ourselves behave in certain ways and succeed in bringing about desired effects, people modify their expectations about their own behavior. The third influence, verbal persuasion, refers to attempts to change expectations by providing new or newly motivating information. This paper, for example, is an attempt at verbal persuasion. Lastly, people develop their sense of efficacy, in part, from how distressed, anxious, and tense they feel when faced with the need to perform the behavior. Efforts to decrease his emotional arousal may directly enhance efficacy expectations. When there are satisfactory levels of self-efficacy, the motivation to perform a particular behavior can be increased through the expectations that the behavior will lead to a desirable outcome (outcome expectation) and through incentives (rewards). Reward expectations can be influenced by observing others receive rewards (vicarious reward) or by being rewarded oneself (direct reward). Rewards may come from external sources, such as awards, promotions, or professional recognition, or they may come from internal sources, such as the self-satisfaction a health educator might feel after implementing an effective intervention.

Putting Theory to Work

A figure, such as the one included here, can at first glance be overwhelming. However, all of the information contained in Figure 1 aids in making program development decisions, as we shall describe.

Planning

During the planning stage, health educators search for answers to the "why" questions. Why does a particular health education problem exist? For example, why do more women over the age of 50 not get screened for breast cancer? Why do some physicians not routinely recommend to their patients that they stop smoking? Health educators must identify the important factors that contribute to the problem. The answer to these "why" questions aid in the identification of targets for intervention. It is through understanding of the "why" that health educators learn what needs to be changed in order to deal with the problem. Theories aid in answering these "why" questions by directing the attention of the health educator to important explanatory factors.

Why do many health educators fail to utilize available theory as a guide to program development? SLT directs our attention to the factors of behavioral capacity, efficacy expectations, outcome expectations, and incentives in the form of rewards. In order for health educators to choose to utilize theory, they must first possess the requisite skills and information necessary for applying theory to public health problems. Second, health educators must feel confident that they will be able to use theory appropriately, that is, they must have high self-efficacy regarding their ability to perform the behaviors needed to successfully utilize theory. Third, they must believe that developing theory-based interventions will result in good outcomes. For example, they must believe that utilizing theory to guide intervention development will result in interventions that are more effective, more easily evaluated, and/or generalizable than programs that are not explicitly theory based. Lastly, health educators must experience or expect to experience rewards for integrating theories into their program development process. SLT suggests then that the failure of many health educators to utilize theory in program development is due to a combination of health educators lacking skills, and/or lacking confidence about using those skills (self-efficacy), and/or lacking positive outcome expectations. We now have some insight into the "why" questions and have completed the first step of the program development process.

Normally, the next step would be to conduct a needs assessment and review available literature on the problem. Theories help guide needs assessments by pointing to types of information that would be most helpful in guiding program development decisions. In our example, SLT would guide us to assess health educator's skills, outcome expectations, and self-efficacy, regarding applying theory to program development. We would want to ascertain which of the factors suggested by SLT are of the greatest importance among our target population. For example, a need assessment might reveal that most health educators already possess the knowledge and skills needed to use theory to guide practice, but lack either self-efficacy or positive outcome expectations. This information would lead us to focus our intervention on increasing self-efficacy and positive outcome expectations. However, we do not have needs assessment data available to us for our case example, so we include all three factors in our proposed intervention.

Implementation

The implementation stage deals with the "how" questions. How can the important influences on the problem be changed or modified? For example, how does a health educator go about increasing the knowledge of the public about mammography? How does a health educator change physicians' opinions about the effectiveness of their recommendations to stop smoking? The answers to these questions guide the development of programmatic activities. Theories can help answer the "how" questions through their identification of change processes.

The learning processes described by SLT suggest a multipronged program for increasing health educators' use of theory in program development:

1. Increase skill at performing the relevant behavior.
2. Increase self-efficacy regarding performing the behavior.
3. Increase the expectation that a positive outcome will result from performing the behavior (e.g., that a theory-driven program will be effective), and increase rewards for performing the behavior.

Translating goals of this kind into program activities is a creative process. Health educators can use their own considerable ingenuity as well as learn from each other's experiences in achieving these goals. For our example program, we reviewed the literature to find what others had done to increase skill, self-efficacy, and outcome expectations and, based on this review, developed some likely program components. For example, in order to increase skills and thus behavioral capacity, skill-building workshops could be offered at various professional association meetings. These workshops could focus on the skills needed to apply theory to the program development process. By utilizing role modeling and active learning techniques, the relevant skills can be observed and practiced. These workshops will be intended to raise both the objective skill level of health educators, as well as their self-efficacy regarding successfully performing these skills. As part of the self-efficacy enhancing process, facilitators should draw attention to the improvement in performance of the participants, thus ensuring that participants take note of their own skills and attribute their successes to their own abilities.

Initial attempts to modify outcome expectations will rest on verbal persuasion and vicarious experience. Professional communications such as this special issue can serve to disseminate information and motivate health educators. Testimonials from health educators about how using theory strengthened their programmatic efforts may persuade other health educators that using theory is not overly difficult and leads to desired outcomes.

In terms of rewards, we are confident that the development of theory-based interventions will eventually be self-rewarding. As it becomes apparent that the programs being developed are highly effective, health educators will feel satisfied with and reinforced for their efforts. Initially though, external reinforcement might be useful to help motivate behavior change. Perhaps an organization such as SOPHE could sponsor a competition for the best theory-based intervention. The publicity for the competition would also help to establish the integration of theory into practice as a priority for the profession. The winner, along with claiming a prize, could be sponsored to present the intervention at the APHA annual meeting.

Evaluation

Once the targets for change have been identified and the methodologies for intervention determined, an evaluation plan should be developed. Theories can guide the choice of evaluation strategies. Not only do health educators need to know if a program was successful, they need to know why a program was successful, they need to know why it was or was not successful. Knowing why a program worked (or failed) will provide information to help guide future programs. Evaluations that only look at the final outcome (e.g., smoking status or weight loss) will shed no light on why a program had its effects. If it was unsuccessful, where did the program began to break down? Theories, through their identification of important explanatory factors, indicate the factors that need to be measured in order to understand whether or not the hypothesized change process unfolded as planned.

In evaluating our intervention with health educators, we would want to measure the amount of increase in the number and quality of theory-based interventions developed by health educators. In addition, we would need to measure the four explanatory factors: skill levels, perceived self-efficacy at performing the behaviors needed to utilize theory, health educators' beliefs about the usefulness of theory, and both external and internal rewards for using theory to guide practice. Thus, if our efforts were not successful in bringing about an increase in the use of theory, we could look to see which links in the chain were not strongly forged.

Reformulation and Generalization

The last stage of the program development process deals with putting the results of the evaluation to work. A theory-based evaluation serves two purposes. First, health educators can use the evaluation results to formulate or improve their programs. Activities that did not bring about the expected changes in skills, beliefs, or events can be modified. For example, our evaluation might indicate that health educators were convinced of the usefulness of theory, but were not confident in their ability to adequately apply theory. This would suggest the need or improvement in the self-efficacy enhancing portions of the program. This improvement might include incorporating more opportunities for practicing skills and for receiving positive feedback on skill performance.

The second purpose of a theory-based evaluation is to facilitate the adaptation of the program to other programs or populations. One of the reasons health educators often give for irrelevance of theory is that public health programs need to appeal to many specific audiences, in many different contexts. One of the key qualities of a theory is its generalizability to a wide variety of settings. This makes theory-based programs more easily adapted to other target populations. For programs to be generalizable, health educators need to understand why and how they work. Programs cannot be generalized at the level of activities. An activity that worked in one program may not work in another. Only by knowing what those activities are supposed to do and why it is important for those activities to be successful can a program developer effectively replicate or adapt an existing successful program. Through helping health educators better understand the change process that their programs are trying to accomplish, theories allow for successful adaptation of good programs to new problems, audiences, and environments.

For example, in our hypothetical case, we may have developed a set of activities that were quite successful in increasing skill levels and self-efficacy. This set of activities, with some modifications in content, might be adapted for a program geared toward some other desired behavior change in health professionals. Without a tested theory suggesting the importance of skill level and self-efficacy in promoting behavior change, the use of these activities in another context might not occur to us. The time and energy invested in designing programmatic activities can have much greater payoffs if we learn how to generalize successful activities to new contexts.

THE BENEFITS OF THEORY

Theories can provide answers to program developer's questions regarding why people aren't already engaging in the desirable behavior of interest, how to go about changing their behaviors, and what factors to look at when evaluating a program's focus. Our case example illustrated the role of theory in all stages of program development. The case example highlighted the advantages provided by using a well-tested theory to guide our intervention:

1. We had a clear sense of what the targets of our intervention should be (the explanatory factors of the theory: behavioral capacity, outcome expectations, and efficacy expectations) in order to maximize the likelihood of achieving our desired outcome (the use of theory by health educators in the program development process).
2. The theory would have guided a needs assessment by specifying the type of information that would be most helpful in planning our program.
3. The theory provided us with specific ideas about the methodologies or learning activities that would be most effective in modifying the important influences on behavior.
4. Because theories must be coherent and their parts consistent with each other, basing our program on theory made it more likely that the components of our intervention would be consistent with each other, as well as being comprehensive.
5. We had a clear understanding of how to evaluate and improve our program, linking specific activities with important intermediate outcomes that eventually result in the ultimate goal of the program.
6. Lastly, but perhaps most importantly, we were more optimistic that our program would lead to behavior change than we would have been without a theory-based intervention. This confidence stems from knowledge of the success of other SLT-based interventions in the past.

COMMON USAGE REVISITED:
ROOTS OF NEGATIVE MISPERCEPTION OF THEORY

Let us return to two of the least flattering definitions of theory found in common usage. In light of the previous discussion of the value and use of theory in practice, it might be seen as surprising that negative perceptions exist. In fact, however, the course of the negative misperceptions of the nature of theory are quite likely to be the very aspects of theories that make them the most useful: generalizability and testability.

The principle of generalizability may be the source of the first negative common usage definition of theory. This misperception of theory is reflected in Webster's definition of theory as "abstract reasoning" and Roget's definition of theory as "existing only in concept and not in reality." Indeed, one function of theory is to develop general principles from the observation and testing of specific phenomena. The development of general principles from specific observations certainly involves a type of abstract thinking. However, it is an unfortunate misunderstanding that the abstraction involved in theory is antithetical to the practical. As we have mentioned, the generalizability of theory makes it useful in application to a wide variety of settings, populations, and problems. The practitioner's challenge is to take a theory's general principles and apply them to the specific case or problem at hand. This can be difficult. It is easy to become frustrated by having to wade through unfamiliar scientific jargon or decipher poorly defined concepts. Perhaps our frustration with the seemingly inaccessibility of theories causes us to write them off as too abstract. However, theories are built upon observations of specific events and relationships. They are meant to apply to a broad spectrum of specific problems.

The second common misperception is that theory lacks validity or veracity, thus making it useless for practice. The misperception is reflected in Roget's definition of theory as "something taken to be true without proof" and Webster's definition as "an assumption or guess based on limited knowledge or information." Initially, theories do indeed represent educated guesses about how the world works, based on observation of the phenomena under study. Importantly, however, good theories are submitted to rigorous testing to see if they accurately represent the way the world works. The usefulness of a theory to a practitioner is very much dependent on the degree to which it has been adequately, successfully tested.

Perhaps the very fact that theories have to be tested, rather than simply accepted as true representations of the world, raises the suspicions of practitioners. Perhaps the complexity of the evidence resulting from these tests further fuels suspicions about a theory's usefulness. Even if a large body of evidence supports a theory, there will most likely be a few studies that do not. The challenge for the practitioner is to adequately evaluate the evidence regarding a theory. This is not always an easy task. Our frustration with our own lack of time or ability to examine the evidence may lead us to assume that theories are, at best, guesses. The suggestions on practical ways to get information on theories, provided above, may help in this regard. In addition, colleagues in academia can help by making information about various theories more accessible to practitioners.

CONCLUSION

This paper is one component of the intervention described in our case example. The information and arguments put forth here constitute an effort to verbally persuade readers that using theory is not only possible but will lead to desirable outcomes. From our discussion of the definition of theory and its roots in everyday experience and observation we hope that, rather than fearing or being intimidated by theory, readers see the roots of theory in their own belief systems. From our discussion of the uses and benefits of theory we hope that, rather than characterizing theory as abstract and impractical, readers will welcome theory as the practical tool it is. Lastly, we hope that readers see that the generalizability and testability of theories make them more enduring and effective guides to program development than common sense, intuition, or habit.

Clearly, application of well-defined and carefully tested theories to the program development process holds tremendous advantages for health educators in terms of coherence, effectiveness, and evaluation of interventions. On a personal note, the authors have found that there is an additional pleasure that may be experienced in working with theory-based interventions. There is a sense of connection and a satisfaction to be gained in being a part of the development of a cumulative body of knowledge. Applying theory to the program development process demands that one learn about what others have done, what has worked, what has failed. In short, the process of connecting past experience and a large body of knowledge to current activities can be an immensely satisfying experience.

PART II

WHAT IS
THE TEACHER'S ROLE?

TOWARD A NEW MAINSTREAM OF INSTRUCTION FOR AMERICAN SCHOOLS

by Eric J. Cooper,
Vice President, Inservice Training and
Telecommunications, Simon & Schuster School Group

THE NEED FOR INSTRUCTIONAL REFORM

The question of what should be the central focus for education is one that has increasingly been debated in the nation. In the 1970s, the general reaction to students' deficiencies led to renewed public demand for a return to the basics of education and a refocusing on the "three Rs." As interpreted by state legislators, the courts, and school systems, this demand resulted in a reversal of the educational trends of the 1960s—a change from open classroom and student-centered instruction to more traditional classroom and teacher-centered instruction, and a moving away from scientific inquiry models toward the test-driven curriculum and didactic teaching styles that were advocated prior to the curriculum revolution of the 1960s. The resulting curriculum of the current decade stresses minimum skills and continues to produce students who are unable to perform comprehension tasks sufficiently.

Public education remains under fire from the press, from business and community leaders, and from legislators and parents. Xerox Corporation CEO David Kearns has stated that "public education has put this country at a terrible competitive disadvantage. The American workforce is running out of qualified people. If current demographic and economic trends continue, American business will have to hire a million new workers a year who can't read, write or count." Unfortunately, the students who may be most in need, i.e., minorities, are those least likely to receive the educational support necessary for success in the 21st century. They, more so than other populations, are school dependent and, as such, need access to the best teachers, programs, assessment instruments, materials, and schools. Poussaint stated the problem succinctly:

> If it is any consolation, it appears that American education is short-changing just about everyone—rich and poor, urban and suburban, advantaged and disadvantaged, black and every other color. Unfortunately, and this is the dilemma, black students are substantially behind a student population that is, as a whole, far behind where current studies say it needs to be. If the goal is only to reach a national average, black kids will be in the no-win situation of trying to play catch-up. Playing catch-up will not put black students where the Carnegie Forum on Education and the Economy says all students need to be to make it in the 21st century.

It is estimated that, by the year 2000, one out of every three Americans will be non-White, and that one out of every five students in the nation's public schools will be non-White. Yet, given this country's disappointing track record regarding educational reform and its lack of success in educating disadvantaged urban students, there is increasing evidence that some schools and school districts are performing significantly above the norm in teaching minorities. There is a need to move beyond the rhetoric of reform to identify and establish schools that work for minority students as well as for those students who presently make up the majority. There is also a need to move beyond what have been traditionally identified as the drivers of educational reform to practical suggestions for improving educational opportunities for minority students.

The drivers of curriculum that have been the subject of much discussion include tests and textbooks. The impact of these drivers on schooling often clouds the ability of educators to identify a clear direction for instructional change, causing many of them to eventually drive off into an instructional dead end. This dead end may be partially reflected by the following research data:

> *Eighty percent of the knowledge students are exposed to comes from textbooks marked by many flaws.
>
> *A New York public school system discovered that 80 percent of materials in grades 3–12 were inappropriately matched to the academic needs of their students.
>
> *Seventy percent of allocated instructional time may be spent on workbook-type exercises that often bear little relationship to student needs.
>
> *Students often spend more time engaged in workbook activities than in instructional activities with their teachers.
>
> *By popular estimate, 80 to 95 percent of what goes on in the classroom is derived from published instructional material rather than from the active processing of knowledge between students and teachers.
>
> *In an analysis of elementary and secondary instruction, less than 1 percent of instructional time was devoted to students' responding to teacher

questioning that demanded open responses involving reasoning or opinions. Usual student responses were based solely on informational answers to the teacher's questions. In a landmark study, less than 1 percent of instructional time in the later elementary grades was spent on comprehension instruction, though teachers questioned in this study felt that comprehension instruction was an extremely important part of children's learning.

There is an obvious need in this country to move beyond instruction that limits students' academic experiences to the use of poorly developed materials, that engages them in seatwork that may be improperly designed for their academic needs, or that forces them to attend to a series of activities geared to elicit the simple regurgitation of facts and figures. One implication of the above data is that educators need to rethink how classrooms in this country are managed and organized for instruction. We cannot assume that school reform will take hold until we address the objectives and goals of effective schools, that is, schools that sustain high levels of growth for all students.

A likely beginning is with the child. It is at this reference point that cognitive research has made the most progress in the past fifteen years. It is how children think—and ultimately, how all of us think—that has concerned psychologists like Piaget, Vygotsky, and Bruner; philosophers like Aristotle and James; and every good teacher in school systems throughout the country. Cognitive scientists concerned with improving instruction have, as Fredericksen stated, ". . . attempted to describe the psychological processes that occur when one reads, plays chess, solves puzzles, or attempts to solve mathematical problems." The result of this research has been an information-processing theory of cognition that is highly relevant to teaching and that should help educators solve the complex puzzle of how instruction can be improved.

This article will address some of the educational drivers that continue to steer teachers away from improving educational opportunities for minority students, and it will suggest some practical instructional alternatives that support many of the exciting changes underway.

THE DECLINE IN TEACHING THINKING

It is assumed by most observers of the American educational system that schools exist to teach students how to learn. Yet, for some observers this statement is both questionable and controversial. For example, in Florida, many have argued that schools exist to teach students how to pass the SSAT-I and SSAT-II tests. In New York, others have argued that instruction is driven by the state Regents exam. In other states, the concern is that schools exist to help students pass basic competency tests such as the G.E.D.

With the growing debate over the expansion of the National Assessment of Educational Progress (NAEP), one can assume that testing will remain a central issue for those engaged in instructional reform. Yet, no matter how good the test, it is not the same as learning, and tests should not be the primary vehicles for moving education toward some semblance of excellence. Teaching students how to learn is essentially different from teaching them how to acquire information, to memorize, to take a test, or to build upon any other skills.

The need to focus on improving the thinking skills of minority and other students is well documented. Reference to research emerging out of cognitive science is widespread, yet it is mainly the rhetoric about thinking that has flourished. The application of teaching for thinking to classroom practice still lags far behind. Classroom materials in widespread use still emphasize the acquisition of minimal cognitive skills. Teachers and administrators continue to purchase materials that teach low-level basic skills without regard for what students need to learn to exist as active members of the general society. Tests that place "much emphasis . . . on improving students' performance in the 'basic' rudimentary skills that are easiest to teach and test" are continually used.

Reznick clearly articulated a historical perspective on what may begin to answer the question of why the rhetoric of teaching thinking has flourished, while classroom practice has seemingly not followed suit:

> . . . the goals of increasing thinking and reasoning ability are old ones for educators. Such abilities have been the goals of some schools at least since the time of Plato. But these goals were part of the high literacy tradition; they did not, by and large, apply to the more recent schools for the masses. Although it is not new to include thinking, problem solving, and reasoning in someone's school curriculum, it is new to include it in everyone's curriculum. It is new to take seriously the aspiration of making thinking and problem solving a regular part of a school program for all of the population, even minorities, even non-English speakers, even the poor. It is a new challenge to develop educational programs that assume that all individuals, not just an elite, can become competent thinkers.

Over the last decade, we have been more concrete about the improvement of instruction since we have continued to gain knowledge about the processes of learning. However, as Darling-Hammond has pointed out "between 1972 and 1980, use of teaching methods that might encourage the development of higher-order thinking abilities, e.g., project or laboratory work, writing tasks, and student-centered discussions, declined in public schools . . ." The reasons given by Darling-Hammond and others for this decline are based on the observation that many tests, textbooks, and curricula have focused increasingly on minimal skills (e.g., literal comprehension, routine computation, factual recall) rather than skills that lead students to a higher level of thinking (e.g., inferential and critical problem-solving, comprehension, representation, elaboration, inductive inquiry, synthesis, and evaluation). A consequence of this focus is illustrated by NAEP data that suggest that there is "more cause for concern about the ability of students to solve problems requiring higher-level skills and an understanding of basic principles than their ability to recall discrete facts or to perform routine operations."

Given the prevalence of instruction stressing minimal basic skills, there is good reason to consider the implications of recent research on teaching and learning. Concurrently, as a result of the acute problems related to minority performance, there is a need to propose a "new mainstream" for schooling. The purpose would be to help administrators, supervisors, teachers, and parents integrate the new wave of educational reform into the everyday activities of schools that are serving an increasingly diverse student population.

A VISION OF SCHOOL REFORM

Due to the diverse needs of students in this country, educators need to refocus and expand their vision of what should be done in the nation's classrooms. Rather than focusing on the traditional drivers of instruction, this vision should highlight what students have in common and address the patterns of thinking by which people from different cultures, backgrounds, skill levels, and languages learn to learn in a nourishing atmosphere. This should be the ultimate goal of education and is the source for a New Mainstream of instructional reform. This reform will bring together research on cognition, an understanding of how students engage themselves in the learning process, and the delivery of instruction necessary for diverse student populations. Care must be taken to avoid the abuses of segregation, tracking, and an inadvertent separation of minorities into programs which move them away from the mainstream, e.g., some Special Education and Chapter 1 programs.

The proposed New Mainstream consolidates guarantees of student competency with support to extend learning to the limits of a child's potential. To move toward it there is an obvious need to recognize that no one approach to reform will be a panacea for the nation's educational concerns, yet there are specific organizational and instructional arrangements that have proven successful in educating disadvantaged and minority students. Eubanks and Levine, for example, have reported that "such arrangements emphasize provision of educational assistance to improve reading performance through tutoring before school, during lunch, or after school, utilization of teachers' aides, reductions of non-essential time in art, music, or other subjects, formation of smaller in-class groups for low achievers than for other students . . ."

Other researchers such as Benjamin Bloom and Comer have described the importance of linking the home and school in a partnership based on instruction (e.g., the use of graded homework has been identified as a factor related to improved student achievement). Bloom also stressed the importance of developing automaticity in reading and of an instructional focus on teaching higher order thinking processes as integral factors related to student learning.

Still other educators have stressed the reorganizing of schooling as key to school improvement and student achievement. Bensman reported on an inner-city school that reorganized its physical, instructional, and attitudinal constructs in favor of a student centered philosophy; in effect, teachers and students work under the guiding principle "less is more." Content-area instruction was integrated and focused on three subjects (i.e., math, science, and the humanities, including language arts). Higher-order thinking, synthesis and application became the primary goals of classroom activities at the school. Students work in small groups almost exclusively and are taught through such strategies as team teaching, coaching, modeling, and cooperative learning. Community involvement of students which allows them opportunities to apply skills learned in the classroom is an integral activity of the school. The school does not track students into specific learning streams—in fact, all groups are heterogeneous, whereby students performing on different levels of ability work to support each other's learning. High expectations as well as instructional arrangements that lead to cognitive skill development are the central themes of this highly successful inner-city school.

COGNITIVE MODELS OF LEARNING AND TEACHING

Recent cognitive research has provided the field of education with some answers as to how students learn and how they may learn to perform higher-order cognitive tasks. It is this research that has begun to ad dress the transaction by which information is imprinted, communicated, or understood—the how of how we learn.

The imprinting of information seems to follow specific routes from an idea to spoken words, to listening, and to ownership of that idea. These routes form a "cognitive map" from stimulus to understanding. Ausubel and others have postulated that thinking involves the making of maps of knowledge derived from knowledge already understood. It is inferred from this that cognition is a matter of building patterns and of developing strategies to incorporate new information with old, i.e., building networks of information that bridge the gap between what we know and do not know.

Cognitive Research and Reading

It is with respect to comprehension instruction that some of the more dramatic applications of cognitive theory have been consolidated. There are several reasons why this has occurred.

First, reading comprehension involves cognitive processes similar to the processes involved in thinking. For example, even reading recreational material on trains or planes requires a concentrated cognitive act to remember the perils of a Robert Ludlum character as he or she moves from one dramatic situation to another. Thinking is central to reading comprehension, so much so that Pearson and Johnson have stated that "whatever influences general thinking or problem solving ability also influences reading. . . ."

Reading can also be broken down into many identifiable strategies by which information passes from the mind of the reader to the page and from the page into our memories. Research has indicated that readers use many different strategies for understanding what they read, just as map readers may look at the back roads on a map. Readers seem to develop schema that enable them to understand letters, words, phrases, and connected prose while incorporating new data with old. Therefore, to build knowledge one must first have some knowledge to begin with, i.e., one begins with a lump of experience to which one can attach more experience.

Applying this conceptual scheme, this model of how reading is learned involves another connection between mapping and reading comprehension: teaching reading requires an intellectual map through which teachers and learners travel from novice to expert.

Instructional Bridging

In the most current teaching, learning, and cognitive model this map is not linear. To elaborate on this point, Brown has discussed the concept of "expert scaffolding," which involves construction of learning scaffolds deliberately and consciously erected by a teacher and the building of schema with classes of children in an interactive environment. The "expert" provides classroom activities from which students gradually acquire skills; thus, teachers create a laboratory situation in which "novices are encouraged to watch and then to participate before they are able to perform unaided." Within this instructional context, good teaching is based on providing the appropriate clues, not the answers, for the students.

In practice, such scaffolding allows students to build concepts from their discussions; only when these concepts, ideas, or mental constructs are experienced or concretized does a teacher move to develop the students' words into key words, phrases, and prose for improving understanding. When this conceptual model is applied to learning or even to test development, it is the opposite of simply instructing students to fill in the blanks. Instead, teachers build the sentences using appropriately leveled language for the student while devising a process whereby gaps purposely occur, generating questions for which a single answer is usually incorrect. In this context, there are no "right words" to a fill-in-the-blank discussion developed by the teacher. Instead, there are ideas that build up other ideas in a planned way, taking the form of a scaffold which may be as challenging to the tester as to the test taker.

Expert scaffolding lends itself to a wide range of teaching styles, classroom formats, and subject matter. It is particularly useful to comprehension instruction because one rarely attends to the specific strategies; yet, in fact, good readers may use them all the time. Beyond the coding activities of phonics and the memorization of most spelling instruction, the how of reading is mostly unconscious and undirected. However, reading remains subject to direct improvement through mediated instruction. In a classroom structured with this kind of scaffolding, students discover the skills they use, while they use those skills as individuals and as a group.

This is more obvious when we look at some of the strategies and cognitive signposts that appear on the maps developed for improving reading comprehension. Paris listed six reading strategies:

1. understanding the purposes of reading
2. activating relevant background knowledge
3. allocating attention to main ideas
4. critical evaluation
5. monitoring comprehension
6. drawing inferences

These learning strategies are generic in that they reflect technique rather than subject matter. They apply just as much to watching television or movies as to parsing sentences. Yet, they merit direct attention in the classroom both as illustrations of strategic teaching and as demonstrations of applied cognitive research.

The first strategy—to know the purpose of reading comprehension—involves mobilizing some commitment from students before expecting them to deliver on that commitment. It means sharing the need to comprehend, to think, and to understand written text across subject, grade, age, and school. A way to mobilize this activity is to get students to "buy into" the process of learning—a process whereby responsibility for learning is shared by teachers and students alike.

Secondly, rather than using testing as a motivator for learning, teachers might help students to understand the purposes of instruction through interactive and interdisciplinary lessons that build on prior knowledge gained from home and community experiences. More specifically, activating background knowledge means building from clearly understood ideas and bridging this knowledge across to new areas; it means motivating interest from curiosity and celebrating that curiosity with all the reinforcement teachers can bring to bear. Of course, this does not mean that students can only relearn what they already know, but it does affirm Plato's observation that knowledge is a continuous rediscovery of our own insights.

Inspiring such insights is the aspiration and the goal of the New

Mainstream, for new knowledge must be linked, overlaid, and enriched through vocabulary and history. If students do not know what their teachers are talking about as a result of prior exposure to a concept, then they will not understand why, how, or if the introduction of the concept makes any sense. Such an observation is no less relevant for a six-year-old than for a group of professionals. It is the sense of learning that teachers should strive to impart to their students not the mere ability to perform the rote calling of words.

Paris's strategy—to attend to main ideas—is, perhaps, the most frequent strategy used by many teachers and appears on most reading tests and in most textbooks; however, more often than not, the teaching of main ideas is taught out of the context of extended text and is isolated and treated as a separate function of reading comprehension. The appropriate implementation of this strategy requires real concentration on the part of students and should not be viewed as a skimming exercise that teaches them to locate the topic sentence in isolation of "real" reading activities. Examined critically, the main idea strategy is as appropriate for the math, science, or health teacher as it is for the reading teacher. It requires that teachers think along with their students and that they provide examples or models of the concept while also providing feedback. If materials are poorly designed for conceptual understanding to occur, teachers need to carefully guide students through the key concepts which, by the nature of the material, often are somewhat obscure for the reader. However, with good materials, the pursuit should be as interesting as the discovery itself.

The two strategies described by Paris as involving evaluation and monitoring are important for helping teachers and students avoid the inappropriate testing or quizzing that often follows instruction lacking clear purpose and that often stresses basic skills over comprehension and thinking skills. There are very few tests that have these kinds of strategies built into them. An exception related to reading comprehension assessment is "Degrees of Reading Power" (DRP), which was "designed explicitly to assess performance on dimensions other than rote mastery of narrow subskills." As important is the fact that the DRP is an untimed power test which, through its structure, avoids much of the testing bias inherent in timed assessments. The monitoring and evaluation that Paris suggests, as reading or learning strategies, are cognitive and interactional in nature, not easily tested nor easily taught using solely deductive and didactic approaches. Instead, classroom instruction needs to move away from the lecture format to the facilitation of instructional dialogues between students and teachers.

A potential problem related to classroom management when using the strategies stressed by Paris is that they may make for noisy classes. Yet, when people are involved in generating their own ideas, thinking and learning are rarely quiet activities. By their nature, monitoring and evaluating involve a high level of interaction since they often call for judgments and conclusions to be drawn within student/teacher dialogues.

The sixth and last of Paris's strategies is the drawing of inferences. When this strategy is internalized, students begin to control their own learning and assert that control with greater confidence. This transference from teacher to student is best attained when the teacher is willing to share instructional control with the students.

Interweaving Teaching and Learning

The strategies described herein are all on the map of the New Mainstream. They indicate some of the directions—some of the cognitive skills—that one must use as a learner and that, hopefully, students will gain in the course of their schooling. These and, obviously, many other strategies for teaching and learning should be the shared responsibility of schools, teachers, and students at all grade, discipline, and skill levels.

Teaching and learning are reciprocal, not complementary; they represent two sides of the same coin, not two parts of a fitted puzzle. This is a difficult concept to implement in schools and one that opens a host of options that have been available, yet not consistently deployed, in our schools. Thinking about what may be called strategic learning can highlight how teachers might also think about strategic teaching. Teachers may set the direction and do, in fact, chart the map and erect the learning scaffold but they also share in the learning.

CONCLUSION

The suggestions outlined in this article can lead to a New Mainstream of instruction for minority and other students regardless of individual learning differences brought to the classroom. They draw on the expertise of every child for the experiential growth of every other child and of teachers and schools in general. This philosophy for instruction also reflects an educational arrangement based upon heterogeneous and untracked groupings in classrooms; thus, it may help avoid some of the transitional problems related to the pull-out programs that have been found to be disruptive to cohesive learning experiences.

Teaching should not be held as the exclusive prerogative of teachers. For example, reading and learning should not be segmented into a small niche of a large curriculum. Teachers should avoid delegating the passive activities—from blackboard cleaning to collecting papers—while retaining the active learning responsibilities—talking, listening, responding, and analyzing—for themselves. Regrettably, how often has a teacher overheard students asking, "Will it be on the test?" in order to find some purpose for an activity that they see little apparent reason to learn. This is an example of the most obvious misapplication of instruction: If it is only the testmakers that set purpose in schools, education has left the driving to them, and places in their hands the prerogative for choosing the routes, schedules, maps, and destinations for the school system. Classrooms where tests and textbooks may dominate 80 percent of what students are exposed to should be tolerated no longer. Instead, that 80 percent should be focused on mediated classroom discussions that provide for give-and-take interaction among students and among teachers and students.

The instructional changes proposed within this article require teachers who maintain high expectations for students, administrators with creativity and leadership, restructured classrooms for improved management of instruction, and partnerships forged out of participatory decision making with all of the individuals involved in the process of schooling. Cognitive theory as a central theme for this change can be applied without compromise and with major effect. It is a matter of driving or steering carefully through this path I am calling the New Mainstream—a broad stream that encompasses learning theory, student differences, and instructional reform.

Cognitive research has generated a body of knowledge and a library of strategic interventions that are helping to bring a renaissance to schooling. This research has provided us with new fuel for accelerating school improvement, yet it has, thus far, had remarkably little effect on instruction in the nation's schools. Obstacles such as minimal-competency tests and instructional material steeped in lower-order objectives need to be removed. Teachers and administrators unwilling to maintain high expectations for all students need to be retrained or removed. Classrooms that are organized primarily for lecturing by the teacher (where students, because of the seating arrangements, are forced to engage with the backs of their fellow students' heads) need to be restructured. Should we so choose to incorporate the process of learning into the management of schools for instruction, cognitive research provides us with an opportunity to improve schooling.

HOWARD GARDNER ON LEARNING
FOR UNDERSTANDING

by Elizabeth Donohoe Steinberger
Elizabeth Steinberger is a free-lance writer and educational
researcher based in Leesburg, Virginia.

Howard Gardner has challenged not only the ways in which we see ourselves and our children, but also the ways in which we teach and learn. His book, *Frames of Mind*, published in 1983, forwarded his theory of multiple intelligences, which shook the bedrock of traditional cognitive psychology by advocating that each individual is smart in many more ways than can be measured by conventional IQ tests.

In 1991, Gardner attracted national attention in *The Unschooled Mind* by arguing that even the best students in the best schools leave the classroom with flawed theories about how the world works and why people do what they do. Gardner, a professor at Harvard University's Graduate School of Education, believes that schools have substituted various proxies, such as Carnegie units and other credentials, for genuine knowledge, understanding, and achievement.

An author of a dozen books, Gardner has worked with victims of brain disease at the Veterans Administration Medical Center in Boston as well as with highly artistic children at Harvard. Most recently he has directed his efforts toward ATLAS (Authentic Teaching, Learning, and Assessment for all Students), a collaborative project supported by the New American Schools Development Project.

How are teaching and learning being reshaped in ATLAS communities? Gardner describes the reforms he believes are needed for genuine student understanding and achievement in an interview with *The School Administrator*.

STEINBERGER: You have suggested that one of the most striking aspects of educational reform has been the silence about educational purpose. What do you see as being the purpose of schooling in today's world?

GARDNER: We managed to go through several years of reform by focusing on things where there probably wasn't going to be a huge amount of disagreement. One point of agreement was that we need to have kids who have basic skills and who work hard—that was not very controversial.

A second was that if we want teachers to be professional, they have to have more control over their lives and what happens in schools. That was not terribly controversial either.

My analysis suggests, however, that ultimately we have to bite the bullet and say what schooling is for and ask how we know whether we are achieving that. So a couple of years ago, I bit the bullet and said the purpose of education is to enhance students' understanding.

This, in itself, is not controversial, either. But when you ask what is understanding and how do you know whether you have achieved it, these questions become very controversial.

STEINBERGER: What do you mean by "understanding"?

GARDNER: Let's say, for example, you have 16 Carnegie units or that you get a certain score on a standardized test. Can I assume then that you understand something? You might say, "Sure, because those tests test for understanding." But here's where things get really interesting.

Research indicates that most students in most schools, including our best students in our best schools, do not really understand. And you say, "What? The students who get A's, who get good scores on the College Boards, and who go to Ivy League schools don't understand?"

Let me give an example from the sciences. When you ask students who get very high grades and go to very good colleges to explain a physical phenomenon, not only can they not explain it but they actually give the same sort of explanations that four and five-year-olds give.

In mathematics, kids learn how to plug numbers into a formula, but then you give them a problem they have not seen before, most students do not know how to use the formula to solve the problem. In the social sciences, arts, and humanities, a student may well be able to express a complex phenomenon they have encountered in school or a text, but when something complex happens in the real world, they give very simplistic explanations.

This is where my definition of understanding comes in. I consider an individual to have understood when he or she can take knowledge, concepts, skills, and facts and apply them in new situations where they are appropriate. If students simply parrot back what they have been told or what they have read in a textbook, then we do not really know whether they understand.

We can only really determine whether a student understands when we give the student something new and they can draw upon what they have learned to help answer a question, illuminate a problem, or explain a phenomenon to someone else.

STEINBERGER: Where do students get these simplistic notions about their world?

GARDNER: They get them pretty much on their own by being human beings, by having brains, and by trying, during their early years, to make sense of the world. Kids develop very powerful theories about the world when they are young—theories about matter, mind, and life. A theory about matter, for example, is that sweaters keep you warm so they must have warmth in them. But when you leave a sweater outside, it stays cold.

Many of a child's theories are totally intuitive and totally wrong. They are developed without a lot of help, without a lot of teaching. And that is what I call the "unschooled mind," the mind that is developed without any formal education. It is a wonderful mind. However, if all of these ideas were correct, we would never have had to develop disciplines or teach children new things because they would come to school entirely equipped.

STEINBERGER: How do teachers and administrators take the unschooled mind and help the child understand the world and the way people are?

GARDNER: According to the work I have done, these early theories are deeply engraved into our mind. Because many of them are wrong, the purpose of school ought to be to change the engraving so that it is more accurate. Instead what happens is that the engraving gets covered with a very fine powder—the stuff that school is trying to teach.

If you peek into the mind in school, it looks pretty good because you just see the powder. But beneath the powder, the engraving is unaffected. And when you leave school and slam the door for the last time, the powder blows away and the initial engraving is still there. In other words, the unschooled mind is relatively unaffected by school once the individual gets out of the school context.

Although we need teachers and textbooks, they often are not enough. Unless you really confront students' notions about the world and figure out why they believe these theories and what could convince them they are wrong, they will continue to hold onto those ideas.

And so you can simulate things. You really have to help kids challenge the ideas they have. If you leave a sweater outside every day of the year and have kids take the temperature of the sweater everyday, that is going to affirm the notion that the sweater is not inherently warm. You take their stereotypical ways of thinking very seriously, recognize their misconceptions, and deal with them directly.

STEINBERGER: Are there other ways?

GARDNER: There are. These include two institutions I am very interested in. One is an old institution—the apprenticeship. The other is a new institution—the children's museum.

Now I'm not talking about the surface features of apprenticeships and children's museums—with apprenticeships, seven years of indenture and sweeping the floor, or with children's museums, a place you go to on weekends to see big fountains and eat ice cream. I'm talking about the educational wisdom that is embedded in each of these institutions.

In an apprenticeship, you hang around somebody who is an expert, a mentor. You see that person use his or her knowledge in action everyday. Here is where we can get into the marrow of schools.

STEINBERGER: And what about the educational wisdom embedded in children's museums?

GARDNER: What's amazing about children's museums is that you can take kids who seem like total dolts in school and put them in children's museums and suddenly they become very intelligent. They inquire, explore, experiment. They learn things, approach things in their own way, and do their own kind of reflection about what is going on.

I've seen 50 to 60 kids totally engaged and working in a children's museum without any adult around. You don't often see that sort of thing in schools.

STEINBERGER: Both apprenticeships and children's museums suggest that students go outside the traditional school setting. How can we bring more of this type of learning into the classroom?

GARDNER: It's really bringing the habit of mind and the practices associated with those institutions closer to classrooms. If teachers think of themselves as role models—actually using the literacies of their discipline, thinking historically, and carrying out experiments—kids will see that what they are learning really does have a use.

The single most important thing that a superintendent, principal, or teacher can do is to show that learning and knowledge and understanding are important to them. If they can do that, they have crossed the most important river. And if they do not have the time to do that, they are destined to fail in the area of genuine understanding, no matter how clever they are and how good they are with budgets. If they do not communicate that learning and understanding are central, they cannot possibly be effective.

STEINBERGER: So administrators and teachers can serve as experts in learning for the apprentice student?

GARDNER: Yes, but it's not that important that the teacher be the total expert. Teachers shouldn't feel badly if they don't know all the answers. They should feel badly if they cut off the questions.

Children learn a lot when teachers say they don't know—as long as teachers also ask questions, such as how can we figure this out, who can we go to, where could we look it up? What is important is that the teacher, at his or her level of understanding, demonstrate how to learn and use what he or she has learned.

STEINBERGER: Let's turn the tables a bit. You have talked about how children develop flawed theories about how the real world works. What are some of the flawed theories about schools, about how children develop and how they learn?

GARDNER: Everybody—you, I, administrators, and teachers—has flawed notions about school. Perhaps the most profound one is that school has to be the way we adults remember it. Most people feel that if they sat still with worksheets in front of them and handed work in on time, then that's the way school should be.

I'm not saying schools like that are necessarily disastrous, but I can say with great confidence that this type of learning doesn't work anymore.

Another flawed notion is that the teacher is the person who is smart and has all the knowledge and the child is an empty vessel in whom that knowledge is poured. Still another is that kids are bright or dumb. They are born that way and there isn't much you can do about it. The purpose of school, then, is to figure out who the bright ones are and push them through as quickly as possible and to sort out the dumb ones because you really can't do much about them.

And then there's the notion that you have to control things at all times, and that kids have to be kept down because as soon as you turn your back, they'll throw something at you.

STEINBERGER: You said that some of these flawed notions play out in the ways children are labeled as being smart or dumb. How does your theory of multiple intelligences counter such labels?

GARDNER: The notion of intelligence as being a single thing is actually less than 100 years old, but it has exerted enormous influence in this country and others as well.

My research led me to a different perspective. I observed that with both children and brain-damaged patients, strength in one area simply did not predict strength in another area. If I tell you, for example, that somebody is good in music, you can't tell me whether or not he or she will be good with language or science or understanding other people.

My argument is that in evolution we have developed a brain and a mind that can analyze lots of different information. And while every brain and mind can do that, probably no two brains and minds have exactly the same configurations of intelligences.

STEINBERGER: What does this mean for school?

GARDNER: What we have been doing is to teach and assess everybody as though each has the same kind of mind. In school, we appeal to people who have what I call a blend of superficial language and logic—people who are quick and glib and who can talk fast and reason pretty well.

As long as these people stay in school, they do well. But once they walk out into the street, they discover that the skills they have are really not any more essential than other skills for surviving in the world.

If you take the notion of individual differences and multiple intelligences seriously, you have to ask several questions: What curricula do we offer kids? To what extent do we try to configure curricula to children's ways of learning? What kind of assessments should we use to find out whether kids really understand?

There's no reason why everyone has to learn history or math in the same way. And there is no reason why we have to be assessed in the same way. We have different kinds of minds. If I understand a mathematical principle and I can show you it one way, it's really not important that I show it to you in another way.

STEINBERGER: How can schools test for and appeal to so many different intelligences?

GARDNER: A lot of intelligences really can't be tested for, in the sense we usually use the word "test." What we need to do is to create school environments where you can observe a lot about what kids are good at, what interests them, and where they show substantial growth—environments that, in many respects, resemble children's museums.

STEINBERGER: Where might school administrators and teachers start?

GARDNER: Within the educational context, I believe we need to start with the child's strengths. If a child is afraid of a particular area or not very good in an area, the best way to work with that child is to use an area of strength as an entry point.

This not only increases the chances that the child will find some way to the concept—after all, there are many windows in the same room—but, at the same time, it gives the child a sense of what it means to be an expert because an expert is able to think about things in more than one way.

We also might begin to observe children when they are young and share our observations with the children, their parents, and subsequent teachers. In the end, however, we have to be responsible for our own education, and this means knowing what sorts of things we are good at and how we learn best.

STEINBERGER: Are there model schools that are successfully implementing these practices?

GARDNER: There is the Key School in Indianapolis, which is organized around the idea of multiple intelligences. One thing that excites people about the Key School is that the children there are very metacognitive. The children say, "Well, I learn about stuff in this way." They get very angry when the teacher insists on doing things only his or her way.

Another example is a high school in East Harlem in New York City. The kids, who have had many strikes against them, are learning a progressive curriculum and working hard. Graduation is by exhibition, not by test scores. Eighty percent of the kids graduate and go on to colleges.

We also have a new project, currently funded by the New American

age. Understanding takes time, and the greatest enemy of understanding is coverage. If you are determined to cover everything, you guarantee that most kids will not understand.

I find it incredible that we have so many educational leaders—from chief state school officers to governors to presidents to secretaries of education—and none of them talks about what seems to be the most elementary thing: If kids don't understand, then what are we doing?

MASLOW AND FIELD EXPERIENCES IN COMPETENCY-BASED TEACHER EDUCATION

by Allen R. Warner
Director of Field Experiences, University of Houston

Presented as A Special Interest Session at
THE 1975 ANNUAL CONFERENCE
of the ASSOCIATION OF TEACHER EDUCATORS
NEW ORLEANS, LOUISIANA
February 6, 1975

THE NEED FOR A CONCEPTUAL BASE

Even a perfunctory review of the literature on student teaching in the last 75 years leads quickly to the conclusion that there is no comprehensive theoretical rationale for the contributions of student teaching and related direct experiences to the development of a professional teacher (Andrews, 1964, p.30).

Because of the lack of a theoretical base from which to operate, research in student teaching has been criticized as being "highly randomized," leading one writer to conclude: ". . . what we have actually said is something like this: we do not know what we want to happen, but surely it will happen if we give the teacher education students enough exposure" (LaGrone, 1965, p.97).

Conant (1964, p.142) considered professional laboratory experiences the "one indisputable essential element in professional education." But as Silberman has pointed out, this view is primarily based on the opinions of graduates of teacher education programs rather than being rooted in a systematic justification. "To the extent to which they value any aspect of their professional education, teachers generally cite practice-teaching as the most valuable—sometimes the only valuable—part" (Silberman, 1970, p.451).

Within the past few years, professional education has become a more scientific undertaking. One thrust has been directed toward breaking the teacher act down into more specific, definable behaviors. Another thrust has been in the direction of codifying and quantifying those behaviors, and assessing their effects on student learning.

As professional education becomes more scientific in its approach, controversy multiples between "behaviorists" and "humanists." In one corner of the ring are those who see the proper goal of teacher education programs as the production of a teacher who has mastered a variety of teaching skills. The trainee is expected to display a certain minimal degree of competence in his/her behavior as measured against predetermined objectives. Cooper and Weber define competency-based teacher education as follows:

> A competency-based (or performance-based) teacher education program is a program in which the competencies to be acquired by the student and the criteria to be applied in assessing the competency of the student are made explicit and the student is held accountable for meeting those criteria (Cooper & Weber, quoted in Elfenbein, 1972, p.4).

The reader should note at this point that this definition of competency-based teacher education involves only the explicit nature of the objectives of the program, and the accountability of the student for meeting those objectives. Other concepts, such as individual progression and mastery learning, are not given in this definition but are often introduced into discussions concerning competency-based teacher education.

Teacher educators who value teachers possessing a "self-as-instrument" self concept, a view of the teacher as helper, as the ultimate goal of professional education, tend to be in the opposing corner. Arthur Combs may be considered representative of this group. He has argued that, "The production of an effective teacher is a highly personal matter," and "Effective teacher education must concentrate its efforts on meanings rather than behavior" (1972, pp.286–287). Behavior is only a symptom: subjective, idiosyncratic meanings are the causal agents.

Combs has criticized the competency approach for a number of reasons, questioning whether methods of experts can be taught to beginners; whether long lists of competencies cannot be discouraging to the neophyte and the experienced teacher alike, because one never really "arrives." There are always more competencies to be mastered (1965, pp.4–5).

For the self-as-instrument group, becoming a teacher is part of an overall process of "becoming" as a person, part of the development of a total personality. And that process of becoming must "start from security and acceptance" (Combs, 1972, p.287).

Such arguments, however, tend to obscure a deeper difference between these two approaches to the training of teachers. That difference is one of epistemology, of basic assumptions concerning that which is worth knowing. Epistemological assumptions are basic to any view of science, for they outline the rubrics of empirical inquiry.

Competency-based programs, by Cooper and Weber's definition, are organized on the principle of criterion-referenced instruction. This has been outlined earlier, but a further distinction must be made. In criterion-referenced instruction, the basic operational problem is the definition of desirable outcomes of units of instruction, and the statement of those outcomes in behavioral terms. Outcomes stated in this way are known as behavioral objectives, and the basic epistemological assumption of behavioral objectives is that outward behavior is that which is worth knowing, worth studying and measuring.

This assumption is in direct opposition to the position taken by Combs, alluded to earlier, that those entities worth knowing are the subjective, idiosyncratic meanings which cause behavior. This is the phenomenological point of view—that behavior should be considered from within a subject's frame of reference rather than from without.

THE NEED FOR A MORE COMPREHENSIVE PERSPECTIVE

Each of these approaches posits a desirable goal of programs of teacher education and delineates, to a degree, the types and structure of field experiences necessary to obtain that particular end goal. If, for instance, one's ideal picture of a beginning teacher emphasizes primarily measurable, observable basic skills, probably the most efficient method of achieving that end would be to: (1) modularize skill learning packages, giving the trainee the opportunity to develop specific competencies in simulated environments, and (2) to expect the trainee to exhibit those skills gained in later, direct classroom performance.

If, on the other hand, one's ideal beginning teacher is one with a strong sense of purpose, a positive view of self; highly attuned to the needs of individual students; responsive to, and interactive; if this is the case, then the principle of "appropriate practice" would seem to suggest much more direct experiences and less indirect, simulated experience.

In the first case, extreme emphasis on skill development alone ignores other elements of personal development. In the second, skill development is sacrificed because of the lack of control by the teacher trainer over the dynamics of direct classroom experience.

Truth, as is customary, lies somewhere between the extreme poles. The real goal of all teacher educators is a beginning teacher who enjoys working with pupils, who finds great satisfaction helping them learn, and who possesses the requisite skills to accomplish this end. This description is virtually identical with what Abraham Maslow has described as a self-actualized individual.

Maslow has proposed a theory of human motivation that is basically teleological, proposing an inherent human tendency toward self-actualization. Maslow ranks what he proposes to be inherent human needs, in order of decreasing strength:

1. Physiological needs
2. Safety
3. Love and affection
4. Self-esteem and prestige (approval of others)
5. Self-actualization

The point of the hierarchy is that the stronger, basic needs must be satisfied before the weaker, higher needs become important to us. A further point with regards to the hierarchy is that the needs in the hierarchy need not be totally satisfied in order for the individual to become aware of, and concerned about beginning to satisfy, the next higher and weaker need. The degree to which each need must be satisfied before movement to the next higher need occurs is an individual process. For some individuals safety or security is a stronger need than for others.

It is at level four (self-esteem and independence) where there exists a possibility for integrating, at least theoretically, the two opposing points of view ("competency" vs. "becoming") with regards to the goals, and therefore the structure, of clinical experiences. Maslow has from time to time referred to "competence" as an important ingredient in obtaining and maintaining a sense of self-esteem and independence. One must view himself as a competent human being in order to gain self-esteem.

STUDENT TEACHING

At what level of concern are teacher-trainees as they complete their training? David Aspy has suggested that there is a considerable discrepancy between what teacher educators expect of teacher trainees in clinical experience, and what teacher trainees are in a position to give. Reviewing a number of studies concerning anxieties expressed during teacher training and during initial years of teaching, Aspy concluded:

> . . . the majority of our student teachers are operating in fear as they enter their final phase of teacher training. According to Maslow, they would be operating at the safety level, which means they are concerned with their own survival at a time we are asking them to give to others (Aspy, 1969, p.304).

Do other data support this view? Dussault (1970) reviewed studies from 1931 to 1968 which utilized professional laboratory experiences (almost exclusively student teaching) as the independent variables and attitude changes on the part of teacher trainees as the dependent variable. He found a number of positive changes:

— positive changes in self-concept
— greater acceptance of others
— greater reality-orientation
— less self-depreciation
— improvement in teaching skills
— improved ability to work with children
— better understanding of children
— greater self-autonomy and decision-making
— greater correlation between perceptions of ideal and actual own teaching role
— more positive perceptions of ideal and actual teachers
— decrease in professional anxieties

Assuming that the desired outcome is a teacher who enjoys working with students, who is open to new ideas and approaches, who begins to develop his own personal idiosyncratic teaching style, and so on, the "bad news" effects of student teaching are:

— less openness to experience
— adoption of accepted practices
— adoption of cooperating teacher's methods of teaching
— adoption of cooperating teacher's methods of classroom housekeeping
— less logical consistency of ideas about education
— more negative perception of child behavior
— more custodial pupil-control ideology

Sorenson and Halpert (1969) found that 70 percent of the student teachers who they studied experienced "considerable psychological discomfort" at the beginning of the student teaching experience, and 20 percent carried that discomfort with them to the end of the assignment. The researchers identified five stress factors. Two of these dealt with the nature of discomfort: physical discomfort and irritability, and feelings of personal inadequacy and uncertainty about the teaching role. Two more factors were identified as sources of discomfort: disagreement between the student teacher and the supervising teacher concerning teaching practices, and perceived differences in personality between student teacher and supervising teacher.

The fifth factor which Sorenson and Halpert identified concerned the relationships between the student teacher and pupils. The researchers were unsure whether to assign this variable to either a source of discomfort, or nature (or type) of discomfort. They refer to this scale as "dislike of students."

STUDENT TEACHING AND
SAFETY-LEVEL BEHAVIOR

Do the results of research given above support Aspy's charge that teacher trainees are operating at a safety level of behavior during the final phase of their training?

Answering this question requires, first of all, operationalizing the term "safety" in this specific context. What constitutes safety here? What is the goal of the organism (in this case, the student teacher)?

Student teaching is usually a terminal experience in a teacher education program. The student teacher is often in the final semester of his undergraduate college career. What is his most immediate goal? To graduate. To complete the program. In order to complete his college career, he must complete student teaching. The diploma constitutes the consummation of sixteen years of schooling. It represents a considerable amount of effort and the allocation of numerous resources. Reaching that goal constitutes immediate perceived safety.

How does one succeed in student teaching? Whose expectations must be met? Daily, the supervising teacher. Occasionally, the university supervisor. It is not surprising then that the student teacher should model a considerable amount of his classroom teaching behavior after that of the supervising teacher—that the supervising teacher becomes a "significant other" to the point where disagreements between student teacher and supervising teacher result in, as Sorenson and Halpert phrase it, "considerable psychological discomfort."

What of the pupils in the student teacher's charge? The supervising teacher, the university supervisor, and the entire educational staff back at the university want the student teacher to like the children he is teaching, to help those children learn, to show respect for their abilities.

But the student teacher sees a necessity of presenting himself to his evaluators as poised, confident, in control of his classes. This type of image is, after all, vital to success. The students don't quite understand. With a new person in charge of the class, the rules change. The children test, probe, explore this new leader to determine the limits he will place on their behavior. And the novice teacher views this pupil behavior as a threat to reaching the goal that is so close after so many years, the diploma.

It is to be expected that, upon completing this stressful experience, the positive changes in attitude identified by Dussault would also follow. Having successfully completed student teaching experience with all its strains, it is to be expected that the student teacher will feel better about himself. He has conquered. He will feel better about teachers in the field. He has, after all, adopted many of his supervising teacher's methods in order to succeed.

Almost everyone does succeed in student teaching. Johnson (1968) found that 86 percent of responding institutions reported failing 1 percent or less of their student teachers on the first assignment. But in succeeding, some less than desirable attitudes have been fostered. One intention (or objective) was for the student teacher to use the skills gained in earlier training, to test them, to use them in developing his own idiosyncratic teaching style. But instead, he simply adopts many of the methods of his supervising teacher. The status quo lives.

Another objective was to open the student teacher's mind to experience. The stresses of the situation have instead made him less open.

The student teacher was supposed to develop a fairly rational philosophy concerning education and his own teaching. He was so busy meeting everyone's expectations, however, that he had little time to attempt to synthesize the theory he had been taught on campus with the practices he was expected to display in the classroom. He ended the experience with less logical consistency of his ideas about education that when he began.

The trainee was supposed to learn to like the age-group of children he was preparing to teach as a career. But with all the other stresses, all the other expectations he had to meet, the pupils really got in the way. They, after all, were not the ones to make the final evaluation. And much of the final evaluation rested on how well he controlled or guided them. The pupil's attempts to determine the "new rules" with the new leader were not perceived a natural phenomenon but rather a threat to success, to safety.

And finally, under the stresses of the situation, the trainees began to question whether teaching was really the type of career to which he would like to devote his life. But this was the last semester of the senior year! It was much too late to change. So he made it through, he did what was expected of him, he got the degree. Then perhaps he took a teaching job. And perhaps for just a year or two until he found something more exciting, more personally fulfilling.

The reader at this point may feel that the writer is painting an overly dismal picture of student teaching. But the previous discussion did not wander from the findings summarized by Dussault, those of Sorenson and Halpert, and an additional consistent research finding—that 50 percent of the people who enter teaching do not stay in teaching longer than ten years.

The question remains: Does student teaching have to be this way? At least one study suggests that it does not. Fuller, Pilgrim and Freeland (1967) reported the results of an experiment which involved providing counseling and close supervision to student teachers. The researchers identified six developmental stages during the student teaching experience.

In the first stage, trainees were concerned about the question "Where do I stand?" This initial stage concerned placements, school rules, identifying and ascertaining the expectations of various supervisory personnel.

The second stage involved concerns about the student teachers' perceptions of their adequacy in the teaching role. Anxieties about subject-matter adequacy and class control were highly evident.

A desire to determine the causes of deviant behavior on the part of students was evidenced in the third stage, while the fourth stage exhibited a desire for evaluation, for feedback, from supervisors, parents, principals, and other teachers.

In the fifth stage, trainees began to display a concern for what their pupils were learning as opposed to what they were being taught. Finally, student teachers reflected a full concern for their pupils and began to achieve new understandings of themselves through their relationships with pupils.

Two points need to be made with regards to this study. The first is that these developmental stages parallel rather nicely the sequence of Maslow's theory of motivation, or at least the intermediate stages (safety, love and belongingness, esteem). The first two stages obviously fit quite well into ego-centered safety concerns. Stages three through five exhibit a movement from safety to belongingness, from ego-centered concerns to concerns about others. And the final stage shows the beginnings of a synergic environment—one in which the needs of the individual (in this case, the teacher trainee) and the needs of those about him are both being satisfied by the mutual relationship.

The second point to be made concerning this study is that few schools of education exist that can afford such close supervision and counseling on a regular basis with their student teachers. The results of the research summarized by Dussault, and the study by Sorenson and Halpert, suggests that most student teachers do not advance beyond the fourth developmental stage: concerns for feedback, for evaluation.

SKILLS AND SAFETY

Microteaching and simulation, as supplements to direct classroom experience in teacher education, have a number of advantages toward helping the trainee increase his cognitive skills. And a more broad repertoire of teaching behaviors should result in the gratification of a number of broadly defined safety needs. It would be expected that, having a broad repertoire of teaching skills, the trainee should, in the student teaching experience, exhibit somewhat less anxiety about his abilities in the teaching role. And it might also be expected that the trainee would exhibit less modelling after the teaching behavior of the supervising teacher.

But this is conjecture. These questions have not, to the present writer's knowledge, been researched. Much of the research that has been accomplished on microteaching and simulation has dealt with matters such as whether or not the trainee actually acquires the skills presented, whether or not he considers simulation and microteaching as relevant to conditions he will face in the classroom.

At present, then, the best that can be said is that microteaching and simulation have considerable potential toward gratifying a number of safety-related concerns of the trainee in the instructional role.

If the general aim, however, is to assist the trainee in reaching a level of esteem in the instructional role, a level of general attitudinal orientation in which the trainee finds the teaching role personally rewarding, there is an intermediate need-stage yet to be addressed.

LOVE AND BELONGINGNESS

Aspy (1969) has noted the desirability of promoting feelings of belongingness among teacher trainees, suggesting that trainees should have the opportunity to establish close personal relationships with at least one teacher educator from the teacher training institution. Dussault's summary of goals of professional laboratory experiences includes "acceptance and appreciation of other people."

To what group should teacher educators encourage the trainee to feel that he "belongs"? He should begin to feel himself a member of the profession, certainly, by the completion of his training. Research on student teaching, reviewed earlier, suggests that trainees complete student teaching with more positive attitudes toward teachers in the field than was the case prior to student teaching. And yet, 50 percent of the teaching force leaves teaching within ten years.

Of all the factors which may cause a teacher to leave the teaching profession, what lasting bonds of affection (or belongingness) encourage one to remain in teaching? Close relationships with teacher educators may be valuable adjuncts to training, but are at best transitory. Such relationships will probably terminate when the trainee leaves the institution. If modeling of teaching behavior is any indication, trainees tend to develop a rather close relationship with supervising teachers. But this relationship is again, in the majority of cases, transitory.

It would seem, then, that the only lasting bonds of attachment are those between the trainee and the type of child he is preparing to teach. Of all the institutional dysfunctions identified earlier in this paper which might cause individuals to leave the teaching profession, a vital ingredient which would cause one to remain in teaching would be positive view of the children with which he works. One may decide to become a teacher because of previous experience with admirable people in the teaching profession. One may successfully complete training because of a close relationship with various supervisory personnel. But one will probably not stay in teaching very long simply out of admiration for other teachers with which one works. Social encounters with other teachers over coffee, over lunch, or after hours are simply not sufficient if one is not attracted to the day-by-day work of helping children learn.

In simpler terms, if one does not like the type of child he is preparing to teach, he may not take a teaching position in the first place. And if he does take a teaching position, he will probably not last long (by his own choice or that of others). This sort of general affection for the type of child one is preparing to teach (or, in behaviorist terms, an approach tendency), is not a quality that can be trained. Yet if it is as important to the holding power of the teaching profession as the previous discussion has suggested, the necessity of fostering such feelings should be recognized and implemented in preservice training.

Can student teaching prove to be a useful activity through which to foster positive perceptions of pupils on the part of trainees? Research evidence, reviewed previously, suggests that student teaching has not been particularly successful at achieving this goal in the past. Results have been at best, inconclusive; and at worst, negative. Using the Minnesota Teacher Attitude Inventory as a data-gathering device has produced evidence of approximately even distributions of studies which show positive changes in relationships with students, negative changes, or no significant change at all. A fairly consistent finding, according to Dussault (1970), is that student teachers tend to have a more negative view of pupil behavior at the end of student teaching than was once the case at the outset of student teaching.

EARLY DIRECT EXPERIENCE

If belongingness needs of teacher trainees—defined in this context as the development of positive perception toward the type of pupil the trainee is preparing to teach—are to be addressed so that the trainee may have the opportunity of gratifying such needs, neither microteaching, simulation, nor student teaching would appear to be a viable option.

Developing positive relationships with pupils necessitates physical encounter and interaction between the trainee and pupils: direct experience. Yet there is precious little evidence of the effects of direct experience aside from student teaching—a terminal activity in teacher education. Virtually no research has been done with regards to attitude changes of potential teachers resulting from early, direct contacts with pupils.

Speculation, then, becomes the order of the day.

What types of direct classroom experience are available? There are two generic types of direct classroom experiences: observation and participation. The trainee can watch, or he can do something. The trainee has, however, been observing teachers at work since the age of five or six. Additional unstructured observation, by itself, can probably add little to helping the trainee answer questions concerning his feelings about himself in the teaching role. Nor can observation alone allow the trainee to interact with pupils, to decide for himself whether working with pupils is a world of work to which he would like to commit his time and energies, or to develop positive relationships with pupils.

If, on the other hand, the reader will consider direct, participative experience as an early learning device—might not the same sorts of outcomes identified by Dussault as the results of student teaching be anticipated as results also of such early experience? That is, might teacher educators not expect such early, direct, participative experience to have positive effects of greater reality-orientation, positive changes in self-concept, less self-depreciation, and so on, on the part of trainees? And might not the negative effects, especially modelling behavior after the practices of personnel in the field, be better brought out early when such effects can be dealt with in later training, than left only as an effect of a terminal experience in the program? Broadening the cognitive teaching skills of the trainee after an initial reality-contact (through microteaching and simulation) should be more productive because the trainee would have a more concrete frame of reference concerning the teaching role.

One negative effect of direct experience identified by Dussault's review was that of more negative perceptions of pupil behavior on the part of the trainee. If the previous analysis in this paper has been correct—that this effect of student teaching has been, to a considerable extent, the result of trainees having to meet a plethora of supervisory expectations while working with entire classes—might not the opportunity to work with individual pupils, or small groups of pupils, with much less expected of the trainee in terms of skill learning or display, increase the opportunity for trainees to develop *positive* relationships with pupils? Gratification of belongingness needs is then also potentially addressed.

A further advantage of early, direct, extensive, participative clinical experience could be posited. If the trainee is viewed in a Maslovian sense—as a human being with a measure of free will who must be provided an optimum degree of freedom of choice—then such early reality-contact, if it is an initial experience in the teacher preparation program, can provide a solid basis for the trainee to decide whether or not teaching is a career to which he wishes to commit his time and energies. In providing an opportunity for the trainee to explore the instructional role in a low-threat environment, an opportunity is also set forth for the trainee to explore the less apparent complexities of the teaching role—hall duty, lunchroom duty, faculty meetings, instructional planning, and so forth. The trainee then has a considerable amount of information on which to base very personal questions of commitment, and sufficiently early in the program so that he can, if he so desires, shift to another area of professional training—another world of work more consonant with his own needs and desires—with little penalty.

PHASES OF CLINICAL EXPERIENCE

With these considerations in mind, field experience might most profitably be conceptualized in terms of successive phases—each phase with differing objectives, and experiences provided to accomplish those objectives. For the purpose of this analysis, three phases will be suggested: an exploratory phase; a skill-acquisition phase, and a skill-testing and revision phase.

Exploratory Phase

In the exploratory phase, the primary objective is to provide the trainee who has made an initial decision to become a teacher, the best, most realistic information possible on which to base his decision as to whether or not to continue in teacher training. At the end of this initial phase, the trainee would be held accountable for making an initial commitment to continue training. Or, conversely, to select himself out of the program at a sufficiently early stage so that he can seek a world of work more appropriate to his own needs.

If this exploratory phase also contains certain conditions, those trainees who decide to continue their training can potentially gain more than decision making information: they can gain a measure of readiness for subsequent training as well. If, for instance, the exploratory phase contains the basic generic elements of student teaching—direct, participative experience—then teacher educators might also expect that most of the effects of student teaching (as outlined by Dussault earlier) would also be the result of this early direct experience. Those trainees who decide to continue training should evidence, as a group: an enhanced self-concept; better understanding of children; greater reality-orientation, and so on. These positive effects can only enhance later training.

If the previous analysis presented in this paper has been correct—that negative effects such as less openness to experience, more negative perceptions of pupil behavior as residual effects of student teaching are primarily caused by the trainee having to respond to too many expectations at once—then these effects of student teaching need not be effects of the exploratory stage. If the trainee is given limited instructional tasks to accomplish which virtually guarantee success—such as one-to-one tutoring, perhaps later at the judgment of the supervisor leading small group discussions, and perhaps under close supervision leading an entire class in a learning activity—the effect that might be anticipated is that the trainee will be more open to experience and less negative concerning pupil behavior.

The point, then, is that by assuring the safety of the trainee, an opportunity is being provided for the trainee to address questions of belonging as well. In being given a low-threat environment in which to explore the instructional role, the trainee at the same time is being given the opportunity to develop positive relationships with pupils. The complexities of the teaching role with regards to leading whole classes have been lessened, but with trainee-pupil interaction still possible.

In order for the trainee to acquire the optimum amount of information on which to base decisions concerning further commitment to the teaching profession, this exploratory stage should not be limited only to working with students. Non-instructional activities which consume so much of the teacher's time in actual practice (typing, paper grading, planning, hall duty, and so on) are also integral elements of the teaching role. To be honest with the trainee demands that the trainee be exposed to such activities as part of this exploratory stage. The primary purpose of the exploratory phase is to allow the trainee the opportunity to develop positive relationships with pupils representative of the age group he is preparing to teach. Because this phase is early in the program, the trainee also has the opportunity not to develop positive relationships with pupils, and to select himself out.

Most certainly, these purposes or objectives should be made explicit, clearly spelled out, to the trainee at the beginning of the exploratory phase. The trainee should not have to expend his energies attempting to determine what is expected of him in this phase, because that uncertainty itself can be the cause of considerable anxiety and coping behavior.

The denouement of the exploratory phase should come at the end. At this point, trainees should be confronted with a conscious rational decision based on the opportunities provided: whether or not to continue preparing to become teachers. This initial commitment is a statement of intention, not a contract. The trainee always retains the option of divorcing himself from the program at a later date. And the trainee's intention certainly need not be in the form of a written document. Most important, the trainee must be addressed with the proper questions, clearly and explicitly, perhaps phrased as follows:

> Over the past few weeks you have been allowed the opportunity to explore the teaching role. You were given this opportunity because you had expressed an interest in teaching as a career. Hopefully, you have found out through that experience that teaching is more than it may have appeared to you in your role as a student. Helping pupils learn is a vastly complicated undertaking, and teaching a class is by no means all there is to the role of teacher.

> The professional staff in the school of education at this institute has considerable experience in the field of education. They can help you become a better, more skilled teacher. But they cannot make you want to teach, nor can they make you like the type of child you are preparing to teach. Both of these qualities are essential, and you are the only one who can answer these questions.

> If you decide to continue preparing to teach, the next phase will require that you acquire a variety of skills to help you function more effectively as a teacher. And in student teaching, the final phase, you will be expected to display some of those skills in your teaching behavior. These skills are not required for the purpose of "fitting" you into the mold of a good teacher, but rather to supply you with "tools" to help you become more effective as a teacher.

> If you have decided at this point that you do not wish to continue in teacher preparation, then this experience was also beneficial for you. You now have the opportunity to contact your advisor and revise your pro-

gram so that you may prepare for an occupation more in line with your interests.

Skill-Acquisition Phase

Having provided the trainee with opportunities to attend to the gratification of safety and belongingness needs within the instructional context during the exploratory phase, those trainees who decided to continue training should be ready to address the acquisition of skills related to the teaching role.

PHASES:	EXPLORATORY	SKILL ACQUISITION			SKILL TESTING AND REVISION
	UNRE STRU CTUR ED OBSE RVAT ION	EARLY DIRECT EXTEN SIVE PART ICIP ATIVE CLINICAL EXPERIENCE	STRU CTUR ED OBS ERVA TION	IND- IRECT CLIN- ICAL EXPER IENCE	TERMINAL DIRECT EXTENSIVE PARTICIPATIVE CLINICAL EXPERIENCE
1. DECISION ON TEACHING CAREER	P	P	S	S	I
2. GRATIFICA- TION OF SAFETY NEEDS IN INSTR- UCTIONAL ROLE	I	P	I	P	S
3. GRATIFICA- TION OF BELONG- INGNESS NEEDS IN INSTRUCTION- AL ROLE	S	P	I	I	S
4. GRATIFICA- TION OF ESTEEM NEEDS THROUGH SKILLS ACQUISITION	I	I	P	P	S
5. TESTING (BY TRAINEE) OF INSTRUCTIONAL SKILLS, REVIS- ION INTO PERSON- AL TEACHING STYLE			I	S	P
6. DEVELOPMENT OF DECISION MA- MAKING SKILLS	S	P	I	P	P
7. TESTING OF TRAINEE BY INSTITUTION FOR PURPOSES OF CERTIFICATION			S	S	P
P-PRIMARY OBJECTIVE S-SECONDARY OBJECTIVE I-INCIDENTAL LEARNING					

FIGURE 1. MAJOR OBJECTIVES TO BE REALIZED FROM CLINICAL EXPERIENCE IN TEACHER EDUCATION

In this phase, techniques such as microteaching and simulation become extremely valuable. Both simulation and microteaching rely heavily on selectivity. The teaching act is broken down into constituent elements, and this simplification allows analysis. The complex stimuli inherent in the classroom environment are categorized, separated. The trainee is provided with a safe environment in which to attend to stimuli relevant to a particular category. He is given a relatively safe environment in which to practice decision-making skills (simulation), or specific teaching behaviors (microteaching). The result of such training is a broadening of the cognitive skills of the trainee. And the more skilled he is, the more confident he should tend to be during the student teaching phase. With this confidence should come less defensiveness under stress, and less tendency to "model" his teaching behavior after that of the supervising teacher (some modelling is probably unavoidable, if only because the supervising teacher is an important evaluator in the student teaching phase).

Skill-Testing and Revision Phase
(Student Teaching)

In the first phase, the trainee was given the opportunity to gratify safety and belongingness needs in the instructional context, and at the end of that phase was given the opportunity to make a rational decision concerning the desirability of the teaching role in terms of his own potential for growth.

In the second phase, the trainee was supplied with skills of teaching and decision-making. In effect, the purpose here was to gratify esteem needs through providing the trainee with a degree of technical expertise in the instructional role.

The final phase the present author has termed skill-testing and revision. In the past, this phase has variously been referred to as apprenticeship, practice teaching, student teaching. The functions which are suggested for this stage are:

1. Opportunities for the trainees to test the skills gained in the previous phases against the dynamics of full professional role assumption.
2. Through testing and evaluation, opportunities for the trainee to explore various skill combinations, and on the basis of experience to revise them.
3. Opportunities for the teacher preparing institution, through its supervisory personnel, to determine the final adequacy of the teaching candidate for purposes of certification.

PHASE OBJECTIVES

It may be useful for the reader to have the objectives of the three recommended stages summarized and presented in tabular form. Stated from the perspective of that which the trainee is expected to accomplish,

1. To utilize the best information available as a basis for personal decision to become or not to become a teacher.
2. To begin to gratify needs of safety and belongingness in the instructional role so as to develop readiness for skill training.
3. To gratify esteem needs through the development of technical expertise, the acquisition of instructional skills.
4. To test instructional skills against the dynamics of classroom teaching, to revise those skills, and to integrate them into a personal teaching style.
5. To develop decision-making skills.
6. To meet the requirements of the teacher training institution for purposes of certification.

The relationship between the various phases, activities within those phases as discussed above, and the objectives given, can be charted as shown in Figure 1.

QUESTIONS I WOULD ASK MYSELF
IF I WERE A TEACHER

by Carl R. Rogers
Resident Fellow, Center for Studies of the Person,
La Jolla, California

I have been asked to talk about humanizing education for gifted children and since most of you in this audience are dealing with programs for the gifted and talented I shall try to point my remarks in that direction. However, I believe that what I have to say applies to education for children with various labels because all children have tremendous potentialities, far more than are released. Those of you, however, who are privileged to work with youngsters who seem to have the greatest potentialities are indeed fortunate. You have a rare opportunity.

In many ways I am ill fitted for the task I have been given. I have never taught an elementary or high school class and only a relatively small number of undergraduate college students. I simply do not know at first hand the kind of situations you face every day in your classrooms. So I have wondered whether I have anything to contribute.

It has seemed to me that perhaps I could simply raise with you the questions that I would ask myself if I were given responsibility for the learnings of a group of children, gifted or otherwise. Suppose I was to be thought of as their teacher. I have tried to think about the questions I would ask myself, the things I would try to learn, the things I might try to do. How would I meet the challenge posed by such a group?

What Is It Like?

I think the first question I would raise is: What is it like to be a child who is learning something significant? I believe the most meaningful answer I can give is to speak from my own experience.

I was a very good boy in elementary and high school. I got good grades. Frequently I annoyed my teachers by being clever enough to get around the rules they had set up, but I was not openly defiant. I was a very solitary boy with few friends, isolated from others by a very strictly religious home. My family moved from a suburban setting to a large farm with acres of woodland when I was 13. At that time the Gene Stratton-Porter books were popular, which involved a wilderness setting and made much of the great night-flying moths.

Shortly after we moved to the farm I found a pair of luna moths—great pale green wings with purple trimmings—on the trunk of an oak tree. I can still see the spread of shimmering green with its iridescent lavender spots, bright against the shaggy black bark. I was enthralled. I captured them, kept them, and the female laid hundreds of eggs. I got a book on moths. I fed the baby caterpillars. Though I had many failures with this first brood I captured other moths and gradually learned to keep and sustain the caterpillars through their whole series of life changes; the frequent molting of their skins, the final spinning of their cocoons, the long wait until the next spring when the moths emerged. To see a moth come out of its cocoon with wings no bigger than a thumbnail and within an hour or two to develop a five to seven inch wingspread was fantastic. But most of the time it was hard work; finding fresh leaves every day, selected from the right varieties of trees, emptying the boxes, sprinkling the cocoons during the winter to keep them from drying out. It was in short, a large project. But by age 15 or 16 I was an authority on such moths. I knew probably twenty or more different varieties, their habits, their food, and those moths which ate no food during their lifespan. I could identify the larvae by species. I could spot the big three to four inch caterpillars easily: I never took a long walk without finding at least one caterpillar or cocoon.

But it interests me as I look back on it that to the best of my recollection I never told any teacher and only a very few fellow students of this interest of mine. This consuming project wasn't in any way part of my education. Education was what went on in school. A teacher wouldn't be interested. Besides I would have so much to explain to her or him when after all they were supposed to teach me. I had one or two good teachers whom I liked during this period, but this was a personal project, not the thing you share with your teacher. So here was an enterprise at least two years in length, scholarly, well researched, requiring painstaking work and much self-discipline, wide knowledge and practical skills. But to my mind it was, of course, not a part of my education. So that is what real learning was like for one boy.

I am sure that significant learning is often very different—for girls, for the ghetto child, for the physically handicapped child. But keeping this aspect of my own childhood learning in mind, I would try very hard to find out what it is like to be a child who is learning. I would try to get inside the child's world to see what had significance to him. I would try to make school at least a friendly home for such meaningful learning wherever it might be occurring in the child's life.

Can I Risk Myself in Relationship?

A second cluster of questions I would ask myself would run along these lines: Do I dare to let myself deal with this boy or girl, as a person, as someone I respect? Do I dare reveal myself to him and let him reveal himself to me? Do I dare to recognize that he/she may know more than I do in certain areas—or may in general be more gifted than I?

Answering these questions involves two aspects. One is the question of risk. Do I dare to take the risk of giving affirmative answers to the queries I have raised? The second aspect is the question of how this kind of a relationship can come about between the student and myself. I believe the answer may lie in some type of intensive group experience, a so-called communications group, human relations group, encounter group, or whatever. In this kind of a personal group it is easier to take the risk because it provides the sort of psychological climate in which relationships build. An experience in such a group would make almost impossible the following statement by a gifted black student. "My Utopia is to get to the point where I can retreat into my dream world because I have learned that I can't find happiness with human beings."

I think of a very moving group (recorded on film*) in which a teacher, a narcotics agent, and a convicted drug addict were participants. At the conclusion of this group Russ, a high school student, said with wonderment in his voice "I've found that a teacher, a cop, and a drug addict are all human beings. I wouldn't have believed it!" He had never found such a relationship with teachers in school.

We have found much the same thing in our conferences on humanizing medical education. Here one of the outstanding learnings is that of the physicians-in-training—discovering that their department chairmen, medical school deans, and faculty members are human beings, persons like themselves. They regard this as incredible. We had the same experience in dealing with the Immaculate Heart school system, both the high school and college levels, where students and teachers were able to relate as persons, not as roles. It was a totally new experience on both sides.

Although I have seen the highly positive results of an open and personal relationship between learner and facilitator, this does not mean that it would be easy for me to achieve it in every class or with every student. I know from experience that to show myself as I am—imperfect and at times admittedly defensive—seems like a great personal risk. And yet I know that if I could answer this second cluster of questions in the affirmative—if the relationship between myself and my students was truly a relationship between persons—much would be gained. If I was willing to admit that some students surpass me in knowledge, some in insight, some in perceptiveness in human relationships, then I could step off the pedestal of the "teacher" and become a facilitative learner among learners.

Discovering Interests

Another question I would ask myself would be, "What are the interests, goals, aims, purposes, passions of these students?" I would want to ask the question not only collectively but individually. What are the things that excite him or her and how can I find these out?

I may be over-confident, but I think the answer to this question is an easy one. If I genuinely wish to discover a student's interest I can do so. It might be through direct questions. It might be through allowing free discussion. It might be by creating a climate in which it is natural for interests to emerge. Although young people have been greatly deadened by their school experience, they do come to life in a healthy psychological atmosphere and are more willing to share their desires.

It impresses me as I think back that I can recall no teacher who ever asked me what my interests were. That seems an amazing statement, but I believe it is a true one. Had a teacher asked, I would have told him about wildflowers and woodland animals and even about the night-flying moths. I might even have told him about the poetry I was trying to write or my interest in religion, but no one asked.

Although nearly sixty years have gone by, I remember one question a teacher pencilled in the margin of a freshman theme. I had written, I believe, about something I had done with my dog, and alongside the description of some action I had taken the teacher wrote, "Why Carl?" I have always remembered this marginal note but it is only in recent years that I realized the reason for the memory. It stands out because here is a teacher who seemed to have a real personal interest in knowing why I, Carl, had done something. I have forgotten all other wise comments written on my themes but this one I remember. To me it shows how rarely it comes across to a student that a teacher really wants to know some of the motive and interests which make him tick. So if I were a teacher I would like very much to make it possible for students to tell me just these things.

The Inquiring Mind

A fourth question I would ask myself is "How can I preserve and unleash curiosity?" There is evidence to show that as children go through our public school system, they become less inquiring, less curious. It is one of the worst indictments I know. The provost of the California Institute of Technology has told me that if he could have only one criterion for selecting Cal Tech students it would be the degree to which they show curiosity. Yet it seems that we do everything possible to kill, in our students, this inquisitiveness, this wide ranging, searching wonder about the world and its inhabitants.

It has been pointed out that if you transplant a five-year-old boy into a foreign country where he is surrounded by peers who speak a language different from his own, it will only be a short time before he is conversing readily, speaking with the proper native accent, and within months quite at home in the new language. Yet if we try to teach a foreign language to a five-year-old the process is incredibly slow. The curiosity, the desire to find out, is now missing.

A professor who I know in a California university is finding his way of preserving the zest of inquiry. He writes me, "I want to tell you about some of the outcomes your Freedom to Learn has had for me and my students . . ." He tells how he decided to adapt each of his psychology courses to make them freer. He continues, "I was careful to explain to the students the assumptions underlying the approach we were going to try. I further asked them to consider seriously whether or not they wanted to take part in such an 'experiment'. (My courses are elective, so no one is required to take them.) No one decided to drop out. We—the class and I—created the course as we went along. (There were sixty in the class.) It was the most exciting classroom experience I have ever had, Carl! And, as it turned out, the students were equally excited. They turned in some of the best work (papers, reports of research, class oral projects, etc.) that I have ever seen from undergraduates. Their excitement was contagious. I found out later, from several different sources, that the students in the course were constantly being asked by roommates, by peers in the cafeteria, etc. 'What did you do in class today?' 'How is the course going?' I had a constant stream of students requesting to visit the class.

"Their own evaluations of the course at the end (I have saved these) were consistently positive: 'I have never learned so much in any course I have ever taken.' 'This is the first time anyone ever asked me what I wanted to learn, and it was exciting to discover I do want to learn.'

"Perhaps the most meaningful evaluation for me came from those students who said that they had not learned as much as they could have, but that this was their own fault: they took the responsibility for it. There is so much more to tell, Carl, but I don't want to belabor the point. What I did want is that you know how enthusiastically these students responded to the opportunity to learn—in how freeing it was for me as a fellow learner."

Resources?

Another question I would be asking myself is, "How can I imaginatively provide resources for learning—resources that are both physically and psychologically available?"

I believe that a good facilitator of learning should spend up to 90%

of his preparation time in making resources available to the young people with whom he or she works. To a large extent with all children, but outstandingly with bright children, it is not necessary to teach them, but they do need resources to feed their interests. It takes a great deal of imagination, thought, and work to provide such opportunities.

My son is a physician. Why? Because in a forward-looking school in the junior year of high school each student was given a number of weeks and considerable help in trying to arrange a two-week apprenticeship. My son was able to obtain the consent of a physician who found himself challenged by the naive but often fundamental questions of a high school boy. He took Dave on hospital rounds and home visits, into the delivery room and the operating room. Dave was immersed in the practice of medicine. It enlarged his very tentative interest into a consuming one. Someone had been creative in thinking about resources for his learning. I wish I could be that ingenious.

Creativity

If I were a teacher I hope that I would be asking myself questions like this: "Do I have the courage and humility to nurture creative ideas in my students? Do I have the tolerance and humanity to accept the annoying, occasionally defiant, occasionally odd-ball qualities of some of those who have creative ideas? Can I make a place for the creative person?"

I believe that in every teacher education program there should be a course on "The Care and Feeding of Infant Ideas." Creative thoughts and actions are just like infants—unprepossessing, weak, easily knocked down. A new idea is always very inadequate compared to an established idea. Children are full of such wild, unusual thoughts and perceptions, but a great many of them are trampled in the routine school life.

Then too as the work of Getzels and Jackson showed, there is a difference between those students that are bright and those who are both bright and creative. The latter tended to be more angular in their personalities, less predictable, more troublesome. Can I permit such students to be —to live and find nourishment—in my classroom? Certainly education— whether elementary, college, or professional training—does not have a good record in this respect. So Thomas Edison is regarded as dull and stupid. Aviation only came about because two bicycle mechanics were so ignorant of expert knowledge that they tried out a wild and foolish idea of making a heavier-than-air machine fly. The educational professionals would not waste their time on such nonsense.

I would hope that perhaps in my classroom I could create an atmosphere of a kind often greatly feared by educators, of mutual respect and mutual freedom of expression. That, I think, might permit the creative individual to write poetry, paint pictures, produce inventions, try out new ventures, without fear of being squashed. I would like to be able to do that.

Room for the Soma?

Perhaps a final question would be, "Can I help the student develop his feelings for life as well as his cognitive life? Can I help him to become what Thomas Hanna calls a soma—body and mind, feelings and intellect?" I think we are all aware of the fact that one of the tragedies of present-day education is that only cognitive learning is regarded as important.

I see David Halberstam's book, *The Best and the Brightest*, as the epitome of that tragedy. The men who surrounded Kennedy and Johnson were all gifted, talented men. As Halberstam says, "if those years had any central theme, if there was anything that bound these men, it was the belief that sheer intelligence and rationality could answer and solve anything." Certainly they learned that viewpoint in school. So this complete reliance on the cognitive and the intellectual caused this group of brilliant men to lead us little by little into an incredible quagmire of war. The computers omitted from their calculations the feelings, the emotional commitment, of little men in black pajamas with little equipment and no air force, who were fighting for something they believed in. This omission proved fatal. That factor was not put into the computers because McNamara and the others had no place in their computations for the feeling life, the emotional life of individuals. I would hope very much that the learning that took place in my classroom might be a learning by the whole person—something difficult to achieve but highly rewarding in its end product.

Concluding Summary

Let me conclude by stating these questions in somewhat different form— the questions I would ask if I were a teacher or a counselor or an administrator; the questions I would ask myself if I had the responsibility for facilitating the learning of young people.

1. Can I let myself inside the inner world of a growing, learning person? Can I without being judgmental, come to see and appreciate this world?
2. Can I let myself be a real person with these young people and take the risk of building an open, expressive, mutual relationship in which we both can learn? Do I dare to be myself in an intensive group relationship with these youth?
3. Can I discover the interests of each individual and permit him or her to follow those interests wherever they may lead?
4. Can I help young persons preserve one of their most precious possessions—their wide-eyed, persistent, driving curiosity about themselves and the world around them?
5. Can I be creative in putting them in touch with people, experiences, books—resources of all kinds—which stimulate their curiosity and feed their interests?

6. Can I accept and nurture the strange and imperfect thoughts and wild impulses and expressions which are the forerunners of creative learning and activity? Can I accept the sometimes different and unusual personalities which may produce these creative thoughts?

7. Can I help young learners to be all of one piece—integrated—with feelings pervading their ideas and ideas pervading their feelings, and their expression being that of a whole person?

If, by some miracle, I could answer yes to most of these questions, then I believe I would be a facilitator of true learning, helping to bring out the vast potential of young people.

PART II: WHAT IS THE TEACHER'S ROLE?

Compare and contrast Gardner's conception of the role of the school with Cooper's suggestions for educational reform.

_____

_____

_____

_____

_____

_____

STEINBERGER ARTICLE

Discuss Gardner's critique of IQ testing.

_____

_____

_____

_____

_____

_____

Discuss Gardner's concept of understanding.

_____

_____

_____

_____

_____

_____

COOPER ARTICLE

Briefly discuss the following:

Teacher Thinking

_____

_____

_____

_____

_____

_____

Cognition and Reading

_____

_____

_____

_____

_____

_____

Instructional Bridging

_____

_____

_____

_____

_____

_____

WARNER ARTICLE

Consider your own development as a teacher (teacher-in-training). Briefly discuss both the stage at which you feel you are presently functioning and your development through previous stages.

_____

_____

_____

_____

_____

_____

_____

_____

_____

_____

_____

_____

_____

_____

_____

_____

_____

_____

ROGERS ARTICLE

Briefly discuss the following:

1. Knowing the Child

_____

_____

_____

2. Relationship between teacher and pupil

_____

_____

_____

3. Interest

_____

_____

_____

4. The Inquiring Mind

_____

_____

_____

5. Creativity

_____

_____

_____

PART III

PSYCHOLOGICAL THEORIES AND THEIR APPLICATIONS

SECTION A: LEARNING THEORIES

MISTAKES AND OTHER CLASSROOM TECHNIQUES: AN APPLICATION OF SOCIAL LEARNING THEORY

by Harriet C. Edwards
California State University, Fullerton

Social learning theory provides ideas and techniques for teaching complex thinking skills such as mathematical problem solving. The theory behind the concept of the teacher as a model is surveyed and illustrated with descriptions of classroom techniques employed by the author. These techniques include taking advantage of classroom mistakes to model thinking and problem solving. Student evaluation results indicate that instructor credibility is unaffected by the use of these techniques.

INTRODUCTION

As teachers, we wish to do more than present to our students the established ideas and facts of our fields. We want to give them a sense of how one thinks and creates within the discipline, to impart the tools of scholarship. In my field, mathematics, this concern has led to an increased focus on the teaching and learning of problem solving. Researchers have directed much attention to the executive functions and metacognition involved in problem solving, that is, the solver's awareness of thinking processes and of progress toward a solution (Schoenfeld, 1985). In addition to these procedural matters, attitudes and emotions surrounding mathematical problem solving also have been addressed in the active field of mathematics education research (Silver, 1985). In fact, the concern with thinking patterns and scholarship extends well beyond the technical sphere. Studies have compared and contrasted styles of learning and thinking in scientific and humanistic disciplines, to the benefit of students in both areas (Tobias, 1990).

83

Teaching the skills of scholarship is no easy task; in some fields, such as mathematics, special courses exist for that purpose. A single course devoted to problem solving or critical thinking may speed the learning process, but such complex behavior is best learned by integrating it into everyday course work. Can we incorporate the teaching of these thinking skills into our regular classes? A large body of research indicates that we can, with a few simple techniques.

In this article, I will describe the social learning theories and studies of Bandura, Vygotsky, Meichenbaum, et al., and discuss their applications in the classroom. I have used these theories as the basis for techniques that involve (a) taking advantage of classroom mistakes, both spontaneous and planned, to illustrate the problem-solving process; (b) acting out the process of reaching a solution, to make explicit the thinking skills that usually are employed silently; (c) expressing feelings, to show ways of coping with emotions; and (d) modeling self-talk, to help students develop new thinking patterns. As each technique is introduced, I will explain its background in social learning theory and describe supporting experimental results.

Much of the discussion is based on my experience teaching mathematics, but the theories and ideas are applicable to many disciplines. The discussion is directed primarily to instructors who teach mostly in the demonstration and lecture format, because the ideas can be implemented incrementally and effectively in that teaching style. For those engaged in other teaching formats, the theoretical framework introduced in this article can help direct the development of new techniques.

THE THEORY

Bandura's social learning theory emphasizes vicarious learning, or learning through observation (1977, 1986). In most cases, the observer performs the learned behavior embellished with his or her own idiosyncrasies, rather than imitating precisely the model's actions. This indicates that the observer has processed and integrated what was modeled. Such flexibility in learning is well suited to the teaching of intellectual skills such as mathematical problem solving and critical thinking, because the student must adapt the learned behavior for use in similar, but not identical, situations.

It should be noted that social learning theory differs significantly from the behaviorist theory that has dominated education over the past several decades. Behaviorist theory stresses that the learner must directly experience and practice the skill. Further, the skill usually is broken down into smaller, easily acquired subpatterns, and after each part is learned, the entire complex behavior pattern is reassembled. One of the major proponents of these techniques was Gagne (1965), who described highly detailed 'learning hierarchies.' In education, behaviorist theory found its purest expression in the 'programmed texts' that were once popular.

Problem solving, however, calls for improvisation, a skill not easily taught with behaviorist methods. The patterns of solution must be created by the solver before they can be executed, and the rules of finding these patterns are fuzzy at best. When attempting to apply such ill-defined rules, trial and error and the ability to find and cope with error become extremely important. Therefore, the flexibility of vicarious learning as described by Bandura is particularly apt for acquiring problem solving skills.

Bandura's theories were applied to effect changes in complex, ill-defined behaviors in a study on the improvement of academic skills (Kunce, Bruch, & Thelen, 1974). A group of disadvantaged adults enrolled in a basic education class were shown videotapes of model students handling situations similar to those that these adults might encounter at school. The tapes covered skills such as test taking and the scheduling and organizing of study time. The models not only demonstrated the skills, but also verbalized a determination to cope with academic problems via the use of these skills, and then talked about what they were doing. The effect of the videotapes on the adult students was measured by variables related to academic achievement such as class attendance, test scores, and willingness to continue with education. Students exposed to the models showed significant improvement, indicating that they had acquired some of the modeled skills and learned to apply the skills appropriately in their own lives.

Techniques and Applications of the Theory

Mistakes

Many instructors know the uncomfortable feeling that occurs when a student finds an error in the presentation or a difficulty arises while demonstrating a problem. The legendary professor, upon discovering a mistake in the lecture, says to the students, 'I just made that mistake to see if you were all on your toes!' It is an old, but revealing, story. The embarrassed instructor does not want to admit that mistakes (indeed dumb mistakes) can be made even by the expert. Yet in mistakes lurk valuable opportunities to improve student understanding. By openly displaying our reactions to a mistake, we can demonstrate not only the problem-solving process, but also the coping mechanisms for dealing with the emotions that accompany mistakes.

Most instructors present themselves as masters of a subject when they lecture, offering only one neat, final path to the answer and seldom indicating that several correct solutions may be possible. When the correct solution or conclusion is discussed, it usually is presented as a series of steps, each justified by the application of some rule or fact. The reasoning behind the method of arriving at the answer or conclusion rarely is discussed. Heller and Hungate (1985) describe this kind of teaching as follows:

> Too often, instructors jump from reading a problem statement to writing on the board an already completed solution, skipping the qualitative analysis, strategic decisions, and explanations of why and how each step was

done. Missing too are the mistakes, tentativeness and exploration that are all parts of problem solving.

An alternative is to present a 'coping model' to demonstrate that mistakes are a normal part of intellectual life and that it is important to develop the ability to suspect, detect, and correct errors. When we discover a mistake, rather than expressing discomfort, we can explain how we found it. Even minor mistakes should be pointed out, because they too can lead to incorrect results. After stating why we believe that an error has been made, we can demonstrate the checking routines we use to find the mistake. For example, errors creep into mathematical calculations very easily, so mathematicians develop techniques for anticipating common slips that may arise from habits such as simplifying expressions as we go or eliminating unnecessary negative signs. We also know our own predisposition to make certain mistakes and check for those idiosyncratic errors if there is a problem. By sharing small tricks for preventing or finding mistakes, we can help students who may not have developed these skills or even thought to develop them.

Over the years, I have made the usual quota of mistakes in the classroom, either in working a problem that I have not had a chance to prepare or in following student suggestions for solutions. I have learned to take advantage of mistakes to discuss subtle points of mathematical reasoning that I would not have included in a planned lecture. For example, I have demonstrated the value of using the redundancy of the information one generates as a means of checking work long before arriving at a complete solution. By going through the process of solving the problem rather than just presenting a prepared solution, I model problem-solving skills that could not be explicated effectively in a lecture. For those familiar with first-semester calculus, the appendix provides an example of how a classroom mistake was handled.

As we plan lectures, we can include discussions of illuminating past errors. After all, mistakes do not happen that often in a well-prepared class, and we may not want to wait until an interesting mistake appears spontaneously. In more advanced classes, as we work out the solutions to problems we plan to present, we can preserve and reenact our first attempts (including dead ends and errors), so that students can see how an expert generates a first approach and then modifies it if that attempt does not work. In mathematics classes, this can be especially helpful in showing students how to generate proofs, because the arguments presented in texts tend to offer few clues to their development. In many fields, paradigms and methodology have changed over time. By highlighting and modeling some of these arguments and conflicts, the instructor can demonstrate the uncertainty and ambiguity so important to most intellectual endeavors as well as the skills needed to think through to an intelligent conclusion or solution.

Of course, one might ask how mistakes affect the instructor's credibility. Do students lose confidence in a teacher who stumbles occasionally when solving a problem? No instructor wishes to appear ignorant or unprepared, and both common sense and research indicate that as a model's status decreases, so does learning from that model. The message that mistakes are a fact of mathematical life would be lost if students did not perceive the instructor as credible.

Fortunately, my experience, as documented in student evaluations, indicates that even when mistakes are highlighted and discussed in class, the students' perception of the instructor's expertise is not damaged. I examined the responses of my students to two items on the standard student evaluation form: demonstration of knowledge of the subject and preparation for each class meeting. Although it can be argued that students are unqualified to judge a professor's command of the material or quality of preparation, these items do accurately represent the students' perceptions, and it is their perceptions that matter. The mathematics instructors in my department tend to receive high ratings on these items, with an average of 3.7 on knowledge and 3.6 on preparation (4=highest, 0=lowest). After my first semester of teaching, my ratings stabilized in a range from a .10 standard deviation below the department mean to .25 above. This pattern has persisted over eight semesters, so I conclude that my credibility is little affected. It appears that if mistakes occur in the context of a well-prepared and organized presentation, the instructor's expertise is still respected.

Coping with Emotions

When I deal with a mistake in the classroom, I model far more than mathematical skills and techniques. As I work through a problem and include mistakes, students see an expert in the field not only solving a problem, but also, like them, feeling puzzled and frustrated, yet working through to a solution. This demonstration of emotion, or affect, is an important classroom tool. Any mathematics problem worth doing does not present its solution readily. Like an artist facing a blank canvas, the mathematician needs courage to make a start. The first approach often is incorrect, so one must not only find and correct the mistake, but also handle the accompanying disappointment and frustration. For students who have seen the instructor perform only flawlessly, the real experience of problem solving can make them feel incompetent and defeated. Therefore, it is important to help students develop the ability to cope with the anxiety that surfaces in the learning process.

Accordingly, in class I act out my responses to the emotions that arise from my work. I point out the things I dislike doing (such as long, tedious calculations) and share the joy of discovering an ingenious smooth argument. I express disappointment when I make a mistake and frustration when I cannot solve a problem immediately. When I am unable to answer a student's question or to solve a problem on the spot, I explain that it may

Schools Development Corporation, called ATLAS, (Authentic Teaching, Learning, and Assessment for all Students). It is a consortium among Ted Sizer's Coalition of Essential Schools at Brown University, Jim Comer's School Development Program at Yale University, the Education Developmental Center in Newton, Mass., which is run by Janet Whitla, and my own group at Harvard, Project Zero.

STEINBERGER: How does ATLAS propose to restructure schooling?
GARDNER: At the very center of ATLAS is the child. Education is personalized and makes sense to the child. Students graduate not because of Carnegie units but because they can exhibit knowledge and understanding of what is important.

The curriculum grows out of essential questions human being have asked since the beginning of time. The focus is on uncoverage—not coverage. Less is more, so kids can go into things deeply.

Also at the center are authentic learning experiences. These are practices that aren't done just to satisfy a state requirement or because it was done to you, but rather practices that you can justify because kids are going to learn from them. It's very important in ATLAS schools that you have flexible policies so that experimentation is allowed.

In the very early stage of developing an ATLAS school, we emphasize the creation of organizational management structures where everybody in the community who has a stake in the school gets together and talks and argues and reaches a consensus, without blame, about what the important things in the school are, about how to achieve them, and about how to make sure everybody is on board.

STEINBERGER: What can superintendents, principals, teachers, and parents do to cultivate authentic learning and genuine understanding in their schools?
GARDNER: It's easy to sit at Harvard and tell everybody what to do. I'm mindful of the enormous problems faced by so many teachers and administrators. They are problems that I frankly would not know how to handle.

That being said, I don't think there is any way for people in American schools today to be successful unless they are focused on the education of kids. Schools have to decide what to leave out, what's not important, what's the bonus you can do later, and then really focus on what I call the meat and potatoes. This means tackling important questions and reaching deep understanding.

If people don't want understanding, they have no reason to defend what they are doing except to say they are keeping kids off the streets. And since shootings go on in schools, too, keeping kids off the streets is not such a huge deal.

Once you decide that understanding is your focus, then how you think about everything changes, including the notions of curriculum and cover-

take time to find the solution to an intriguing problem. I set the problem aside for a while and report back to the class as soon as I figure out the answer. This shows that the correct solution or argument may not always be right at hand and that patience is needed to unravel a difficult problem.

As students see an expert displaying the negative emotions they feel and yet eventually achieving success, they are encouraged to persist in their own work. Experiments based on Bandura's work support this notion. The experiments studied the characteristics of the successful model in treatments of phobia or avoidant behavior, from snake phobia (Bandura, 1972; Bandura, Jeffery, & Gajdos, 1975) to test anxiety (Jaffe & Carlson, 1972; Sarason, 1973, 1975). The therapies involved anxious subjects viewing live or videotaped models performing those tasks that the subjects avoided. The difference between the models was how they performed the task: either competently and confidently from the start (a mastery model), or hesitantly and fearfully at first, but then gaining ability and confidence (a coping model). The coping model produced better results. In one experiment (Meichenbaum, 1971), models differed not only in mastery versus coping behavior, but in whether they spoke aloud their thoughts and feelings while they performed the tasks. Although little difference was observed in the ability to perform tasks between those who saw the verbalizing or the silent models, those who saw the verbalizing, coping model reported a significant decrease in fear compared to all other subjects. In an experiment with test-anxious subjects (Sarason, 1975), the models chatted about exam situations with subjects before administering a test. Again, the model who admitted to test anxiety but also explained how to deal with the problem produced the greatest improvement in the subjects' test scores.

Self-Talk

Why is the coping model more successful? Why should verbalizing one's attitudes and emotions have an impact? Why should presenting oneself as a coping model be more effective in dealing with anxiety (a common phenomenon in science and mathematics courses)? Why should talking about the problem-solving process change the way students think? One possible answer can be found in the study of relationships between speech, thought, and action. We express our thoughts to one another through speech, and it is generally agreed that words affect our thoughts and actions. But how this influence occurs and how it might be applied to teaching and therapy are still open questions.

The Soviet psychologist Vygotsky attempted to answer these questions by formulating a theory of the development of thought and language (1962, 1978). Starting with the assumption that social influences are of paramount importance, Vygotsky considered speech first and foremost a social, communicative act. A child's egocentric speech (singing, talking to self, etc.) is a stage in the process of turning the social aspects of speech inward, culminating in the silent phenomenon of inner speech. In particular, Vygotsky theorized that much of a child's behavior at an early age is regulated by the speech of the adults around it, and that the shift toward inner speech reflects the child's taking over and internalizing control of its behavior. The process of internalizing social speech continues into adult life. A number of mathematics educators (Noddings, 1985; Schoenfeld, 1985) have cited Vygotsky in their work, but few have mentioned the recent development of self-talk techniques that are based on Vygotsky's theories.

Meichenbaum has been a leading developer and applier of self-talk techniques. In one of his early experiments (1977), he used such techniques to teach impulsive school children how to slow down and work carefully on a task. Meichenbaum modeled reflective behavior by performing tasks in front of the children, while constantly talking aloud to himself. He then encouraged the children to imitate his behavior but to use self-statements that came naturally to them. He first trained the children to speak aloud to themselves as they worked, saying, for example, 'Okay, what is it I have to do? . . . I have to go slowly and carefully . . . Good, I'm doing fine so far. Remember, go slowly . . . Even if I make an error I can go on slowly and carefully . . . Finished, I did it!' (Meichenbaum, 1977, p. 52). After they had established the habit of speaking aloud to themselves, Meichenbaum encouraged the children to drop their speech to a whisper, and finally to work in silence, but to continue talking to themselves in their minds. After the treatment, the children showed significant improvement on tests for impulsivity, and follow-up tests several months after instruction indicated that the gains had persisted.

Other researchers applied Meichenbaum's self-talk techniques to teach seventh grade girls who were having problems with mathematics and math anxiety (Genshaft, 1982). The self-talk method was modeled for the students, who were then encouraged to become aware of their own negative self-statements, to change these to positive statements, and to use the positive statements as they worked. After the students had developed their own collections of self-instructions, they were encouraged to generalize their new self-statements to other anxiety-producing situations. After a few weeks of practice, the students were given diagnostic tests, the results of which were equivocal. Both experimental and control groups improved on applications, but only the experimental group showed significant improvement in computation.

There is evidence that people also assimilate self-statements without explicit instructions to do so. In Meichenbaum's experiments with snake phobia (1971), some subjects spontaneously borrowed the coping models' verbalizations as they performed tasks during post-testing. The phenomenon of unintended social learning was documented further in an experiment in which students watched videos of model students solving problems (Henderson, Landesman, Atkinson, & Kachuk, 1983). The models made occasional mistakes, but used self-statements attributing success to careful work and perseverance, for example, "I wouldn't have made that error if I had been more careful," or "I can get it if I just stick with it." A questionnaire that assessed the students' success and failure attributions indicated that those students who had been exposed to the models were more likely to believe that their own efforts, rather than luck or the kindness of the teacher, were responsible for success. The results of these experiments suggest that coping self-statements can be learned vicariously and without reinforcement.

In fostering self-guidance through internalized speech, are we training students to be like us, the recognized experts? The distinction between what the expert actually does and what may be taught in order to produce such expert performance is particularly important in science and mathematics. Expert problem solvers may not engage in the self-talk that could aid their students, or if they do, it may be an unconscious act. Therefore, teachers must first become aware of the speech they should model before they can encourage self-talk in their students. An inservice program for teachers, described by Gibney and Meiring (1983), attempted to develop this awareness:

> The purpose of the . . . institute was to use problem solving as the vehicle to influence teacher and student behavior, expectations and attitudes in the classroom. Initially, teachers were given experience in problem solving by being introduced to puzzling and perplexing situations to which they had not been previously exposed. While confronting these challenges, they were led to examine their own thinking to become consciously aware of methods they were employing (whether successful or not), and to label techniques which were helpful in making headway toward resolving problems.

Participants devoted much time to discussing not only the problems they had been assigned to solve, but also the problem of teaching problem solving. As the institute progressed, "they personally experienced the frustration and challenge of applying mathematics . . . [that] helped them perceive the need for teaching an aspect of mathematics to which they had never been sensitive." They began to develop and discuss strategies for solving problems as well as ways to teach those strategies in the classroom.

Demonstrating self-talk is at the heart of my classroom techniques. The classroom mistake presents the opportunity for me to talk through a problem, and in some cases, to verbalize emotions and the accompanying coping responses. I teach students to talk to themselves as they work on problems, to move their lips as they read a mathematics text, so that they can develop new habits of self-talk. I use these techniques even more extensively in my office, where I can help individual students to construct self-talk regimens tailored to their idiosyncratic needs. Self-talk can be useful in considering mathematical concepts (e.g., "I shouldn't just read the word 'logarithm,' but remind myself what that means."), regulating oneself during calculations (e.g., "Take each step in turn, don't rush. I'll finish this correctly if I'm careful."), and developing positive attitudes toward problem solving (e.g., "Okay, so I don't know what to do right away; I don't have to give up. I'll start by rereading the problem and making sure I know what each word and phrase means."). When students work in my office, I instruct them to make such statements aloud and to keep speaking quietly to themselves as they work at home. A number of students report that they have been helped significantly by self-talk.

Conclusion

The techniques described are only the beginning of changes in our teaching that can be derived from social learning theory. As we become more familiar with these ideas, new ways of teaching will develop naturally, and the skilled actions of the good teacher will be better understood.

By showing how we talk to ourselves as we work and think, or by acting out problem-solving strategies that could be useful to our students, we can transmit the skills of scholarship that are essential to our work yet seldom taught in the classroom. In verbalizing our feelings and attitudes and how we cope with them, we give students permission and freedom to experience ups and downs as they study and work. Our mistakes, when shared, illuminate much of the real, everyday experience of study and scholarship, and give students the tools and the courage to apply their own talents.

Appendix

The following is an example of a mistake that became a useful teaching opportunity. One of my students was unable to find a correct solution to this first-semester calculus problem:

> Find all local maxima, minima, and points of inflection of
> $y = \sin x + 1/2 \sin 2x$
> and use these to sketch a graph on $[0, 2\pi]$.

If I had prepared a solution in advance, I would have calculated the derivative $y' = \cos x + \cos 2x$, found where the derivative was zero, calculated the second derivative, and written down its zeroes. Then I would have evaluated y'' at the critical points to apply the second derivative test, and having assembled this information, would have sketched the graph quickly and correctly. But as we worked this problem in class, the process was quite different. The students told me what had been done, and I sketched the graph, inserting information and refining the graph as information was collected. First we found that the zeroes of the original function were at $x = 0$, π, 2π, by rewriting the function as

$$y = \sin x + \sin x \cos x = \sin x \,(1 + \cos x).$$

This allowed us to determine easily where the function had positive or negative values. We then computed

$$y' = \cos x + \cos 2x = \cos x + 2 \cos^2 x - 1$$

which can be considered as a quadratic expression in $\cos x$. A student suggested that we could solve the related quadratic equation

$$2w^2 + w - 1 = 0$$

to find the critical points. Finding the roots at $w = -1$ or $\frac{1}{2}$ led us to conclude that $x = \pi$, $\pi/3$, or $5\pi/3$ were critical numbers. Noticing that the quadratic expression changes sign at $w = -1$ and $w = \frac{1}{2}$, we concluded that we had local extrema at all our critical points. But when we went back to our graph, we found trouble: At $x = \pi$, the function was changing sign and decreasing, so no local extremum was possible! This was the point at which the student had stopped, not knowing what to do. The inconsistent result indicated that a mistake must have occurred, but we did not know what the mistake was and had to start looking for it. We checked the arithmetic and algebra and found no problem. After a few more minutes of fruitless searching, we were too puzzled and annoyed to think productively any longer, so we tabled the problem and continued with the class. Later we found the mistake, which turned out to be a subtle flaw in reasoning: We had inappropriately deduced sign changes in the equation $2\cos^2 x + \cos x - 1 = 0$ from the simplified version $2w^2 + w - 1 = 0$. We heaved a collective sigh of relief and happily finished the graph.

The mistake gave me a valuable opportunity to teach some subtle mathematics and problem-solving techniques. I illuminated the pitfalls of reasoning from simplified equations, a lesson that I would not have included in a planned lecture. In addition, I demonstrated the value of developing the solution by drawing the graph as one progresses through the problem, using the redundancy of the information one generates as a means of checking work. By going through the process of solving the problem rather than just presenting a prepared solution, I served as a model of problem-solving skills.

THEORY TO PRACTICE: SELF-EFFICACY RELATED TO TRANSFER OF LEARNING AS AN EXAMPLE OF THEORY-BASED INSTRUCTIONAL DESIGN

by Jan B. Carroll
Colorado State University

A Training Specialist Certification Program illustrates an example of theory to practice. Transfer of learning as a responsibility of instructional design and delivery, and Bandura's social learning theory and its component part, self-efficacy, are examined. Four instructional methods, practice, modeling, suggestion, and climate-setting, are discussed in relation to principles from the theory literature and from practice. Understanding theory-based methods gives instructors the basis for effective adaptation in many diverse circumstances and encourages positive transfer of learning.

The field of adult education, especially designing and delivering adult learning programs, is often derived from effective practice. Effective practice requires an understanding of the theoretical underpinnings of instructional methods. Simple recognition that something works or that it feels good is not enough for instructors' effectiveness in adapting content delivery from one situation to the next. An example of theory-based methods is constructed by first examining transfer of learning and its relationship to social learning theory. Second, some methods associated with Bandura's (1977) four sources of information about self-efficacy are considered.

While instructors will recognize the four instructional methods as applicable to numerous and various content areas, the example presented here is illustrated with commentary on actual practice. A university within the mountain plains region offers instruction for subject-matter experts in how to train others in the mid-1980s and the four component classes and an internship opportunity are offered several times each year through the university's Division of Continuing Education.

TRANSFER OF LEARNING

Baldwin and Ford (1988) defined positive transfer of learning as "the degree to which trainees effectively apply the knowledge, skill and attitudes gained in a training context to the job" and, further, the degree to which learning behavior is generalized to the job context and maintained over time. They identified training inputs, including training design, as one factor affecting transfer. Parry (1990) corroborated with similar factors which help or hinder transfer of learning from workshop to workplace, including instructional factors. These references substantiate the awareness of participants in the Training Specialist Certification Program that transfer of learning is, at least in part, connected to instructional design and delivery. Theory-based designs and delivery have a greater capacity to assure transfer of learning than those which are only technique-based, so social learning theory and its self-efficacy component are examined in reference to transfer of learning.

SOCIAL LEARNING THEORY AND
SELF-EFFICACY

Self-efficacy is one variable identified by Gist (1989), Wood, Bandura & Bailey (1990), Taylor, Locke, Lee & Gist (1984), Stumpf, Brief, Hartman (1987), and Marx (1982), which may intervene between learning and performance. Perceived self-efficacy, according to Bandura (1982), is "concerned with judgments of how well one can execute courses of action required to deal with prospective situations." Furthermore, "given appropriate skills and adequate incentives . . . efficacy expectations are a major determinant of people's choice of activities, how much effort they will expend, and of how long they will sustain effort in dealing with . . . situations" (Bandura, 1977). This theory has been tested with phobias about snakes and the dreaded situations experienced by agoraphobs and acrophobs (Bandura, 1982). Results indicated that how well learners think they can perform, or take the learning with them for generalization and maintenance over time, will affect how they actually do perform after the learning experience.

According to a social learning view (Bandura, 1977), there are four principal sources of information concerning judgments of self-efficacy: performance accomplishments, vicarious experiences, verbal persuasion, and physiological states. This social learning theory of self-efficacy supports four complementary instructional methods: practice, modeling, suggestion, and climate setting, which can be designed into curriculum to encourage transfer of learning.

PERFORMANCE ACCOMPLISHMENTS/PRACTICE

Personal mastery experiences are one of self-efficacy information and may be the most influential (Bandura, 1982). According to Binder (1990), a confidence gap exists for learners, and practice is the only way it can be closed. Practice which promotes fluency (the mark of an expert) considers the three dimensions of time, sufficiency, and pace, and treats mistakes and errors as learning opportunities. Reference systems and job aids must be integrated so that skills and knowledge can be practiced even beyond perfect accuracy.

Bandura (1977) structured the environment of therapy so that clients could perform successfully in spite of their incapacities. Various aids were used to enhance the environment of learning, including:

* preliminary modeling of activities;
* graduated risk-level;
* graduated time intervals;
* cooperative performance with the instructor or another expert;
* protection to reduce feared consequences;
* variation in complexity of task.

Gendelman (1991) summarized practice in instructional design with three criteria: "be realistic, start out easy and gradually become more complex, be rewarding." The most valuable reward comes to participants when they see themselves doing something useful that they were unable to do before.

Just as Bandura (1977) withdrew aids as treatment progressed, so can instructors encourage and allow participants to succeed unassisted as learning progresses. "Successes raise mastery expectations; repeated failures lower them, particularly if the mishaps occur early in the course of events" (Bandura, 1977).

Instructors in the Training Specialist Certification Program attempt to model as many instructional methods as they present. Risk levels are graduated and most content is presented interactively. A safe environment is emphasized as participants share their expectations and efforts. One course supports the participants as they design and deliver a 30-minute mini-training session in front of instructors and other class members. After all course work is completed, the participants design and delivery a half-day workshop to an audience of their choice, or to one provided by the Division of Continuing Education.

VICARIOUS EXPERIENCE/MODELING

Not all information about self-efficacy comes from performance accomplishments, even though it is a rich and influential source. Many expectations of self-efficacy are obtained through vicarious experience. "Social learning theory asserts that we learn much—if not most—of our behavior vicariously, by watching others and retaining and remembering both what they did and the apparent outcome of that behavior" (Zemke, 1982). According to Bandura (1977), "much human behavior is developed through modeling. From observing others, one forms a conception of how new behavior patterns are performed, and on later occasions the symbolic construction serves as a guide for action." In therapy, clients convince themselves that if another can do it, they can do it, or at least they can improve their own performance. Behavior modeling is usually applied to overt behaviors, while cognitive modeling is used in teaching conceptual skills, judgment, language and thought (Harmon & Evans, 1984).

According to Goldstein & Sorcher (1974), learners should be encouraged to practice, rehearse, or role-play the behaviors they have seen modeled and they should be rewarded for successful performance in order for modeling to be effective. The criteria for successful modeling used in therapy which can be adapted for instruction include:

* models are shown overcoming difficulties by a determined effort;
* models are similar to clients (learners) in characteristics other than modeled situation;
* modeled behavior has clear, rather than ambiguous, outcomes.

As mentioned previously, Training Specialist Certification Program instructors model techniques and methods as they deliver information. Occasionally, difficult group behaviors are exhibited and instructors make the determined effort required to manage the situation. Videotaped behavior models, not currently available in the program, would standardize this component of the training for each section. All instructors are somewhat similar to many participants in age, geographic domicile, variety of experience, and level of education. Outcomes of modeled behavior are thoroughly processed, or discussed, to avoid potential shadows of ambiguity. Finally, all instructors show similar success with similar situations, to broaden the participants' exposure to the modeled behavior. One factor recognized to undermine self-efficacy, however, is the presence of a highly confident individual (Bandura, 1982). Instructors must be aware of over-performing in the classroom, thereby decreasing participants' ability to apply their own routine skills.

VERBAL PERSUASION/SUGGESTION

Suggestion, or verbal persuasion, is widely used in increasing perceptions of self-efficacy because it is easy, inexpensive and readily available. Bandura (1977) cautioned, however, that "to raise by persuasion expectations of personal competence without arranging conditions to facilitate effective performance will most likely lead to failures that discredit the persuaders and further undermine the recipients' perceived self-efficacy." Furthermore, suggestion will be less readily accepted when delivered to those cast in the role of a subordinate. Users of positive feedback as a suggestion technique must be attuned to these cautions; overenthusiastic encouragement and compliments delivered by an authority figure can do more harm than good.

In the Training Specialist Certification Program, participants work collaboratively with instructors and with each other to build on strengths exhibited in designing and delivering instruction. Presenting and group facilitating skills are practiced repeatedly with multiple opportunities for sharing feedback. The mini-training session is structured to support success by allowing participants to 1) choose their own content; 2) determine which methods they will use for delivery; and 3) design and provide an evaluation which will give them the feedback they consider most useful.

PHYSIOLOGICAL STATES/CLIMATE SETTING

An additional source of information about self-efficacy is emotional arousal. The social learning theory-based method associated with instructional design and delivery is climate setting. Participants expect success when they are in comfortable, untaxing environments, free from stress and annoyance. Instructors' attention to physical and psychological needs of participants reduces stress and anxiety by decreasing potential sources of discomfort. Fear-provoking thoughts about ineptitude, frequently based on previous learning experiences, may also be reduced by careful climate-setting. Some details include:

* physical environment (temperature, lighting, acoustics, furniture, etc.);
* set up (arrangement of furniture);
* equipment and supplies;
* setting norms and expectations for learning experience;
* genuineness, acceptance, empathic understanding of participants on part of instructor.

While ideal facilities are seldom available, as class sizes vary and other university needs prevail, every effort is made in the Training Specialist Certification Program to provide a climate conducive to the development of high levels of self-efficacy. Carpeted rooms with ample wall space for charts and posters are requested, along with temperature control and little or no noise distraction from adjoining rooms. Furniture is seldom arranged classroom-style, but in a U, semi-circle, or circle to avoid association with previous, and perhaps fear-provoking, school experiences. Equipment and supplies are typically low-tech and high-touch, utilizing color and graphic design for impact. Instructors exhibit sincere willingness to see others succeed, and are available not only in the classroom, but for consultation during and after the course.

CONCLUSION

The four methods presented—practice, modeling, suggestion and climate setting—are interactive and interdependent, reinforcing each other as well as other learning methods. Their contribution to positive transfer of training may be enhanced or damaged by two other factors: learner characteristics (personal factors), and work environment (organizational factors) (Baldwin & Ford, 1988; Parry, 1990). Further investigation is needed to validate and integrate these other factors.

Reapplication of successful methods to new settings without fully understanding the theory or principles involved relies on luck more than skill. According to Hanna (1988), "When unexpected problems arise, those who are grounded only in techniques may be ill-equipped to get back on track. It is often the understanding of the principle behind the technique that permits responses to keep the system on target." Participants in the Training Specialist Certification Program, attending primarily for acquisition of pragmatic and immediately applicable methods, also receive some theory to enhance transfer of learning.

INTEGRATING SOCIAL LEARNING THEORY WITH EDUCATING THE DEPRIVED

by George R. Taylor
Professor of Special Education and Acting Dean
Division of Education, Coppin State College
Core Faculty, Union Institute

ABSTRACT

The relevance of major concepts associated with social learning theories for teaching deprived and minority children are reviewed; from these concepts postulates are abstracted which are intended to induce further inquiry and research. The paper describes practical application of social learning theories to education, offering the school a common context through which environment, developmental sequence, and early experiences can be understood and reached. These theories enable educators better to understand how deprived and minority children think and feel about themselves, and to become aware of factors in the environment precipitating cognitive and affective problems that may have some bearing on academic performance. A need exists to conduct empirical studies to determine the degree to which social learning theories impact on the academic performances of minority and deprived children. Eight postulates are outlined to stimulate further inquiry and research. The study of social learning theories enables the school to understand how students' cultures and learning styles can be modified to promote expected learning outcomes.

INTRODUCTION

During the last two decades we have witnessed the rediscovery, creation, or the validation of a great diversity of social learning theories. These theories have provided us with a common language with which we can communicate about the affects of social learning theories on academic performance of deprived children.

The study of social learning theories enables the school to better understand both how deprived and minority children think about school related processes and how the children are likely to be feeling about themselves in relation to the process. The school's understanding of both the cognitive and the affective characteristics of deprived children may be termed as "empathic." One way of showing empathy to children is through designing effective classroom environments that considers the cognitive and affect levels of the children (Butler, 1988; Hillard, 1989).

THEORETICAL FRAMEWORK

The major emphasis of social learning theories is primarily on environmental learner interaction. The learning behaviors that are socially accepted, as well as learning which ones are not, is social learning. This view is supported by Stuart (1989). He maintained that social learning theory attempts to describe the process by which we come to know what behaviors should or should not be engaged in when we are in different social situations. The theories themselves are learning theories that have been applied to social situations. These theories have been generally behavioristic rather than cognitive (Bandura, 1977).

The conceptual basis of this research is based upon the social imitation theory of Bandura and Walters (1963). The common threads uniting these theories and concepts are imitation, modeling and copying, and behavior intervention. Deprived or minority children imitate, model and copy behavioral techniques from their environments. These models and techniques are frequently inappropriate for the school environment and create conflict and tension between children and the school. Learning, culture, and behavioral styles of these children should be incorporated and integrated into a total learning packet. Social learning theories also provide a concrete framework for the schools to begin to implement additional social skills strategies into the curriculum.

Purpose of the Study

This study is designed to review major concepts associated with social learning theories and their relevancies for teaching deprived and minority children, and to abstract from these theories and research findings postulates which are intended to induce further inquiry and research.

Transforming the Environment

Many deprived and minority children live in sub-standard environments where they are denied appropriate mental, physical and social stimulations.

These conditions impede normal development in all areas of functioning. Direct and immediate intervention must be made in the social environment of these children if they are to profit sufficiently from their school experiences.

Early Environmental Experiences

Children born in poverty and neglect often suffer from debilitating deprivation that seriously impair their ability to learn. Early prevention programs for these at-risk children and their parents, starting with prenatal care and including health care, quality day care, and preschool education, help prevent learning disabilities and other psychological problems that disrupt later educational efforts (Butler, 1989). A key reason that deprived children have such a high rate of educational failure is that they often lag in physical and psychological development and may be unprepared to meet the demands of academic learning. There is evidence to support that lack of early experiences can affect brain development. Some areas of the brain require adequate stimulation at the right time in order to take on their normal functions. From case studies of deprived children, findings indicate that there may be critical periods for cognitive and language development (Hatch, Thomas, Gardner, and Howard, 1988). Intervention in the early years appears to be the most effective way to improve the prospects for deprived children to receive maximum benefits from their educational experiences.

Impoverishment of a child's early environmental experiences, including any major restriction on play activities or lack of feedback from older individuals, is suspected of retarding his/her social development and learning. Lack of adequate adult stimulation in the early years can lead to the deprived child's developing negative social behavior which may be irreversible. Firstly, in the absence of adequate stimulation and activity, neurophysiological mechanisms involved in learning may fail to develop. Secondly, conditions in impoverished environments, such as the slums, generally do not provide variety and duration of exposure to perceptual-motor experiences compared to children from more affluent environments.

P.L. 99 457 (Part H Infants and Toddlers Program) is designed, in part, to offset some of the above deprivation by assisting states in setting up early intervention programs, for children birth through age 2 who need special services. Early intervention services include the following skills: physical, mental, social and emotional, language and speech, and self-help skills. Special education services may be provided to children age 3 and older who have a special need, such as a physical disability, partial or total loss of sight, severe emotional problems, hearing or speech impairment, mental handicap, or learning disabilities.

Many deprived and minority children will be classified as disabled and will have many of the listed characteristics. Nevertheless, services provided by P.L. 99 457 should be extended to deprived and minority children and their families. The key is early intervention, which should be designed to treat, prevent and reduce environmental factors which may impede social growth and development.

Learning Styles

There is no one common definition of learning styles, however, researchers have considered learning styles from four dimensions: cognitive, affective, physiological, and psychological. The cognitive dimension of learning styles refers to the different ways that children mentally perceive and order information and ideas. The affective dimension refers to how students' personality traits—both social and emotional—affect their learning. The physiological dimension involves the senses and the environment. Does the student learn better through auditory, visual, or kinesthetic/tactile means? And how is he/she affected by such factors as light, temperature, and room design? The psychological dimension involves the student's inner strengths and individuality. How does the student feel about himself/herself? What way can be found to build his/her self-esteem (Butler, 1988)?

Hillard's research indicated that educational dialogue in recent years has given substantial attention to the question of the importance and precise meaning of style in teaching and learning, particularly for minority groups. Style differences between teachers and students and between students and the curriculum have been cited as explanations for the low academic performance of some minority groups (Hillard, 1989).

Home and Environmental Conditions

Research reported by Erikson as early as 1959, supported that environments characterized by mistrust, doubt, limitation, feeling of inferiority and powerlessness are environments that contribute to identify confusion and inhibit the development of the mature individual (Erikson, 1959). In support of Erikson's view, Ayer (1989) wrote that children need the home base of family life in order to grow up healthy and strong. They need to be listened to and understood, nurtured and challenged by caring, committed adults. Parents need to contribute to their children's self-esteem, self-activity or self-control through appropriate modeling strategies.

If a child's early development status and its early home environment are both low, there is an increased likelihood of poor developmental outcomes. The home environment should be where the child receives support, experiences love, and acquires important skills in becoming a productive, happy, sociable and emotional person. The home environment is the foundation for further development within the child. Experiences from the home must be integrated with the school curriculum for meaningful experiences to occur, which will necessitate including the family, and the community in the education process (Kagan, 1989; Bradley, 1989).

Practical Application of Social Learning

Theories to Education

Social learning theories offer the school a common context through which environment, development sequence, and early experiences of minority and deprived children's development can be understood and researched. These theories enable educators to better understand how deprived children think, how they feel about themselves, and to become aware of factors in the environment precipitating cognitive and affective problems which may have some bearing on academic performance. The relationship between social learning theories and their various concepts toward learning and academic performance of minority and deprived children is not well established. Most research reported today simply indicated that there is a casual relationship. There is a need to conduct empirical studies to determine to what degree social learning theories impact on the academic performances of minority and deprived children. Several postulates have been formulated to stimulate and provide further inquiry and research.

Postulate I.

Over time individuals tend to develop habitual ways of responding to experiences.

Individuals are a product of their environments. They imitate experiences to which they have been exposed. Personality is conceived as a product of social learning. Its development is largely a function of the social conditions under which one grows up. Some social learnings are much more important than others for deprived children. There is frequently a conflict between the social values of deprived children and school. This is chiefly due to the school not being tolerant of the cultural and behavioral styles of deprived and minority children.

Social skills should be taught to children who need them, and in some instances should supercede academic skills. Appropriate social skills must be taught and modeled for many deprived children before a meaningful academic program can be pursued. The school should be cognizant of the fact that many of the habits developed by deprived and minority children are well entrenched. Consequently, surface attention will not have a sufficient impact on changing negative habits. A planned coordinated and integrated program will be needed.

Postulate II.

Style is learned, learned patterns can be either changed or augmented, but can not be ignored. Style tends to be rooted at a deep cultural level and is largely determined by prior experiences and motivation.

Misunderstandings of behavioral style can lead to misjudging students' language abilities, intelligence and establishing rapport and communication. Style is directly associated with cultural values and has been changed over a span of time. Modifying style is a slow and arduous process, and may never be fully realized. A proper sensitivity to style can provide a perspective for the enrichment of instruction for all children for the improvement both of teacher-student communication and of the systematic assessment of students. The schools must become more sensitive to style out of basic respect, and for their tremendous potential for learning (Hillard, 1989). Additionally, a person can use more than one style and can be taught to switch styles when appropriate. According to Deal (1990) the core problems of the schools is not technical but spiritual and social. A climate for growth depends upon healthy, fertile social relationships where the styles and experiences of deprived and minority children are recognized. The notion that each culture has made significant contributions to mankind should be highlighted by the school and integrated into the curriculum.

Postulate III.

Learning depends upon the following factors: drive, response, cue, and reward.

The principal theoretical concept drawn from this postulate are reinforcement values and expectations. The primary assumption is that the tendency for behavior to occur in any given situation is a function of the individual's expectations of reinforcement in that situation and of the value of the reinforcements.

Reinforcement values and expectations of minority and deprived children are different than the values expected from the school. What has been successful in the deprived child's environment may be a source of conflict in the school. In essence, these children have frequently been reinforced by what the school may term "negative behaviors." Deprived and minority children historically have responded to behaviors which have brought them success in their environment. The goal driven behaviors, responses to events and the cues, which they have developed are frequently a means of survival in their environments. These behavior work well for them, until they attend school. At school the copying and imitative tendencies learned at home by deprived children are generally not tolerated or accepted by the school, causing frustration, poor self-image, and sometimes aggressive behavior. It is incumbent upon the school to recognize and accept this fact and to develop strategies to modify, adapt, and gradually promote, what is considered to be "appropriate social behavior" through the use of behavior intervention techniques and other strategies.

Postulate IV.

Children receive and order information differently and through a variety of dimensions and channels.

Diggory (1990) implied that the school is not sensitive to the various personal learning styles that pupils have developed and mastered during the developmental stages. Making sense out of the world is a very real and active process. During early childhood children master complex tasks according to their own schedules and without formal training or intervention.

Upon entering school, children are regimented and required to follow specific school rules, which often conflicts with their styles and modes of learning. Diggory (1990) further outlined that the child and school conceive learning differently. The school is mostly concerned with verbal and written expressions and standardized tests results. Accordingly, many of these activities are strange to children and many have not developed sufficient background or skills to master them. If the school is to be successful in meeting the needs of children, especially those from diverse backgrounds, deprived children must be given an activity role in their own learning by structuring activities which are relevant and meaningful to them. Additionally, teachers must be free to experiment with various models of instruction.

The role of the school should not be to fill children with information, but to help them construct understanding about what they are doing. Children's competence, their ability to make meaning from their environment to construct knowledge, or form generalizations, to solve problems and to associate and transfer knowledge is seldom encouraged by the school.

The concept that style requires a pedagogical response, especially at the point of applying special teaching strategies, appears to be a sound approach. It is widely believed that such an approach ought to be attempted and that when they are made, teaching and learning will be more successful.

Some children are concrete learners while others are abstract learners, some focus on global aspects of the problem while others focus on specific points. Ideally, a student should be flexible enough to do both. Since schools traditionally give more weight to analytical approaches than to holistic approaches, the student who does not manifest analytical habits is at a decided disadvantage (Hillard, 1989).[1]

---

[1]Ed. note: Original document did not contain Postulate V.

Postulate VI.

Early intervention and parental involvement are essential for preparing deprived children to master school tasks successfully.

There has been strong support from the Federal government to include the family in the early educational process of the handicapped child. The passage of the Education of the Handicapped Act Amendments of 1986 (P.L. 99–457) established guidelines for the relationship among federal, state, and local education agencies to provide professional resources to handicapped children and their families. The federal government created guidelines for the educational community in developing and implementing a comprehensive, coordinate, multidisciplinary, interagency program of early intervention services for infants, toddlers and their families (Gallagher, 1989).

A significant percentage of deprived children may be classified as disabled, or have handicapping conditions so severe that they will meet the guidelines specified for services under P.L. 99–457. Generally, deprived children live in sub-environments which stifle growth and development. P.L. 99–457 will allow many deprived children to receive services early, thus preventing or eradicating many of the handicapping conditions which will manifest themselves later.

Postulate VII.

Individuals in mismatched environments often leave the environment or become less productive in it.

Individuals are influenced by the elements within their environments. An individual who lives in an environment that is a good match for his needs and abilities will likely be more productive and prone to stay and will achieve academically. Individuals in mismatched environments, such as deprived children often have trouble transferring values from one environment to another; therefore, many leave school when they reach the legal age. Deprived children, as well as all children, do a great deal of learning outside the classroom. They have accomplished a vast amount of non-academic learning before they enter school, and continue to learn non-academic sources while they are enrolled. Historically, the schools have not tapped this great learning resource. Values, styles, and concepts that deprived and minority children bring to the schools must be matched and integrated into their own social reality if school experiences are to be meaningful.

Postulate VIII.

Most learning is social and is mediated by other people, consequently children should work in groups as much as possible.

There are many group experiences designed to promote social growth among and between children. One of the most promising techniques is cooperative learning. It appears to be a promising technique for improving the social skills of deprived children. Cooperative learning promotes:

1. Positive interdependence
2. Face to face interaction
3. Individual accountability
4. Interpersonal and small group skills
5. Group processing
   (Johnson and Johnson, 1990; Kagan, 1990 and Schultz, 1990).

Most deprived children do not meet academic success, due partly to their inability to implement the above social skills or techniques. These techniques are designed to reduce student isolation and increase students' abilities to react and work with other students toward the solution of common problems. The school should experiment with various forms of cooperative learning strategies to improve social skills of deprived and minority children.

CONCLUSIONS

The impact of personality temperament, cognitive styles, sociological influences, and ethnic background may all influence development and learning of minority and deprived children. The study of social learning theories enables the school to both understand how these students' cultures and learning styles can be modified to promote expected learning outcomes, as well as how these students feel about themselves in relationship to learning. This understanding of matching the cognitive and affective process in designing learning experiences of minority and deprived children appear to be realistic and achievable within the school.

Deprived and minority children generally differ from their counterparts not only in cognitive functioning, but also in interaction to other people. Their abilities to function satisfactory in social groups, and in dispositions, habits, and attitudes customarily associated with character and personality are usually below expected levels. They have fewer and less rigid controls over their impulses and have learned hostile and destructive patterns of behavior. Deprived children often seem unable to respond to classroom instruction. Growing up poor, many of them seem unable to learn the skills and attitudes that they must have in order to escape from poverty. The majority of them never will become fully integrated unless early intervention is attempted (Matsueda, 1987). Intervention should begin early and cover all aspects of human behavior as well as support services. Services provided for handicapped children, under P.L. 99-457 (Part H Infants and Toddlers Program) should be extended to minority and deprived children and their families.

Some observations that are relevant to minority and deprived children:

1. Seem generally unaware of the "ground rules" for success in school.
2. Are less able to learn from being told than are their counterparts.
3. Are often unable to make simple symbolic interpretations.
4. Tend to have shorter attention spans, consequently have problems in following directions.
5. Are unable to use language in a flexible way.
6. Tend to have little concept of relative size of objects outside of their environments.
7. Are less likely to perceive adults as people to whom they can turn for help.
8. Seem to have a low level of curiosity about things.
9. Seem to project a low self image.
10. Have experiences within a very narrow range.

The difficult part of teaching is not developing appropriate learning strategies for minority and deprived children, but dealing with the great influx of children who come from emotionally, physically, socially and financially stressed homes. This is not a school problem alone, society in general must assume the major responsibility for these environmental atrocities. The school is responsible to the extent that it has not changed its approach to teaching minority and deprived children over the last several decades, in spite of the vast amount of research and literature on innovated teaching techniques and strategies successfully employed. School experiences for minority and deprived children are usually unrelated to the experiences they bring to school and do not adequately address the aforementioned observations outlined. Life in school is mostly teacher-centered textbook-dominated, restrictive, impersonal, and rigid (Goodlad, 1984).

These issues and more must be addressed by the school if it is to become responsive to the educational needs of minority and deprived children. The position advanced by the Committee for Economic Development (1987) stated that, "for imperative moral and practical reasons, then, our commitment to the young must go beyond political rhetoric; it must produce a well planned continuum of programs for children from birth through adulthood." This statement appears to be appropriate for the school to promote in providing equal education opportunities for all children, including minority and deprived.

A SYSTEMATIC INSTRUCTIONAL DESIGN STRATEGY DERIVED FROM INFORMATION-PROCESSING THEORY

by Margaret E. Bell

Information-processing theory describes how humans perceive, organize, and remember the vast amounts of sensory data in the environment. The importance of the theory for instruction is its focus on learning as a complex, multi-stage event. Briefly summarized, the three major stages identified by the theory are (1) the reception of information, (2) its transformation into a symbolic code, and (3) its retention (Kintsch, 1974).

The implications of these stages for instructional design are yet to be fully explored (Gagne, 1980). Current research, however, indicates that different instructional strategies can lead to qualitatively different ways of processing information. Mayer and Greeno (1972) found that the formula method for teaching the concept "binomial distribution" led to internal connections. That is, students formed links between one aspect of the new information and some other characteristic of the material (Mayer, 1979). In this relationship, the original structure of the material is not altered. In contrast, the concept method of teaching led to external connections; i.e., links between the new material and the knowledge system already in the student's cognitive structure.

With regard to encoding, research indicates the importance of verbal cues that are learner-generated. Referred to as verbal elaboration, these cues have greatly increased reading comprehension (Doctorow et al., 1978; Wittrock, 1974). In addition, visual elaboration or the practice of generating vivid associative images can also enhance retrieval of information. Children's paraphrase recall of prose passages was increased by training them to illustrate passages with stick-figure cartoons (Lesgold, McCormick, and Golinkoff, 1975). Moreover, Gagne and White (1978) suggest that systematic approaches to the teaching of episodes and images be included in the classroom instruction. In the past, the use of imagery as a processing aid has been neglected in favor of directly teaching verbal knowledge.

Further instructional development is needed, however, with regard to both the processes of encoding and retrieval (Gagne, 1980). In particular, Gagne notes that systematic design procedures for activating the learner's propositional knowledge and organizing schema have yet to appear (Gagne, 1980). The major purpose of this article is to suggest such a design procedure and to illustrate its application.

An important design consideration with regard to encoding and retrieval is that the two processes are directly related. In fact, the process of encoding is one in which new information is summarized or categorized in some way for later recall. Therefore, planning strategies that anchor the new information to the learner's store of previously-acquired knowledge is important. Information that is poorly integrated into the learner's knowledge is difficult to retrieve. Furthermore, only partial information is available to the learner (Norman, 1970).

More importantly, what is retained in long-term memory is not some "written tablet" of what is learned. Instead, it is a summary code that compresses the information into a label. Therefore, the process of recall is not the revival of an existing relationship. Rather it is the construction of a relationship, much as sentences are constructed by the individual. This model of memory is analogous to the model implemented by paleontologists: from a few available bone fragments, a dinosaur may be constructed (Neisser, 1967).

The theory and research indicate that a major goal for instruction is insuring the quality of the learner's processing strategies. Therefore, while providing objectives and advance organizers is important, this procedure alone is insufficient. In addition, instructional design procedures must include the following: (1) analysis of the new learning into a network of closely-related information, (2) development of additional anchoring knowledge for the information to be learned, and (3) the design of encoding exercises that provide the learner with opportunities, for elaboration and reconstruction.

Instructional Design Strategy

The suggested instruction design strategy derived from the theory and research is described below:

1. Establish the internal connectedness of the terms and concepts to be learned. How are the concepts related to each other? Which new terms are synonyms and which are extensions or superordinates to other concepts? How many terms are being used with regard to the same concept? Which terms have maximum utility for establishing links with the learner's prior knowledge? Can some terms be deleted or deferred? Is there a logical order to learning the concepts and/or terms based on their definitions?

2. Establish the external connectedness of the terms and concepts to be learned. What synonyms of the new terms may the students already know? How is the new information an extension or subdivision of what has already been learned? What incidents in the students' experiences may be related to the new concepts? How will the new concepts assist students in re-interpreting prior experiences?

3. Develop advance organizers for the new material to be learned. Select either comparative or expository organizers or a combination of the two. Comparative organizers provide the mechanism of relating new and unfamiliar information to existing knowledge (Mayer, 1979). Expository organizers, on the other hand, provide the mechanism for generating logical relationships in the new material (Mayer, 1979). The information generated in design step one (see above) provides the necessary components for expository organizers, while the information developed in design step two contributes to comparative organizers.

4. Develop additional anchoring knowledge for the new concepts using the balance of the information prepared in design step two. This anchoring knowledge will be used throughout the implementation of instruction to facilitate later retrieval.

5. For the concepts to be learned, identify the concept attributes and the potentially confusing non-attributes. This information will be used in preparing examples for illustration and also in step six.

6. Develop situations that make use of visual and verbal elaboration. Design open-ended examples for the students to verbally complete; develop adjunct questions; design visual displays of examples or situations about which students can develop episodes. The information generated in design step five contributes to the design of situations as well as the writing of adjunct questions.

An Instructional Example

The instructional design strategy for the concepts "prejudice" and "discrimination" and the function of each step are illustrated in Figure 1.

Discussion

The design strategy described in Figure 1 accomplishes several goals. First, it meets the criteria mentioned by Gagne (1980). That is, it includes (1) the planned presentation of retrieval events (see steps six and seven), and (2) it encourages learners to manage some aspects of their own learning. In addition, it reduces the amount of relevant information related to these concepts which otherwise might be included. More importantly, the design strategy may be implemented in either an inductive or deductive sequence. Thus, it provides comprehensiveness, while remaining flexible.

Figure 1

Analysis of the Concepts "Prejudice" and "Discrimination"

Instructional Design Strategy	Function
(1) Establish the internal connectedness of the concepts.	(1) This relationship for the two concepts provides the framework for designing the instruction. The belief/action sequence is used throughout.

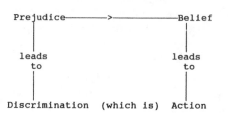

(2) Establish the external connectedness of the concepts.	(2) Facilitates development of advance organizers.

Prejudice———>———prejudgment; bias
                 stereotype; misjudgment
                 mental set & attitude
Discrim-———>———biased treatment; unfair
ination   treatment based on pre-
                 judgment; denial of
                 opportunities and rewards
                 to members of some group

(3) Develop an advance organizer using   (3) Facilitates encoding.
    information in design step two.

"Discrimination is a particular type of
unfair treatment. It results from pre-
judice, which is a misjudgment of (a)   Comparative organizer
group(s) in society. This mental
attitude and the unfair treatment that
it lead to (discrimination) prevent   Expository organizer
individuals from enjoying the benefits
of society. These benefits include
equal opportunities and rewards such as   Expository organizer
good housing, quality education, and
good jobs. Prejudice and discrimination
are harmful because their consequences   Expository organizer
include emotional, social, and economic
ill effects.

Figure 1 (continued)

Analysis of the Concepts "Prejudice" and "Discrimination"

Instructional Design Strategy	Function
(4) Develop anchoring knowledge for the concepts from the information in design steps one and two.	(4) Facilitates encoding and retrieval.
Prejudice——>—Belief—>——Association of assumed characteristics with some groups as a basis for judging them inferior	The concept relationship identified in design step one is further refined by adding detailed information. The "prejudice/belief" relationship is now defined as in the parallel "discrimination/action" relationship.

Examples: "Women are too emotional to be good administrators."

"Blacks are irresponsible."

"Indians are lazy."

Discrimination—>—Action—>—"Unfair treatment based on prejudice

Examples: "Women are too emotional to be good administrators; therefore, they should not be hired for advanced positions."

"Blacks are irresponsible-don't trust them with anything important."

"Indians are lazy; they will steal from you."

"A store owner believes that black children are there to steal and white children are there to buy (prejudice). He treats white children like customers and black children like thieves."

Figure 1 (continued)

Analysis of the Concepts "Prejudice" and "Discrimination"

Instructional Design Strategy	Function
(5) Identify concept attributes.	(5) Provides additional information for elaboration and encoding.

prejudice: prejudgment based on alleged demonstrated behavior
-- used as a basis for differential treatment

discrimination: differential treatment resulting from the attitude
-- rewards and opportunities are assigned on the basis of irrelevant criteria
-- maintains political power structure
-- maintains economic status quo
-- maintains social status
-- provides scapegoat

(6) Design learner rehearsal situations that use substitutions	(6) Places learner in the situation of actively managing his or her learning during the encoding process.

"Why do these examples or pictures represent prejudice?"

"What are the assumed characteristics on which the prejudgment is made?

"What is the stereotype being presented?"

"Why are these actions examples of discrimination?"

"How do these actions evolve from prejudice?"

"What about the action that qualifies it as an extension of prejudice?"

(7) Design learner rehearsal situations that use elaboration.	(7) Implements the technique of learner-developed episodes in elaboration; facilitates retrieval of concepts.

Introduce a situation or sequence with one or two preliminary statements. Then have the students visually and/or verbally complete the situations as representing prejudice and discrimination.

 Illustration: Driver in heavy traffic becomes angry at woman driver and . . .

PART III, SECTION A: LEARNING THEORIES

EDWARDS ARTICLE

What is the classic attitude toward mistakes made in the classroom?

_____

_____

_____

_____

Describe Edwards' alternative (coping model) approach to the classic attitudes toward mistakes.

_____

_____

_____

_____

Briefly discuss the following from the Edwards Article:

Coping with emotions

_____

_____

_____

_____

Self-Talk

_____

_____

_____

_____

PART III, SECTION A: LEARNING THEORIES

CARROLL ARTICLE

Briefly discuss the following:

Practice

_____

_____

_____

_____

Modeling

_____

_____

_____

_____

Suggestion

_____

_____

_____

_____

Climate Setting

_____

_____

_____

_____

PART III, SECTION A: LEARNING THEORIES

CARROLL ARTICLE (continued)

Describe a classroom lesson that integrates the four methods discussed in the
Carroll article.

_____

_____

_____

_____

_____

_____

_____

_____

_____

_____

_____

_____

_____

_____

_____

_____

_____

_____

_____

_____

PART III, SECTION A: LEARNING THEORIES

TAYLOR ARTICLE

Briefly discuss the following:

1. Learning Style

_____

_____

_____

_____

_____

_____

_____

_____

_____

2. Changing Learning Patterns

_____

_____

_____

_____

_____

_____

_____

_____

_____

3. The role of the school

_____

_____

_____

_____

_____

_____

_____

_____

_____

_____

_____

4. Value Transfer

_____

_____

_____

_____

_____

_____

_____

_____

_____

PART III, SECTION A: LEARNING THEORIES

BELL ARTICLE

Bell states "providing objectives and advance organizers is important, (but) this procedure alone is insufficient" in insuring learning? What else is required to insure learning? Design a "mini-lesson" to illustrate the use of these additional steps in helping students to learn.

_____

_____

_____

_____

_____

_____

_____

_____

_____

_____

_____

_____

_____

_____

_____

_____

_____

_____

_____

_____

SECTION B: COGNITIVE DEVELOPMENT

THE SCIENTIFIC FOUNDATION OF EDUCATION

by Constance Kamii
University of Illinois at Chicago Circle
and University of Geneva

Piaget's theory is so original and has so many aspects that it has influenced many people in a wide variety of fields, such as logic, physics, ethology, psycholinguistics, cybernetics, and education, to name only a few. As an educator who has been profoundly influenced by him, I would like to focus this evening on an important point he makes about education, and discuss the recent "back to the basics" movement as an example of this point.

Piaget (1965) said that education is not a profession that is respected in our society, and pointed out that medicine, law, and engineering have much more prestige. To say that teachers are not respected because they make less money than doctors, lawyers, and engineers is to focus only on the symptoms. The real cause of the problem, Piaget said, is that education is a profession that is not based on a solid body of knowledge. Medicine is based on a vast amount of scientific research and theory. Law is likewise based on a highly explicit and systematized body of knowledge, and attempts are constantly and rigorously made in law to avoid contradictions. Engineering, too, is based on a vast amount of scientific research and theory. Education, by contrast, is in a prescientific or early scientific stage that I think resembles Aristotle and Ptolemy's astronomy. Aristotle and Ptolemy rejected the view that the sun might be the center of our system, and upheld the common-sense theory that the sun and other planets revolve around the earth. Because education does not have a scientific base, educators jump on bandwagons when new fads appear, and they change their beliefs with the public as the old pendulum swings. The recent "back to the basics" movement is one more example of this sad state of the profession.

Education is a profession that developed over the centuries by personal opinions called philosophies and by trial and error and by tradition,

121

to meet certain practical needs. To educate the young generations of their society, teachers have used their best common sense. But a profession cannot develop on the basis of common sense alone. We now have many situations in which one person's common sense is the diametric opposite of another person's common sense, and the disagreement ranges from what to teach at what age to everything else, such as the desirability of behavioral objectives and testing programs. Just as agriculture and medicine advanced with scientific research and theory, education can go forward only by raising fundamental questions once again and getting scientific answers to these questions. The two fundamental questions are: "How do children acquire knowledge?" and "How do they learn moral values?"

I stated earlier that education is in a prescientific or early scientific stage. The reason for this statement is that some educators have tried to base their practice on various scientific theories such as behaviorism. Essentially, behaviorism views "learning" as the internalization of knowledge and moral values from the environment, and explains "learning" by reinforcement. Its implication for educators is that if we want children to become able to do something, we have to reinforce correct answers with reward and repetition, and sequence objectives to maximize success.

But there are many counterexamples that make even the layman skeptical of behaviorism. For example, if Johnny cries and the teacher holds him, this comforting does not reinforce Johnny's crying. Instead of learning to cry more by having this behavior reinforced, Johnny gets over his upset and goes on to something else that is more interesting than crying. Children's learning to walk and talk also disproves behaviorism. Children do not need reinforcement from adults to learn how to walk and talk, nor do they need a sequence of objectives that maximize success. Encouragement helps, but if toddlers fall down, they get up and try to walk again even if they are not encouraged by adults. Besides, failure is necessary to learn how to walk. Toddlers need to know how they fall if they are to figure out how to avoid falling. Learning to talk also comes out of children's initiative and errors. No programmer would teach children to say "My foot hurt," "I brang my lunch today," or "I thinked it in my head." But teachers know that children go through these errors. Children make these errors because they are intelligent and can think, and I would worry about a child who did not make these errors. Some children even surprise us by learning to read, without any teaching or reinforcement on the part of the parents or teachers at the day care center. In my research on first-grade arithmetic, I found out a month ago that, without any teaching or reinforcement on the teacher's part, almost all the children in the class knew by heart the sums of 2+2, 5+5, and 3+3. More than half the class also knew the sum of 4+4. The children played dice games and card games, and they learned these sums by heart without any lesson, worksheet, drill, or reinforcement.

These examples contradicting behaviorism illustrate the process by which all sciences develop. In astronomy, "the" scientific truth before the publication of Copernicus's heliocentric theory in 1543 was Ptolemy's geo-centric theory. But many astronomers were bothered by counterexamples. The calendar of the time was sometimes off, and predictions about the planets' positions were constantly wrong. Grappling with these contradictions, Copernicus ended up by proposing a theory in diametric opposition to the common-sense theory of his day. The scientists of his time reacted by laughing him off the stage. But today, only 400 years later, no one doubts the truth of the heliocentric theory.

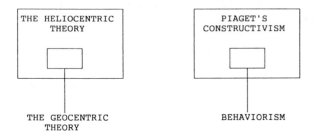

The relationship between behaviorism and Piaget's theory is analo-gous to the relationship between the geocentric theory and Copernicus's he-liocentric theory. Behaviorism and the geocentric theory both grew out of common sense, and Piaget and Copernicus both revolutionized common sense. Both invented their theories by trying to overcome the contradictions presented by the prevailing view. In each domain, the later theory stated the opposite of the earlier theory, but the earlier theory was not eliminated. The earlier theory became a particular case within the new theory. In the weather forecast, for example, we still hear of the time the sun rises and sets. Within the listed perspective of the earth, it is still true that the sun rises every morning, but from a broader perspective, it is no longer true that the sun goes around the earth. Behaviorism is likewise still true within cer-tain limits. For example, if we want to teach toddlers not to go out into the street, behaviorism is clearly still true and highly useful. If we want to teach children to memorize the multiplication tables, likewise, behaviorism is still as true as the sunrise every morning. But, within the broader per-spective of children's acquisition of knowledge and moral values, it is no longer true that these are learned by reinforcement and well-sequenced ob-jectives.

Let us return to the two fundamental questions educators must ask: "How do children acquire knowledge?" and "How do they learn moral val-ues?" Piaget studied these questions scientifically. He concluded that both knowledge and morality are constructed from within by each child in in-teraction with the environment, rather than being learned directly by inter-nalization from it.

An example might help to understand the child's construction of knowledge from within. Once, when I came face to face with a 5-year-old black girl in a day care center, the child greeted me by saying, "Hi, Chinese." I responded by saying that I was Japanese and not Chinese, and asked her "What are you?" The girl said that she was black, whereupon I asked, "Are you an American?" She said "yes," and I told her that I, too, was an American. The girl was amazed and asked, "Is that because you are black?" We see the constructive process in this example. For this child, all blacks were apparently American, and all Americans were conversely black. When I told her I was an American, she reasoned that I had to be black if I was an American. The construction of knowledge is such a complicated business, and anybody who is around children can see that knowledge is not acquired directly by internalization from the environment.

The second question educators must ask is how moral values are learned by children. Piaget concluded in 1932, almost 50 years ago, that moral values and rules, too, are constructed from within by each individual rather than being learned directly by internalization from the environment. Piaget made a distinction between morality of autonomy and the morality of heteronomy. Autonomy means "being governed by oneself," while heteronomy means "being governed by somebody else." Piaget asked many children whether it was worse to tell a lie to a grownup or to another child. An example of the morality of heteronomy is the 6-year-old who answered that it was worse to lie to a grownup. When Piaget asked why, the child replied, "Because adults can tell it isn't true." An example of the morality of autonomy is the 12-year-old who answered, "Sometimes you almost have to tell lies to a grownup, but it's rotten to do it to another fellow." Autonomous people have their own convictions about why it is bad to tell lies.

If we want children to become heteronomous adults, the best way is to use behavioristic principles, that is, reward and/or punishment. Behaviorism (the small square in the figure) is a very limited theory that can explain heteronomy and aspects of our behavior that we share with animals, such as motor skills and certain habits. If we want children to become autonomous adults, we need a broader, more powerful theory that goes beyond reward and punishment (the large square in the figure).

Teachers who want to foster the morality of autonomy must think of ways that encourage children to construct their own moral values for themselves. If a child tells a lie, for example, the teacher must avoid punishing him, look him straight in the eye instead, with great affection and skepticism, and say, "I really can't believe what you are saying because . . ." This communication of a point of view makes the child think about what he has to do if he wants to be believed and trusted. If there is a good human relationship between the child and the teacher, the child may, over a period of time, construct for himself the value of honesty. Adults who have constructed their own conviction about the desirability of honesty can resist the temptations of the reward system. They become like Elliot Richardson, who was the only one on Nixon's cabinet in the Watergate Cover-Up Affair who refused to tell lies and handed in his resignation. Autonomy is not only more moral than heteronomy; it is also more intelligent than heteronomy. Autonomy, in other words, is indissociably moral, intellectual, social, and emotional in nature.

Most educators and parents are still at a prescientific stage of holding the common-sense belief that the way to raise children to become moral is by being strict. The detention hall, having to write 50 times "I will not talk in class," grades, gold stars, and citizenship awards are examples of the reward and punishment schools still use to get children to be "good." The behavioral objectives and tests that are imposed on teachers in the "back to basics" movement are based on a scientific theory, but a theory that was surpassed decades ago, when Piaget published *Judgment and Reasoning in the Child* in 1924, *The Child's Conception of the World* in 1926, *The Child's Conception of Physical Causality* in 1927, *The Moral Judgment of the Child* in 1932, *The Origins of Intelligence* in 1936, *The Construction of Reality* in 1937, and many other volumes that are too numerous to mention. I am not against the 3 Rs. I am, in fact, all for them. But reading, writing, and arithmetic must be taught in ways that fit the way children honestly think, and not with behavioral objectives that are foreign to the way they learn.

Science never goes back to an earlier stage. Once we believe in the heliocentric theory, we cannot go back to the old geocentric theory. Once we understand quantum physics, likewise, we cannot go back to the physics of Aristotle, Galileo, and Newton. Once we understand non-Euclidean geometry, similarly, we cannot go back to the limited views of Euclid's geometry. I have seen many behaviorists, associationists, and empiricists change over Piaget's theory as I did, but I have never heard of a Piagetian who became a behaviorist. When you hear of "back to basics," therefore, you know that a profession that can shamelessly go back to what did not work before is obviously not based on scientific knowledge. Science only goes forward and always builds on what is already known. If educators understood learning and development scientifically, the profession would go forward and not backward any more.

I have insisted so far that education must become more scientific. But I am not saying that education must become a pure science. Piaget said that education is and must remain an art, just as good medicine still is and must remain an art. Doctors must take into account the possibility of various side effects, as well as the patient's fears, dependency needs, and need for independence. Medicine is thus an art involving guesswork and human factors, but it is an art based on a vast amount of scientific knowledge. Education must likewise become an art that is based on scientific research and precise theoretical links.

I am not saying that medicine is fully developed or that doctors always know what they are doing. What I am saying is that educators must learn from the rigor of more advanced professions. Piaget left behind a

towering theory about how each individual and the entire human race construct knowledge and moral values. Every educator must wake up to this
theory and compare it for himself with the scientific merits of all the other
theories that explain how children acquire knowledge and become responsible citizens. Piaget's theory may then become widely accepted as being
more adequate than the geocentric theory. Piaget left for us the tools with
which to move forward. It is now up to us to make use of these tools.

PIAGET TAKES A TEACHER'S LOOK

by Jean Piaget and
Eleanor Duckworth

To quote any number of late-night talk show hosts, "Our next guest needs no introduction." So it is with Jean Piaget, today's dominant force in child psychology and educational theory. The unique nature of the following "guest appearance" does, however, deserve explanation. The traditional Piaget discourse, by his own admission, is abstract and rarely concerned with classroom application. But Piaget willingly abandoned that posture in a recent chat with long-time associate Eleanor Duckworth of the Atlantic Institute of Education, Halifax, Nova Scotia. On special assignment for LEARNING, Duckworth asked Piaget to examine for LEARNING's audience some of the specific implications for teachers in his life's work. His suggestions were drawn from the original 15,000 word transcript by Odvard Egil Dyrli of the University of Connecticut. They follow.

ELEANOR DUCKWORTH: To begin with, from your point of view, what do you think you have to offer educators? Why do you think educators get so enthused about your work?
JEAN PIAGET: It's a mystery. I don't know what happened. In Geneva no one pays any attention.

DUCKWORTH: There is an increasing tendency to sell kits to teachers so they can present to children the same types of tasks that you have used in your research, as if this is what the children should be doing. That seems to me a rather limited view.
PIAGET: Yes, of course it is. And if the aim is to accelerate the development of these operations, it is idiotic.
　　I would say that the only step in the right direction such kits repre-

127

sent is to provide the children with actual objects. I have been even more distressed by examples brought to my attention where American educators thought it useful to present a host of objects in the form of photos or films, as if looking at these would somehow constitute contact with the objects themselves. Manipulation of materials is crucial. In order to think, children in the concrete stage need to have objects in front of them that are easy to handle, or else be able to visualize objects that have been handled and that are easily imagined without any real effort.

Teachers should select materials that make the child become conscious of a problem and look for the solution himself. And, if he generalizes too broadly, then provide additional materials where counter-examples will guide him to see where he must refine his solution. It's the materials he should learn from.

DUCKWORTH: Should you, the teacher, then, know what you want the child to understand from such materials?

PIAGET: Yes, I think so, as long as the child is not told. But still you should be on the lookout for the unexpected things to develop, and make sure he can pursue these, too.

DUCKWORTH: What about in cases where you really don't know what will happen? Is it realistic to present these and expect that the child will be able to raise his own questions?

PIAGET: As long as the material is simple enough so that the child can indeed raise questions that he can answer for himself.

DUCKWORTH: Do you think that raising questions is just as important as knowing how to solve them?

PIAGET: Yes, I do.

DUCKWORTH: Would there be any way of facilitating a child's tendency to ask questions? Or do you simply try not to kill it.

PIAGET: You could facilitate it mainly through having a multitude of materials available that raise questions in a child's mind without suggesting the answers.

DUCKWORTH: Do you know if there is any systematic development in the levels of the questions children ask?

PIAGET: It depends to some degree upon the subject matter. In the ideal situation, the questions the child asks himself and the reactions he discovers are always in the context of the possibilities opened by his findings at the preceding level. Of course, this requires materials in each area that encourage a progression. That is, once the child has answered the previous question, he will be likely to ask himself a new question. The teacher's role then is to make certain that the materials are rich enough to allow simple questions at the beginning, with solutions that each time open new possibilities.

DUCKWORTH: Once the child has succeeded in a particular task, as you suggest, does it go without saying that he will ask the next question?
PIAGET: No, not at all, though eventually this should take place. But if the teacher discreetly changes the situation slightly, thereby preventing the child from succeeding immediately in the next step, the child will wonder why he was more successful the first time and not the second. So now it becomes a question of understanding.

I have a horror of teaching methods that are predetermined. This was a great weakness of the Montessori approach—closed materials. Take, for example, lining things up in order of length. She started with a fine idea, but she ended up with form boards! Each piece fits in its place, and that's as far as you can go. Whereas, in fact, you can order all sorts of different things.

If the material is just a set of sticks of different lengths, for example, there are unlimited variations. In addition to the arrangement with equal differences from one element to the next, sticks could also be arranged so that the line of the tops would be convex, or concave, or a combination. Children might find such variations themselves or they could be asked to copy a given series or to continue it. This is just one example of the many Montessori materials that offer such limited possibilities.

DUCKWORTH: I can see in this particular case that the materials are limited. What would be the general criteria which define material as being closed or open?
PIAGET: Well, it is closed in the sense there are few possibilities.

DUCKWORTH: One point that is important to Montessori teachers is that children must do things correctly. If they are not able to do a task correctly, then they must wait until later. That seems another contrast with you, since you have always taken such an interest in errors.
PIAGET: Yes, I think children learn from trying to work out their own ways of doing things—even if it does not end up as we might expect. But children's errors are also instructive for teachers. Above all, teachers should be able to see the reasons behind errors. Very often a child's errors are valuable clues to his thinking. As Seymour Papert says, a child always answers his own question correctly; the cause of an apparent error is that he did not ask himself the same question that you have asked him.

DUCKWORTH: When we were discussing kits at the onset, you suggested that explicitly teaching operations is probably not a very fruitful form of pedagogy.

PIAGET: Yes, conservation of number, for example, is a notion children always create for themselves. So why spend the effort to cram it into their heads?

DUCKWORTH: If teachers should not be trying to teach operations, then what is the value in knowing about your work?

PIAGET: It is essential for teachers to know why particular operations are difficult for children, and to understand that these difficulties must be surmounted by each child in passing from one level to the next. It is not the stages that are important; it is rather what happens in the transition. Teachers must understand, for example, why responsibility cannot be taken for granted with 4-year-olds, and why 12-year-olds have difficulty reasoning from hypotheses. What changes take place from one level to the next, and why does it take so much time?

Too many people take the theory of stages to be simply a series of limitations. That is a disastrous view. The positive aspect is that as soon as each stage is reached, it offers new possibilities to the child. There are no "static" stages as such. Each is the fulfillment of something begun in the preceding one, and the beginning of something that will lead on to the next. It is just as disastrous, moreover; to assume that a child has or has not reached a certain stage just because he is a certain age. The ages I have mentioned are only averages. Any child may be a year or so beyond or behind the average capabilities reached by most children his age.

DUCKWORTH: Is it possible that one child may develop much more slowly than another child, but go further in the long run? Because he spends time exploring all the possibilities at each new level?

PIAGET: Yes, certainly. This is still full of mystery, but it seems probable that assimilation that is done too rapidly does not result in a structure that can be generalized as readily to apply to other situations.

DUCKWORTH: I think there is still another misinterpretation of your stages. I have heard people refer to a child who has some difficulty in arithmetic and attributed the problem entirely to some stage he may not yet have reached. Aren't there other factors to consider besides the stages of intellectual development?

PIAGET: Yes, of course. In a great many cases, it's just the language we use is bad. We simply do not make ourselves understood. I have often questioned children who have been identified as being very poor in mathematics. If I gave them problems and made sure they knew what I was talking about, they solved them very well. Then afterwards I told them that was arithmetic, and they were amazed. It could be another world. I do not believe in aptitudes and nonaptitudes in mathematics and science that differentiate children at the same intellectual level. What is usually involved is either aptitudes or nonaptitudes to the teacher's approach.

DUCKWORTH: Do you believe that there are fields in which aptitudes exist?

PIAGET: I think that in the artistic world there exist people who are more or less visual or more or less audio-motor.

DUCKWORTH: Do you think this kind of aptitude is innate, or is it influenced by childhood experiences?

PIAGET: That's difficult to say, but I would not be surprised if it were innate. It's possible, though, that experiences have to be taken into consideration. I myself am not visually oriented at all.

DUCKWORTH: This distinction bothers me a bit. When teachers say that some children are visual and others are auditory, it seems to me that they are presupposing that the only way for children to learn is through words—either through reading or being told.

PIAGET: No, of course not. I was talking about artistic aptitudes. No, of course, we learn through our actions too.

DUCKWORTH: Do you think that there are things that must be taught to every child, or do you think that it does not really matter what is learned, as long as the child is involved intellectually?

PIAGET: My position is somewhere between these two. There are, of course, some things that are commonly useful, that we all should know fairly automatically. Proportions, for example.

DUCKWORTH: Well, suppose that a child reaches the age of 14 and has never been taught about proportions and has never needed them until now, but at 14 years of age he finds himself faced with a problem requiring the use of proportions. Wouldn't he be able to create them for himself at this point?

PIAGET: Yes, of course.

DUCKWORTH: It seems to me from one point of view that if we teach it to them now as a skill they may need later, then when they are called upon to use it, they won't even recognize that this is what they need.

PIAGET: Yes, I agree. But of course when I say teach, I mean an active teaching method and not just a verbal transmission.

DUCKWORTH: Could we say that the child is sufficiently intelligent to create for himself his own way to understand a particular subject? It is not necessary for the teacher to cut everything up into small pieces and do the intellectual work for the child. The child must do the work himself.

PIAGET: This is certainly the ideal. The teacher should rather center upon studying the way the child solves problems for himself, and provide suitable materials to assist him as necessary.

DUCKWORTH: For many years now you have urged teachers to actually do some of your experiments rather than to simply read about them. I have often had teachers do this; it's always exciting. Still, it is not always easy to find the relationship between these very pretty games and what they do in the classroom.

PIAGET: The relationship is that behind what we observe there are ten times more things that we suspected. It is essential for teachers to see that behind a child's apparent understanding, and all the more so behind his lack of understanding, there is a world of mechanisms that remain unknown in direct observations.

It must be emphasized strongly that pedagogy cannot be deduced from psychology directly. Teachers themselves must function as research workers—if they are free to do so.

In the United States maybe they are freer than in Geneva. In Europe there is a great difference between a doctor and a teacher. The doctor has his procedures, which are scientific, drawn from medical research, while the teacher is under the orders of a state that dictates to him his methods and his programs. So he is not free to alter them. But if teachers are free enough, they must develop an experimental pedagogy that is not limited to such small problems as trying to find out if one reading method gives better results than another reading method. They have to look at greater questions—what should be taught, what should not be taught, and so forth. Such an experimental pedagogy would utilize observations and experiments of all the various programs to determine why they were successful in certain cases and failed in others. Teachers who have worked with different materials and approaches, therefore, must learn to confront each other and discuss the advantages and disadvantages of each. And this can only be the work of educators. Knowing about our psychological findings is only one necessary aspect; they must also know about teaching and children.

DUCKWORTH: Can I ask you one more question? It is a big one, but maybe you can give a small answer. Once a child acquires language, what part does that play in his thinking?

PIAGET: Come on! Well, I will answer you with a story I read somewhere. A journalist asked a physicist what he thought of interdisciplinary research, and the physicist said, "You remind me of the lady who was sitting beside a great painter at dinner and asked him, 'Master, what do you think about art?' and the painter answered, 'My dear madam, wouldn't you have one slightly smaller question?'" As for the relationship between language and thought! . . .

PIAGET'S THEORY AND SPECIFIC INSTRUCTION: A RESPONSE TO BEREITER AND KOHLBERG

by Constance Kamii

The present paper draws pedagogical implications from Piaget's theory in the light of Bereiter's critical response to Kohlberg's view against specific instruction. It argues that instruction can be more specific in some ways than Kohlberg suggested, e.g., in the teaching of social knowledge and in the structuring of cognitive processes that will eventually result in logical thinking. It shows the relevance of Piaget's theory to early childhood education and argues that specific instruction should take place within a developmental context and within the framework of a broad theory of knowledge.

In the above article, Bereiter (1970) responded critically to Kohlberg's conclusion against specific instruction (Kohlberg, 1968). Although Bereiter did not make a convincing case in support of specific instruction, his article did have the effect of causing me to reread Kohlberg's paper in a new light. This reexamination led to the conclusion that the educational implications Kohlberg drew from Piaget's theory were too general. This paper is written to present some other implications that can be drawn from Piaget's theory.

I attempt first to indicate that the three areas of knowledge delineated by Piaget (social, physical, and logico-mathematical knowledge) suggest

Ed. note: At the time this paper was written, Constance Kamii was Curriculum Director of the Ypsilanti Early Education Program, which had been in operation since September, 1967, and was created primarily for the development of a preschool curriculum based on Piaget's theory. She studied under Piaget, Inhelder, and Sinclair at the University of Geneva in 1966–1967 in preparation for this project.

where instruction should be specific and where it should not be. The term "specific instruction" is then to be interpreted to refer to the teacher's knowing specifically when to teach something and when not to teach it. The final part of the paper presents other educational implications that can be drawn from Piaget's theory with regard to the context within which I believe specific instruction must take place.

Before going on to the main part of the paper, I would like to point out that both Bereiter and Kohlberg did not push their analyses far enough to be useful to the curriculum builder. Bereiter did not make a convincing case partly because he did not address himself to the real issue. The question Kohlberg raised was not whether or not instruction should be specific, but how early education could be conducted to be of long-term benefit. Having shown that Kohlberg's statements could be questioned, Bereiter did not attempt to specify any principle to guide the policy maker in deciding what to teach at what age so as to produce long-term gains. It is hoped that he will advance his arguments further toward a general theory of instruction that will be broad enough to generate a curriculum for early childhood education.

I am in agreement with Kohlberg's view that the Piagetian approach does not give rise to great optimism about the extent to which preschool education can compensate for the lack of "massive general types of experience." However, I am of the opinion that cognitive stages are more modifiable than Kohlberg seems to believe. Kohlberg gave an overly pessimistic outlook and said almost nothing about how a theory of instruction could be based on Piaget's theory. The only pedagogical principles he gave are the following:

1. Intellectual development can be accelerated by "employing cognitive conflict, match, and sequential ordering of experience" and "active and self-selective forms of cognitive stimulation."
2. ". . . Piaget and his followers have systematically studied the development of preschool children's play, their conversations with one another, their conception of life, of death, of reality, of sexual identity, of good and evil. The implications of these and other themes for the broader definition of preschool objectives are taken up elsewhere (Kohlberg and Lesser, in preparation)."
3. ". . . limited specific staining experiences cannot replace the massive general types of experience accruing with age."

These principles hardly show even to the most sympathetic reader how Piaget's theory can be applied to actual teaching. Kohlberg intended to describe the pedagogical principles elsewhere, but it is easy to see how the few points he did sketch invited the criticism that his article showed a "theoretical dead end." I sketch below a few directions in which this epistemological theory can be developed into a theory of instruction.

SPECIFIC INSTRUCTION AND THE THREE AREAS
OF KNOWLEDGE

Piaget delineated three areas of knowledge according to their respective sources. They are social knowledge, which comes from people; physical knowledge, which comes from physical phenomena; and logico-mathematical knowledge, which is structured from the internal cognitive structure that the child has already built. Each will be described below in order to show how this framework enables the teacher to know the kind of content that can be taught as specifics.

The ultimate source of social knowledge is people, and the child can acquire it only from people. Some examples are:

1. All the names of objects, animals, people, and ideas, both in spoken and written forms.
2. Saucers go under cups, and not under pencils.
3. Tables are not to stand or sit on.
4. Girls wear skirts, and boys wear pants.
5. We eat three meals a day.
6. My telephone number is (123)-456-7890.
7. December 25 is Christmas Day.
8. Washington, D.C., is the capital of the United States.

It can be seen from the above examples that the nature of social knowledge is rather arbitrary, and that specific feedback from people is essential for the child to build social knowledge.

The ultimate source of "truth" in physical knowledge is physical phenomena. The child finds out about most physical phenomena by acting on objects and observing the objects' reactions. Some examples are:

1. This cup will go down (not up) if I let go of it, and it will break because it is made of porcelain.
2. Balls bounce when they are dropped on the floor, but cups do not.
3. Pennies sink in water.
4. Wheels roll, but blocks do not.
5. If there are five marbles on one side of the balance, there will have to be an equal number on the other side to make it balance.
6. The light will go off when I turn off the switch.
7. Plants die if they are not watered.

While social and physical knowledge is built from sources that are external to the child, logico-mathematical knowledge is structured from the internal consistency of the system that the child has already built. Some examples are:

1. If I take out 10 cups and 10 saucers, there will be as many cups as saucers even if their spatial arrangement is changed.

2. If A is bigger than B, and B is bigger than C, A is bigger than C.
3. There are more animals in the world than there are dogs.
4. If all men are mortal, and Socrates was a man, Socrates was mortal.

In the logico-mathematical realm, the child's knowledge is based on his own reasoning rather than on external sources. In the above examples, the older child "knows" that there have to be as many cups as saucers without reestablishing the one-to-one correspondence. He "knows" that A has to be bigger than C without empirically comparing the two. He "knows" that there have to be more animals in the world than there are dogs without actually counting them. He "knows" that Socrates must have died without checking the empirical fact.

It can be seen from the above distinction that in social and physical knowledge learning is both specific and based on feedback from external sources. These are the areas in which instruction can and should be specific. If the child is wrong in social knowledge, he can simply be told the social rule (e.g., Christmas is not December 24). If he thinks that a ball will break when it is dropped, he can find out the truth by dropping the object and studying the regularity of the object's reaction. The child is not made unsure of himself when he is flatly contradicted in social and physical knowledge. In the logico-mathematical realm, however, teaching is more delicate. Even if a three-year-old could somehow be taught the conservation of number, such teaching is likely to make him unsure of his beliefs unless he can anchor the learning in the total system of how he thinks.

The statement that instruction can be specific in social and physical knowledge does not imply that the child can learn specific facts without a logical structure. In fact, according to Piaget, every concept is related to every other concept that the child has acquired. Instruction must, therefore, be anchored in the total system of how the child thinks so that the development of one concept will affect the development of the entire network in an integrated way. For example, knowing that "girls wear skirts" or that "porcelain broke today, yesterday, and the day before yesterday" requires the ability to classify and to structure the regularity of events over time. Piaget's theory thus permits the analysis of knowledge into three major areas and suggests how the mutual interdependence among the three might be used to strengthen each other. Through the teaching of social and physical knowledge, it is often possible to facilitate the organization of logico-mathematical structures. The details of a preschool curriculum based on this framework are being developed, and are outlined in Kamii and Radin (1970), Sonquist, Kamii, and Derman, (1970), and Kamii (in press).

SPECIFIC INSTRUCTION IN A DEVELOPMENTAL CONTEXT

Piaget's theory is the only one in existence that demonstrates the continuity of cognitive development from birth to adolescence. It shows how the most abstract hypothetico-deductive thinking of the adult evolves out of the infant's sensorimotor intelligence. The educational implication of this continuity is that the objectives of preschool education should be not only the mastery of specific content and processes but also the consolidation of previous acquisitions and the preparation of abilities that will take two, three, or more years to appear. The term "specific instruction" in this developmental context changes its meaning to refer to the teacher's knowing specifically why she teaches (or does not teach) certain things during the preschool years.

Inhelder has conducted learning experiments in Geneva to find out, among other things, how logical structures are acquired and to what extent operations can be taught. The conclusion stated in Inhelder, Bovet, and Sinclair (1967) is that learning is possible within the limits imposed by the child's developmental level at the time teaching is initiated. The early pre-operational child progresses only to a slightly more advanced pre-operational level. The child who is at an intermediary pre-operational level to begin with usually reaches the threshold of operations with the same general method of instruction. The child who is very close to the operational level reaches it very quickly. In other words, children progress from one stage to another within the pre-operational period, i.e., from one stage of being "wrong" to another stage of being "wrong," before they become able to reason logically like adults.

The implication of the above conclusion is that specific instruction must be specific from the learner's point of view, rather than from the adult's point of view. As can be seen in the teaching experiment described in Sinclair and Kamii (1970), the pre-operational child learns in ways that adults do not expect, and specific instruction must be careful not to impose adult logic, thereby making the child skip the intermediary stages that he needs to go through.

The administration of Piagetian tasks to the children taught by Englemann illustrates what pre-operational children learn when specific instruction imposes adult logic (Kamii & Derman, in press). In this experiment, Englemann taught the concept of specific gravity to six-year-old children to demonstrate that formal operations could be taught to pre-operational children. The children were found unmistakably to have learned to "explain" that certain objects float on water "because they are lighter than a piece of water the same size," and that other objects sink "because they are heavier than a piece of water the same size." However, when the questions were changed to nonverbal tasks, it was found that the children were thinking just like any other pre-operational children. For example, they were asked to sort a number of objects into "things that you think will float" and "things that you think will sink." Typically, they put large and/or heavy objects in the category of "sink," and small and/or light objects in the category of "float." For example, some children put the large candle in the "sink" pile, and the tiny birthday candle in the "float" pile.

It was concluded, therefore, that the children had not really learned the concept of specific gravity. In fact, the imposition of adult logic may even have stifled their ability to think. When faced with a hard question, they seemed to mentally search through their memory to find any rule that might fit the facts. Thus, when a needle was predicted to float, but was found to sink, the children simply changed their "explanation" from "it's lighter than a piece of water the same size" to "it's heavier than a piece of water the same size." They did not show any sign of curiosity as to why some small objects sink and why some large objects float.

Inhelder and Piaget believe that, for the solid structuring of the concept of specific gravity, children need to have the following prerequisites:

(1) the conservation of substance, weight, and volume,
(2) class inclusion, and
(3) the seriation of sizes and weights.

In the Piagetian approach to teaching, children thus have to be given the time and freedom they need to build the prerequisite structures, to figure out their own strategy, to mobilize their entire cognitive organization, and to go through the sub-stages they need to go through in order to build a solid foundation for future learning. "Specific instruction" in a Piagetian sense thus takes on the meaning that the teacher has to know:

(1) what to teach and when,
(2) what not to teach and why, and
(3) when to let the pre-operational child be "wrong."

Examples of each situation are given below.

WHAT TO TEACH AND WHEN

A distinction must be made between teaching for the attainment of operations and for the preparation of their eventual attainment. Bereiter and Kohlberg discussed teaching only in the first sense, particularly with regard to whether or not conservation can be taught. I believe that the better strategy for teaching the pre-operational child is to put the emphasis on the preparation of operations.

Piaget's theory stresses the process of reasoning that enables the child to reach the correct conclusion. If the process becomes better structured and more mobile, the child will inevitably achieve the operation. "Preparing the child for operations" thus places the accent on general and specific instruction that aims at the underlying process rather than the final product.

Examples of preparing the child for the acquisition of number concepts can be found in Kamii (1969) and Ezell, Hammerman, and Morse (1969). As can be seen in these papers, we believe that the teaching of conservation of number as such should be avoided, and that educational efforts should focus on the processes that underlie conservation, that is,

(1) making groups and comparing grossly different groups,
(2) arranging, disarranging, and rearranging objects,
(3) linear ordering,
(4) establishing and reestablishing equivalence with provoked correspondence,
(5) temporal correspondence,
(6) reversibility, etc.

Teaching the underlying processes entails refraining from external reinforcement to let the child figure out for himself whether or not his prediction was correct. Social reinforcement and the giving of rules based
on empirical generalization are efficient only in the short run. This statement will be further elaborated in connection with the Piagetian notion of
"learning."

WHAT NOT TO TEACH AND WHY

It is evident from the above discussion that, in my opinion, the conservation of number should not be taught explicitly. Following are two other examples of things not to teach according to the implications that I draw from
Piaget's theory.

1. Teaching the relationships among seconds, minutes, hours, days, weeks,
   months, and years to children who do not have class inclusion.
2. Teaching the writing of letters to children whose representational space
   is not structured enough to even copy squares and triangles (Piaget &
   Inhelder, 1967).

WHEN TO LET THE PRE-OPERATIONAL CHILD BE "WRONG"

As it was stated above, both in teaching experiments and in nature, pre-
operational children progress from one stage to another within the pre-
operational way of thinking, before they achieve concrete operations. It becomes clear, when the invariant sequence of development is examined, that
children's earlier errors are essential stages in the construction of the correct solution. To help children progress, therefore, the teacher must understand the reasoning processes that lead to these errors. Actually, in the case
of Piaget's tasks, it is incorrect to say that children make "errors." For example, when they give a non-conserving answer by basing their judgment
on the level of the liquid in the beaker, they are taking into account one
of the factors that are indeed pertinent to the judgment of quantities. This
evaluation based on height is a step forward compared to judgment that is
based on the color of the liquid or the attractiveness of the container. These
pre-operational ways of thinking are not errors to be eliminated, but pre-

logical modes of evaluation that have to be brought to the fore and integrated with other factors. Specific instruction can thus imply that the teacher should be a skillful questioner who asks just the right question at the right time to make the child figure out his own strategy at his own level.

Bereiter rightly pointed out that Kohlberg did not demonstrate why the invariant sequence should be the major issue in the determination of educational policy on cognitive development. The preceding discussion and what follows hopefully explain why I believe that specific instruction should be based on the child's developmental stage.

SPECIFIC INSTRUCTION AND THEORIES OF LEARNING

Bereiter (1970) stated that "specific learning and cognitive stage development do not refer to different phenomena but rather to the same phenomena, described at different levels of generality and according to different principles." It is argued below that specific learning and cognitive stage development are indeed two different phenomena, and that Bereiter's argument is based on a view of "learning" that differs rather basically from the Piagetian view.

Let us take the conservation of substance as an example of something that can be learned either by specific instruction or without any teaching. Bereiter and Kohlberg both discussed conservation in a narrow sense in isolation from the total structure that Piaget calls "intelligence." In contrast, Piaget and Inhelder use the conservation task as a kind of thermometer to explore the structure and network of schemes that are inside the "black box." Conservation is thus not just conservation, but an indicator of an internal structure that has become coherent and reversible.

The conservation of substance is achieved shortly after the conservation of number. In other words, the latter indicates the beginning of reversibility of thought. About the time the conservation of substance is achieved, a host of other abilities also emerge—class inclusion, operational seriation, arithmetic operations, mental images that are mobile, geometric operations, a system of causal relationships in explaining physical phenomena, certain forms of language, etc., just to name a few that fill up many volumes. The common element in all these operations is thought that has become reversible, with the result that the child ceases to be dominated by the static, configurational aspect of what he sees. In other words, it is reversibility of thought that makes the operations possible.

It may be added, parenthetically, that if the above operations seem to appear and disappear at the beginning, as Bereiter pointed out, it is because reversibility of thought is a very gradual achievement, and fluctuation is a characteristic of the child who is at an intermediary stage of approaching the operational level.

Another point in Piaget's theory that is often overlooked is his belief that operations become stable only when they belong together. In fact, to speak of an isolated operation is a contradiction in terms, as an operation cannot exist in isolation. It is this integrated and mobile system that Piaget calls "operational intelligence." Conservation that is achieved through specific instruction, is therefore, a phenomenon that differs from what is the result of the general structure that has become stable and reversible. The issue is neither one of "natural versus induced learning" as Kohlberg sees it, nor one of "rules of greater or lesser scope" as Bereiter sees it, but one of whether or not the operation in question is part of, or an outcome of, a larger whole.

If education is to aim at developing the total structure of intelligence, specific instruction would have to be combined with the more general methods of play, social interaction, and child-initiated learning that Kohlberg and the child developmentalists advocate. This combination could be either consecutive or simultaneous. The crucial question for specific instruction would then become, "What kind of play in what kind of group, what kind of social interaction, and what kind of child-initiated learning?" Bereiter states that the Piagetian view and child developmentalist view may be "unrelated ones, which merely happen to appeal to the same people" (1970). The two views seem to me to converge because Piaget provides a theoretical rationale for the traditional practices that have been defended merely on intuitive grounds.

The most questionable sentence in Bereiter's article may be the following: "If . . . a teacher is interested in educating young children so that they will become better thinkers in the long run, the last thing he need be concerned about is getting them to attain Piaget's stage of concrete operations, since he can be assured they will all reach it anyway without his help." The attainment of concrete operations indicates that the child's intelligence has become more mobile and better structured so that he can now reason logically. The ramifications of this achievement are enormous (e.g., the ability to measure, to add and subtract, to multiply and divide, etc.), and if the child is two years behind in this achievement, he will theoretically have 2,000 hours of class time during which he will assume the role of a "slow learner" at least part of the time.

The above argument showed the relevance of the stage of concrete operations to early education from the standpoint of preventing learning problems. A second argument can be advanced from the point of view of the permanence of the acquisitions found in Piaget's tasks. A third argument can be based on what Piaget and Inhelder found recently about the nature of memory (Inhelder, 1969; Piaget & Inhelder, 1968). In these investigations, the authors found that what is learned in certain pre-operational situations is remembered not only permanently but also in such a way that the accuracy of memory improves over time through cognitive structuring. An example is given below at the risk of grossly oversimplifying the findings.

In an experiment described in further detail in Inhelder (1969), the child was shown 10 seriated sticks (9 to 16.2 cm), and was told to take a good look at them in order to remember what he saw. A week later, and again eight months later, the experimenter returned to the school and asked the child to recall what he had been shown. The memory was expressed with gestures on the desk and in drawings, and these were divided into several pre-operational sub-stages—e.g.,

(1) many lines all of equal length,
(2) many lines of only two different lengths,
(3) many lines of three different lengths,
(4) lines of many different lengths but seriated imperfectly, etc.

Most of the pre-operational children's memory was found to have improved toward the operational stage eight months after the exposure compared to a week after it. (In other words, long-term memory was more accurate than short-term memory.) Piaget and Inhelder (1968) give additional evidence, both empirically and theoretically, that supports the argument that when learning is rooted in the child's total cognitive organization, memory can be used as a powerful ally to produce long-term gains.

Finally, it must be pointed out that the above arguments are part of the broader issue of what different theorists mean by the term "learning." A thorough comparison of Bereiter's and Piaget's views is beyond the scope of this paper, but a few differences can be mentioned. For Bereiter, the essence of learning seems to be the change in the child's behavior. For example, if the child can give conserving answers without being shaken by trick questions, Bereiter would conclude that conservation has been learned. His concern is whether or not the child can apply general rules to specific situations. Piaget is more concerned with how the internal processes become structured because rules that are not rooted in a total structure are not likely to lead to the construction of later structures.

We know very little about how exactly the pre-operational child learns. Nevertheless, the following three principles of learning can be selected from Piaget's theory for their relevance to preschool education:

1. Knowledge is not a copy of reality that is passively received but, rather, the result of an active construction on the part of the child.
2. Every concept the child possesses at a given time is related to the network of all the other concepts that he has built.
3. Assimilation and accommodation entail the necessity of the pre-operational child's going through one stage after another of reasoning "illogically" before he becomes able to reason logically.

The pedagogical implication of the above principles of learning seems to indicate that teaching must somehow take into account the pre-operational child's total cognitive structure even when the content and strategy of teaching are specific. This principle goes counter to Bereiter's philosophy of defining the specific criterion of learning in operational terms and setting out to reach the behavioral goals as efficiently as possible. The Piagetian objectives of instruction are broader, and the visible accomplishments come more slowly. This Piagetian approach can be criticized as being too unstructured and too idealistic to prepare the disadvantaged child for elementary school as it exists today. However, for the long-term benefit of the individual children as well as for the maximum development of society's human resources, I feel that the Piagetian approach is more defensible than Bereiter's.

In conclusion, Bereiter's view of specific instruction is not completely in disagreement with the Piagetian view. The two schools of thought converge with regard to the teaching of social knowledge, but not with regard to logico-mathematical knowledge. I have attempted to show above that logico-mathematical knowledge be taught by empirical generalization and social reinforcement as if it were learned in the same way as social knowledge. The teaching of physical knowledge, too, is a delicate art, since it is inextricably related with logico-mathematical structures.

The relative merits of the two approaches can be determined only through long-term longitudinal comparisons. The problem to guard against in such comparisons is that each school of thought has its own theoretical framework for evaluating "learning" as it defines its own goals of instruction. The solution to this problem is a continuous exchange of evaluators. Since the state of the art in evaluation is as primitive as it is in theories of instruction, the different schools of thought have much to learn from each other through the in-depth exchange of views, evaluators, and researchers for many years to come.

VYGOTSKY'S THEORY:
THE IMPORTANCE OF
MAKE-BELIEVE PLAY

by Laura E. Berk
Professor of Psychology at Illinois State University

In most theories of cognitive development, the social and the cognitive make contact only minimally. Rather than being truly joined and interactive, they are viewed as separate domains of functioning. At best, the social world is a surrounding context for cognitive activity, not an integral part of it. Early childhood educators have a long tradition of regarding what the young child knows as personally rather than socially constructed—a tradition that follows from the massive contributions of Piaget's cognitive-developmental theory to our field.

The ideas of the Russian developmental psychologist Lev Vygotsky, who early in this century forged an innovative theory granting great importance to social and cultural experience in development, have gained increasing visibility over the past decade. In Vygotsky's ([1933] 1978) sociocultural theory, the "mind extends beyond the skin" and is inseparably joined with other minds (Wertsch 1991, p. 90). Social experience shapes the ways of thinking and interpreting the world available to individuals. And language plays a crucial role in a socially formed mind because it is our primary avenue of communication and mental contact with others, it serves as the major means by which social experience is represented psychologically, and it is an indispensable tool for thought (Vygotsky [1934] 1987). A basic premise of Vygotsky's theory is that all uniquely human, higher forms of mental activity are jointly constructed and transferred to children through dialogues with other people.

Vygotsky's ideas are stimulating a host of new ways to educate young children that emphasize opportunities for discussion and joint problem

144

solving. A central Vygotskian concept that has played a formative role in these efforts is the zone of proximal development, which refers to a range of tasks that the child cannot yet handle alone but can accomplish with the help of adults and more skilled peers. As children engage in cooperative dialogues with more mature partners, they internalize the language of these interactions and use it to organize their independent efforts in the same way (Berk, 1992). According to sociocultural theory, supportive guidance from adults that creates a scaffold for children's learning is essential for their cognitive development. Such communication sensitively adjusts to children's momentary progress, offering the necessary assistance for mastery while prompting children to take over more responsibility for the task as their skill increases (Wood & Middleton, 1975; Wood, 1989). Furthermore, cooperative learning—in which small groups of peers at varying levels of competence share responsibility and resolve differences of opinion as they work toward a common goal—also fosters cognitive maturity (Forman, 1987; Tudge, 1992).

These Vygotskian ideas about teaching and learning have largely been implemented in academically relevant early childhood contexts, such as literacy, mathematics, and science (Moll, 1990; Forman, Minick, & Stone, 1993); but a close look at Vygotsky's writings reveals that they recur as major themes in his view of play. Although Vygotsky's works contain only a brief 12-page statement about play, his discussion is provocative, innovative, and ahead of his time. In accord with his emphasis on social experience and language as vital forces in cognitive development, Vygotsky ([1933] 1978) emphasized representational play—the make-believe that blossoms during the preschool years and evolves into the games with rules that dominate middle childhood. Vygotsky accorded fantasy play a prominent place in his theory, granting it the status of a "leading factor in development" (p. 101), as the following frequently quoted remarks reveal:

> Play creates a zone of proximal development in the child. In play, the child always behaves beyond his average age, above his daily behavior; in play it is as though he were a head taller than himself. As in the focus of a magnifying glass, play contains all developmental tendencies in a condensed form and is itself a major source of development. (p. 102)

As we discuss Vygotsky's theory and the research stimulated by it, we will see that he situated play squarely within a sociocultural context. Adults and peers scaffold young children's play, nurturing the transition to make-believe and its elaboration throughout the preschool years. Representational play serves as a unique, broadly influential zone of proximal development within which children advance themselves to ever higher levels of psychological functioning. Consequently, Vygotsky's theory has much to say to teachers about the importance of promoting make-believe in preschool and child care programs.

DEVELOPMENT AND SIGNIFICANCE OF MAKE-BELIEVE PLAY

Vygotsky began his consideration of the importance of play by suggesting that if we can identify its defining features, we can gain insight into its functions in development. To isolate the distinctiveness of play, Vygotsky explored characteristics regarded by other theorists as central to playful activity and found them wanting. For example, the common assumption that play is pleasurable activity is not specific to play. Many other experiences, such as eating a favorite treat, being granted the individual attention of a parent, listening to an exciting story, are at least as gratifying and sometimes more so than is play. Furthermore, certain playful experiences—games that can be won or lost—are not pure fun for the child when they result in disappointing outcomes.

A second way of understanding play is to highlight its symbolic features, as Piaget ([1945] 1951) did in his characterization of make-believe as a means through which children practice representational schemes. Yet symbolism is another feature that is not exclusive to play. Both Piaget and Vygotsky noted that it also characterizes language, artistic, and literacy activities during the preschool years.

Vygotsky concluded that play has two critical features that, when combined, describe its uniqueness and shed light on its role in development. First, all representational play creates an imaginary situation that permits the child to grapple with unrealized desires. Vygotsky pointed out that fantasy play first appears at a time when children must learn to postpone gratification of impulses and accept the fact that certain desires will remain unsatisfied. During the second year, caregivers begin to insist that toddlers delay gratification (e.g., wait for a turn) and acquire socially approved behaviors involving safety, respect for property, self-care (e.g., washing hands), and everyday routines (e.g., putting toys away) (Gralinski & Kopp, 1993).

The creation of an imaginary situation in play, however, has often been assumed to be a way in which children attain immediate fulfillment of desires not satisfied in real life. Vygotsky pointed out that this commonly held belief is not correct. A second feature of all representational play is that it contains rules for behavior that children must follow to successfully act out the play scene. Games that appear in the late preschool period and flourish during the school years are clearly rule based. Even the simplest imaginative situations created by very young children proceed in accord with social rules, although the rules are not laid down in advance. For example, a child pretending to go to sleep follows the rules of bedtime behavior. Another child, imagining himself to be a father and a doll to be a child, conforms to the rules of parental behavior. Yet a third child playing astronaut observes the rules of shuttle launch and space walk. Vygotsky ([1933] 1978) concluded, "Whenever there is an imaginary situation, there are rules" (p.95). A child cannot behave in an imaginary situation without rules.

These attributes of play—an imaginary situation governed by rules—provide the key to its role in development. According to Vygotsky, play supports the emergence of two complementary capacities: (a) the ability to separate thought from actions and objects, and (b) the capacity to renounce impulsive action in favor of deliberate, self-regulatory activity.

SEPARATING THOUGHT FROM ACTIONS AND OBJECTS

In creating an imaginary situation, children learn to act not just in response to external stimuli but also in accord with internal ideas. Infants and very young children, Vygotsky ([1933] 1978) explained, are reactive beings; momentary perceptions trigger their behavior. A baby who sees an attractive toy grabs for it without delay. A toddler runs after a ball that has rolled into the street without considering consequences. "In play, things lose their determining force. The child sees one thing but acts differently in relation to what he sees. Thus, a condition is reached in which the child begins to act independently of what he sees" (p. 97).

Just how does imaginative play help children separate thought from the surrounding world and rely on ideas to guide behavior? According to Vygotsky, the object substitutions that characterize make-believe are crucial in this process. When children use a stick to represent a horse or a folded blanket to represent a sleeping baby, their relation to reality is dramatically changed. The stick becomes a pivot for separating the meaning of "horse" from a real horse; similarly, the blanket becomes a pivot for distinguishing the meaning "baby" from a real baby. This adjustment in thinking occurs because children change the substitute object's real meaning when they behave toward it in a pretend fashion.

Vygotsky emphasized that young children have difficulty severing thinking—or the meaning of words—from objects; they do so only gradually. Indeed, such research reveals that object substitution becomes more flexible as children get older. In early pretense, toddlers use only realistic objects—for example, a toy telephone to talk into or a cup to drink from. Around age 2, children use less realistic toys, such as a block for a telephone receiver. Sometimes during the third year, children can imagine objects and events without any direct support from the real world, as when they say to a play partner, " I'm calling Susie on the phone!" while pretending to dial with her hands or without acting out the event at all. By this time, a play symbol no longer has to resemble the object or behavior for which it stands (Bretherton et al., 1984; Corrigan, 1987).

According to Vygotsky ([1930] 1990), in helping children separate meaning from objects, the pretending of early childhood serves as vital preparations for the much later development of abstract thought, in which symbols are manipulated and proposition evaluated without referring to the real world. And in detaching meaning from behavior, make-believe also helps teach children to choose deliberately from among alternative courses of action. This capacity to think in a planful, self-regulatory fashion is also strengthened by the rule-based nature of play, as we will see in the following section.

RENOUNCING IMPULSIVE ACTION

Vygotsky pointed out that the imaginative play of children contains an interesting paradox. In play, children do what they most feel like doing, and to an outside observer, the play of preschoolers appears free and spontaneous. Nevertheless, play constantly demands that children act against their immediate impulses because they must subject themselves to the rules of the make-believe context or the game they have chosen to play. According to Vygotsky ([1933] 1978), free play is not really "free"; instead it requires self-restraint—willingly following social rules. As a result, in play the young child displays many capacities that "will become her basic level of real action and morality" in the future (p. 100). By enacting rules in make-believe, children come to better understand social norms and expectations and strive to behave in ways that uphold them. For example, a child occupying the role of parent in a household scene starts to become dimly aware of parental responsibilities in real situations and gains insight into the rule-governed nature of the parent-child relationship (Haight & Miller 1993).

When we look at the development of play from an early to middle childhood, the most obvious way in which it changes is that it increasingly emphasizes rules. The greater stress on the rule-orientated aspect of play over time means that children gradually become more conscious of the goals of their play activities. Vygotsky ([1933] 1978) summarized, "The development from games with an overt imaginary situation and covert rules to games with overt rules and a covert imaginary situation outlines the evolution of children's play" (p. 96). From this perspective, the fantasy play of the preschool years is essential for further development of play in middle childhood—specifically, for movement toward game play, which provides additional instruction in setting goals, regulating one's behavior in pursuit of those goals, and subordinating action to rules rather than to impulse—in short, for becoming a cooperative and productive member of society. Play, in Vygotsky's theory, is the preeminent educational activity of early childhood.

IMPACT OF IMAGINATIVE PLAY ON DEVELOPMENT

Was Vygotsky correct in stating that make-believe serves as a zone of proximal development, supporting the emergence and refinement of a wide variety of competencies? A careful examination of his theory reveals that the benefits of play are complex and indirect; they may have taken years to be realized (Nicolopoulou, 1991). Still, considerable support exists for Vygotsky's view that play contributes to the development of a diverse array of capacities in the young child.

Sociodramatic play, the coordinated and reciprocal make-believe with peers that emerges around age 2½ and increases rapidly until age 4 or 5, has been studied thoroughly. Compared to social nonpretend activities (such as drawing or putting together puzzles), during social pretend activities, preschoolers interactions last longer, show more involvement, draw larger numbers of children into the activity, and are more cooperative (Connolly, Boyle, & Reznick, 1988). When we consider these findings from the standpoint of Vygotsky's emphasis on the social origins of cognition, it is not surprising that preschoolers who spend more time at sociodramatic play are advanced in general intellectual development and show an enhanced ability to understand the feelings of others. They are also seen as more socially competent by their teachers (Burns & Brainerd, 1979; Connolly & Doyle, 1984).

A growing body of research reveals that make-believe play strengthens a variety of specific mental abilities. For example, it promotes memory. In a study in which 4 and 5-year-olds were asked either to remember a set of toys or to play with them, the play condition produced far better recall. Rather than just naming or touching the objects (strategies applied in the "remember" condition), children who played with the toys engaged in many spontaneous organizations and uses of the materials that enabled them to memorize effortlessly (Newman, 1990). In this way, play may provide a vital foundation for more sophisticated memory strategies mastered during middle childhood that depend on establishing meaningful relationships among to-be-remembered information. Other research confirms that opportunity to engage in fantasy play promote children's storytelling and story memory (Saltz, Dixon, & Johnson, 1977; Pellegrini & Galda, 1982).

Language is also greatly enriched by play experiences. As children engage in play talk, they often correct one another's errors, either directly or by demonstrating acceptable ways to speak. For example, in enacting a telephone conversation, one kindergartner said, "Hello, come to my house please." Her play partner quickly countered with appropriate telephone greeting behavior; "No, first you've got to say 'what are you doing?'" (Ervin-Tripp, 1991, p. 90). Vocabulary expands during make-believe as children introduce new words they have heard during recent experiences. One 4-year-old playing nurse remarked to an agemate, "I am going to give you a temperature" (p. 90). Although her first use of the term was not correct, active experimentation increases the chances that she will notice more about the context in which "temperature" is applied and move toward correct usage. Furthermore, the linguistic skills required to express different points of view, resolve disputes, and persuade peers to collaborate in play are numerous. Play offers an arena in which all facets of conversational dialogue can be extended.

Make-believe also fosters young children's ability to reason about impossible or absurd situations—a finding highly consistent with Vygotsky's emphasis that fantasy play assists children in separating meaning from the objects for which they stand. A repeated finding in the cognitive development literature is that through much of early and middle childhood, thinking is tied to the here and now—to concrete reality; but under certain conditions, young children attain a "theoretical" mode of reasoning.

Consider the following syllogism: All cats bark. Rex is a cat. Does Rex bark? Researchers had a group of 4- to 6-year-olds act out problems like this with toys. A second group of children were told that the events were taking place on a pretend planet rather than on Earth. A control group merely listened and answered the question. Children in the two "play" conditions gave more theoretical than factual responses and were also able to justify their answers with theoretical ideas—for example, "In the story, cats bark, so we can pretend they bark" (Dias & Harris, 1988, 1990). Entering the pretend mode seems to enable children to reason with contrary facts as if they were true—findings that provide striking verification of Vygotsky's ([1933] 1978) assumption that in play, the child is well "beyond his average age, above his daily behavior" (p. 102).

Finally, young children who especially enjoy pretending or who are given encouragement to engage in fantasy play score higher on tests of imagination and creativity. When children use play objects in novel ways, the objects seem to stimulate the discovery of new relationships and enhance children's ability to think flexibly and inventively (Kansky, 1980; Pepler & Ross, 1981).

In sum, fantasy play contributes to social maturity and the construction of diverse aspects of cognition. For people who have questioned whether play activities, so indigenous and absorbing to children, must be curbed in favor of more "productive" activities or whether play constitutes a powerful zone of proximal development, the findings just reviewed clearly grant play a legitimate and fruitful place in children's lives.

SCAFFOLDING CHILDREN'S
MAKE-BELIEVE PLAY

The Piagetian view, dominant for the past three decades, claims that make-believe emerges spontaneously when children become capable of representational thought. Piaget and his followers assumed that children lack the cognitive competencies to share play symbols with others—both adults and peers—until well into the preschool period (e.g., Fein, 1981). Not until recently have researchers seriously addressed the social context of children's play experiences. Their findings challenge the notion that fantasy play is an unprompted phenomenon arising solely from tendencies within the child.

Instead, new evidence suggests that make-believe, like other higher mental functions, is the product of social collaboration.

ADULT-CHILD PLAY

Twenty-four-month-old Elizabeth is being carried upstairs for a diaper change by her mother.

Elizabeth: My going Sherman Dairy. (Sherman Dairy is the family's favorite dessert restaurant.)
  Mother: You're going to Sherman Dairy?
Elizabeth: Yeah.
  Mother: Is Andrew the cook? (Andrew is a 4-year-old friend who is playing with Elizabeth's sister.)
Elizabeth: Yep. (Pause) My cook.
  Mother: (Putting Elizabeth on the changing table and beginning to change her) You're the cook? You can cook with your dishes, right? Do you have some pots and pans?
Elizabeth: Yep.
              (Adapted from Haight & Miller, 1993, p. 46)

In the play sequence above, 2-year-old Elizabeth initiates a make-believe scenario in which a trip upstairs for a diaper change is transformed into a journey to buy ice cream. Her mother encourages her to expand the imaginative theme and act it out with toys. The play episode is elaborated and sustained as her mother asks questions that help Elizabeth clarify her intentions and think of new ideas.

Vygotskian-based research on play emphasizes that make-believe is, from its beginnings, a social activity (El'konin, 1966; Garvey, 1990). In Western industrialized societies, play first appears between caregivers and children; children initially learn pretense and games under the supportive guidance of experts. From these interactions, children acquire the communicative conventions, social skills, and representational capacities that permit them to carry out make-believe on their own.

In the most extensive study of caregiver scaffolding of make-believe, Haight and Miller (1993) followed the development of pretend play at home of nine middle-class children between 1 and 4 years of age. Social make-believe was common across the entire age span, consuming from 68% to 75% of the children's total pretend time. Furthermore, mothers were the children's principal play partners until 3 years of age. By age 4, children played approximately the same amount of time with their mothers as they did with other children (siblings and peers). Children's pretending with mothers, however, was not caused by a lack of child playmates at the youngest ages. Several investigations reveal that 1- and 2-year-olds who have fairly continuous access to other children prefer to play with their mothers (Dunn & Dale, 1984; Miller & Garvey, 1984). These findings confirm the Vygotskian view that play with caregivers gradually gives way to play with peers as children's competence increases.

Further evidence that caregivers teach toddlers to pretend stems from Haight and Miller's observation that at 12 months, make-believe was fairly one sided; almost all play episodes were initiated by mothers. From age 2 on, when pretending was better established, mothers and children displayed mutual interest in getting make-believe started; half of pretend episodes were initiated by each. At all ages, mothers typically followed the child's lead and elaborated on the child's contribution. Thus, although pretense was first introduced to 12-month-olds by their mothers, it quickly became a joint activity in which both partners participated actively in an imaginative dialogue and in which the adult gradually released responsibility to the child for creating and guiding the fantasy theme.

Children's object substitutions during make-believe are also largely traceable to episodes in which their mothers showed them how to engage in object renaming or suggested a pretend action to the child (Smolucha, 1992). By the time their children are 2 years old, mothers talk more about nonexistent fantasy objects, a change that may prompt children to widen the range of object substitutions in their play (Kavanaugh, Whittington & Cerbone, 1983). Furthermore, many parents and early childhood teachers surround children with toys designed to stimulate pretend themes. By offering an array of objects specialized for make-believe, caregivers communicate to children that pretense is a valued activity and maximize opportunities to collaborate with them in integrating props into fantasy scenes.

CONSEQUENCES OF SUPPORTIVE CAREGIVER-CHILD PLAY

In their longitudinal study, Haight and Miller (1993) carefully examined the play themes of mother-child pretense and found that it appeared to serve a variety of functions, including communicating feelings, expressing and working through conflicts, enlivening daily routines, and teaching lessons. These diverse social uses of caregiver-child play suggest that adult support and expansion of preschoolers' make-believe should facilitate all the developmental outcomes of play already discussed, although as yet, no systematic research on the topic exists.

Accumulating evidence does show that children's make-believe play with their mothers is more sustained and complex than is their solitary make-believe play. One- to 3-year-olds engage in more than twice as much make-believe while playing with mothers than while playing alone. In addition, caregiver support leads early make-believe to include more elaborate themes (Dunn & Wooding, 1977; O'Connell & Bretherton, 1984; Zukow, 1986; Slade, 1987; Fiese, 1990; Tamis-LeMonda & Bornstein, 1993;

Haight & Miller, 1993; O'Reilly & Bornstein, 1993). In line with Vygot-sky's zone of proximal development, very young children, for whom make-believe is just emerging, act more competently when playing with a mature partner than they otherwise would. In Haight and Miller's study, suggestive evidence emerged that mother-child play promotes effective child-child play. Children whose mothers ranked high in pretending when their chil-dren were 1 year old ranked higher in peer play at 4 years. And children of the most enthusiastic and imaginative parents were among the most highly skilled preschool pretenders.

CRITICAL FEATURES OF ADULT-CHILD PLAY

Although mother-child play has been granted considerable research atten-tion, a search of the literature revealed no studies of teachers' participation in young childrens' play. Yet evidence on the effect of adult-child play sug-gests that it is vital for teachers in preschool and child care programs to en-gage in joint play with children.

Teachers' effective playful involvement with children requires early childhood environments that are developmentally appropriate. Especially important are generous adult-child ratios, a stable staff that relates to chil-dren sensitively and responsively, and settings that are richly equipped to offer varied opportunities for make-believe. These factors are critical be-cause they ensure that teachers have the necessary time, rapport, and play props to encourage children's imaginative contributions and to scaffold them toward social pretend play with peers.

At the same time, adults walk a fine line in making effective contri-butions to children's pretense. The power of adult-child play to foster de-velopment is undermined by communication that is too overpowering or one sided. Fiese (1990) found that maternal questioning, instructing, and in-trusiveness (initiating a new activity unrelated to the child's current pattern of play) led to immature, simple exploratory play in young children. In contrast, turn taking and joint involvement in a shared activity resulted in high levels of pretense. Furthermore, adult intervention that recognizes children's current level of cognitive competence and builds on it is most successful in involving children. Lucariello (1987) reported that when 24- to 29-month-olds were familiar with a play theme suggested by their mother, both partners displayed advanced levels of imaginative activity and constructed the scenario together. When the theme was unfamiliar, the mother took nearly total responsibility for pretense.

PROMOTING SOCIAL PRETEND PLAY
WITH PEERS

At preschool, Jason joins a group of children in the block area for a space shuttle launch.

"That can be our control tower," he suggests to Vance, pointing to a corner by a bookshelf.

"Wait, I gotta get it all ready," states Lynette, who is still arranging the as-
tronauts (two dolls and a teddy bear) inside a circle of large blocks,
which represent the rocket.

"Countdown!" Jason announces, speaking into a small wooden block, his
pretend walkie-talkie.

"Five, six, two, four, one, blastoff!" responds Vance, commander of the
control tower.

Lynette makes one of the dolls push a pretend button and reports, "Brrm,
brrm, they're going up!"

(Berk, 1993, p. 311)

When pretending with peers, children make use of the many competencies they acquire through their play with adults. Yet pretend play with
peers must also be responsive and cooperative to result in satisfying play
experiences and to serve as a zone of proximal development in which children advance their skills and understanding. According to Goncu (1993),
social play with peers requires intersubjectivity—a process whereby individuals involved in the same activity who begin with different perspectives
arrive at a shared understanding. In the play episode just described, the
children achieved a high level of intersubjectivity as they coordinate several roles in an elaborate plot and respond in a smooth, complementary
fashion to each other's contributions.

The importance of intersubjectivitiy for peer social play is suggested
by the work of several major theorists.

Piaget ([1945] 1951) notes that for children to play together, they
must collectively construct play symbols. Likewise, Vygotsky ([1933]
1978) claimed that in pretense with peers, children jointly develop rules
that guide social activity. And Parten (1932) labeled the most advanced
form of peer social participation cooperative play, in which children orient
toward a common goal by negotiating plans, roles, and divisions of labor.

Recent evidence indicates that intersubjectivity among peer partners
increases substantially during the preschool years, as the amount of time
children devote to sociodramatic play rises. Between 3 and 4½ years, children engage in more extensions and affirmations of their partners's messages and fewer disagreements, assertions of their own opinions, and
irrelevant statements during play (Goncu, 1993). Interestingly, preschoolers
have much more difficulty establishing a cooperative, shared framework in
"closed-end" problem solving, in which they must orient toward a single
correct solution to a task (Tudge & Rogoff, 1987). Here again is an example of how children's competence during play is advanced compared to
other contexts. By middle childhood, the social skills mastered during sociodramatic activities generalize to nonplay activities.

When we look at the features of harmonious child-child play, the relevance of warm, responsive adult communication for encouraging such play becomes even clearer. Even after sociodramatic play is well underway and adults have reduced their play involvement, teachers need to guide children toward effective relations with agemates. Observational evidence indicates that teachers rarely mediate peer interaction except when intense disagreements arise that threaten classroom order or children's safety. When teachers do step in, they almost always use directive strategies, in which they tell children what to do or say (e.g., "Ask Daniel if you can have the fire truck next") or solve the problem for them (e.g., "Jessica was playing with that toy first, so you can have a turn after her"). (File, 1993, p. 352)

A Vygotskian-based approach to facilitating peer interaction requires that teachers tailor their intervention to children's current capacities and use techniques that help children regulate their own behavior. To implement intervention in this way, teachers must acquire detailed knowledge of individual children's social skills—the type of information teachers typically gather only for the cognitive domain. When intervening, they need to use a range of teaching strategies because (like cognitive development) the support that is appropriate for scaffolding social development varies from child to child and changes with age. At times the adult might model a skill or give the child examples of strategies (e.g., "You could tell Paul, 'I want a turn'"). At other times, she might ask the child to engage in problem solving ("What could you do if you want a turn?") (File, 1993, p. 356) In each instance, the teacher selects a level of support that best matches the child's abilities and momentary needs and then pulls back as the child acquires new social skills.

Children can be socialized into sociodramatic play by a variety of expert partners. In a recent comparison of the make-believe play of American and Mexican siblings, Farver (1993) found that American 3½- to 7-year-olds tended to rely on intrusive tactics; they more often instructed, directed, and rejected their younger siblings' contributions. In contrast, Mexican children used more behaviors that gently facilitated—invitations to join, comments on the younger child's actions, suggestions, and positive affect. In this respect, Mexican older siblings were similar to American mothers in their scaffolding of play, a skill that appeared to be fostered by the Mexican culture's assignment of caregiving responsibilities to older brothers and sisters.

These findings suggest that multi-age groupings in early childhood programs offer additional opportunities to promote make-believe and that older siblings from ethnic-minority families may be particularly adept at such scaffolding—indeed, they may be as capable as adults! Because of their limited experience with the caregiving role and their more conflictual relationships with siblings, children from ethnic-majority families may need more assistance in learning how to play effectively with younger peers. In classrooms with a multicultural mix of children, children of ethnic minorities who are skilled at scaffolding can serve as models and scaffolders for agemates, showing them how to engage young children in pretense.

CONCLUSIONS

The vast literature on children's play reveals that its contributions to child development can be looked at from diverse vantage points. Psychoanalytic theorists have highlighted the emotionally integrative function of pretense, pointing out that anxiety-provoking events—such as a visit to the doctor's office or discipline by a parent—are likely to be revisited in the young child's play but with roles reversed so that the child is in command and compensates for unpleasant experiences in real life. Piaget underscored the opportunities that make-believe affords for exercising symbolic schemes. And all theorists recognize that pretense permits children to become familiar with social role possibilities in their culture, providing important insights into the link between self and wider society.

Vygotsky's special emphasis on the imaginative and rule-based nature of play adds an additional perspective to the viewpoints just mentioned—one that highlights the critical role of make-believe in developing reflective thought as well as self-regulatory and socially cooperative behavior. For teachers who have always made sure that play is a central feature of early childhood curriculum, Vygotsky's theory offers yet another justification for play's prominent place in programs for young children. For other teachers whose concern with academic progress has led them to neglect play, Vygotsky's theory provides a convincing argument for change—a powerful account of why pretense is the ultimate activity for nurturing early childhood capacities that are crucial for academic as well as later-life success.

ANDRAGOGY:
IMPLICATIONS FOR SECONDARY
AND ADULT EDUCATION PROGRAMS

by Norene F. Daly

The study of andragogy, while relatively recent in the United States, is a well developed science in Europe. Ingalls (1973) reports the first use of the word andragogy in the literature:

> The word was first used by a German grammar school teacher, Alexander Kapp, in 1833, to describe the education theory of the Greek philosopher, Plato. Kapp distinguished Andragogy from Social Pedagogy (basic remedial education for disadvantaged or handicapped adults) referring to Andragogy as the normal and natural process of continuing education for adults. (p. 10)

In Canada, Europe, and some countries of South America, theorists have evolved a comprehensive framework for the study of andragogy during the past several decades. In 1970, the University of Amsterdam established a Department of Pedagogical and Andragogical Sciences. Students enrolled in the six year program may obtain a doctorate in Andragogy. Curriculum in andragogy is embodied in the social sciences "in order to provide an opportunity for prospective students to be trained a) for research in the field of andragogy and b) for academic professions in the variegated field of andragogical activities." (p. 18)

In "The Role and Training of Adult Educators in Poland," Jindra Kulich (1971) summarized the development of training programs in andragogical science which have been established at universities in Poland. Kulich (1967) also reviewed the development of andragogical programs in Czechoslovakia.

Rehder (1971) related recent developments in adult education in Canada to andragogical theory. Course work leading to a graduate or undergraduate degree at Yugoslavian universities is detailed by Savicevic (1968, 1970). Andragogy is a well structured discipline in Yugoslavia. Savicevic (1968) lists ten interdisciplinary studies which are currently available at the University of Belgrade:

1. General Andragogy—The study of the subjects and tasks of andragogy.
2. Andragogical Didactic—The study of the processes of learning and education.
3. Andragogical Research Methodology—The study of research methods and techniques and their application to adult education.
4. Industrial Andragogy—The study of adult education in industry.
5. Military Andragogy—The study of education in the army.
6. Penologic Andragogy—The study of problems of adult education in penal institutions.
7. Family Andragogy—The study of adult education for family life.
8. Comparative Andragogy—The study of the system, theory, and practice of adult education on a comparative basis.
9. History of Andragogy—The study of adult education in historic perspectives.
10. Social-Health Andragogy—The study of adult education in health institutions. (p. 53)

Simpson (1964) traces the development of andragogical theory and content in England where the science has been established since the nineteenth century. In a later work Simpson (1972) reports: "Andragogical knowledge has to cover such a diversity of phenomenon, such a wide range of teaching-learning situations, that it is difficult to establish any principle or methodology which can be applicable to all." (p. 163)

In Germany, Poggeler (1957) is the primary theorist in the field of andragogy, and in Switzerland the development of andragogical theory has been traced by Hanselmann (1961).

Malcolm Knowles introduced the theory of andragogy to American adult educators in 1968 and has made it the central theme of his work since that date. He has sought to organize andragogical theory into a comprehensive process framework.

During the last decade, the theory and practice of andragogy have gained greater acceptance largely through Knowles' application of it to a variety of fields. A review of the literature reveals the use of andragogical theory in Junior College Biology Teaching (Mader, 1972); training in the Health Sciences (McTernan, 1974); the training of Social Workers (Gelford, 1975); and, the development of staff training programs for state and local Social Service agencies (Ingalls, 1973). To date, it has been most widely used in the training of adult educators involved in Adult Basic Education Programs (Adult Basic Education Teacher Workshop, 1972), (Komins,

1973); church related adult education programs (Institute for Continuing Education, 1977); and sales promotion seminars (Knowles, 1970).

As the field of adult education continues to grow during the next decade, andragogical theory will no doubt become a moving force in American education as it has in Europe and Canada.

Andragogy—
Theoretical and Philosophical Bases

In *The Modern Practice of Adult Education—Andragogy Versus Pedagogy*, Knowles (1970) sought to differentiate between pedagogy and andragogy and explained the etymological derivations of the terms:

> Pedagogy is derived from the Greek stem paid- (meaning 'child') and agogos (meaning 'leading'). So 'pedagogy' means, specifically, the art and science of teaching children. Andragogy . . . is based on the Greek word aner (with the stem andr-) meaning 'man.' Andragogy is, therefore, the art and science of helping adults learn. (p. 37)

Knowles (1968) viewed the term "pedagogy of adult education," as a semantic contradiction. (p. 351)

Variant spellings of the term which appear in the literature include androgogy an androgology.

The distinction between andragogy and pedagogy is basic to an understanding of andragogical theory. Knowles (1970) attempted to elucidate this distinction:

> Andragogy is premised on at least four crucial assumptions about the characteristics of adult learners that are different from the assumptions about child learners on which traditional pedagogy is premised. These assumptions are that, as a person matures, 1) his self-concept moves from one of being a self-directing human being; 2) he accumulates a growing reservoir of experience that becomes an increasing resource for learning; 3) his readiness to learn becomes oriented increasingly to the developmental tasks of his social roles; and 4) his time perspective changes from one of postponed application of knowledge to immediacy of application, and accordingly his orientation toward learning shifts from one of subject-centeredness to one of problem-centeredness. (p. 39)

A summary of the basic distinctions between andragogy and pedagogy is contained in Table 1. The seven steps in the andragogical process model are compared with the elements of the pedagogical content model in Table 2.

It may be argued that the principles of andragogical theory, embodied

TABLE 1
A COMPARISON OF ASSUMPTIONS OF TEACHER-DIRECTED (PEDAGOGICAL)
LEARNING AND SELF-DIRECTED (ANDRAGOGICAL) LEARNING

ASSUMPTIONS

About	*Pedagogical* Teacher-directed	*Andragogical* Self-directed
Concept of the learner	Dependent personality	Increasingly self-directed organism
Role of learner's experience	To be built on more than used	A rich resource for learning
Readiness to learn	Varies w/levels of maturation	Develops from life tasks & problems
Orientation to learning	Subject-centered	Task or problem-centered
Motivation	External rewards and punishments	Internal incentives, curiosity

Source: Institute for Continuous Education, Adult Educators
"Expansion" Workshops Handbook.

in the process model, represent merely "good teaching." While this may be true, it is their systematic organization and application to teaching which is considered to be essential.

Holt (1975) recognized the dichotomy inherent in the application of the andragogical process model:

> There are some subtleties lurking in the communication of andragogy. The basics are simple; almost so simple as to be classed among the catalogs of conventional wisdom. However, conventional wisdom or no, a sufficiently high number of both secondary and higher education classes are conducted contrary to the principles of andragogy to suggest that the concept has not functionally seen the light of day in academia. If the concept is a matter of conventional wisdom, behaviors to enliven that concept aren't. (p. 24)

Porter (1972) reflected upon the adolescent's orientation toward learning and the fact that the "traditional" secondary school may not be addressing itself to the adolescent's educational needs:

> The adolescent is faced with a number of distractions and new feelings which alter his previously held views of education. Physiologically, he has new sensations and desires experiences as a result of the body changes. Perhaps more important is his psychological development which allows him to visualize a better world and a better way of life. In his

TABLE 2

A COMPARISON OF PROCESSES OF TEACHER-DIRECTED
(PEDAGOGICAL) LEARNING AND SELF-DIRECTED
(ANDRAGOGICAL) LEARNING

PROCESS ELEMENTS

Elements	*Pedagogical* Teacher-directed learning	*Andragogical* Self-directed learning
Climate	Formal authority, oriented, competitive, judgmental	Informal, mutually respectful, consensual, collaborative, supportive
Planning	Primarily by teacher	By participative decision-making
Diagnosis of needs	Primarily by teacher	By mutual assessment
Setting goals	Primarily by teacher	By mutual negotiation
Designing a learning plan	Content units, course syllabus, logical sequence	Learning projects, learning content sequenced in terms of readiness
Learning activities	Transmittal techniques, assigned readings	Inquiry projects, independent study, experimental techniques
Evaluation	Primarily by teacher	By mutual assessment of self-collected evidence

Source: Institute for Continuous Education, Adult Educators
"Expansion" Workshops Handbook.

search for identity, he may or may not see education as a suitable vehicle. In his desire to integrate his idealism with a world filled with conflict and falsity, education does not always aid him in reaching his goal. In such a world, education may not shed light on critical issues. In short, the typical secondary-school student often finds little assistance from his traditional educational experience. (p. 138)

In 1971, the United Nations Educational, Scientific and Cultural Organization (UNESCO) embarked upon the task of developing a conceptual model of lifelong education. The model envisioned by UNESCO would incorporate many of the components of the andragogical process model. Both have their basis in John Dewey's vision of education as a lifelong process. Dewey (1938) expanded this vision in his discussion of the principles of continuity and interaction as the longitudinal and lateral aspects of experience:

Different situations succeed one another. But because of the principle of continuity something is carried over from the earlier to the later
ones. As an individual passes from one situation to another, his world, his
environment, expands or contracts. He does not find himself living in another world but in a different part or aspect of one and the same world.
What he has learned in the way of knowledge and skill in one situation becomes an instrument of understanding and dealing effectively with the situations which follow. The process goes on as life and learning continue.
Otherwise the course of experience is disorderly, since the individual factor that enters into making an experience is split. . . . Continuity and interaction in their active union with each other provide the measure of the
educative significance and value of an experience. (p. 44)

Parkyn, (1973) described the UNESCO conceptual model of lifelong
learning with its basis in Dewey and andragogical theory and identified
what he referred to as "untenable" assumptions underlying education systems. These may be viewed as being largely characteristic of the traditional
pedagogical model. They include the assumption that:

Children should be taught those things that they will need to know
when they are adults. . . . There is a partial truth here. There are many
basic things that can be learned then, and that remain permanently valuable. There are, however, many things needed in adulthood that it would
be a waste of time and a waste of life to teach in childhood. . . . Curriculum content of this kind too often fills a large part of school time when it
is thought that the education in childhood adequately prepares people for
their adult lives. . . . Much of the common distaste for education when
school days are past can be attributed to the premature and irrelevant content of the curriculum of many school systems. (p. 13)

The role of the teacher in the educative process is another of the areas
identified by Parkyn as retarding the acceptance of the concept of lifelong
learning:

When teachers were regarded as the repositories of the body of
knowledge that had to be passed on to the learners, the teaching aspect of
education was emphasized to the detriment of the learning aspect, the
heuristic or discovery method of learning was neglected, and mass instruction took precedence over individualized learning. (p. 13)

Another assumption detailed by Parkyn which he considers to be a
"more fundamental error" is "the tendency of the school to isolate learning
from the context of immediate action." This is an assumption which was
also questioned by Bruner, (1960) in *The Process of Education.* (p. 43) Liv-
ingstone (1943) referred to this divorce between theory and practice as

leading to the paradox that "Youth studies but cannot act; the adult must act but has no opportunity of study; and we accept the divorce complacently." (p. 43)

In detailing the fundamental aims of a conceptual model of lifelong learning as envisioned by UNESCO, Parkyn includes the following:

> First, the education of childhood and adolescence now need to aim at producing not educated people but educable people, people who have both the capacity and the incentive to continue their education throughout their lives. It will aim at producing people who are able to choose and control as far as possible their own course of development and who therefore, will need to have a breadth of experience as a basis on which to make those adult choices of vocation and life-style that so profoundly influence their subsequent lives. It will aim, too, at producing people who are adaptable in changing circumstances, who realize the provisional nature of knowledge, the tentative nature of decisions, and the need for constant evaluation of the results of their action. Such people need to have the confidence to try new things without undue fear of making mistakes, but with the wisdom to be willing and able to judge the consequences of their choices and hence to learn from them. (p. 17)

The implications of andragogical theory and the conceptual model of lifelong learning for the education of adolescents are drawn by Knowles (1970):

> The differences between children and adults are not so much real differences, I believe, as differences in assumptions about them that are made in traditional pedagogy. Actually, in my observation (and retrospection), the child starts fairly early to see himself as being self-directing in broadening areas of his life; he starts accumulating experience that has increasing value for learning; he starts preparing for social roles (such as through part-time jobs) and therefore experiencing adult-like readinesses to learn; and he encounters life problems for which he would like some learnings for immediate application. Therefore, many of the principles of andragogy have direct relevance to the education of children and youth. (p. 53)

Like Parkyn (1973), Knowles sees the lag in applying andragogical theory to education systems that are firmly embedded in the pedagogical content model. He cites recent developments in curriculum which seem to "start with the concerns of the students and engage them in a process of largely self-directed discovery," but observes:

> These developments are quite piecemeal, and the practitioners have lagged far behind the curriculum theorists in helping students learn how to learn rather than just teaching them what they 'ought' to know. What is

required, if youth education is to produce adults who are capable of engaging in a life-long process of continuing self-development, is a whole new set of assumptions about the purpose of youth education and a new technology to carry out that purpose. I can foresee that the result would be a more andragogical approach to the education of children and youth. (1970, p. 54)

The concept of the adolescent as an evolving adult capable of engaging in the andragogical process is supported by an examination of Piaget's theory of adolescent learning:

> Adolescent thought has achieved an advanced state of equilibrium. This means, among other things, that the adolescent's cognitive structures have now developed to the point where they can effectively adapt to a great variety of problems. These structures are sufficiently stable to assimilate readily a variety of novel situations. Thus, the adolescent need not drastically accommodate his structures to new problems. . . . Piaget does maintain . . . that by the end of adolescence, the individual's ways of thinking, that is, his cognitive structures, are almost fully formed. While these structures may be applied to new problems with the result that significant knowledge is achieved, the structures themselves undergo little modification after adolescence. They have reached a high degree of equilibrium. (Ginsburg and Opper, 1969, p. 203)

Allen Tough, of the University of Toronto, reported results of research which examined the independent learning projects of 10-year-olds, 16-year-olds, and adults. Tough's findings support the recognition of the secondary student as an evolving adult more receptive to andragogical teaching than the child:

> By the time a person reaches the age of 16 . . . some clear changes have occurred. During his hours away from school and homework, the 16-year-old spends far more time at sustained learning efforts than he did at an earlier age. These efforts are marked more clearly and strongly by the intent to learn. Also, he learns more often in order to handle effectively his new responsibilities and the major problems and decisions that are not faced by a 10-year-old. In many ways the 16-year-old is closer to the adult than he is to the 10-year-old. (1971, p. 24)

The Polish educator, Lucjan Turos (1969), stressed the generic and historical roots of pedagogy and andragogy and theorized that andragogy must build upon pedagogy in the way in which the adult grows out of, and builds upon, his childhood.

Houle (1972), commenting upon the viability of andragogy as a distinct science, also recognizes the implications for the teaching of adolescents.

> If pedagogy and andragogy are distinguishable, it is not because they are essentially different from one another but because they represent the working out of the same fundamental processes at different stages of life. . . . The definition of adult education . . . could easily be rephrased to apply to young people or indeed to all mankind, but, if so, it would encompass the full range of educative experiences in the earlier as well as the later years of life. . . . It must be applied in ways which are appropriate to the immaturity of the learners, even as, in other situations, the educator of adults who adopts a system devised for children has to adjust it to fit the requirements of men and women. (p. 222)

In specifying the characteristics which distinguish traditional and progressive education, Dewey (1938) might have been referring to the basic distinctions between pedagogy and andragogy:

> To imposition from above is opposed expression and cultivation of individuality; to external discipline is opposed free activity; to learning from text and teachers, learning through experience; to acquisition of isolated skills and techniques by drill, is opposed acquisition of them as means of attaining ends which make direct vital appeal; to preparation for a more or less remote future is opposed making the most of the opportunities of present life; to static aims and materials is opposed acquisition with a changing world. (p. 19)

Almost forty years after they were written, Dewey's words seem to have had little impact upon traditional pedagogy. However, as the concept of lifelong learning and andragogical theory gain greater acceptance, perhaps his vision will become a reality.

In summary, andragogy has its theoretical and philosophical bases in the work of Dewey (1938), Erikson (1950) (1959), Bruner (1961), Maslow (1954) and Rogers (1951).

> Andragogy combines elements from humanist psychology with a 'system approach' to learning. . . . Like the humanists, he [Knowles] believes that methods and techniques involve the individual most deeply in self-directed inquiry. (Srinivasan, 1977, p. 13)

PART III, SECTION B: COGNITIVE DEVELOPMENT

BERK ARTICLE

1. Briefly discuss the following:

Play and the Zone of Proximal Development

_____

_____

_____

_____

The critical aspects of play

_____

_____

_____

_____

The social context of children's play experiences

_____

_____

_____

_____

2. Contrast Piaget's and Vygotsky's views of the role of play in children's development.

_____

_____

_____

_____

PART III, SECTION B: COGNITIVE DEVELOPMENT

DALY ARTICLE

Daly draws a distinction between the way children learn and the way adults learn. Is this distinction one with which Piaget and other developmental psychologists would agree, or would they maintain that principles of andragogy also apply to children? Refer to your text, the other articles in this section, and class discussion when formulating your answer to this question.

_____

_____

_____

_____

_____

_____

_____

_____

_____

_____

_____

_____

_____

_____

_____

_____

_____

_____

_____

SECTION C: SOCIAL AND PERSONALITY DEVELOPMENT

SPECIAL TOPIC:
MAPPING THE MORAL DOMAIN

BOUNDING THE CONTROVERSIES: FOUNDATIONAL ISSUES IN THE STUDY OF MORAL DEVELOPMENT

by Peter H. Kahn, Jr.
Colby College, Waterville,
Maine, USA

Abstract. By drawing on four foundational issues in the study of moral development—moral definition, ontogeny, variation, and epistemology—this article offers a means for bounding moral development controversies, in the sense of defining their parameters and clarifying the conflicts. Numerous controversies are examined, to provide a sense of the robustness of the analyses. These controversies include debates between character-education and social-cognitive theorists concerning moral education, claims of gender differences and charges of sex bias in moral development research, differing interpretations of cross-cultural data, tensions embedded in anthropological theories of cultural relativism, and attempts to move from empirical findings to statements of value. In addition, attention is paid to how the four foundational issues can and often should be brought together in moral theory and research.

Presumably uncontroversial is the proposition that the moral development literature abounds in controversy. From some anthropological accounts, for instance, we learn that devout Hindus believe that it is immoral for a widow to eat fish, or for a menstruating woman to sleep in the same bed with her

husband [Shweder et al., 1987]. Other accounts document that members of
the Yanomamo tribe of Brazil at times practice infanticide, and that the
women are occasionally beaten, shot with barbed arrows, chopped with
machetes or axes, and burned with firebrands [Hatch, 1983, p.91]. Some
theorists use such illustrative accounts of moral diversity to argue against
the proposition, supported by others, that on important dimensions the
moral life is similar across cultures. Some theorists also use such accounts
to argue against the proposition, again supported by others, that one culture
can morally judge another culture.

Many such controversies in the literature (spanning the fields of psychology, anthropology, sociology, philosophy, and education) reflect persistent and persuasive differences in theoretical perspective. These differences
can neither be easily dismissed nor reconciled. However, some of these
controversies become more complicated, if not muddled, than they need be
because they confuse what I will refer to as foundational issues in the study
of moral development. In the first section of this article, I briefly characterize four such issues. The first entails the definition of morality, the second moral ontogeny, the third individual and cultural moral variation, and
the fourth moral epistemology. In the second section, I suggest that while
the content of moral development controversies can vary widely, their
sources are often bounded by one or more of these issues, and that moral
theorists and researchers have sometimes confused or confounded evidence
that pertains to two or more of these issues. In addition, I pay attention to
how these issues can and often should be brought together in moral theory
and research.

FOUR FOUNDATIONAL ISSUES

Moral Definition

One fundamental issue in the study of moral development is how to
define the term "moral." In philosophy, three broad approaches traditionally
have been taken: consequentialist, deontological, and virtue-based. Briefly
stated, consequentialist theories maintain that a moral agent must always
act so as to produce the best available outcomes overall [Scheffler, 1982].
Utilitarianism, dating from John Stuart Mills and more recently defended
by Smart and Williams [1973], is the most common form of consequentialism. In its simplest form, utilitarianism proposes that a moral agent should
act so as to bring about the greatest amount of utility (for example, happiness) for the greatest number of people. In contrast, deontological theories
maintain that there are some actions that a moral agent is forbidden to do,
or, in turn, must do, regardless of general consequences or utility. Moral
theories ranging from Kant's [1785/1984] work in ethics to current work
by Rawls [1971], Gewirth [1978], and Dworkin [1978] are largely of this
type. For example, Kant's maxim that a moral agent should never treat an-

other human being merely as a means but always as an end develops the idea of a rationally derived respect for person. Both consequentialist and deontological theories are centrally concerned with answering the fundamental question, "What ought I to do?" In contrast, virtue-based theories are centrally concerned with answering the fundamental question, "What sort of person ought I to be?" where the focus is on long-term character traits and personality [Louden, 1984]. This tradition dates back to Aristotle's delineation in *Nichomachean Ethics* of the ethical virtues (for example, courage, temperance, wisdom, and justice), and is developed in current work by, for instance, MacIntyre [1984] and Foot [1978].

Moral Ontogeny

A second issue in the study of moral development is how to explain moral ontogeny, or the developmental process. Drawing on characterizations by Turiel [1983], Piaget [1966], and Langer [1969], four general types of explanations can be provided for moral development. The first is an endogenous explanation—that moral development occurs largely through internal mechanisms. Included are innatist and maturational theories [Rousseau, 1762/1979; Neill, 1960/1977], and sociobiological theories [Dawkind, 1976; Trivers, 1971; Wilson, 1975]. The second is an exogenous explanation—that moral development occurs largely through external mechanisms. Included here are behaviorist theories that focus on stimulus-response mechanisms and operant conditioning [Watson, 1924/1970; Skinner, 1974] and social-learning theories that focus on modeling and imitation [Bandura, 1977; Rushton, 1982]. The third type of explanation is interactionist, involving both endogenous and exogenous forces. For example, Freud [1923/1960] proposed that the conditions for moral development arise when the child's instinctual desires come into conflict with environmental constraints. Finally, the fourth type of explanation reflects a structural interaction theory. As proposed by Piaget [1932/1969, 1983] and elaborated by Kohlberg [1971], Turiel [1983], Langer [1969], and others, moral development is theorized to occur through the equilibration of mental structures, driven by the interaction of individual and environment. For each of these types of explanations for moral development, differing views can be taken with respect to the extent, rate, sequence, and invariance of development. Extent refers to how far development proceeds, rate refers to how fast development proceeds, sequence refers to the order of the developmental progression, and invariance refers to whether that order is necessarily sequential.

Moral Variation

A third issue in the study of moral development is how to interpret moral variation, i.e., empirically-assessed differences in moral practices and beliefs across individuals, groups, or cultures. Documenting moral variation is part of the stock and trade of anthropologists. A few examples were noted at the outset of this article, involving Hindu beliefs and Yanomamo practices that differ from Western ones. Research of this sort directly addresses the question of how the moral life is similar or different across cultures or among individuals within a culture.

Moral Epistemology

A fourth issue in the study of moral development is how to conceptualize moral epistemology, i.e., the limits and validity of moral knowledge. Often at stake is whether it is possible for a moral statement to be objectively true or false, or for a moral value to be objectively right or wrong, or good or bad. A wide variety of positions have been taken. For instance, some believe that moral knowledge corresponds with or approaches a correspondence with a moral reality that exists independent of human means of knowing [R. N. Boyd, 1988; Sturgeon, 1988]. Others believe that moral knowledge can be objectively grounded by constructing rational principles that strive for coherence and consistency while building on the common ground and specific circumstances of society [Dworkin, 1978]. Still others believe that the only thing that can be said of moral knowledge is that it can be true subjectively for an individual or culture depending on that individual's or group's desires, preferences, and goals [Rorty, 1982; Dewey, 1929/1960; Ayer, 1952; Mackie, 1977]. Finally, some believe that any moral knowledge is unattainable, even in a weak sense. This is the full skeptic's position (see Nagel, 1986, for a characterization).

BOUNDING THE CONTROVERSIES

These four foundational issues—moral definition, ontogeny, variation, and epistemology—can be combined in six distinct paired combinations. Controversies concerning moral development often involve four of these combinations. In this section, I show how this is the case by examining a variety of controversies and highlighting how the controversies can be clarified and at times resolved by distinguishing between foundational issues.

Controversies Involving Moral Definition and Moral Ontogeny

In the opening to Plato's [1956] *Meno*, Menon asks Socrates:

> Can you tell me, Socrates—can virtue be taught? Or if not, does it come by practice? Or does it come neither by practice nor by teaching, but do people get it by nature, or in some other way? [p.28]

In effect, Menon offers Socrates a choice of developmental mechanisms. Menon asks if virtue develops by exogenous forces (by practicing or teaching), by endogenous forces (by nature), or in some other way. In response, Socrates says that he is in no position to answer, as he does not know what virtue is. Thus Socrates, as he is wont to do, embarks on a dialogue that is centrally concerned with the essence of a thing. In other words, Socrates analytically distinguishes the ontogenetic question from the definitional one and argues that the latter needs as much attention as possible before addressing the former.

The distinction, let alone ranking of priorities, is not always made in the current literature. For instance, the recent US Secretary of Education, Bennett [Bennett and Delatree, 1978], has argued vigorously against the cognitive-developmental approach to moral education, as embodied in the work of Kohlberg [1971]. Though it is not made explicit in his writing, Bennett's position differs from Kohlberg's in two distinct ways. First, Bennett and Delatree [1978] provide a different definition of morality than does Kohlberg:

> In fact, it must be doubted whether what Kohlberg describes is really morality at all. Morality takes place among human beings and not among disembodied bearers of "rights," who are incessantly engaged in squabbling about them. Morality is concerned with doing good, with sacrifice, altruism, love, courage, honor, and compassion, and with fidelity and large-mindedness regarding one's station, commitments, family, friends, colleagues, and society in general. [p.97]

Without worrying about Bennett and Delatree's misunderstanding of what Kohlberg means by rights [D. Boyd, 1979, 1986, 1989], it is clear that while Kohlberg provides largely a deontological definition of morality that emphasizes rights and justice, Bennett and Delatree provide largely a virtue-based definition, including such virtues as sacrifice, altruism, love, courage, honor, compassion, and fidelity. Granted, to this list Bennett and Delatree might add virtue of justice. But from their perspective, the justice construct is conceived largely in terms of habits and dispositions, rather than rational judgments and decision-making processes. It is partly for this reason that Bennett and Delatree disagree with Kohlberg's educational efforts in creating a just community.

Second, Bennett and Delatree build on a different explanation of developmental process than does Kohlberg, one that is largely exogenous. Moral development occurs through the transmission of those who know (adults) to those who do not (children). Bennett and Delatree [1978], for instance, end their essay as follows:

> Finally, according to . . . Kohlberg, there is no place for stories and lessons, no place for the passing on of knowledge and experience. Children are invited to a world where it is a travesty and an imposition for anyone to tell them the truth. [p.98]

This exogenous view emphasizes the transmission (passing on) of moral knowledge and is compatible with character-education views. For example, Wynne [1986, p. 4] argues that the "transmission of moral values has been [and should be] the dominant educational concern of most cultures." According to this view, transmission occurs best through good role models [Wynne, 1989a], and by demanding from children obedience to authority, while moral reasons and justifications "merely serve as a form of intellectual courtesy" [Wynne, 1989b, p.2]. In contrast, Kohlberg's structural-interaction view has led him and others to propose pedagogy that involves students in critical thinking about and active participation in moral issues and problems.

This is not the place to discuss the strengths or limitations of the views proposed by these theorists. However, in such discussions clarity can be achieved by independently addressing issues and assessing arguments that pertain to the two foundational issues, moral definition and moral ontogeny. Indeed, this is the tact partly taken in a recent response to Wynne [Kahn, 1990] in which I argue that one can accept the importance of role models in shaping a child's life without accepting an exogenous developmental theory.

A distinction between these two foundational issues can also help to clarify a complexity that has been part of extensive debate regarding gender and moral development initiated by Gilligan [1982]. Here I wish simply to point out that Gilligan has intertwined two fundamentally distinct claims. The first claim is that Kohlberg has too narrowly defined the moral domain in terms largely of deontology, excluding an alternative definition based on an ethic of care. Based on this dispute over moral definitions, Gilligan's second claim is that males and females undergo different developmental progressions. These two issues of definition and ontogeny are independent since one does not imply or contradict the other. One could accept a different moral definition than Kohlberg's (or Gilligan's), and find or not find developmental differences between males and females. Likewise, one could accept Kohlberg's (or Gilligan's) definition and find or not find developmental differences.

If we accept that the same individual can draw on different moral perspectives and that such perspectives may develop by different means, a research approach is needed that takes seriously the relations between definitional and ontogenetic issues. One such approach has been proposed by Shweder [1990; Shweder et al., 1987], who distinguishes three different codes of moral discourse. Roughly characterized, code 1 focuses on justice, code 2 on duty, and code 3 on virtue. A strength of this approach is that by distinguishing different moral definitions, it allows for analyses of different moral development processes. While these processes, in turn, have not yet been adequately characterized by Schweder [see the critique by Turiel et al., 1987, pp.220–233], they do reflect important considerations, for example in the ways that construct knowledge may depend on socially transmitted beliefs, customs, and taboos.

I have taken another approach to this problem in a recent study of children's obligatory and discretionary moral judgments [Kahn, in press]. Obligatory judgments were defined as generalizable requirements not contingent on societal rules or laws and largely justified on the basis of justice and welfare. In turn, discretionary moral judgments referred to those for which moral action, while not required of an agent, is nevertheless conceived of as morally worthy based on concerns of welfare and virtue (for example, benevolence, sacrifice, and supererogation). The point here is that by drawing a distinction based on two different moral definitions, deontological and virtue, it was possible to analyze developmentally the intrapersonal coexistence and relations between different moral orientations. This same approach is being used in a current study [Kahn, in preparation] on children's moral reasoning about environmental issues. It is hypothesized that judgments about why one should protect the natural environment (for example, why one should protect Prince William Sound from oil spills) can tap both obligatory moral judgments (that an oil spill harms individuals who are dependent on the local fishing economy) and discretionary moral judgments (that the consequences reflect a wrong, inharmonious relation between individuals and the land).

Controversies Involving Moral Definition and Moral Variation

Anthropological accounts of the practices and beliefs of various cultures provide important data that directly bear on the questions of whether the moral life is similar or different across cultures. At first blush, it may seem self-evident that cultures differ morally. For instance, among the practices van der Post [1958/1986] documents of the Bushmen of the Kalahari Desert is that they abandon their elderly, either to be attacked by animals or to sure starvation. Such a practice differs sharply from the treatment accorded the elderly in Western cultures. Likewise, in the case of the examples described earlier, Westerners, unlike devout Hindus, do not generally believe that it is immoral for a widow to eat fish, or for a menstruating woman to sleep in the same bed with her husband. Nor do Western men engage in the practice of shooting women with barbed arrows, chopping them with machetes or axes, or burning them with firebrands, practices documented among the Yanomamo tribes.

Yet what is crucial in analyzing such anthropological data is to pay close attention to varying moral definitions. A simple analogy may prove helpful. Modifying an example used by S. Langer [1937/1953], consider four men's suits. One is made of cotton, the second wool, the third polyester, and the fourth silk. Each is also cut to a different size. Now we ask, are these four objects the same? If by object we mean the material, then the answer is no. But if by object we mean their function as a suit, then the answer is yes. Thus the answer to whether there is variation or similarity between objects depends on how we define what we mean by an object.

So, too, with morality. Depending on how morality is defined, and anthropological data are collected, one is led to varying conclusions about moral diversity. For instance, the example of the Bushmen practice of leaving their elderly to die appears fundamentally different from Western practices. But as van der Post [1958/1986] further describes the Bushmen's intentions, motivations, social context, and environmental constraints, their practice seems less foreign. The Bushmen are a nomadic people that depend on physical movement for their survival. Elderly people are left behind only when they can no longer keep up the nomadic pace and thereby jeopardize the survival of the entire tribe. When the tribe is thus forced to leave an elderly person behind, they conduct parting ceremonies and ritual dances that convey honor and respect. The tribe also builds the elderly a temporary shelter and provides a few token days of food. All these additional practices convey an attitude of care and concern for the elderly, and felt loss at their impeding death—a death that is unavoidable should the tribe as a whole be able to survive.

Such an analysis does not negate differences between Bushmen and Western cultures. On a behavioral level, both cultures do engage in different practices regarding the care of the elderly. But the analysis also points to similarities. Both societies show care and concern for their elderly. Both societies also balance that care with the well-being of society as a whole. (Note, for instance, that as some of our medical practices become more extensive and extraordinarily expensive, we face the problem of how to weigh the benefits of elderly patients with the corresponding costs to society.) Thus, if morality is defined and analyzed in terms of a deontic idea of promoting the good for the greatest number, then in some respects Bushmen morality may well resemble the morality reflected in Western culture.

It is this type of analysis that Turiel et al. [1987] provide of the anthropological data of Hindu culture collected by Shweder et al. For instance, Shweder et al. found that devout Hindus believe that harmful consequences would follow from a widow who ate fish. (The act would offend her husband's spirit and cause the widow to suffer greatly.) Similarly, harmful consequences were believed to follow from a menstruating woman who slept in the same bed with her husband. (The menstrual blood is believed poisonous and capable of hurting the husband.) While such beliefs themselves differ from those in Western culture, the underlying concern for the welfare of others is similar.

If it is accepted that an analysis of moral variation depends on but is analytically separate from moral definition, the following generalization can be proposed. Definitions of morality that entail abstract characterizations of justice and welfare tend to highlight moral universals, while definitions that entail specific behaviors or rigid moral rules tend to highlight moral cross-cultural variation. Typically, theorists who strive to uncover moral universals believe they are wrestling with the essence of morality, with its deepest and most meaningful attributes. Thus, for instance, in the *Meno*, when Menon defines virtue in terms of many different virtues depending on a person's activities, occupation, and age, Socrates asks:

If I asked you what a bee really is, and you answered that there are many different kinds of bees, what would you answer me if I asked you then: Do you say there are many different kinds of bees, differing from each other in being bees more or less? Or do they differ in some other respect, for example in size, or beauty, and so forth? Tell me, how would you answer that question? [p.30]

Menon replies: "I should say that they are not different at all one from another in beehood" [p.30]. This is exactly what Socrates wants to say about virtue, and what we could say about the essence of "suits" in the case of the earlier analogy.

In contrast, theorists—and I take Shweder to be of this position—who strive to characterize moral variation argue that by the time one has identified a common moral feature that cuts across cultures, one has so disembodied the idea into an abstract form that it loses virtually all meaning and utility. For instance, consider once again the example of devout Hindus who believe that by eating fish a widow hurts her dead husband's spirit. Is the interesting moral phenomenon that Hindus, like ourselves, are concerned with not causing others harm? Or, as Schweder might argue, is the interesting moral phenomenon that Hindus believe in spirits that can be harmed by earthly activity?

I believe that both questions have merit, and that a middle ground offers a more sensible and powerful approach, one that allows for an analysis of universal moral constructs (such as justice, rights, welfare, and virtue) as well as allowing for the ways in which these constructs are expressed in a particular culture at a particular point in time. Granted, a particular construct may reflect a high level of abstraction and yet not be universal. For example, the virtue of chastity presumably does not apply to all cultures. Yet it is precisely in the examination of such phenomena that this approach is productive. [For further discussion of these issues, see Dunker, 1939; Asch, 1952; Hatch, 1983; and Spiro, 1986; for additional studies based on this approach, see Friedman, 1989; Helwig, 1989; and Turiel et at., 1990.]

Consider as an illustration a study by Hollos et al. [1986] examining social reasoning of Ijo children and adolescents in Nigerian communities. The study reports on various Ijo beliefs that differ from Western ones, such as the belief that the spirit of ancestors can be harmed by adultery, or by a menstruating woman touching the food she serves her husband—not unlike the beliefs of the devout Hindu reported by Schweder et al. Such beliefs, in addition to those proscribing such acts as murder and stealing, are termed in the Ijo language "ologho" and either have supernatural sanctions or are considered to be of universal applicability. In contrast, the term "miyen ya" refers to "customary behaviors that are considered normal by members of the community, such as not eating with the left hand or greeting older people first" [p.357]. Interviews with Ijo children and adolescents established that they, like children and adolescents in Western countries [Davidson et al., 1983; Nucci and Nucci, 1982a, b; Smetana, 1981, 1989], distinguish between moral and conventional concepts, where the former refer to prescriptions of a noncontingent nature pertaining to obligations in social relations and the latter to regulations contingent on the constituted system of social arrangements.

This research approach—one that is sensitive to both universal and cultural influences—is applicable not only to cross-cultural work, but to research within our own culture as well. For example, in a study by Friedman [1988], adolescents' conceptions of property rights pertaining to electronic information were found to entail universal abstract components alongside of specific variation in the application of those rights. The variation was, in part, found to depend on assumptions about the social context. For example, some students said that copying computer software to give away did not violate the author's property rights because they assumed that by publishing the program the author implicitly gave consent to have the program copied. Other students said that such copying violated the author's property rights because they assumed explicit consent from the author was required. Friedman proposed that such varied assumptions were related in part to cultural conventions that were not well established for new technologically related property such as computer software.

Controversies Involving Moral Variation and Moral Epistemology

In various critiques, Kohlberg's theory has been charged with sex bias. For instance, Baumrind [1986] has argued that had Kohlberg's research shown that higher stages of moral reasoning are equally distributed among sexes then "there could be no charge of sexual . . . bias against the Kohlberg system" [p.520]. However, on Baumrind's interpretation the findings do show that men score higher than women on Kohlberg's moral reasoning dilemmas, and thus she concludes sex bias exists in the theory.

An empirical finding for or against sex differences cannot, however, by itself, establish sex bias. This fact can be illustrated by considering six examples. In the first example, identical to one used by Walker [1984], it is assumed that sex differences are empirically shown to exist for number of eyes (virtually all men and women have two eyes). In both cases we can say that no sex bias exists in our system of measurement and counting. But this is not a conclusion that can be empirically derived from negative findings regarding sex differences; in the first example sex differences are present, not absent. The same reasoning applies to Kohlberg's work. If Kohlberg's research showed no sex differences, it could follow that the theory was either sex-biased, should it be that men (or women) were more morally developed, or not sex-biased, should it be that men and women were morally equal. Similarly, if Kohlberg's research showed sex differences, it could follow that the theory was either sex-biased, should it be that men and women were morally equal, or not sex-biased, should it be that men (or women) were more morally developed. Thus the fallacy should be clear. Baumrind assumes there are no sex differences, and charges bias if research finds them, and yet, by her approach, prejudges an answer to precisely the research question. In other words, empirical findings that pertain to moral variation are directly used to judge the validity of Kohlberg's theory (with respect to sex bias), when instead judgments of validity should be established by drawing on epistemological criteria, such as predictability, disconformation, and coherence, in consort with evidence.

A more distinct and pervasive confusion between moral variation and epistemology occurs in the often heated and confusing controversy regarding cultural relativism. This confusion can be highlighted by considering Herskovits' theory. According to Herskovits [1972]:

> . . . cultural relativism is a philosophy that recognizes the values set up by every society to guide its own life and that understands their worth to those who live by them, though they may differ from one's own. Instead of underscoring differences from absolute norms that, however objectively arrived at, are nonetheless the product of a given time or place, the relativistic point of view brings into relief the validity of every set of norms for the people who have them, and the values these represent. [p.31]

In addition Herskovits writes:

> The very core of cultural relativism is the social discipline that comes of respect for differences—of mutual respect. Emphasis on the worth of many ways of life, not one, is an affirmation of the values in each culture. [p.33]

Thus Herskovits puts forth the philosophical position that cross-cultural practices and beliefs differing from one's own deserve respect and validation. Most notable, for purposes here, is the explicit justification that Herskovits provides for this view:

> For it is difficult to conceive of a systematic theory of cultural relativism—as against a generalized idea of live-and-let-live—without the pre-existence of the massive ethnographic documentation gathered by anthropologists concerning the similarities and differences between cultures the world over. Out of these data came the philosophical position, and with the philosophical position came speculation as to its implications for conduct. [p.33 emphasis added]

Note that it is the established empirical claim of cultural variation that leads Herskovits to the epistemic claim that every culture's practices and beliefs are equally valid.

At this time, at least two broad interpretations of Herskovits' theory have been advanced. The more traditional interpretation [Williams, 1972; Spiro, 1986; Turiel, 1989] is that Herskovits asserts contradictory propositions. By asserting that the values and beliefs of different cultures are equally valid and cannot be judged from the perspective of any single culture, Herskovits commits himself to what he says cannot be done, namely establishing a judgment that transcends purported cultural biases. Said differently, the proposition that morality is subjective because different people hold different moral beliefs inappropriately draws on a statement of moral variation to support an epistemic claim.

Another interpretation of Herskovits' cultural relativism has recently been advanced by Fernandez [1990], although a good part of his interpretation appears inadvertently consonant with the more traditional one. According to Fernandez, Herskovits distinguished between cultural relativism and ethical relativism. Cultural relativism refers to "the way things are— facts learned by many years of ethnographic fieldwork in a great diversity of cultures" [p.44]. Ethical relativism refers to how things ought to be. According to Fernandez, Herskovits did not confuse the two: "In short, it is a 'logical distortion' of the anthropological position to reword into an implicit moral premise explicit propositions based on extensive ethnographic knowledge of how cultures work" [p.144]. If Fernandez stopped here, the interpretation would be clear: Herskovits was only concerned with documenting moral variation, and his theory said nothing about how to judge that variation, let alone about the epistemic standing of such a judgment. Yet such a position is quite unsettling to many (is their no objective basis by which to judge Nazi Germany?), and was apparently unsettling to Herskovits. Thus, according to Fernandez, Herskovits' theory of cultural relativism was not, after all, a theory of ethical indifference, but a "tough-minded" theory [p.148] that did not condone "man's inhumanity to man" [p.148]. At this point, of course, a problem arises in that this added proposition leads directly to the very contradiction noted by Herskovits' critics. After all, who decides and on what basis, what counts as inhumanity in a different culture?

At the conclusion of his essay, Fernandez offers a response to this problem. He suggests that what has to date been characterized by critics such as Williams [1972] as a naive contradiction should be reconceived as, and thus transformed into, a meaningful paradox:

> [I]n a discipline such as ours in which complex, overdetermined creatures propose to study other complex and overdetermined creatures by means of an apparently absurd and surely paradoxical method, participant-observation, perhaps the best way we can do, in the case of such overarching, virtually existential issues as this one of how to treat 'otherness,' is transform dilemmas into paradoxes. And perhaps in that transformation—the coming to a thoroughgoing apprehension of the paradoxical in human affairs to which it leads—lies the only true and lasting relief from intolerance and

the best remedy we can devise for dealing with 'man's inhumanity to man.' [1990, p.160].

As far as I can understand, this provocative passage means that the paradox that arises (given that a theory of cultural relativism is itself a non-relativistic theory) reflects the human condition, and is part of that with which people must struggle for there to exist human consideration of divergent cultures.

Naive contradictions or meaningful paradox? The point here is not to argue for or against a theory of cultural relativism, but to recognize that any stance partly hinges on how one understands the relation between the foundational issues of moral variation and epistemology. Directly drawing on variation to establish a subjective epistemic claim creates clear problems. Thus the challenge for those who seek to generate a convincing theory of cultural relativism is to provide a rich and compelling account that can ease the tension that occurs when fusing both foundational issues.

Controversies Involving Moral Ontogeny and Moral Epistemology

In the *Emile*, Rousseau [1762/1979] presents paradigmatic examples of an epistemological fallacy. Consider the following propositions:

> Do you wish to be well guided? Then always follow nature's indications. [p.363]
> Everything that hinders and constrains nature is in bad taste. [p.367]
> I am persuaded that all the natural inclinations are good and right in themselves. [p.370]
> What is, is good. . . . [p.371]

The fallacy inherent in these propositions, whose explication is sometimes credited to Hume [1751/1983] though more often to Moore [1903/1978], is that facts do not logically imply value. Conterexamples make this clear. A baby can be born with an infection, a fact that describes the baby's condition; but that fact does not logically imply that the infection is good, or that a doctor's efforts to hinder the infection is, in Rousseau's terms, in "bad taste." Similarly, a person can naturally acquire AIDS, but it does not logically follow that the disease is good. The fallacy is part of an epistemological enterprise because it draws on empirical evidence in an attempt to establish the validity of moral knowledge of the good and the right.

Now and again, this fallacy pervades current arguments. For example, Sperry [1988] claims that inherent in the human cognitive structure is an elaborate system of innate value preferences, and that these preferences are directly embodied in future preferences and provide the basis for knowing the rightness of particular moral decisions. Thus Sperry claims that current concepts of cognitive processing make it possible not only to explain mentalistic phenomena (such as moral and religious beliefs), "but to go from fact to value and from perception of what 'is' to what 'should' be" [p. 610]. However, as noted by Pirolli and Goel [1990], Sperry's claim still falls prey to the naturalistic fallacy. For example, it is often believed that our inherent nature includes not only, as Hume proposed, a general sympathy for all human kind, but some level of aggression as well, as reflected in Freud's [1930/1961] theory of an original and self-subsisting aggressive instinct. Assuming that all natural preferences are not moral, it then becomes even clearer that morally right preferences cannot logically be derived from the natural.

At times, Kohlberg comes close to committing the naturalistic fallacy as defined here. In one essay, Kohlberg and Mayer [1972] say that the moral principles underlying stage 6 of his theory . . .

> represent developmentally advanced or mature stages of reasoning, judgment, and action. Because there are culturally universal stages or sequences of moral development (Kohlberg and Turiel, 1971), stimulation of the child's development to the next stage in a natural direction is equivalent to a long-range goal of teaching ethical principles. [p. 475]

To the extent Kohlberg and Mayer mean to say that because there are universal stages of moral development it therefore follows that the latter stages are more moral than the earlier stages (thus providing long-range pedagogical goals), they commit the fallacy. After all, it could be claimed that as people get older they, by and large, get more politically conservative; but it does not follow from this proposed developmental progression that political conservatism is a more adequate political theory than political liberalism. Hence, the claim for the more advanced status of the "higher" stages is not supported by establishing a developmental progression.

Rather, such a claim is supported by other philosophical considerations. For instance, Kohlberg follows a view proposed long ago by Baldwin [1899/1973] that a more adequate moral theory will take into account a larger group of people. Based on this philosophical criterion, Kohlberg's stages do increase in moral adequacy. In stage 1 there is moral consideration only for the self (punishment avoidance). In stage 2, there is consideration for another person, but only instrumentally (instrumental hedonism). In stage 3, there is consideration for family members and other personal relations (good boy or good girl orientation). And, finally, by stages 5 and 6, there is consideration for humanity from a universal perspective. This stage progression also highlights another criterion, that is hierarchical integration. Kohlberg proposes that the higher stages subsume the earlier stages. For instance, the legal codification emphasis of stage 4 includes consideration for self, other, and family, but it attempts to correct for the unfairness that can arise from basing moral judgments largely on interpersonal considerations (e.g., the unfairness of a judge who gives his family member or friend preferential treatment). It is in this sense—in which the central organizing principle of an earlier stage becomes an element in a more inclusive organizational framework—that stages represent transformations of moral knowledge, rather than simple replacements of one moral view with another.

While these philosophical criteria are arguably plausible criteria in helping to evaluate the relative adequacy of various moral theories, their plausibility does not follow logically from the claim that they are observed ontogenetically. In fact, Kohlberg himself elsewhere says as much. In his 1971 article provocatively titled, "From is to ought: How to commit the naturalistic fallacy and get away with it in the study of moral development," Kohlberg says that there are forms of the naturalistic fallacy that he does not commit. One of these is "assuming that morality or moral maturity is part of man's biological nature," and another is that the "biologically older is necessarily the better" [p.222]. The first is the fallacy that Sperry commits. The second is fallacy I characterized earlier using the analogy of the progression from political liberalism to conservatism. Instead, Kohlberg says that the "form of the 'naturalistic fallacy' which we are committing is that of asserting that any conception of what moral judgment ought to be must rest on an adequate conception of what it is" [p.222].

At this point Kohlberg moves beyond what most theorists take to be the naturalistic fallacy, and what I have in mind when arguing for the distinction between moral ontogeny and moral epistemology. Instead, Kohlberg draws on Piaget's [1971a, b, c] theory of genetic epistemology. In this theory, Piaget argues against the view that philosophy can stand apart from psychology in identifying valid knowledge, for such knowledge is tied to its psychological genesis and requires scientific methods of verification. Thus for Piaget [1971b] the "first rule of genetic epistemology is therefore one of collaboration [between philosophy and science]" [p.8]. Now, as Piaget develops this theory, I think he runs into problems. For though he seeks collaboration, Piaget [1971a] in fact sets psychology above philosophy. While both are modes of knowledge, the former "is higher than the other, because it attains the essential, while the other is 'lower,' as it is either merely verbal or incomplete knowledge . . ." [p.79]. But I do not take Kohlberg to go this far. Rather Kohlberg seems to place psychology and philosophy on an equal footing. To the extent that Kohlberg is successful in bridging the two disciplines, so does he successfully bridge moral ontogeny and epistemology.

CONCLUSION

By drawing on four foundational issues—moral definition, ontogeny, variation, and epistemology—I have portrayed a means for bounding moral development controversies, in the sense of defining their parameters and clarifying conflicts. Numerous controversies have been examined to provide a sense of the robustness of the analysis. I do not wish, however, to overstate my case. While it is true that some of the controversies arise from straight-forward conceptual mistakes (and need not be perpetuated), others have for many decades if not centuries resisted simple means of dismissal, and I have offered no simple means here. Rather, in these latter cases, the foundational issues provide a means for understanding better the nature of the controversies and what is at stake in varying approaches that strive to resolve them.

Indeed, in this regard it is worth noting that the conceptual distinctions themselves share common ground. For example, the problems that arise from confusing moral ontogeny and epistemology are often similar to those that arise from confusing moral variation and epistemology. In both cases, a descriptive claim about how the world is empirically can lead to an epistemic claim about what ought to be and about the validity of such judgments. More generally, if we accept that the issues of definition and epistemology entail a philosophical stance, and variation and ontogeny a psychological stance (broadly conceived to include cross-cultural psychology), then many of the controversies in the moral development literature arise from difference in how to conceive of the relation between philosophy and psychology.

Toward conceptualizing this relationship, we can draw on current philosophical theory [Williams, 1981, 1985; Nagel, 1986; Scheffler, 1982], which holds that since morality derives from social relations, an adequate moral theory must take into account the nature (including possible limitations) of human agents ('ought implies can'). For instance, Scheffler [1986] seeks a moral philosophical theory in which "the content of morality is constrained by considerations of the agents psychology and well-being, and of the ways in which it is appropriate for morality to enter into an agent's life, and to impinge on his or her thought, deliberations, feelings, and action" [p.537]. Taking this position more broadly, moral psychology and philosophy—while distinct from one another in the ways described in this article—are foundationally interdependent. Moral psychology cannot succeed unless it takes seriously and accurately accounts for the actual social and moral lives of human beings. It is hoped that the conceptual analyses presented her contribute to clear thinking in the difficult task of integrating both disciplines substantively.

A JUST AND DEMOCRATIC COMMUNITY APPROACH TO MORAL EDUCATION: DEVELOPING VOICES OF REASON AND RESPONSIBILITY

by Mary F. Howard-Hamilton
Assistant Professor, Dept. of Counselor Education
University of Florida, Gainesville

School counselors have had a history as change agents in performing virtually every function of their job (Perry & Schwallie-Giddis, 1993). Today, the concept of a comprehensive developmental school counseling program has expanded the role of the counselor and provided additional opportunities to become involved in educational reform efforts (Perry & Schwallie-Giddis, 1993). The school counselor can be instrumental in restructuring the current system, which leads to positive change for student success. As a developer of systematic prevention and intervention programs for all students, the school counselor can be a leader for school improvement through team building and coordinating collaborative efforts.

One example of a redesigned model for shifting school counselors' roles and responsibilities involves working with school personnel to enhance the classroom and school environment. A particular challenge in improving school climate is how to affect students so that an atmosphere of justice and support is of primary concern for all. When children are raised in an environment that is hostile and nonsupportive, they may internalize behaviors that demonstrate a lack of compassion, care, and sensitivity. Consequently, students may not have a sense of personal regard for their teachers, classmates, or school. This article presents models specifically designed to help students to build group cohesion, to encourage them to think and act more compassionately, and to provide them with more leadership opportunities. The "just community" approach and moral dilemma methods based on Kohlberg's (1984) moral development theory are described.

MORAL DEVELOPMENT

Moral development examines moral reasoning and moral judgment, not moral conduct (Reimer, Paolitto, & Hersh, 1983). Moreover, it is a concept that explores what people "think they should do" and is less concerned with what they "would do." According to Kohlberg (1984), moral development occurs in a sequence of three levels, and within each there are two stages that are age-related, although there is nothing absolute about the age at which a child enters a given stage. Each level and stage is defined by abilities that limit and determine the character of what can be learned during that period. These abilities also determine how children view their physical and social world. Each level and stage of moral judgment expresses a different basis for deciding what is the fair or just way to resolve a moral dilemma. The Appendix provides a description of Kohlberg's levels of ethical reasoning.

Moral development through each level and stage occurs as a result of interaction between the children and their environment. Kohlberg (1984) believed that children acquire moral knowledge by psychologically acting on their environment. Situations that encourage children to compare, hypothesize, categorize, and make judgments increase the probability that they will gain an understanding of the objects and the events that surround them. Children are exposed to surroundings including family, friends, and teachers throughout the day, with most of their critical interactions occurring in the classroom. Schools have an excellent opportunity to be agents of change and to positively reshape the learning environment so that everyone has a chance to grow, learn, and value differences.

CURRENT STATUS IN SCHOOLS:
THE HIDDEN CURRICULUM

Currently, schools have been slow making changes in the learning environment; instead, they continue to adhere to traditional methods of discipline, teaching, and counseling. Most school systems are run on authoritarian principles (Sullivan, 1986). Therefore, it is difficult to move students toward the postconventional level when the school system emphasizes lower stages of reasoning and values. Thus, given the emphasis of such systems, an attempt to develop a community of trust, respect, empathy, and cooperation between teachers and students would be difficult to cultivate in such an atmosphere. In his research, Kohlberg (1984) found that children were influenced by groups outside of their immediate family circle. Children who belonged to groups that engaged in moral discussion and dialogue in which there was some responsibility for decisions advanced further in moral character. Often, schools promote covertly prescribed hidden lessons, values, and behaviors through books, multimedia, games, and the teacher's personal pedagogical philosophy (Sadker & Sadker, 1994). One of Kohlberg's (1986) greatest concerns was how to promote development among students when there were pervasive hidden norms or curricula in the schools.

Kohlberg (1983) noted that roles and attributes are prescribed and transmitted through a hidden curriculum from the teacher and the institution to the student. The hidden curriculum approach shapes the lives and moral beliefs of the students in an unconscious manner by teachers and educational institutions covertly defining, discussing, and establishing their educational purposes and procedures (Koger, 1989). This is done by tracking or stratification by ability, gender role differentiation by sex, as well as by promotion or failure through the grading system (Kohlberg, 1983; Sadker & Sadker, 1994).

Another approach to dictating "right" values and morals to students is called the "bag of virtues tact" (Kohlberg & Mayer, 1972). By this approach, children are taught that certain virtues, behaviors, and characteristics are placed in high esteem by others. Unfortunately, these ideas are not always integrated by students. The embodiment of virtues that are right could mold individuals into people with no sense of self-determined identity. In addition, because most schools support an authoritarian and conventional structure, promoting reflective thought is difficult unless the moral atmosphere at the school can be changed.

THE JUST COMMUNITY CONCEPT

Recognizing these issues and observing the students' internalization of traditional beliefs and behaviors, Kohlberg's (1985) ultimate aim was to transform the authoritative atmosphere of the school to a democratic decision-making community. Essentially, Kohlberg (1980a, 1980b, 1985) wanted to develop a just community approach to advance stage judgment. In other words, Kohlberg wanted to develop a community in which students, teachers, and administrators collaborate on establishing of rules and procedures that are viewed as fair and just among them all. The just community approach is one method of promoting moral development at the postconventional level with Stage 6 reasoning abilities.

The just community approach is a " process of democratic schooling that involves collective establishment of rules and responsibility taking in concrete situations instead of hypothetical dilemma discussions" (Oser, 1990, pp.82–83). The just or democratic community was designed according to the following conditions (Reimer et al., 1983, p. 239):

* Student interest must be maintained.
* There must be a clear, flexible procedural order.
* Issues must be raised clearly so that the pros and cons of concrete proposals can be discussed.
* Students and staff must discuss issues by voicing reasons for their stands and not by attacking one another on personal grounds.
* Everyone has to feel that the decisions of the community will be carried

out and will not be subverted by higher authorities or dissenting minorities.

* Establish a community based on democracy and fairness.
* Extend responsibility to all.
* Encourage collective responsibility.
* Create a climate of trust.
* Establish a social contract and constitution.
* Raise the moral level of the group as a group.
* Stimulate individual moral decisions and actions.

A just community approach promotes moral character development and responsibility through (a) living in an atmosphere of fairness and developing relations of loyalty and trust, (b) taking responsibility for making and enforcing rules for all members of the group including yourself, and (c) participating in moral discussion that provides exposure to new and different points of view (Kohlberg, 1985; Power, 1988).

The basic and underlying premise of this unique approach is to promote prosocial behavior that is easier to maintain when rules and norms are discussed openly and applied democratically (Power, Higgins, & Kohlberg, 1989). Furthermore, the just democracy is a community in which there is an altruistic spirit or group attachment among the participants (Powers, 1988). There are certain primary virtues that are advocated in the just community approach, such as caring, trust, respect, involvement, and unified responsibility (Power et al., 1989). These virtues are contained in the rules adopted by community members. For instance, the behavior of students who skip school, vandalize property, or steal from classmates would be discussed by community members in an open and sensitive manner. Subsequently, an assembly would be formed to discuss the group or a collaborative decision would be made about appropriate penalties.

DILEMMA DISCUSSIONS

One particular set of skills embedded in the just community involves the use of dilemma discussions. This approach includes the presentation of open-ended situations for discussion and analysis. The teacher or counselor serves as a mediator for the process. The primary purpose is for students to articulate their reasoning about their decisions. In addition, students are given opportunities to hear the ideas of others. Counselors or teachers focus on clarifying the levels of reasoning, not on lecturing or providing right answers (Paisley & Hubbard, 1994).

Sometimes before, or as part of, building a democratic community in which real-life issues are considered, students need practice with the process of ethical reasoning. Many types of dilemmas are possible. Adult leaders can provide dilemmas specifically constructed around particular content areas. Generally, topics are chosen that are associated with the experience of students and might include choices concerning school, drugs, or relationship issues. Students who are familiar with the process can also be encouraged to create their own dilemmas for discussion. Teachers and counselors can also use existing curricula in social studies, literature, and health education to provoke discussions.

There are several specific strategies that can be used as part of this moral or ethical thinking process (Kohlberg, 1986). One method is "position-taking" in which individuals must choose an issue or policy that they could abide by regardless of their position in society. It is critical that the individuals take into consideration the views of the disenfranchised in society. Another method is called "moral musical chairs," in which individuals take the point of view of everyone involved in a dilemma that would take into account the perspective of all people involved.

Whether creating a democratic environment or using a specifically constructed dilemma for discussion, the preconditions for meaningful dialogue are trust and community that ensures fairness for everyone. Variations of these interventions have been successfully implemented at several schools across the country.

USING THESE IDEAS IN ELEMENTARY AND MIDDLE SCHOOLS

Several successful democratic societies have been established at the elementary school level. One such program was developed and implemented at Birch Meadows School in Reading, Massachusetts (Murphy, 1988). The teachers and students implemented two ongoing programs, circle meetings, and student councils to ameliorate grievous student behavior and peer hostility. The circle meetings, conducted as dilemma discussion groups, were held in each classroom on a daily basis. Dilemma discussions were led by the teacher or counselor. The purpose of each discussion was to help students examine their own moral judgment and the judgment of others (Galbraith & Jones, 1976). Elaborating on the moral dilemmas highlights the different reasoning and judgment used to solve a problem rather than the recommended behavior of the primary character. Students who stated similar beliefs or recommended similar behavior often had a multiplicity of reasons for their recommendations. Discussions mediated by a counselor or a teacher helped the students develop collaborative communication skills. Students sat in a circle and discussed critical concerns or issues with the assistance of an adult leader who was not necessarily their teacher. They were taught to be active listeners, to share opinions, and not to interrupt each other. Issues or specific situations were shared in the classroom and solutions were decided unanimously.

The second activity was implementing a student council with representatives from the primary and intermediate grades who met with the school principal. The council handled discipline issues by appointing students to judge their classmates behavior and levy a sanction or punishment. In addition, the council organized community service and fund raising activities for the entire school. Murphy (1988), the former principal, stated that "our Just Community has enabled almost 400 children to develop a sense of ownership of Birch Meadow School and a sense of responsibility for their classmates" (p. 428).

Two other schools on the elementary level achieved some success with heightening the moral spirit of their respective institutions by incorporating the just democracy and collaborative curriculum concept (Rosenzweig, 1980). Project Change in New York City enlisted the help of teachers to make the just community approach applicable for school-age children (Lickona, 1977). The children in this democratic community shared in the classroom decision-making process (Lickona, 1977; Rosenzweig, 1980). At the University of Pittsburgh's Falk Laboratory School, a complete moral education program similar to the Birch Meadows concept was established and successfully implemented. The program included moral dilemma discussions in each classroom and a schoolwide just community (Kubelick, 1977; Rosenzweig, 1980).

The moral discussion approach has been empirically tested and proven to promote stage growth in students. Research conducted by Higgins (1980), Power, (1988), as well as Power et al. (1989) compared samples of students in traditional school settings with those who participated in a just or democratic community. These students spoke of their institution using the "we" voice and internalized a greater sense of concern and responsibility for the well-being of the school and the policies that were implemented as compared with students in traditional educational settings who tend to be individually focused and apathetic.

A JUST COMMUNITY MODEL FOR
HIGH SCHOOL STUDENTS

I conducted a recent study to assess the effect of a just democratic community approach and value and moral dilemma discussion method on the psychosocial development of academically gifted adolescents (Howard-Hamilton, 1991). The study was conducted in 1991 with 167 gifted high school seniors. The design and implementation of the program are presented to provide a model as well as techniques that can be adapted to fit the needs of students at the elementary and middle school levels.

Several techniques to affect and enhance moral judgment and behavior were used. The students met once a week as a just community in which they had an opportunity to decide curfew hours and discipline sanctions when a peer had violated the program's policies. Students were given an opportunity to talk and listen to each other regarding sensitive issues. Also small-group integrative seminars provided a forum each day for students and faculty to explore and clarify feelings, ideas, and perspectives as they related to day-to-day issues and to the decisions made by the just community. The seminars were similar to a group counseling format with an underlying premise of democratic education (Hayes, 1991). During these seminars, which met five times per week, the faculty leader discussed moral dilemma scenarios and challenged the students to respond using higher stage thinking. Students also wrote in their journals on a daily basis and turned them in to their seminar instructor who provided confidential feedback to them. This written forum allowed students to clarify their own feelings and heighten their capacity to seek resolution to their own problems (Hayes, 1991).

I went back to the summer program in 1993 and taught a class titled Human Ecology. The purpose of the course was to study varying human environments and their cultures as they interact with their environment. For example, the students studied the high school environment and the type of characters and culture that were prevalent in various schools. The college environment was studied along with the various cultures one would expect to find on campuses across the country. The students also learned how individuals interact with their environment and how to embrace cultures different to their own. In addition, the state of the world and its various human ecological forces were studied. The final outcome and goal for this course was to provide the students with information to help transform their current environment (work, home, and school) and become actively engaged in the process of change for a better human ecological environment or just societal community.

Required readings for the course were the *State of the World 1993: A Worldwatch Institute Report on Progress Toward a Sustainable Society* (Brown, 1993), *The Good High School: Portraits of Character and Culture* (Lightfoot, 1983), and *Multicultural Relations on Campus: A Personal Growth Approach* (Parker, Archer, & Scott, 1992). The course curriculum and design adhered to Kohlberg's (1985) guidelines and key elements in the classroom, which were to

(a) establish a nonthreatening atmosphere,
(b) organize time effectively,
(c) encourage peer interaction and dialogue, and
(d) use probe questions when stimulating the dialogue
(Kuhmerker, 1991).

The Socratic and developmental teaching methods were used, with students sitting in a circle and with the teacher functioning primarily as a mediator of class discussion. During the class discussions, there was ample opportunity for guided reflection, support and challenge, as well as for self-disclosure and reflection, as provided by the instructor. Often the students would relate their own personal experiences to some of the issues presented in the text. For example, problems related to gender bias, racism, and peer or family pressures were discussed. The students would listen, share, and come to a collective decision as to how they would handle the presenting problem.

Another component that was intended to enhance the students' learning and promote a sense of care and justice was the role-taking activities that supplemented the textbook material as well as the dialogue in the class. The student served meals in a homeless shelter, went to an African-American wax museum, toured Harlem, New York, and visited an inner city high school, which included an engaging dialogue regarding school policies with the principal. The final class project was a qualitative compilation of poetry and essays on the future of our human environment. The booklet was distributed to all of the students participating in the summer program. The essays, poems, and book critiques ranged in topics from racism and homophobia to gender role socialization and revamping school curricula.

CURRICULUM DESIGN AND RESOURCES

Educating for a just society (Kohlberg, 1980a, 1980b) by implementing the democratic community and dilemma discussion methods can be adapted and redesigned to promote growth among elementary and middle school students. Counselors who are familiar with Kohlberg's (1984, 1985) moral development theory could provide in-service training workshops for teachers and administrators on how to establish a democratic community, lead dilemma discussions, and integrate this material into existing academic curricula. Excellent curriculum materials and moral dilemma stories for elementary and secondary school children can be found in *The Kohlberg Legacy for the Helping Professions* (Kuhmerker, 1991), *Moral Reasoning: A Teaching Handbook for Adapting Kohlberg to the Classroom* (Galbraith & Jones, 1976), and *Teaching Moral Reasoning: Theory and Practice* (Arbuthnot & Faust, 1981). Specifics on how to establish a just community can be found in *Promoting Moral Growth: From Piaget to Kohlberg* (Reimer et al., 1983), *The Kohlberg Legacy for the Helping Professions* (Kuhmerker, 1991), and *Moral Education: A First Generation of Research and Development* (Mosher, 1980). Guidelines from the aforementioned textbooks are provided so that school counselors and educators can note that extensive change in an existing program is not necessary and modifications can be made without disputing the current curriculum design.

When designing a moral dilemma discussion curriculum, there are several key concepts and steps to follow. Galbraith and Jones (1976, pp. 35–36) stated that a moral dilemma story should provide the following opportunities for students:

(a) to consider genuine moral problems,
(b) to experience genuine social and cognitive conflict during a discussion of a moral problem,

(c) to apply their current level of thought to challenging situations,

(d) to be exposed to the next higher level of thought, and

(e) to confront their own inconsistencies in reasoning over a variety of moral issues without someone stressing a right or wrong answer.

If at all possible, realistic moral dilemma stories directly related to the lives of the students should be discussed, followed by opportunities to disagree over the issue facing the primary characters. This type of disagreement and subsequent discussion should cause some cognitive dissonance, thus exposing the student to higher levels of moral reasoning. Moral dilemma stories can be presented through a video vignette from a television show, film segment, textbook reading, or children's literature. The key elements of a dilemma story are as follows (Galbraith & Jones, 1976, pp.38–39):

* Focus—The situation in the dilemma should focus on the lives of the students, the course content, or contemporary society.
* Central character—The dilemma should involve a central character or primary group of characters around which the dilemma is focused.
* Choice—The story or situation must involve a choice for the central character.
* Moral issues—Moral dilemmas revolve around key moral issues such as social norm, truth, life, sex, affiliation, authority, law, contract, civil rights, religion, conscience, and punishment.
* A "Should" Question—Each moral dilemma ends with a specific question that asks about what the character should do in the situation.

Elementary age children should have comprehensible dilemmas read to them (Arbuthnot & Faust, 1981). There should not be more than two or three characters in the story, and the details should be summarized by the teacher or counselor. Before the students discuss the dilemma, make sure all of the issues are clear and ask the children if they understand the terms used in the story. After the dilemma has been presented, the students should be given time to reflect on their personal solutions to the dilemma. Give the students ample discussion time, and the chalkboard should be used to write down the opinion and decisions made by the group members.

Teachers and counselors do not need to be precise in assessing the student's level of moral reasoning to lead a dilemma discussion (Galbraith & Jones, 1976). The students that are at adjacent levels and stages of Kohlberg's (1980b, 1983) model will often confront and challenge each other. It is important for the teacher or counselor to have sound mediation and communication skills to provide support and challenge as well as to have a productive discussion of a moral problem. Concomitantly, teachers or counselors need to look for "teachable moments" by recognizing real-life dilemmas and applying similar discussion techniques. This process allows the students an opportunity to not only broaden their perspective about the issue in the story but to create a situation in which there is balance of reflection and experience. Students can reflect on the moral dilemma discussion by writing in a journal to further explain their points of view or why their views have changed in light of challenges presented by classmates. Students can also personally experience the characters dilemmas by role-playing activities or acting out the story. The just democracy allows students an opportunity to role-play daily dilemmas that occur in their learning environment and to use their newly acquired communication skills.

Just community discussions could be designed to encourage schoolwide collaboration and interaction among students in various grade levels. The conditions for establishing a just community were described earlier on in this article and should be adhered to when implementing this model in elementary and middle schools. The process of a democratic society can be implemented in small groups or classroom or grade levels. By introducing dilemma discussion in the classroom, students should be adequately prepared to actively engage in moral reasoning dialogue when deliberating on issues affecting their educational environment. The issues that are discussed could center around problems, issues, or concerns that have caused some tension among the students, teachers, and staff at the school. Students may be hesitant at first to enforce rules when the just community approach is in place; however, they do "rise to the occasion after several community meetings" (Power et al., 1989, p.139). In their daily interactions with colleagues counselors and teachers should model the discussion techniques that they teach the students (Reimer et al., 1983). In addition, the values adopted among the students in their just community should also be actualized by practicing the newly acquired beliefs and behaviors in society (Murphy, 1988; Power, 1988; Rosenzweig, 1980). Middle school students, for example, could help elementary students establish a just community in their school. Children often listen and respond to teens and older youths rather than adults. This form of peer modeling would provide younger children with a positive figure they may wish to emulate.

SUMMARY

School counselors are in a unique position to effect change and participate in current movements that take a comprehensive approach to preparing youths for their future (Perry & Schwallie-Giddis, 1993). Programs in which students are provided an opportunity to be a part of a democratic just community and to actively engage in moral dilemma discussions have been positively affected behaviorally and psychologically. In many instances these students have become the promoters of instilling voices of reason and responsibility among our youth. The process of journal writing, reflective thought, dilemma discussion on moral issues, role-taking, and just community discussion groups provides students with an opportunity to find the tools to transform their environment and actively engage in the process of change for an altruistic society. Furthermore, the experience of participating in just communities could lead to caring relationships and moral commitment (Kohlberg, 1985). Structured group dialogue, which provides opportunities for students to vent their frustrations verbally without the use of gangs or physical retaliation, could become commonplace among today's youth. The effect of the moral development curriculum on the level of reasoning of one participant can be summarized in a poem written for the Human Ecology class memoirs.

Untitled
by
Sunny Lee

Oh! my sister
how can we argue over such superfluous things?
Even knowing that people are dying,
we are so wrapped up in our tedious traumas,
we don't want to open our eyes.
There are people out there dying of AIDS, hunger, violence,
how can we fight over such superfluous things?
Are we going to let our children see the world always black or white?
Isn't it time for us to come together in unity, under one belief, one body,
    one God?
Why are we always pointing the finger at him or her with different skin
    color?
Aren't we all created equal?
Even with affirmative action there's anger, discrimination, racism that's
    alive.
Why are we always complaining
about the injustices, inequality?
Let's speak up to the world,
not with guns or knives
but with understanding and less frustration.
Oh! my sister,
don't be discouraged if it doesn't work.
Don't start calling people
JAP, CHINK, SPIC, NIGGER, YANKEE . . .
Just be calm and try to understand them.
We are all the same regardless of color or race.
I love you not because of your color
but for who you are.
Don't change for me because of the society,
I love you just the way you are
regardless of your color.

APPENDIX

Kohlberg's Stages of Moral Development

Level I: The Preconventional Level

At this level, moral value resides in external, physical happenings (e.g., bad acts) or in physical needs (e.g., food to eat), rather than in either person or standards.

Stage 1: Obedience and punishment orientation
> Egocentric deference to superior power or prestige, or in a trouble-avoiding set. A moral decision is based on whether the person will be punished for the action.

Stage 2: Naively egoistic orientation
> Right action is based on instrumental hedonism. The person's attitude is based on a "selfish" or "how can I gain" motive, only occasionally satisfying others' needs.

Level II: The Conventional Level

At this level, moral value resides in performing good or right roles, in maintaining the conventional order, and in meeting the expectations of others.

Stage 3: Social conformity or good-boy orientation
> An orientation to approval, and to pleasing and helping others.

Stage 4: Authority, law or legal sanction, and social order maintaining orientation
> An orientation to doing one's duty, showing respect for authority, and maintaining the given social order. Individual makes the decision based on legal sanctions or law and order.

Level III: The Postconventional Level

At this level, moral value resides in conformity by the self to share (or sharable) standards, rights or duties.

Stage 5: Social contract based on principles or consequentialism
> There is a recognition of an arbitrary element or starting point in either rules or expectations, for the sake of agreement.

Stage 6: Conscience or universal ethical principles
> An orientation not only to actually ordained social rules but to those principles of choice that involve an appeal to the equality of human rights and respect for all human beings.

Adapted from *Value as the Aim of Education* (p.8), by N. A. Sprinthall & R. L. Mosher (1978). New York: Character Research Press.

CREATING A POSITIVE MORAL CLIMATE WITHIN THE PUBLIC SCHOOL CLASSROOM: AN APPLICATION OF MORAL REASONING THEORY TO PRACTICE

by J. T. Binfet, MA

Editor's Note: Each new generation of teachers must discover and test the applicability and "personal fit" of the educational theories and practices that they have studied in their teacher education program. J. T. Binfet shows how he is making many ideas associated with "open education" and with "just communities" his own. It is therefore no surprise that he listens to—and shares with us—the voices of his students as well.

Although research on Kohlberg's "just communities" has received much attention, descriptions of the application of Kohlberg's theory to elementary and junior high school settings is scant. Indeed, the specific practices in the elementary classroom that create the direct and indirect conditions necessary for moral development have not been clearly outlined or established. This paper describes how I apply my interpretation of Kohlberg's moral reasoning theory to my sixth and seventh graders.

Kohlberg (Kohlberg et al., 1984) postulates that the transition from preconventional to conventional reasoning (i.e., from stage 2 to 3) takes place between the ages of nine to thirteen. This transition from pre to conventional reasoning is most receptive to educational intervention. Specifically, the stimulation of moral reasoning can be fostered via moral discussions and the creation of a nurturing moral climate.

Kohlberg (in Galbraith, R. & Jones, T., 1976) argues that the development of moral reasoning is best fostered when the students have the opportunity to participate in an environment that is characterized by the following conditions:

* participation in group decision making;
* exposure to moral conflict;
* role-taking opportunities;
* exposure to a level of moral reasoning higher than their own;
* opportunity that allows the consideration of both fairness and morality.

Kohlberg (in Galbraith, R. & Jones, T., 1976) further differentiates between direct and indirect conditions. Discussion of a moral dilemma is an example of a direct condition. The indirect conditions include the climate, atmosphere, or ethos that characterize not only the individual classroom, but the school as a whole.

The strategies a teacher uses to create a nurturing learning environment are part of the "hidden curriculum" for many young children. For my sixth and seventh graders, I encourage awareness of, and participation in, the creation of the classroom environment.

The Physical Structure of the Classroom

The contents and appearance of our classroom reflect the interests of my students as well as myself. There are environmental posters on the walls, an aquarium of rescued "feeder" goldfish (petshop goldfish that are used as food for other fish), and numerous plants. The plants play an especially important role in creating a calm and natural environment for the students.

In my classroom students are allowed to sit where and with whom they choose. It is my belief that teachers do not truly know the friendship dynamics of the students well enough to determine with whom a child will work best. Students are asked to reflect on which of their classmates are fun to fool around with, and which are students with whom they think they can work well.

Just as the dynamics of student friendships change, so too does the seating arrangement. Most student groups have four to six participants, pairs of students and students sitting by themselves are rarer.

I give students feedback on how I feel their self-chosen groupings are working out, and encourage students that have selected teammates poorly, to reflect on whether and why they may need to move their desk. The seating arrangement is predominantly student governed, and so the layout of the classroom varies. Allowing students to sit where and with whom they choose sends the message that I, as their teacher, believe they are mature and responsible enough to make a decision that affects not only their learning potential, but also their perception of themselves as responsible adolescents.

First Name Basis

It is a common belief that having students address teachers as Mr. or Mrs. automatically assures a certain degree of respect for the teacher. I don't believe that, and I explain to my students that I am not on a pedestal merely because I am a teacher; we are on an equal level, but students and teachers have a distinctive job to do, and I outline my job as a teacher and theirs as a student very clearly. Using each others' first names helps us establish rapport and fosters productive work.

Greetings

Each morning when the students arrive, I make sure to establish eye contact and say hello to each student individually. I do the same at the end of the day. This may appear trivial, but it sends a clear message to the students that I acknowledge their presence and am glad to see them.

Random Assignment of Tasks

Students often complain that teachers regularly select their favorites for specific classroom activities or errands. In an attempt to combat favoritism—I keep a large goldfish bowl on my desk that holds the name of each student, written on a popsicle stick. Anytime someone needs to be selected, I shake the bowl and randomly choose a student. My name is also on a popsicle stick, so I stand ready to do the same chores I ask my students to do.

Personal Journals

Students are asked to keep a journal on a regular basis. The journal is a booklet in which students respond to personal and classroom issues, and voice opinions, questions and complaints. To give some structure to journal entries, I usually write a question on the board to which I encourage students to respond. Typical questions are:

* Describe your behavior, and the behavior of the class, when I was away and you had a substitute teacher.
* How is your group working and how could your work habits be improved?
* Evaluate the field trip we just went on, as well as your behavior on the bus.
* What did you do this weekend?

I read every journal entry and respond to each student individually and privately. I often use my comments in the journal as a means of regulating the classroom management problems. I may ask a student to explain his/her behavior. I also use the personal journal to congratulate or encourage students for work or for their behavior in class.

Students generally enjoy writing in their journals, and tell me things that are truly important to them. In essence, the journal serves as a running dialogue between myself and my students.

Students are expected to employ the same writing standards—such as using appropriate punctuation and paragraphs—in the journals as in all other written work. It merits noting, however, that the writing in the personal journal is never corrected or edited. This is not to say that I do not note, for myself, repeated spelling or grammatical errors, but I absolutely do not correct any of the text.

Here are examples of student journal entries and my response:

> Student: I didn't contribute to the sub having a terrible day. I helped her in the morning. I took in the people's permission slips and money for "Stop." I even (had) suggestions on how to get the class under control but she refused to listen to me. She said "No, this is my way," even though her way didn't work. She has very different teaching habits. A bit too different for some of us to handle. (Andrea, 7th grade)

> Teacher: I appreciate your trying to help the sub out. You certainly behaved responsibly. You must realize, Andrea, that working in an unfamiliar class such as ours can be a different experience for a substitute teacher. Once again, I appreciate your efforts to keep things in order. Thanks, Ty.

*   *   *   *   *

> Student: I would give myself a C+ or B– because I got up a lot and talked too much. We were always making noises with candy bags or talking. The whole class deserves a C or a B–. I have lots of hockey games in my life. But I wish you would ask me to read. (Bryan, 6th grade)

> Teacher: Bryan, I apologize for neglecting to ask you to read. I think partly it is because I felt you never enjoyed reading aloud and I didn't want to stress you by 'putting you on the spot.' Henceforth I will ask you to read. You have my word. Thanks for letting me know. Anything else I should know?

I have found the Personal Journal an effective means of communicating with students. It provides for the expression of feelings and ideas that they might not otherwise have the opportunity or comfort level to express when talking directly to the teacher.

Class Meetings

Whenever the need arises, we have a meeting to discuss and regulate classroom-related issues. In order that such meetings run smoothly, it is important that the expectations of the tone of such meetings be established prior to the beginning of discussion. Students are reminded that no put-downs are allowed, that students must speak one at a time, and are to remain respectful of their classmates and myself at all times. I instruct the class on how to disagree in a manner that focuses on the topic being discussed rather than on a personal attack of the student who raised the issue.

Moral Discussions

In addition to the classroom issues, we discuss controversial topics stemming from newspaper articles. I instruct the students that they may not "sit on the fence," but must take a stand on one side of the issue. I do this because I have found that discussion tends to stagnate otherwise. We spend a great deal of time talking about justifying points of view, rather than merely stating one's position. Frequently I ask students to take the perspective of a classmate, or to paraphrase a view expressed by a classmate.

Creating Moral Dilemmas

Students are asked to write their own dilemmas as part of our Language Arts Program. All dilemmas are written so as to adhere to the criteria established by Marvin Berkowitz (1991). Many of the submitted dilemmas, like the one quoted below, deal with peer pressure:

> Jack's Dilemma
> Jack is not a very cool person. He's actually quite a loser. So one day when the gang that used to beat him up decided to accept him into their group, Jack was really shocked. He thought about how cool the gang was but they also got into a lot of trouble, like smoking and drinking. Jack really wanted to be cool but he didn't know if it was worth getting into trouble over. Should Jack join the gang and be cool or should he go on being a loser and refuse the gang's offer? (Murray, 7th grade)

Report Cards

At each reporting period students are asked to write two report cards, one for themselves and one for me, their teacher. Blank report cards, identical to the ones usually sent home to parents, are used and students are instructed on how to follow the format that addresses both social and academic achievement. Once again, this practice provides an opportunity for students to reflect, in writing, on their own achievement and on their relationship with me as their teacher. For me it is invaluable to gain insight into the students' perceptions of our shared reality. Here is an excerpt from a seventh grader's self-assessment:

> Rosaline has been working very well in class. She does well in French and English. At times, she is difficult to handle, but only when she

is wrongly accused of a bad deed. She is very helpful and cooperative. She is kind and respectful to others in her group and her class. Overall, I think Rosaline has worked very well this term.

Teachers who encourage students to evaluate them must keep in mind that students can often be brutally frank when assessing teacher performance and competence. Such evaluation is only possible when a safe and nurturing environment exists in the class. Feedback on teacher performance can be shared with the whole class in summarized form. The following examples illustrate typical "Teacher Report Cards":

Ty, you are a good teacher but you should keep the chatting with Mr. Smith and Mr. Jones to a minimum. Your work habits are fine. I suggest you try to print a little neater. In gym, there are people who are not as athletic in some things as others. Don't forget that. (7th grade)

Ty is a good teacher most of the time. But sometimes he gets kids mixed up and the kid who did nothing gets in trouble for nothing. Ty is always clear on instructions. Ty is always fair like how he gives us warnings. Ty manages the classroom really well because students hardly ever get into trouble. (6th grade)

Not only are the "Teacher Report Cards" invaluable to me for insight into how students perceive me, they also send the message to students that their opinions are valued and play a role in shaping the direction of the class.

The benefits of a positive moral classroom climate are many. Many discipline problems disappear when classroom management is a matter of shared responsibility. Allowing students a variety of avenues through which their voice and views are heard, respected, and valued, contributes directly and indirectly to their moral development.

SOCIAL AND MORAL DEVELOPMENT THROUGH COMPUTER USE: A CONSTRUCTIVIST APPROACH

by Batya Friedman
Mills College

Abstract: This paper draws on a constructivist perspective on social and moral development to examine how children's social interactions with computer technologies can be used to promote their moral education. Four types of social interactions with computers are emphasized: those that facilitate discussion of social and moral issues, cooperation and peer resolution of conflicts, perspective taking, and assumption of responsibility for consequences of actions. Methods are discussed that encourage these types of social interactions through the overall social organization of the computer classroom and through individual computer activities. (Keywords: computer uses in education, cooperation, moral development, social development.)

While popular views of the computer nerd—the isolated "brainy" youngster who relates better to a machine than to people—persist and have some validity, recent research suggests that computer use can be an intensely social activity (Becker, 1984; Friedman, 1988; Hawkins, Sheingold, Gearhart, & Berger, 1982; Littlejohn, Ross & Gump, 1984; Muller & Perlmutter, 1985; Turkle, 1984; and for a review, Webb, 1988). This paper draws on a constructivist perspective to examine this activity, taking up the issue of how children's social interactions with computer technologies can be used to promote their social and moral development. From this perspective four types of social interactions with computers are of particular interest: those that facilitate discussion of social and moral issues (Blatt & Kohlberg, 1975; Nucci, 1982), cooperation and peer resolution of conflicts (Devries & Goncu, 1987; Piaget, 1932), perspective taking (Selman, 1980), and assumption of responsibility for consequences of actions (Kohlberg, 1980, 1985). The following discussion develops ideas on the ways educators can encourage these types of social interactions both through the social organization of the computer classroom and through specific activities that can be done on computers.

THE SOCIAL ORGANIZATION OF THE COMPUTER CLASSROOM

Before specifically discussing the social organization of the computer classroom, a few words need to be said about self-government in a noncomputer classroom, for the former draws much from the latter. As described in detail elsewhere (Kohlberg, 1980, 1985; Power, 1988), students in classrooms organized around student self-governance determine many of the policies that regulate their own classroom activities and thus gain experience with democratic and consensus decision-making processes. Moreover, through assuming responsibility for their policy decision, students confront the relationship between their policy decisions and the resulting consequences affecting themselves and other students. The teacher's primary role in a student self-governing classroom is to facilitate the self-governance process; for example, to help students become aware of and understand issues when they arise, ensure that all students have an opportunity to voice their views in policy-setting meetings, and help students articulate and clarify their views. Teachers as members of the self-governing community may also act as advocates, influencing both the selection of issues for which students set policy and the range of acceptable agreements.

The basic tenets of students self-governance can readily carry over to the computer classroom (see also Friedman, 1986). After all, on some dimensions computers simply represent an additional tool and resource that gets used and allocated like other tools and resources in a classroom, such as typewriters, reference books, or musical instruments. For example, consider a classroom where a computer is used to set up an electronic bulletin board that students can use to discuss issues, share information, leave messages for particular friends, and so forth. Like a regular bulletin board, the computer bulletin board raises several policy issues that need to be determined. These include when information on the bulletin board can be read, who can add information, what type of information will be allowed, and who will remove information and under what circumstances.

However, two unique aspects of computer use help to provide unique circumstances for students' social and moral development. First, the consequences of actions involving computer use are often "invisible" or at least difficult to identify (e.g., does making one copy of one piece of school software for performing school computer work at home cause any harm?). Second, given the newness of computer technologies, many consequences of computer use are initially unknown or unintended (e.g., creating a program that unknowingly acts as a computer virus on a class computer). It is in part because of these ambiguities that students, like members of society at large, find themselves in particularly challenging circumstances when establishing computer policies. For example, in determining a privacy policy for students' use of electronic mail, little relevant social policy pertaining to electronic information as mail exists at the societal level, let alone at the school level. Thus, like philosophers and lawmakers, students must draw on their fundamental understandings of privacy rights to develop specific policies for this new situation. In turn, circumstances like these provide opportunities for students not only to develop morally but also to make decisions about a socially and computationally powerful technology, and thus to mitigate a belief many people hold that one is controlled by, rather than in control of, technology.

While the classroom structure of self-governance supports students as they address these unique circumstances involving computers, teachers also play an important role. Most notably, teachers extend themselves as facilitators. For example, teachers can help students identify the less salient consequences of actions mediated by computer technologies, such as who is affected by an action involving the technology and how that individual is affected. Further, drawing on research by Turiel (1983), Nucci (1982), and Friedman (1989), teachers can help students to distinguish between the moral and pragmatic components within their own computer use. For example, when considering a privacy policy to regulate access to student computer files, moral concerns for protecting students' privacy need to be coordinated with pragmatic concerns stemming from educational goals (e.g., if teachers are to evaluate students' work and provide feedback they must be able to access that work). Teachers can help students recognize both types of concerns and their relative importance. Thus a possible privacy policy for student computer files might allow teachers and the student author, but no one else, to examine the contents of a student's file. This policy both serves the pragmatic ends of education and protects the student's privacy from other students. While perhaps a seemingly unusual privacy policy, note, for instance, that this particular student policy parallels, at least in practice, one in use in some newsrooms, where editors electronically browse and copy reporters' computer files that contain stories in progress (Kling & Iacono, 1989).

When extending student self-governance to computer classrooms, teachers also face problems of when and how to establish boundaries for students' decisions. Two general situations arise. In the first, the computer technology and its effects are contained within the classroom or school. Here, as in nontechnological environments, the general guideline that no individual be overly harmed as a result of the student-determined policy suffices. The consensus or democratic process functions as an initial, though not necessarily foolproof, check against the implementation of such overly harmful policies. This situation would be the case for, say policies concerning the ownership and privacy of student computer files or the management of information on a school-wide electronic bulletin board. For example, precisely because only students are affected, a student-generated policy to permit copying of student-authored software would be within acceptable bounds, assuming that all students participated in the policy's development. In fact, students might favor such a policy for their own programs, because trading and modifying computer code can be an efficient and exciting method to master programming skills.

In the second situation, students' computer use extends beyond that of the classroom and school. The use of commercial computer software and telecommunications linking the school to the outside community are two common examples. In these circumstances, the effect on individuals outside the school must be considered, and, as the individuals affected are not present to represent themselves, the teacher must ensure that students' policies do not impact negatively on these individuals' interests. Thus a student-generated policy to make unauthorized copies of commercial software to sell to other students at the school would be outside the boundary of acceptable policies because it financially harms the programmer who is not present to agree or disagree.

SPECIFIC ACTIVITIES ON THE COMPUTER

With a focus on promoting students' social and moral development, let us turn now from the social organization of the computer classroom to individual computer activities. Some experience with cooperating and the value of cooperation can be introduced with computer simulations or games in which the most successful playing strategies involve cooperating with others. For example, in *The Other Side*, a computer simulation by Tom Snyder Productions, students work in teams to build the economy of their own country while working toward building a bridge (representing peace) between their own and a rival country. To succeed best with both goals, the two teams, both with independent and mutual interests, must at times evolve a cooperative strategy. Moreover, within their teams, students must develop this strategy through negotiation with peers. A similar emphasis can be found in *Our Town Meeting*, also by Tom Snyder Productions, where three town agencies (each composed of a group of students) with agency-specified goals find that cooperative strategies are ultimately most effective for all agencies involved.

While also encouraging cooperation, another genre of computer activities that additionally fosters peer discussion and peer resolution of conflicts entails the distribution of labor among a group of students who share a common goal involving the technology. Typically, students are given rough guidelines within which they must negotiate the division and coordination of labor for the group, as well as monitor and resolve disputes concerning the equity of individual work and contribution. For example, in the context of a computer programming course a group of students might be given the goal of writing one large collaborative computer program. In this situation students must decide what program modules to create, who will take major responsibility for each module, how to fit the modules together, and, once together, how to remove the errors. In the process of negotiating these "programming" issues, students have significant opportunity for co-operation and discussion, and this peer dialogue plays a necessary role in ensuring students' success with their endeavor. Similarly, given the shared goal to collect data in a microcomputer-based science lab (where the computer functions as a instrument to aid with data collection), several measurements, such as temperature and elapsed time, might need to be made simultaneously. As a group, students must decide who will have responsibility for taking each measurement and coordinating the record keeping. Discussions among peers about how to divide up tasks, how to ensure all measurements are made, and what to do if there are missing or inaccurate measurements, are likely to occur. Like the collaborative programming example above, this activity provides opportunities for peer discussion, cooperation, and resolution of differences of opinion. Moreover, these collaborative computer-based activities largely parallel the working conditions of many technical professionals when they work with computers.

Classroom computer use can also enhance perspective taking by introducing students to alternative perspectives through the use of computer simulations. Well-designed computer simulations allow students to explore hypothetical situations from multiple perspectives and to follow different courses of action for each. Such simulations can also help students to understand the consequences of their actions for themselves, other individuals, and the larger society. For example, a simulation on the topic of school bullies might allow students to interact with fictional characters (all peers) in the roles of bully, bully's target, bully's friend, and uninvolved observer. For each character, the simulation might highlight the character's motivations, concerns, and assumptions pertaining to an instance of bullying. The program would allow students to investigate multiple courses of action for each character as well as the character's perspective on that course of action. Thus, students could explore what happens when the bully's target decides to run away, stay and tolerate the bullying, or stay and fight back.

While such computer simulations highlight the possibility of alternative perspectives for a given situation and the relationship among individuals' decisions, actions, and consequences, a word of caution about their limitations is needed. Specifically, no computer simulation can fully escape program bias. That is, at some level, normative positions determined by the program designer are embedded in the simulation. For instance, in the example about bullying, the simulation necessarily provides specific consequences that result from the target's decision to run from the bully. Perhaps the consequences are jeering and teasing from family and peers for acting as a coward, or perhaps praise for wisely assessing and avoiding a dangerous situation, or perhaps some combination of both. Each of these possible consequences, which contributes to each character's perspective, may or may not mesh with the student's own experiences or cultural expectations. Thus, the simulation faces two problems. One is providing a single "right" consequence for a given decision and action; the second is providing consequences that lack cultural or experiential validity for the student. Both of these problems can be partially overcome by designing the simulation so that it provides multiple outcomes whenever possible and links these outcomes to specific social contexts. A simulation so designed, in addition to providing access to alternative perspectives and clarifying the relationship among decisions, actions, and consequences, can be used to help students examine how a principle may lead to divergent behaviors depending on the social context. For example, a principle of nonviolence could lead a student to stand her ground without physically retaliating against the bully or, in a situation likely to escalate to nonconstructive violence, to physically leave the area of conflict.

While computer simulations provide access to alternative perspectives through hypothetical situations, telecommunications put students in direct contact with peers of widely different backgrounds. With technologies designed to support remote communication and social interaction, such as electronic mail and bulletin boards, students can bridge cultural (e.g., Afro-American, Asian, Hispanic), economic (e.g., lower to upper class), and regional (e.g., inner city, suburban, rural) boundaries to share ideas, discuss issues of common interest, and collaborate on academic projects. Using electronic mail, for example, students from two geographically distant classrooms might collaborate on joint projects, such as a science experiment or newspaper. In the case of a joint newspaper, students from both classrooms might write editorials on the same national issue, such as federal support for farmers or environmental controls to highlight regional perspectives. These editorials, reflecting students' regional views, could be printed side by side in the paper. Furthermore, students in one classroom could act as editors for students in the other classroom. In so doing, students will need to consider how their criticism will be perceived by the students receiving it and how to accommodate different viewpoints in places of disagreement.

Similarly, electronic bulletin boards can be used to put students into contact with other students and with members of the larger electronic information community. To promote peer communication, an electronic bulletin board could be set up between two remote classrooms, which would allow students to share and discuss ideas on any topic initiated by teachers or students. Extending the earlier discussion of electronic bulletin boards, students from both classrooms can collectively determine policies for how information on the electronic bulletin board should be managed. Concerning communication with the electronic information community, students can participate in existing community electronic bulletin boards on topics of relevance. For instance, in the course of studying the AIDS epidemic, students might access the AIDS bulletin board in San Francisco to discuss with those inflicted with the disease their perspectives on the epidemic, including issues such as job discrimination and inadequate health services. Thus, through direct interactions with others via telecommunications, students gain opportunities for insight into cultural, economic, regional, and situational differences.

A CLOSING NOTE

As with any piece of curriculum, specific computer activities designed to support student interactions and cooperation are not fool-proof. They will fall short of their goals in the hands of a teacher who prefers, for example, a quiet classroom, individual student work, and limited student decision-making. Granted, at times it will be appropriate for students to work on specific computer activities by themselves. However, even in these situations individual activities can still occur in the overarching context of a classroom organization, such as self-governance, that supports students' social interactions in their use of the technology.

DISCOVERING THE NONINTELLECTUAL SELF: ABRAHAM H. MASLOW'S HUMANISTIC PSYCHOLOGY

by Sam Reese
Elementary General Music Teacher
Iowa City Community Schools, Iowa City, Iowa

One of the most intense of the current debates in education concerns the problem of formulating a view of man. Professional educators have discovered that before we can build an effective educational program, we must articulate a view of man, so that our educational approach will be consistent with the nature of man and his needs. Neither the behavioristic view of men nor the Freudian view seems to be appropriate for the values emphasized by music education. But Abraham H. Maslow set forth a view of man that seems to be amazingly consistent with the goals and purposes of music education. We music educators might profit a great deal from a careful study of the basic premises of Maslow's humanistic psychology.

The proponents of the various views of man base their arguments on the literature of three basic schools of psychology—behaviorism, Freudianism, and humanism. Behaviorism, through its investigation of the external forces that affect man's behavior, has produced a view of man that is primarily mechanical and deterministic. The behaviorists maintain that man is basically a product of external influences. Thus, there is little room in the behavioristic view of man for subjective experiences—experiences that cannot be measured, predicted, or accounted for by a physical explanation. The behaviorists are rarely interested in feelings of freedom, joy, love, or purpose in life or in the perception of beauty, value, and meaning. Nor do they consider these experiences essential to an overall view of man. Behaviorism says that man is controlled, that he is not free.

Freudianism, on the other hand, has delved into the deepest, innermost realms of the psyche. All experiences that are not a product of the ego or the intellect are considered diseased or pathological. For Freudians, the subconscious and the unconscious aspects of the psyche are dangerous and must ultimately be brought under control by man's intellectual or egoistic capacities.

A school of thought is now developing in psychology that offers an alternative to the views of man set forth by behaviorism and Freudianism. This new approach is being called humanistic psychology, or the Third Force. According to Maslow, who helped to conceive and nourish this alternative, humanistic psychology is an attempt to account for the "higher-order elements of the personality such as altruism and dignity, or the search for truth and beauty." It is possible that humanistic psychology can provide a firm rationale for the continued or increased study of music in our public schools by showing that the "search for truth and beauty" is a necessary and integral part of man's total psychological make-up.

A major theme of Maslow and the other humanistic psychologists is that aesthetic perceiving and creating should be a central aspect of life and education rather than a peripheral one. "Maslow believes that the development of truly healthy individuals and of a healthy society demands an important place for 'preverbal, ineffable, metaphorical, primary process, concrete experience, intuitive and aesthetic types of cognition.'" Thus, in contrast to the behavioristic or the Freudian view, Maslow's view of man tends to be holistic, placing as much importance on the nonintellectual, emotional, and sensual aspects of man as on his intellectual or rational capacities. This view of man implies that aesthetic, emotional, and nonintellectual experiences should be as much a part of education as the training of the intellect.

During recent years, Western education has heavily emphasized the intellectual aspects of man almost to the exclusion of emotional, intuitive, and aesthetic experiences. A typical day for an elementary school student includes training in such disciplines as math, social studies, language arts, and science, with perhaps short sessions of music, art, or physical education. This over-emphasis on the intellect has been largely a result of the overwhelming influence of science on modern Western culture. Maslow developed some insights into epistemology by investigating the psychology of science and analyzing the way science has affected Western man's view of reality and, therefore, Western educational philosophy and practice.

Maslow drew distinctions between two basic kinds of knowledge, calling them experiential knowledge and spectator knowledge. He described experiential knowledge as "experiencing . . . something in its own right and its own nature. This experiencing, for instance, of a person or of a painting, can grow deeper, richer, more complex and yet can remain within the object that one is trying to understand better." This is basically the way we know or understand a piece of music or a work of art. We attempt to understand the work in its own right and do not seek an external or utilitarian reason to value the work. When we know a composition in an experiential manner, we are seized, grasped, and absorbed by it. There is a breakdown of the boundaries of our egos and intellects. We no longer experience a separation between us (the subject) and the composition (the object).

Spectator knowledge, on the other hand, implies that the knower is removed from the known. This kind of knowledge is usually called intellectual, rational, objective, analytical, or conceptual. Maslow gave this slightly demeaning description of spectator knowledge: "It means looking at something that is not you, not human, not personal, something independent of you the perceiver. It is something to which you are a stranger, a bystander, a member of the audience. You the observer are, then, really alien to it, uncomprehending and without sympathy and identification. . . ."

Maslow felt that for our time and situation a more experiential, receptive style of perception needs to be stressed. He wrote, "For the moment we intellectuals in the West who have heavily and exclusively overvalued abstractness in our picture of reality, even to the point of synonymizing them, had better redress the balance by stressing concrete, esthetic, phenomenological, non-abstracting perceiving of all the aspects of reality, including the useless portions of it."

In this statement, Maslow implied that the orthodox consciousness of Western man—the way Western man sees and experiences himself and the world around him—is a severely diminished reality. Theodore Roszak, another spokesman for the new humanism, has pointed out that ". . . our conscious relations with the world have become almost exclusively those of a spectator looking on and listening in from a hypothetical vantage point which has the feeling of lying outside the experience." Because of the influence of scientific objectivity on our culture, we no longer have any sense of participation or involvement in the world around us or in our own lives. We not only feel removed from our environment but also sense alienation from the nonintellectual and irrational parts of ourselves. Western man has forgotten that what science can measure is actually only a small portion of what man can know. Roszak has said, "There are . . . other kinds of knowledge, those born of sensuous penetration, loving participation, ecstacy, transcendent aspiration. But that way lies art, joy, wisdom, salvation . . ."—not science. It is time we realize that the scientific ideal of objectivity has been carried too far and has contributed to our common disease of alienation. As artists and educators, we can use the powerful ability of music to bring about nonintellectual, intuitive, experimental knowledge. Through music, we can help our children experience the involved type of knowledge characteristic of the aesthetic experience.

The scientific act of knowing is the forcing of everything personal out and away from our experiencing. As Roszak has pointed out, "It is no mere coincidence that this devouring sense of alienation from nature and one's fellow man—and from one's own essential self—becomes the endemic anguish of advanced industrial societies. The experience of being a cosmic absurdity, a creature obtruded into the universe without purpose, continuity or kinship, is the psychic price we pay for scientific 'enlightenment' and technological prowess."

Because of the scientific ideal of objectivity, we have ceased to be whole persons. We have forgotten that we are more than an intellectual and logical apparatus, that we are also capable of feeling and sensing and participating directly in the world. However, there are those who are saying that science is too narrow and that we must begin investigating and reevaluating other ways to know and experience.

Many wise remedies have been offered for the sickness caused by our scientific objectivity. Maslow called for a "hierarchical integration" of many modes of knowing. He felt we should balance both experiential and spectator knowledge, being careful not to let either type of knowledge become dominant. But since spectator knowledge is currently stressed heavily in Western culture, we must now begin to create an equality between the two ways of knowing. Maslow said, "In our culture and at this point in history, it is necessary to redress the balance in favor of spontaneity, the ability to be expressive, passive, unwilled, trusting in process other than will and control, unpremeditated, creative . . ."

It is the ability of aesthetic experiences to help create new, nonintellectual, experiential ways of knowing that make music and art education so important for our times. Aesthetic experiences can play a major role in developing a more experiential style of perception. Fully experiencing a work of art often requires receptivity, a surrendering of the ego, and a restraint from intruding or interfering with the work of art. Such experiences force us to use other parts of ourselves than our intellect. According to Maslow, "You can listen to organ music judiciously, calmly examining it to hear how good it is and whether it is worth the money you paid for the ticket. Or you can suddenly get caught up by it and become the music and feel it pulse through your insides, so that you are not in some other place. If you are dancing and the rhythm 'gets you,' you can slip over to being inside the rhythm. You can identify with the rhythm. You can become its willing instrument."

Because of a widespread inability to perceive experientially, the quality of life in this country often becomes cold and alienated. One of the solutions called for more and more insistently is that our schools place more emphasis on the arts and aesthetic experiences. The current heavy emphasis in our public schools on an intellectual education for our children only promotes the continuation of a narrow consciousness and a rigid, alienated lifestyle. As Maslow said, ". . . if we hope for our children that they will become full human beings and that they will move toward actualizing the potentialities that they have, then, as nearly as I can make out, the only kind of education in existence today that has any kind of faint inkling of such goals is art [aesthetic] education."

Maslow's psychology implies that we, as music educators, have an important mission to carry out for our times. Our task is to help balance the intellectual education of our children with badly needed nonintellectual experiences. Maslow pointed out that music and rhythm and dancing are excellent ways of moving towards the discovery of one's nonintellectual self. These experiences put a person in touch with his body. "We are built in such a fashion that this kind of trigger (music, rhythm, dancing), this kind of stimulation, tends to do all kinds of things to our autonomic nervous systems, endocrine glands, to our feelings, and to our emotions."

Many music educators are beginning to use a eurythmic approach more extensively in their teaching—an approach that attempts to create a connection between the child's body and experiences with music. During eurythmic activities, the child learns to respond physically to music, feeling the music in a way that reaches deeper than mere surface understanding. Through eurythmics, the child feels his whole physical self become involved with sound, not just his intellect.

Many people feel that we have lost touch with our bodies and that our experiencing has become too "head-oriented." We have forgotten how to experience and respond with our whole bodies. Roszak has written, "At once we see what is most repressed—and surely more so in our culture than in any other—is the body's organic nature, which is the body's whole reality. . . . Our head experiences in the mode of number, logic, mechanical connection; our body in the mode of fluid process, intuitive adaption; it sways to an inner purposive rhythm. . . ."

The recent movement to increase the number of creative experiences offered to our children is another attempt to develop more experiential, nonintellectual modes of knowing. Creativity has its roots in deeper parts of ourselves than we normally exercise in our everyday intellectual, egoistic consciousness. It is during the creative experiences, when the generally unused intuitive and nonintellectual parts of our selves are exercised, that our selves are most integrated. In his writings, Maslow emphasized many times the value of creativeness to a healthy, human life. Roszak has pointed out that ". . . life becomes grey indeed if they (creative energies) cannot be exercised, since, to an important degree, we come to know ourselves and to orient ourselves morally and metaphysically through the projection of freely imaginative contents. Traditionally, such projections have brought much wisdom up with them out of the depths of the psyche."

Music educators have been an important force in bringing about a more creative approach to education. Typical creative experiences in elementary music include creating new words to an old tune, creating short original songs, creating rhythmic and melodic ostinatos to songs and recordings, creating and making original scores for sound composition, and improvising melodies and rhythms. Maslow placed particular importance on improvisational types of experiences. He emphasized the importance of the primary process level of creativity—the beginning, inspiration, insight stages of creativity. This is the stage of creativity where the intellectual, controlling ego is left behind and the deeper realms of the psyche emerge into consciousness. Since the improvisational exercise demands "on-the-spot" creativity, there is no time for careful selection or control by the intellect, and more spontaneous faculties must be brought into action. Therefore, improvisational experiences must provide means for exercising the nonintellectual parts of the child's psychic make-up and contribute to the making of a more complete human being.

The psychology of Abraham Maslow has strong implications for music educators. Maslow's struggle to create an alternative to behaviorism and Freudianism and to provide a healthy acceptance of the irrational and nonintellectual in our view of man has resulted in an ever-increasing recognition of the importance of aesthetic perceiving and experiencing. Many people are becoming aware that it is important for modern man to break out of the bounds of our diminished, desacralized, scientific view of reality. We must begin developing new ways of knowing and experiencing if we are going to reduce the extent of our alienation of ourselves and the world around us. The arts provide an important means for attacking this problem. Maslow's psychology should provide music educators with a sense of a crucial mission to be accomplished—providing healthy, feeling-ful, nonintellectual experiences for our children so they can become whole persons instead of incomplete, alienated intelligences.

MASLOW'S CONCEPT OF PEAK EXPERIENCE EDUCATION: IMPOSSIBLE MYTH OR POSSIBLE MISSION?

by Nancy Wilgenbusch, Ph.D.
College of Saint Mary
Omaha, Nebraska

All of us reading this relate in some manner to the educational process which impacts upon the person wishing to become a teacher. Teaching itself is a serious endeavor, but teaching teachers to teach is of frightening importance. Margurger once said, "If we take ourselves too seriously, we jeopardize our sanity. If we don't take ourselves seriously enough, we jeopardize our mission." I'm more concerned today about our mission than about our often discussed sanity.

I have chosen a very familiar person's work to illuminate; one whose writings are well known and highly respected. His efforts in behalf of humanistic psychology and the resultant need theory, are in the repertoire of virtually all teachers. However, one concept postulated by Abraham Maslow has been insufficiently examined—the concept of peak experiences in education.

Maslow was not an educator in the true sense of the word—rather he was a psychologist.

Maslow, writing in the 1930's, had two distinct psychological camps to choose from. The dominant fields of personality theory were freudianism and behaviorism. Maslow's contemporaries were aligned in one camp or the other. Maslow actually ended up rejecting both stances. In a conversation with Maslow, Mary Hall related his thoughts, "I wanted to prove that human beings are capable of something grander than war, and prejudice and hatred. I wanted to make science consider all the problems that nonscientists have been handling—religion, poetry, values, philosophy, art."

Maslow felt that these two positions, freudianism and behaviorism,

220

should be integrated into the "whole" truth. The result was the third force psychology. Maslow postulated, "There is now emerging over the horizon a new conception of human sickness and of human health, a psychology that I find so thrilling and so full of wonderful possibilities that I yield to the temptation to present it publicly even before it is checked and confirmed, and before it can be called reliable scientific knowledge."

Maslow defines a need as ". . . namely that its absence produces illness." He enlarged this definition as he described a basic need as a characteristic which:

1. absence breeds illness
2. presence prevents illness
3. restoration cures illness
4. unmet state leads the deprived person to attempt to meet it over other satisfactions.

Other principles involved in his unique need theory include:

1. The human being is motivated by a number of basic needs which are species-wide, apparently unchanging and genetic or instinctual in origin.
2. Needs are the true inner nature of the human species, but they are weak, easily distorted, and overcome by incorrect learning, habit, or tradition.
3. The higher need is a later phyletic or evolutionary development.
4. Higher needs are later ontogenetic developments.
5. The higher the need the less imperative it is for sheer survival, the longer the gratification can be postponed, and the easier it is for the need to disappear permanently.
6. Living at the higher need level means greater biological efficiency, greater longevity, less disease, better sleep, appetite, etc.
7. Higher needs are less urgent subjectively.
8. Higher need gratifications produce more desirable subjective results, i.e., more profound happiness, serenity, and richness of the inner life.
9. Pursuit and gratification of higher needs represent a general healthward trend, a trend away from psychopathology.
10. The higher need has more preconditions.
11. Higher needs require better outside conditions to make them possible.
12. A greater value is usually placed upon the higher need than upon the lower by those who have been gratified in both.
13. The lower needs are far more tangible, more localized and more limited than are the higher needs.
14. The inner nature (need structure) of man is good or neutral rather than bad.
15. The needs exist in a hierarchy.

Maslow's description of the seven basic categories of needs are found in detail in his original writings. These categories represent Maslow's basic need theory but later, as the result of further research, he added a concept of growth or what he called Being-values or B-values. These are higher needs and are active as meta-motivators. These values are:

1. Wholeness	8. Beauty
2. Perfection	9. Goodness
3. Completion	10. Uniqueness
4. Justice	11. Effortlessness
5. Aliveness	12. Playfulness
6. Richness	13. Truth, Honesty
7. Simplicity	14. Self-Sufficiency

Maslow's later research continued to reflect his firm belief in the transcendent nature of man, and while his mission was not defined in terms of education, he eventually was persuaded to draw some educational implications of the humanistic psychologies. Maslow stated, "We speak then of a self, a kind of intrinsic nature which is very subtle, which is not conscious, which has to be sought for, and which has to be uncovered and then built upon, actualized, taught, educated. The job of the (teacher) is to help a person find out what's already in him rather than to reinforce him or shape or teach him into a prearranged form, which someone else has decided upon in advance, a priori."

Maslow has described two types of learning (and therefore two types of teaching) extrinsic learning and intrinsic learning. The extrinsic learning is the predominant type in our educational system. It focuses upon the "impersonal or arbitrary associations." The teacher decides what is important to learn and any pay off the student hopes to get will have to reflect this. As Maslow puts it, "In this sense the learning is extrinsic to the learner, extrinsic to the personality, and is extrinsic also in the sense of collecting association, conditionings, habits, or modes of action." The obvious question becomes one of whether anything can actually be taught or learned if the process remains a passive one for the student. Maslow went on to say, "This kind of learning too easily reflects the goals of the teacher and ignores the values and ends of the learner himself. It is also fair, therefore, to call such learning amoral."

The second type of learning is a rarer type, seldom to be seen or practiced in our modern classrooms. This type of learning explores the intrinsic selves, uncovers basic identities, values and learnings. It involves people in truth making. The experiences include those in which we learn who we are, what we value, what we are committed to.

As teacher educators, we must be involved in helping the teacher examine the differences between these two types of learning and somehow become instrumental in helping them make the gigantic "leap of faith" out of "reality" into "realness."

The key to this end, lies in the concept of peak-experience education. Dennis and Powers in writing about consummatory (peak) experiences state that Maslow saw peak experiences, "basically as moments of intense joy and insight. Such experiences are characterized by a temporary loss of a sense of time, space, and self awareness. Once it is over, a person has the conviction that something valuable and important has happened."

The peak experience is a very unique happening. The following are distinguishing features of peak experiences.

1. The universe is perceived as all of one piece, and the individual feels he belongs in it—everything seems to "hang together."

2. These moments are characterized by a particular kind of cognition which Maslow calls "Being cognition" (B-cognition). The person, in a sense, surrenders and submits himself to the experience. An example Maslow offers of this type is that of a mother giving her undivided attention in loving ecstasy to her newborn infant. By repeated examination the mother becomes conscious of the richness of every detail in regard to her child in a many-sided awareness.

3. Perception in the peak experience is childlike in that the experience continues to be as fresh and as beautiful as if it were the very first time.

4. The experience is felt as a self-validating moment which carries its own intrinsic values with it. The person, for example, may consider it so valuable as to make life worth-while by its occasional occurrence.

5. An absence of projecting human purpose on the object of perception further characterizes such experiences. The experience is welcomed as an end in itself rather than a means experience. The state brought on, therefore, by such happenings is so delightful that the individual is not concerned about whether it leads to anything further or not.

6. A person undergoing the experience feels an unusual sense of time-lessness and spacelessness. Reality is thus perceived, "Under the aspect of eternity." The individual, for instance, can feel a day passing as if it were only a few minutes.

7. The whole of reality in such moments is perceived as only good and desirable, with never an element of evil or pain. The person at the peak may be described as godlike in contemplating the whole of being and in seeing evil as a product of limited or selfish vision and understanding.

8. Conflicts and inconsistencies are resolved in the experience. The person himself becomes more integrated by a momentary loss of fear, anxiety, defense, and control. He becomes more his real self and feels that he is the creative center of his own universe.

9. Through continued peak experiences, the individual becomes progressively more loving, honest, and motivated.

Maslow describes peak experiences as, "An episode, or a spurt in which the powers of the person come together in a particularly efficient and intensely enjoyable way, and in which he is more integrated and less split, more open for experience, more idiosyncratic, more perfectly expressive or spontaneous, or fully functioning, more creative, more humorous, more ego-transcending, more independent of his lower needs, etc. He becomes in these episodes more truly himself, more perfectly actualizing his potentialities, closer to the core of his Being, more fully human."

EDUCATIONAL IMPLICATIONS

The implications of peak experiences and their relationship to education are outlined as follows:

* Peak experiences are integral to a humanistic theory of teaching.
* Peak experiences can bring newness, excitement and enthusiasm to our classrooms.
* Peak experiences theory should be taught to student teachers.
* Time should be devoted in our education curricula for the purpose of discussing the ways to encourage the occurrences of peak experiences.

Maslow stated, "Using peak experiences as an intrinsic reward or goal at many points in education is a very real possibility, and congruent with the whole philosophy of the humanistic educator. At the very least, this new knowledge can help wean teachers away from their frequent uneasiness with, and even disapproval and persecution of these experiences. If they learn to value them as great moments in the learning process, moments in which both cognitive and personal growth take place simultaneously, then this value can be transmitted to the (student). He in turn is then taught to value rather than to suppress his greatest moments in illumination, moments which can validate and make worthwhile the more usual trudging and slogging and 'working through' of education."

Obviously, the aesthetic peak experience can't be summoned or forced to occur, rather the educational arena should be open to its occurrence and recognize the situation when it arises and most importantly, allow them to happen.

Orr and Miller have lamented about the emergent class of intellectuals who have learned to think without assent, who have become morally paralyzed knowing all the options, being able to explain the logic of each, and of understanding that the outcome depends on one's starting point. Thinking without assent actually refers to thinking without drawing any implications of what the idea represents, no good or bad, moral or immoral, right or wrong. These authors feel that thinking without assent is a moral pathology and that higher education's mission should speak to a reversal of this trend. Peak experiences are the highest, purest form of assent. The peak experience is the antithesis of this moral paralysis.

Writing in 1941, Sorokin observed that, "when a sensate society with its cult of experience and its exultation of cynicism enters the final period, the agents of change are the true believers who turn against jadedness and sophistication and who find a belief-filled place to stand. These change agents will be responsible for idealistic eras that will renew cultural energies."

Returning to a belief-filled place to stand requires an acknowledgement of the fully human responses to situations. These brief and valuable moments are peak-experiences.

Maslow writes, "esthetic perceiving and creating and esthetic peak-experiences are seen to be a central aspect of human life and of psychology and education rather than a peripheral one."

"We must learn to treasure the 'jags' of the child in school, his fascinations, absorptions, his persistent wide-eyed wonderings, his Diongsian enthusiasms. At the very least, we can value his more diluted raptures, his 'interests' and hobbies. They can lead to hard work, persistent, absorbed, fruitful, educative. And conversely, I think it is possible to think of the peak-experience, the experience of awe, mystery or of perfect completion, as the goal and reward of learning as well, its end as well as its beginning. If this is true for the great historians, mathematicians, scientists, musicians, philosophers, and all of the rest, why should we not try to maximize these students as sources of peak-experiences for the child as well?"

CURRICULUM COMPONENTS

Teacher education curricula needs to have components included which will help in developing this concept.

* Education method courses should include a segment on peak experience theory. This would involve a review of Maslow's and other key authors writings on peak experiences.

* In-class discussion and group work would focus next upon the identification and analysis of the student teachers' own peak experiences. Specifically, the following method is proposed:

   1. Have each student teacher write down on paper a brief description of examples of peak experiences they have had. Include the feelings that were felt during the peak experiences.

   2. Place these examples as given on a flip chart or overhead projector. List as many as the group wants to share.

   3. Next list the attributes that these experiences had in common. (For instance, the situation all "involved someone else," "weren't planned," "shared a sense of timelessness.") Place these on a flip chart also.

   4. Next ask the group to point out which of these attributes would or would not be valid for a classroom. (Experience has been that all of the attributes could be valid and appropriate for a classroom.)

   5. Ask the group to discuss how teachers could create opportunities
      or environments for these peak experiences to occur.

* Key elements of an environment conductive to the occurrence of peak
  experiences can be identified. Examples of these key elements are:
   1. Being aware of peak-experiences when they are happening.
   2. Be flexible in the classroom.
   3. Allow for interactive communication.
   4. Change the classroom environment to a discovery mode.
   5. Have a planned period of interaction which has no defined be-
      havioral objectives.
   6. Act as a role model which reacts with enthusiasm and insight.
   7. Be creative and encourage creativity.
   8. Allow for errors. People need an environment free from fear of
      making mistakes.
   9. Create a teaching environment which responds wholistically to
      the student. Relate to all needs of the learner.

Peak experiences are an important part of our lives. They give substance and direction to the necessary, more plodding, part of daily living.
These experiences are elusive and infrequent but as teachers we must be
aware of them as personal and professional motivators. Our teacher education curricula would be missing an important element without including a
focus upon peak experiences.

THE DEVELOPMENT OF THE EGO: IMPLICATIONS FOR EDUCATIONAL SETTINGS

by Helen M. Gore-Laird

When Cynthia, aged twenty and the mother of three young boys, entered a program for homeless single mothers, the counselor noted in her report that Cynthia was a bright young woman with the potential to succeed in the program. The counselor recorded in her notes that Cynthia needed an opportunity to receive job training in order to live independently. The program would provide Cynthia day care, job training, and an apartment to aid in her transition to independent living.

After Cynthia had been in the program a few months, the counselor noted that Cynthia often broke the rules of the program. When confronted with infraction allegations, Cynthia would lie to protect herself and her family. She would attempt to manipulate conversations and situations in order to divert attention from herself. Her manipulations were often designed to get her counselor and other staff members divided in their perception of the situation. Cynthia never saw herself as wrong. All blame for her actions was externalized. She expressed the belief that she was "perfect" at everything she did. She was the perfect student, the perfect client, and the perfect parent.

In counseling sessions, Cynthia would only give information that she thought the counselor wanted to hear. However, she often became argumentative and hostile when her views were challenged. Cynthia abided by the rules of the program when she felt it was to her advantage. For example, if she was asked to comply with the rules or lose her apartment, she complied.

Was Cynthia's behavior indicative of "mental illness," or was she exhibiting behavioral indicators of her developmental level? If one were to analyze Cynthia from a psychoanalytic point of view, one might say that she was exhibiting signs of borderline personality disorder. Otto Kernberg (1985), a psychoanalyst, would state that Cynthia was exhibiting a "weak ego." In Freud's psychosexual theory, her Ego would resort to defense mechanisms to cope with severe threats to the Id. Erik Erikson's theory of psychosocial development would trace her behavior to unfavorable crisis resolution of an earlier stage of development, thus compromising her ego strength. On the other hand, a developmental perspective, such as Loevinger's theory of ego development, would maintain that Cynthia was operating from a low level of ego development.

Loevinger's approach leads to the following questions. "What does the concept of the ego encompass?" "How is ego defined?" There are many ways to study and analyze the concept of ego which could provide answers to these questions. This paper will focus on Jane Loevinger's concept of the ego, the process through which the ego develops, and the identified stages of ego development. Finally, Loevinger's theory will be applied to educational settings.

LOEVINGER'S THEORY

Loevinger (1976) stated that the concept of ego development has origins in ancient Greek, Hebrew, and Hindu cultures. The use of the word "ego" in the English language can be traced back to 1789 (Webster, 1991). Most often the term "ego" is associated with Sigmund Freud. When the word Ego is described in terms of Freud's psychoanalytic theory, it is used in conjunction with the concepts of the Id and the Superego. The psychoanalytic conception of the ego is that of an organization or structure which interacts with reality and seeks to fulfill the Id's needs in a manner that is acceptable to the outside world. Loevinger (1976) departs from the psychoanalytic view that the ego is derived from the processes of frustration and renunciation of drives. Rather, she identifies with Alfred Adler's view that the ego derives from a spontaneous striving for self-realization. Like Adler, Loevinger understands the ego as a single function. For her, the ego is a master trait. The level of the ego at which one functions indicates how one faces problem-solving, how one forms opinions about the self and others, and how one makes meaning and sense out of life experiences.

Loevinger's (1987) theory has in common with the cognitive developmental theories of Piaget and Kohlberg the notion that thought is fundamentally structured rather than being an amorphous progression of concepts. Loevinger believes, as did Piaget and Kohlberg, that each person constructs his/her own cognitive framework from birth to death. The quality of reasoning associated with each structure or framework, not the specific elements within the framework, is the most important aspect of psychological development. In other words, it is more important to examine the manner in which a person reasons through a problem than to scrutinize the specific contents of the problem or its resolution.

Loevinger adheres to the argument that cognitive development (as described by Piaget) is necessary but not sufficient for ego development. In other words, higher levels of cognitive development are necessary but not sufficient to achieve a higher level of ego development. For example, one may attain formal operational logic but still operate from a lower level of ego development than would be indicated by that level of cognitive ability.

The ego is an abstract concept rather than a real entity which can be located, touched, and physically examined. Although Loevinger's concept of ego development is abstract, it is related to and based upon observation of behavioral traits. However, for Loevinger (1976), the ego cannot be studied from the perspective of behaviorism. Her theory of ego development takes a holistic view of the person. For her, the sum of all behavioral traits cannot be added together to form a picture of the whole. Like other cognitive-developmental theorists she believes that the whole is more than the sum of its parts. She views development of an individual as progressing through qualitatively distinct stages rather than in quantitative terms.

The quest for coherent meaning in experience is the essence of ego functioning (Hy and Loevinger, 1996). The ego retains its stability by disregarding any aberrant information. That is, information a person cannot readily assimilate or accommodate is ignored. When the person is developmentally ready to receive a challenge to his world view, then the ego is placed into disequilibrium. That is, the ego stability (equilibrium) is shaken. However, since the ego system wants to maintain stability, the person accommodates to the environment and constructs a new cognitive structure. This new structure constitutes the next stage of development. This need for stability (equilibrium) of the ego in Loevinger's theory is explained in terms of selectivity and flexibility (1976).

The new structures created by the process of selectivity (assimilation) and flexibility (accomodation) are evident in Loevinger's description of the development of hierarchical stages. That is, one must completely construct the current stage before one can move to the next level. Ego development occurs by a progressive restructuring of one's relation to one's environment. Each stage builds on, incorporates, and transmutes the previous stage. Each stage has an inner logic that accounts for its stability and equilibrium.

Because she does not have data from all cultures, Loevinger (1987) makes no claims of universality for her theory. However, her stages have been found to apply to everyone of all ages in all cultures from which there are data. Given these findings and Loevinger's association of her theory with Piaget and Kohlberg's theories, it is not unreasonable to assume universality. Universality assumes that the nature of development is such that no other sequence or pattern of growth stages is possible. Not everyone will go through all the defined stages of development because developmental growth is dependent on both environmental and genetic elements. For example, a severely retarded person could not be expected to reach the higher levels of ego development because of his/her limited cognitive capacity.

Loevinger, like Piaget and Kohlberg, identifies four causal factors involved in the development of the ego: heredity, physical experiences, social 'transmission' of knowledge, and equilibrium. These four causal factors are the mechanism by which change in the organism occurs. As an interactionist theorist, Loevinger maintains that innate capacities enable one to interact with one's physical environment. The expectations of one's culture are socially communicated through the social environment. Socially communicated knowledge comes from outside the person. Examples of socially communicated knowledge, in Piagetian terms, must reflect two strands of social influence that operate in opposing directions. One strand makes reasons unnecessary (heteronomy); the other makes exchange of reasons necessary (autonomy). Examples of heteronomously communicated knowledge are sibling names, appropriate dress, holidays, and all pre-given knowledge that requires no reasons. Communicated expectations for autonomy include assumptions that one will negotiate the rules of the game of marbles, justify a choice made, explain a request made and in general exchange reasons (Piaget, 1932/1965; 1965/1995). The understanding of transmission of social knowledge is dependent upon both the maturational level and the experience of the child. Equilibrium helps to maintain a balance between heredity, environmental experiences, and the accumulation of social knowledge. As Loevinger (1976) has noted, "equilibrium stresses the naturalness of a structure" (p. 34).

To understand Loevinger's stages of ego development one needs to conceptualize ego development as a sequence of structural changes that are stimulated by the interaction of an organism with its environment. It is through one's ability to change and adapt to his/her environment that one is able to change the way s/he makes sense of the world. That is, one's interpretation of reality and the way one responds to the environmental stimuli are functions of one's level of ego development.

Loevinger has organized these structural changes in ego development into nine stages. The identification of these stages emerged from many years of work. The beginning of Loevinger's theory was rooted in a project to measure mothers' attitudes toward problems of family life (Loevinger, 1987). What emerged from that study was the beginnings of a developmental theory. As Loevinger (1987) stated, "the skeletal conception that we began with has become a set of full-bodied character sketches of typical persons at each stage" (p. 226).

Loevinger has developed the Sentence Completion Test (SCT) as a method of assessing ego development. The SCT is comprised of 36 sentence stems. Subjects' responses to these stems are individually assigned to one of the nine stages by matching them with response categories provided in a scoring manual (Loevinger, et al, 1970).

STAGES OF EGO DEVELOPMENT

Loevinger's stages of ego development can be divided into three major levels—1) pre-conformist; 2) conformist; 3) post-conformist. Each level is subdivided into stages. Descriptions of the stages are based on general characteristics of the stage based on the theoretical foundations of the Sentence Completion Test, the psychometric measure of ego development.

PRE-CONFORMIST LEVEL

The Pre-social and Symbiotic Stage

The symbiotic stage is a theoretical stage which cannot be measured by the Sentence Completion Test. This first stage of development is divided into two segments—the Pre-social Stage and the Symbiotic stage. Both of these stages are pre-language stages. In the first stage, the baby is undifferentiated from its world. Its first task is to begin the process of differentiating itself from its environment. Should a child remain at this stage long past the appropriate time for differentiation to have occurred, he or she would be referred to as autistic. In the Symbiotic and Pre-social stage, the baby retains a symbiotic relation to the mother, as the differentiation process of distinguishing self from non-self advances. Near the end of this stage, language begins to emerge.

The Impulsive Stage

As a child enters the Impulsive Stage, the familiar words known to all parents manifest themselves. The empathic "No!" or "Me do it!" emerge to help affirm the self as a separate identity. At the beginning of this stage, the child acts on impulse. He sees an object and reaches for it without thought of consequences. He responds to his physical needs and is dependent on others for control of those impulses. People are valued for what they can give. They are seen in terms of dichotomies of good/bad, dirty/clean, love me/hate me, and so forth. Judgments of morality are seen as "good to me" or "mean to me." Persons in this stage will evaluate other people solely on what they give or withhold. Loevinger states that individuals are rarely in this stage past high school.

The Self-Protective Stage

As a person enters the Self-Protective Stage, impulse control is evidenced as the individual learns to anticipate immediate, short-term rewards and punishment. This person has learned an appreciation for the rules of the world given the boundaries of the world for that particular individual. S/he knows and understands that it is to his/her advantage to abide by the rules. However, s/he expects immediate gratification from external sources. S/he views interpersonal relations as exploitive and, therefore, becomes distrustful and self-protective (hence the name of this stage). Opportunistic hedonism describes persons at this stage.

Individuals at this stage of ego development play the zero-sum game: what somebody gains, somebody else loses. They do not like getting into trouble and attribute their own unacceptable behavior as being caused by others. For example, a person operating from this self-protective stage might excuse his/her behavior by saying, "I was with the wrong crowd" or "I hit her because she made me angry."

Young children will cling to rituals and traditions to maintain stability during this stage. Adults at this stage will resort to "hostile humor." An example of hostile humor would be ethnic or sexist jokes that are hurtful. Loevinger (1987) states some adults at this stage "deserve to be classed as psychopathic personalities" (p. 227). However, most adults at this stage can live in normal society with successful results.

CONFORMIST LEVEL

Conformist Stage

At the Conformist Stage individuals take a giant step towards identifying their own welfare with the "membership" of an identified group. In order for this to occur a strong element of trust needs to be established. An individual accepts rules because the group accepts the rules. The identified group could be family, peers, one's school, one's town, or one's nation. A person operating at this stage of ego development knows the difference between "feeling bad" mentally and "feeling bad" physically.

Disapproval is a powerful sanction for a person at this stage. Right or wrong is determined by the rules of the identified group. If an individual breaks the rules, his/her action is considered wrong. Individuals perceive themselves as conforming to social norms whether the rules are formally written or implicitly held. Groups are defined in terms of who is in and who is out. The individual dichotomizes groups into categories based on us/them or we/they. The Conformist values niceness, helpfulness, and cooperation with others. A key concept at this stage is that belonging makes one feel secure.

The Self-Aware Stage

As a person continues to construct more complex understandings of his/her world, s/he moves to the Self-Aware level in Loevinger's theory. Loevinger (1976, 1987) states that this is the modal level for adults in our society. An individual operating from the self-aware stage demonstrates an increase in self-awareness and an appreciation for multiple possibilities in situations. S/he is open to examining the self because s/he is liberated from the notion of "what I ought to be." Individuals are now able to realize that they don't always have to live up to societal norms. This is taking a step away from the Conformist mode of operating. Yet, this level contains many of the same characteristics of the Conformist Stage. Exceptions and contingencies to the rules are allowed for, but only in terms of stereotypic and demographic categories such as age, gender, martial status, and race, rather than in terms of individual differences that stress differences in traits and needs.

POST-CONFORMIST LEVEL

The Conscientious Stage

The shift into the Conscientious Stage is another major move in terms of Loevinger's ego development process. The internalization of rules is complete at this stage. People at this stage evaluate and choose rules for themselves. An individual operating from this stage has constructed self-evaluated standards by which s/he lives. Thus, a person can decide to break a rule or law if it does not meet with one's own code. An example of this would be the "conscientious objector." But in the 1960s it would have been hard to distinguish a person who was truly in the Conscientious Stage based on the outward behavior of "conscientious objector" from a person who was conforming to what he perceived as a norm for his peer group. A person at this stage feels so responsible for other people that, at times, s/he feels compelled to intervene in order to prevent the other from making a mistake. Achievement is measured by one's own standards rather than by someone else's standards.

Persons at this stage do dichotomize moral acts, but do so in terms of abstract concepts. They think in terms of polarities such as trivial versus important, love versus lust, or dependent versus independent. Motives and intentions are considered when judging behavior. In terms of perspective taking, people functioning at the Conscientious Stage can see from the other's point of view. This new found perspective-taking ability allows them to view experiences within the broader social context, although this aspect becomes more prominent in the later stages.

The Individualist Stage

At this stage a heightened sense of individuality and concern for emotional dependence emerges. An individual operating from this stage has an increased ability for tolerance of self and others. This toleration stems from a recognition of individual differences and the complexities of life situations. An individual at this stage is able to differentiate between the inner self and the outer self. Conflict moves to an internal position. For example, a person would be more concerned about emotional dependence rather than physical and financial dependence. A person is able to see the multiple roles s/he holds. For example, a woman would see herself as wife, mother, daughter, housekeeper, career woman, lover, and so forth. There is an increasing ability to accept paradox and contradictions.

The Autonomous Stage

The mark of this stage is the capacity to acknowledge and cope with inner conflicts such as conflicting needs, conflicting duties, and the conflict between needs and duties. Loevinger (1976) notes that the person at the Autonomous Stage does not have more conflicts than those at lower stages but "rather he has the courage (or whatever other qualities it takes) to acknowledge and deal with conflict rather than ignoring it or projecting it onto the environment" (p. 23). A person at the Autonomous Stage will see reality as complex and multifaceted. A high tolerance for ambiguity exists here. A parent at this stage of development would be willing to let his/her children make their own mistakes, but recognizes the limitations of autonomy and the need for emotional interdependence. The aspiration at this stage is to be realistic and objective about the self and others. Abstract social ideals such as justice are held.

The Integrated Stage

This represents the highest stage identified by Loevinger. She acknowledges that this is the hardest stage to describe. Like other structural developmental theorists before her, such as Kohlberg, Fowler, and Selman, Loevinger views the highest stage as being largely theoretical in nature. The existence of actual people in this stage is rare. Another problem in describing this stage lies in the psychologist's own limitations as a possible hindrance to understanding. (For example, psychologists themselves who are not at this stage of understanding would have a difficult time understanding it.) The new element of this stage is consolidation of a sense of identity. Loevinger states that probably the best description of someone at this stage is provided by Maslow in his description of the Self-Actualizing person.

IMPLICATIONS FOR EDUCATIONAL SETTINGS

Loevinger's theory initially was used solely for theoretical purposes. However, her theory does have implications for applied educational settings. Thus far, the field of counseling psychology has been the primary user of Loevinger's theory in the applied setting, and the methods used in counseling psychology can aid in establishing sound educational practices. The work of clinical psychologists Robert Kegan and Mary Baird Carlsen, which draws on Loevinger and other structural developmentalists, can give educators developmentally appropriate techniques that can be applied in the educational setting.

Carlsen's client-centered approach points to methods for creating an educational environment which is student-centered, whereby the teacher creates opportunities that allow students to learn and grow. Carlsen (1988) stated, "A therapist is a teacher as he or she offers thoughts and ideas, shares learning material and models, and stimulates the client to think, feel, and act in entirely new ways" (p. 126). Methods used by Carlsen that can be transposed into the classroom setting include setting aside time for students to disengage from activity and be alone with their thoughts, and for daydreaming. It can also mean encouraging students' openness to explore anything. It certainly includes insuring conditions that promote both alertness to surroundings and the discipline to stay with projects to completion. Life stories can be shared in the classroom through the use of writing activities such as journal keeping and autobiographies. Critical thinking can be promoted through dialogue and dialectical questioning. Behavioral tasks, such as worksheets and readings, can be assigned when appropriate to promote learning.

Carlsen uses whatever she thinks will work to widen her clients' perspectives on the world and give her clients a larger repertoire of skills, interests, and contacts. She employs what she calls "systematic eclecticism" in a manner that "honors and interacts with the broad spectrum of human thinking, feeling, and behavior—an eclecticism which is aiming for system within the concept of cognitive developmental process" (p. 129).

In other words, Carlsen has in her method bag techniques from many different disciplines, but she makes informed choices on what to use in her therapy sessions. She understands the underlying processes of cognitive developmental theory and this allows her to know what method to select, why she is using it, what she hopes to accomplish, and a way to evaluate a particular technique.

Kegan (1982) incorporates into his therapy practice the tenets of developmental theory. He states that the contribution "developmental theory makes to schooling is its exposure of the child's 'natural curriculum,' an active process of meaning-making which informs and constrains the child's purpose" (p. 255). From Kegan's perspective, the role of the teacher would be to engage students in the process of learning, to join the students in exploring what they understand about the world, and to provide challenges to the students' world views. Kegan recognizes the need for a psychological support system to enable the development of the individual. The psychological supports provide a medium in which the developing organism can thrive. This psychological support system forms what Kegan terms a "holding environment." In the classroom this would mean that the teacher would provide a community in which the child feels he belongs and in which the community is assured of the student's continued participation. Another way of stating this is that the classroom community has ways to recognize that a person grows and changes.

Both Carlsen and Kegan would state that the best use of Loevinger's theory in the educational setting is to be able to recognize the level of ego functioning of the individual but not let the stage be the focus of the interaction with the child. Rather, the interaction should focus on the individual in such a way as to promote and allow the opportunity for the developmental process to occur. Educators incorporating the types of methods used by Carlsen and Kegan allow students to be the creators of their own knowledge rather than the receptacles of transmitted knowledge. It also honors the students' ability to think for themselves.

Two temptations exist when attempting to apply Loevinger's stages of ego development in the educational setting; both can lead to erroneous applications of her theory. The first temptation is to see the stages as a ladder to be climbed. Loevinger's work suggests that there are special attributes of ego functioning at the different stages of development. This can be demonstrated by examining how people reason. Loevinger would state that each stage of ego development presents a distinctly different way or pattern of reasoning. Therefore, the criteria for what is moral for the person operating from the conformist stage of ego development is qualitatively different from those employed by the person operating at the autonomous stage of ego development. The greatest pitfall in failing to understand this concept is that a teacher may attempt to get students to exhibit the concrete behaviors of a "higher" stage and fail to enable the student to internalize the characteristics of that stage. In other words, one cannot force someone to a higher stage.

The second temptation is to view persons at the highest stage as the best adjusted. Higher stages of development are not necessarily better, although they are more adaptive because of the ability to have a greater tolerance for complexity, see things more broadly, and select from a greater variety of possible actions. However, well adjusted individuals can be found at all stages of development. For example, children exhibiting a self-protective stage of development can be viewed as well-adjusted. On the other hand, an adult operating from the self-protective stage may be seen as maladjusted from society's point of view.

The essence of Loevinger's developmental theory does not lie in the account of stages but in its capacity to elucidate the on-going process of adaptation. Thus, it is not the stages that should be the focus in an educational setting but the process of development which gives rise to the development of increasingly adaptive stages.

Thus, when applying Loevinger's theory to the educational setting it is important to remember that the purpose of determining an ego stage level for an individual is not to judge the individual but to understand how the person is reasoning. The goal then for educators is to provide an atmosphere that promotes development and learning. From a cognitive-developmental perspective one can modify Carlsen's goals for therapy into goals for education. Those goals are as follows:

* To join each student where s/he is.
* To create a genuine dialogue.
* To face and use crisis experience as the energy for constructive change.

* To teach, facilitate, and reinforce critical thinking processes.
* To model, stimulate, and encourage dialectical thinking patterns.
* To foster meaning-making.
* To facilitate a sense of unity, continuity, and the "real me" in creating a life that is meaningful.

Loevinger's theory of ego development provides one way to view the developing individual. Understanding the developmental level of a student enables the educator to join the student where s/he is. The educator can develop appropriate methods that will enable the student to grow and change. The development of the individual is an open-ended process born in the interaction of the physical and social environment on the one hand and the emerging cognitive capabilities on the other. When educators recognize this process they are able to provide students with curricula that are challenging but not frustrating and provide the guidance and support necessary to enable each individual to develop.

Assumption of responsibility for consequences of one's own actions

_____

_____

_____

_____

_____

_____

REESE ARTICLE

Distinguish between experimental knowledge and spectator knowledge

_____

_____

_____

_____

_____

_____

What is the role and importance of aesthetics in Maslow's approach to education?

_____

_____

_____

_____

_____

_____

PART III, SECTION C:
SOCIAL AND PERSONALITY DEVELOPMENT

WILGENBUSCH ARTICLE

Explain the difference between intrinsic and extrinsic learning.

_____

_____

_____

_____

Briefly describe the characteristics of peak experiences and their implication for education.

_____

_____

_____

_____

Briefly describe the curriculum components that help develop peak experiences.

_____

_____

_____

_____

Explain Maslow's use of the term "need."

_____

_____

_____

_____

PART III, SECTION C:
SOCIAL AND PERSONALITY DEVELOPMENT

GORE-LAIRD ARTICLE

Briefly discuss the relation of Piaget's theory of cognitive development to Loevinger's understanding of ego development.

_____

_____

_____

_____

_____

_____

_____

George is fifteen years old. He belongs to a gang that is very important to him. He feels that the other gang members accept him. George feels secure when interacting with members of his gang, and he has pride in his relationship with this group. George also accepts all the rules that the group sets forth. What Loevinger stage of development would best describe George? Justify your answer.

_____

_____

_____

_____

_____

_____

_____

_____

_____

PART III, SECTION C:
SOCIAL AND PERSONALITY DEVELOPMENT

GORE-LAIRD ARTICLE (continued)

Explain why Loevinger's stage theory of ego development is qualitative.

_____

_____

_____

_____

_____

_____

_____

_____

_____

_____

Briefly discuss the use of Loevinger's theory in an educational setting.

_____

_____

_____

_____

_____

_____

_____

_____

_____

PART IV

COMPARISON OF THEORIES

THEORIES OF LEARNING AND DEVELOPMENT FOR ACADEMICS AND EDUCATORS

by Sidney Strauss
School of Education
Tel Aviv University

Several theories of learning and development are presented: nativism, behaviorism, structuralism, information processing, the naive theories approach, the sociohistorical approach, and two interstitial theories—a neo-Piagetian and a nonuniversal developmental theory.

I claim that the notions of learning and development are not fixed and agreed on. Instead, they are defined by the theory in which they are embedded.

The aspect of the various theories are discussed with respect to educational practice. Tensions between academic psychology and educational practice about learning and development are also discussed.

The articles that comprise this special issue are presented within the theoretical frameworks of learning and development.

There has been considerable debate about definitions of learning and development and their places in theories of psychology and educational practice. Much of what is said about definitions of learning and development depends on the theory of the speaker's persuasion. In this article, I lay out various positions about learning and development as they pertain to theories that imbue cognitive, developmental, and educational psychology. Then I address tensions between these positions and educational practice.

THEORETICAL POSITIONS ABOUT LEARNING AND DEVELOPMENT

Debate about learning and development has energized the fields of cognitive, developmental, and educational psychology over the distant and not too distant past. Its roots often lay in issues about: origins (i.e., With what do infants come into the world?), how what infants are born with changes over time, and relations between the individual and the environment. Theorists' positions about learning and development result from the various stances taken with respect to these issues.

I briefly summarize the issues with respect to several theories. Due to space limitations, my summaries will have a bottom line ring to them, and there will be little in the way of developing and justifying claims. The theories I review are: nativism, behaviorism, structuralism, information processing, the naive theories approach, the sociohistorical approach, and two interstitial theories—neo-Piagetian theory and a theory of nonuniversal development.

Nativism

Nativists are within the rationalist philosophical tradition. Radical nativists, such as Fodor (1980), argue that infants are born with complete and abstract knowledge about aspects of the world. Using language as an example, the argument is that infants are born with a universal grammar (UG). They are also born with learning devices that allow any child to learn, in my example, any language.

Radical nativists argue that, in principle, there is no development. This is because, in their view, it is impossible to get from less to more powerful mental structures. Because this is impossible, one must engineer an infant who has the most powerful structures from birth. The moment radical nativists take that position, there can be no development because the most powerful structures are in place from the very beginning.

Changes that take place, then, must be learning, and learning must be deductive. Here the argument is that, very roughly, children deductively test hypotheses about their environment (e.g., their language) and get feedback about whether or not their hypotheses are confirmed or disconfirmed. And where can these hypotheses come from? From the complete UG with which they are born.

The radical nativists place the greatest emphasis on the individual and the innate knowledge each of us is born with. The environment is the place where the hypotheses about the world get tested.

In short, the radical nativists argue that one is born with complete, abstract knowledge, which leads him or her to the position that development cannot occur; deductive learning is the explanation for change; and the individual's innate knowledge is the main part of individual-environmental interactions.

There are nativists of another stripe, those who are not advocates of the radical position (Carey, 1985; Gelman, 1990; Karmiloff-Smith, 1992; Mandler, 1992; Spelke, Breinlinger, Macomber, & Jacobson, 1992). They claim that infants are born with considerable innately specified knowledge about their world, learning takes place within the constraints set by those specifications, and mental constructions occur within these constraints.

One candidate for mental constructions that are built off the innate knowledge are the representations humans construct about their world (Karmiloff-Smith, 1992). What this means is that people internally represent their external environment (i.e. we mentally appropriate it). We then represent our representations (or rerepresent our environment) via various languages. This rerepresentation is constructivistic. In short, there are emerging positions suggesting that one can be both a nativist and a constructivist or a "rational constructivist," to use Gelman's (1990) terminology.

Behaviorism

The radical version of behaviorism (Bijou & Barer, 1961, 1965; Skinner, 1953) is that infants are born with neither knowledge nor organization. With respect to what knowledge and equipment the infant brings into the world, behaviorism occupies the pole at the other extreme of the continuum occupied by the radical nativists. Behaviorists claim that infants are born with capacities to discriminate aspects of the environment, respond to it, generalize, and so on.

Because their position is that infants are born unstructured with respect to knowledge, radical behaviorists are unlikely to claim that the child will eventually have mental structures as such a claim would force them to find an explanation regarding how an unstructured mental system becomes structured. In this view, then, there is no development, only learning.

As for learning, radical behaviorists argued that the capacity to form associations inductively in a lawful way is the basis for the knowledge gained about the world. The environment impinges on us, and we form associations about it in such a way that the more we are exposed to a particular environment, the stronger the association, and the closer the aspects of the environment are in time and space, the more likely the association will be formed. The former is called the law of frequency, and the latter is called the law of contiguity.

The behaviorists have the environment as the main interlocuter in the relations between the individual and the environment. The external environment is what is to be noted and copied internally.

In short, the radical behaviorists claim that development does not occur because there are no cognitive constraints on the system, laws of inductive learning are the sole explanation for cognitive change, and the environment is the main aspect of individual-environment interactions.

Structuralism

Structuralists, such as Piaget, argue that infants are born with a weak structure of reflexes that transforms itself over time. Relations between the structure of reflexes and mental structures on the psychological plane have to do with the biological roots of psychological development. How one goes from one to the other is, of course, a puzzle yet to be solved by structuralists.

Because structuralists posit that infants begin life with a structure, the likely ensuing position is that one's future cognitions will also be structured. The issue then turns to the direction and nature of development from relatively weak to relatively powerful mental structures. The enduring core position taken from Piaget and his followers is that qualitatively different structures are transformed in an invariant sequence (Beilin, 1985, 1992).

Learning, in the structuralist view, is the application of mental structures to new content. Mental structures limit what can be learned. One cannot apply a mental structure that does not exist or has not yet been constructed. In this sense, development sets constraints on learning.

Structuralists maintain an intermediate position between the radical nativists and the radical behaviorists about individual-environment relations. They are avowedly interactionist in the sense that there is a subtle give and take between the environment and the structure. This occurs in what D. Klahr (personal communications) once called the Batman and Robin of Piagetian psychology: assimilation and accomodation. Piaget's interactionism was not a compromise between the extremes held by radical nativists and radical behaviorists, who had already staked out a claim for a dominant role for the individual or the environment. It was, instead, a principle position that saw the structure adapting the environment to its constraints while accommodating itself to the subtle differences of the environment.

In this special issue, Cecilia Wainryb and Elliot Turiel (1993) take the structuralist position when describing their work on the meanings of learning and development for social concepts.

In sum, structuralists claim that development occurs, and what develops are structures; learning is constrained by development; and individual-environment relations are interactionist.

Information-Processing Approaches

Information-processing theories are somewhat atheoretical. They are, of course, part of a general worldview, but they are not explicitly ideological in the sense that the three previous theories are (Bruner, 1985).

The theories I present emphasize developmental aspects of information processing, but these aspects are not a prerequisite for information-processing approaches (e.g., Newell & Simon, 1972). Information-processing approaches that do deal with development are quite varied: production systems (Klahr, 1984), rule assessment (Siegler, 1981), skill acquisition (Fischer, 1980), and so on. There does not seem to be consensus among these approaches about how much knowledge the child is born with and how it is organized. Yet, there are some unifying themes to which most information-processing advocates adhere. One is that thinking is information processing. Others are the emphasis placed on the ways children represent knowledge, how they transform information, and the processing limitations that constrain the inductive inferences they can make about their world.

What develops according to these approaches? The answer depends on the approach, of course, and given the space limitations, I can only hint at what has been offered to this question.

The novice-expert shift is a candidate for what develops. Knowledge representation has been described in term of novice-expert dimensions. The novice's knowledge representation differ from the expert's on a number of dimensions: their knowledge base, its organization, problem solving, and so on. These dimensions set limits on what and how much can be learned. For example, a child who has a larger knowledge base about a particular domain and whose knowledge representation is deeper than another child will learn more about new material when it is presented.

Another candidate for what develops is working memory limitations. There is controversy about whether or not working memory changes. Among those who believe there are age-related working memory changes is Robbie Case (1993), who writes about this in his article in this issue. The argument is that working memory limitations set constraints on the inductive inferences that can be made.

In these two examples, the development aspect pertains to constraints placed on the information-processing system, be they processing constraints on knowledge representation and organization or working memory constraints.

Learning can be the result of several processes that occur alone or in concert. Among them are strategy construction (Siegler & Shipley, 1987), automatization (Case, 1984), encoding (Siegler, 1981, 1984), and generalization (Klahr, 1984). To demonstrate what this means, I use automatization as an example. Case argued that within the information-processing constraints on working memory, children are able to learn new material through automatization. When one does that, space is freed up in working memory for other information to be taken into account. Notice that the information-processing capacity has not changed here. Instead, within the constraints of that capacity, one can deal with more information by, say, automatizing processing.

The bulk of the information-processing approaches places the burden of the individual-environment relations on the environment. Physical input from the environment gets transformed as it makes its way to where it eventually is stored. But there is no question that the individual also plays a role here in that knowledge representation of the new material will influence what and how much will get learned.

In sum, information-processing approaches are somewhat atheoretical. Many do not make the claims about the nature of the knowledge and its organization that infants are born with. Some approaches claim that development occurs with respect to changes in the constraints on the information-processing system that limit the kinds of inferences that can be made. Learning overcomes processing constraints via mechanisms such as automatization, generalization, and encoding. And the environment is the dominant factor in environment-individual relations.

Naive Theories Approach

There has been considerable controversy over the years about what cognitive and developmental psychologists should search for: domain-general or domain-specific systems. This either-or view restricts debate, but that is the way people in the field cast it these days. Researchers will probably look for the synthesis, and one recent attempt has already been made by Karmiloff-Smith (1992).

There are certainly good reasons to look for domain-general systems, and the person who manages to describe one grabs the brass ring on the carousel. Diverse data and phenomenon that can be described by a model fulfill the sought-after criteria of parsimony and power. That description has been the aim of most cognitive and developmental psychologists. Piaget, Freud, Newell, and others have taken this time-honored approach.

There has also been a countermove in cognitive and cognitive developmental psychology that takes a different read on these matters (Gardner, 1983). Considerable evidence, both empirical and analytic, suggest that knowledge is compartmentalized and domain specific. Knowledge organization for, say physics, does not have much overlap with knowledge organization for, say, the social domain. For a review of positions on this area of controversy, see Wellman and Gelman (1992).

Within the naive theories approach to cognitive development and learning, Carey (1985) proposed a rather advanced theory. She claimed that children have theory-like conceptual structure. Theories are characterized by their abstractness and law-like coherence, the phenomena in their domains, their explanatory mechanisms, the ways they produce interpretations of evidence and more. The number of such domains is limited: biology, mechanics, language, space, number, and a few others.

Carey (1985) further claimed that concepts in particular domains are part of larger naive or lay theories about that domain. One of the tasks of developmental psychologists is to determine the nature of these naive theories about the domains under study.

Carey (1985) also claimed that because concepts are embedded in naive theories, conceptual change, which can be understood as development, can be viewed as similar to theory change in domains. For example, aspects of theory change in the sciences serve as a way to think about how the development of lay theories occurs to children (and adults).

Carey (1985) viewed learning, through instruction in the widest sense of this term, as the engine that drives development. Instruction, both formal and informal, leads to knowledge acquisition that leads, in a yet undetermined manner, to cognitive development.

In this special issue, Susan Carey and Carol Smith (1993) discuss children's changing epistemologies of scientific experiments within the naive theories perspective.

In short, the perspective is that children form concepts within large domains that have theory-like qualities. Development of concepts occurs in ways that resemble theory changes in disciplines. And learning through instruction may lead to development.

The Sociohistorical Approach

The sociohistorical position, as advanced by Vygotsky (1978, 1987), maintains a two-track position about human cognitive processes: the natural and the cultural. Natural processes follow the path of maturation, and the role of the individual's biological underpinnings is paramount. The environment supplies information for those underpinnings to get played out. These lower mental processes are not reflective and are the result of direct, personal experience with the environment.

For the cultural track, the social environment is crucial, as are the tools that are used for understanding and engaging the environment. There are two basic kinds of tools: material and psychological. Material tools mediate between the individual and nature. For example, screwdrivers (not the drink) have a handle designed to fit the individual's hand and an edge built to fit the material world. The screwdriver mediates between the individual and nature, both literally and metaphorically.

Psychological tools mediate between individuals in their social interactions. There are signs, symbols, and discourses. They are also used by individuals to change their own psychological processes. This is the kernel of Vygotsky's (1987) general genetic law of cultural development. He claimed that all functions appear twice: among people as an interpsychological category and within the child as an intrapsychological category (Wertsch & Tulviste, 1992).

In this issue, Alex Kozulin (1993) elaborates on the power of psychological tools in human cognition. He uses literary concepts as the vehicle to explicate his ideas; in so doing, he argues that literary devices, such as a genre, serve the same role as theories in scientific concepts. He also shows how Vygotsky (1978, 1987) used literature to develop his theory.

The roles of culture are essential when discussing the sociocultural approach. Having said this, I now turn to the roles of learning and development according to this approach. I begin with a caveat. There are at least two main understandings of these terms: Vygotsky's (1987) and his modern-day interpreters.

In Vygotsky's (1978) view, learning goes beyond development and draws development in its wake. Learning in social interactions among individuals happens in the zone of proximal development (ZPD), that battered buzz word that actually has some powerful ideas attached to it. What is learned in concert with others comes to be internalized, and what is learned becomes the new actual knowledge or the new developmental level.

The emphasis on individual-environment interactions for learning and development lean strongly toward the environment side. The environment here is the social environment, of course. Wertsch and Tulviste (1992) noted problems with this emphasis, mostly because of the lack of construction in the ZPD, as Vygotsky (1978) described it. Vygotsky's view of internalization has a ring of absorption, rather than the sound of reconstruction.

As for Vygotsky's modern-day interpreters, there is a sense in which the terms developmental and learning are inadequate to describe what they have in mind. One reason for this has to do with the unit of what they believe changes with age. Newman, Griffin, and Cole (1989) suggested that the unit of analysis for cognitive change is neither invariant mental structures nor the mental process that transforms information. Both exist in the mind of individuals. It is also not in the environment. The unit is in the social interaction between individuals and between them and the environment.

The alternative suggested by Vygotsky's interpreters is to view learning as a social practice, an activity that takes place among people in social contexts. The unit of analysis is located in that nexus. When one takes this view, the notions of learning and development lose their usual meanings.

In this issue, Roy D. Pea (1993) takes the position of the modern-day interpreters of Vygotsky.

Interstitial Theories

Two interstitial theories have taken some positions from different theories. Case's (1985, 1993; also see Case and McKeough, 1990) neo-Piagetian theory has its feet planted in the structuralist and information-processing approaches. His approach is structuralist in that he seeks structural organizations that have properties of stage-like development (e.g., their developmental is sequential, they are qualitatively different from each other, etc.). The point of departure from the structuralist approach in Case's theory is that he uses an information-processing frame to describe the processes that occur when the mental organization deals with information. The move from demanding mental structure via logical and mathematical structures, as did Piaget (1970), to describing them in terms of information-processing systems, led Case to alternate descriptions of cognition and development that are different from Piaget's. Because Case (1993) presents his arguments in this issue, I will not elaborate on them.

Feldman's (1980) interstitial theory of nonuniversal development has elements of both the structuralist and the sociohistorical approaches. He argued that most of cognitive development is about nonuniversals, yet cognitive developmentalists attempt to describe universal development. Ontogenesis proceeds in the following order of intellectual achievements: universal (e.g., number conservation), cultural (e.g., arithmetics), domain specific (e.g., psychology), idiosyncratic (e.g., mathematical models that describe formal operations in Piaget's, 1970, theory), and unique (e.g., those creative changes in models made by an individual that lead to a reorganization of understanding the formal operation stage). The development of societies proceeds in the reverse order, beginning with the unique achievements of individuals who make an impact on their subfields, perhaps on their fields, and, in rare cases, on their cultures.

Several matters arise when one takes Feldman's (1980) position. First, structures and developmental sequences exist in domains. For example, in chess, there are a number of levels of expertise, from the novice to the international grand master. Individuals develop through these stages. Baseball has similar stages; one can develop from the level of sandlot novice through AA and AAA levels arriving, possibly, to the major leagues.

Second, all nonuniversal developments take into account individual differences, creativity, and motivation, and require arranging special situations for learning to occur, such as schools, private lessons, and so on.

The nine theories discussed herein were briefly presented to lay out my interpretation of major theories that have influenced the debate about relations between learning and development. I have attempted to show that the position one takes about what the child is born with has potential to constrain what theorists say about relations between learning and development, mechanisms of learning and development, and the nature of the relations between the individual and his or her environment. I now turn to what all of this has to do with educational theory and practice.

SO WHAT? EDUCATION PRACTICE

I have noted elsewhere (Strauss, 1986, 1987, 1990, 1991) that there are tensions between cognitive developmental psychologists and educators. The reasons for these tensions are varied, and I briefly discussed some of them. Feldman's (1980) theory of nonuniversal development inspired some of what follows here.

Cognitive developmentalists usually search for universal development and for developmental invariants. Piaget's (1970) structuralist theory is emblematic of that search. The question he asked himself was about how novelty arises, and his answer pertained to structural change. That answer was framed within the quest to describe universal structures. These structures develop in an invariant sequence regardless of one's culture, life circumstances, motivation, personal quirks, and such.

The nativists, some information-processing theorists, followers of the naive theories approach, and advocates of aspects of the sociohistorical approach, by and large, search for those universals. Advocates of these theoretical positions search for a level of cognitive development that is much too deep for education to influence. To influence that level of mental structures, we would have to be genetic engineers.

Educators do not search for universal, biologically constrained intellectual achievements that take place in the natural environment. They deal with levels of mental organizations that are at the middle level; that is, they are not as deep as the mental organizations that cognitive and developmental theorists concern themselves with, and they are not close to the behavior mental organizations, such as Siegler's (1981) rules that have little generality. Educators seek a middle-level description of mental organizations that are both able to be changed through instruction and general.

Another focus of tension between cognitive developmental psychologists and educators pertains to relations between the affective domain and cognition. Cognitive and developmental psychologists seek laws of development that occur regardless of motivation, what happened to you in your last class, who is sitting next to you in a class now, and so on. Their quest is for a description of development that takes place regardless of one's motivation or affective state. Children do not learn their mother tongue or construct concrete operations structures because they are motivated to do so.

However, teachers (including university teachers) know that a lack of motivation on the part of students, fear of academic failure (or success), "blocks" about various subject matter, and matters of the heart (e.g., who is sitting next to you in class) influence school learning. Cognitive developmental psychologists are not very helpful in this regard.

Yet another source of tension has to do with individual differences. This topic rarely concerns cognitive and developmental psychologists, who generally seek what unites, not what separates children's cognition and differences, what they seek is above and beyond these differences.

In contrast, teachers are very concerned with individual differences when thinking about how pupils in their classroom learn. The point here is to teach (to foster learning in others) in ways that take into account pupils' different learning styles, preferences of being taught, and so on. Here, too, cognitive and developmental psychologists are not very helpful for educational practitioners.

These and other areas are sources of tension between what is on the agendas of teachers, cognitive psychologists, and cognitive developmental psychologists. I have written elsewhere (Strauss, 1987, 1990, 1991) about how these tensions might be resolved. The thrust of my argument has been that developmentalists could revise their agendas somewhat so that educator's concerns could be part of their research programs; not only could this be done without detriment to their research, but this shift could even enrich them.

Developmental psychologists are beginning to take into account some aspects of these sources of tension. For example, Scarr (1992) recently called for including individual difference in developmental theories. I believe that were the research and theory agendas of cognitive and developmental psychologists to be opened up, some sources of tension between them and educators would be reduced, and both could benefit from this change.

I believe the authors of this special issue are making significant moves in that direction.

THIS SPECIAL ISSUE

The special issue, which is devoted to issues of learning and development, addresses a wide variety of domains and a range of theoretical positions about them. The domains are solid concepts, such as moral judgments and social conventions (Wainryb & Turiel, 1993); numeral concepts (Case, 1993); epistemological concepts, such as epistemology of scientific experiments (Carey & Smith, 1993); literary concepts, such as the genre that can be seen as parallel to scientific theory in the domain of science (Kozulin, 1993); science concepts, such as the concept of light (Pea, 1993); and psychological concepts, such as teachers' understanding of children's learning (Strauss, 1993).

Also, several theories are represented in these works: Wainryb and Turiel (1993) work within the structuralist tradition, Case (1993) presents his work within the neo-Piagetian paradigm, Carey & Smith (1993) take a domain-specific approach to naive theories, both Kozulin (1993) and Pea (1993) are bounded within the sociohistorical frame, and Strauss' (1993) work is a hybrid between the naive theories approach and structuralism.

ACKNOWLEDGMENT

This article is based on working paper No. 92-44 from the Unit of Human Development and Education, School of Education, Tel Aviv University.

VYGOTSKY, PIAGET, AND BANDURA: PERSPECTIVES ON THE RELATIONS BETWEEN THE SOCIAL WORLD AND COGNITIVE DEVELOPMENT

by Jonathan R. H. Tudge and Paul A. Winterhoff
University of North Carolina at Greensboro,
North Carolina, USA

Abstract: In this article we examine the theories of Vygotsky, Piaget, and Bandura as they deal with the relation between the social world and cognitive development. The prevailing belief is that these theories are quite different from each other. We consider a number of factors that contribute to this belief. One is the easy categorization afforded by current 'world views' in psychology—root conceptualizations of the nature of development that are believed to be incompatible. A second factor is that although the theories are far more complex than much of the empirical work based on them, researchers have concentrated on relatively narrow aspects of each theory, in the process magnifying differences between them. We conclude that although the theories have more in common than simple categorizations in much of the research literature suggests, some basic differences nonetheless exist in each theorist's conceptualization of the relations between social and individual factors in development.

Scholars have long been interested in the relations between social factors and cognitive development. In this article, we examine the ways in which three influential theorists (Vygotsky, Piaget, and Bandura) have conceptualized these relations. A number of scholars have pointed to differences between their theoretical positions [Altman and Rogoff, 1987; Azmitia and Perlmutter, 1989; Kuhn, 1978; Mueller and Cooper, 1986; Tudge and Rogoff, 1989], and indeed, the dominant tendency in the field has been to emphasize such differences.

The following contrasts are typically drawn in contemporary reviews, Vygotsky believed that development, a social process from birth onwards, is assisted by others (adults or peers) more competent in the skills and technologies available to the culture, and that development is fostered by collaboration within the child's zone of proximal development. Piaget believed that children are like scientists, working alone on the physical, logical, and mathematical material of their world to make sense of reality. To the extent that they can benefit from interaction, it is with peers rather than with adults, the dominant mechanism driving development being 'cognitive conflict.' Bandura believes that children primarily learn through imitation of models in their social environment and that the primary mechanism driving development is observational learning. Although there is some truth in each of these statements, their simplistic nature blinds us to the richness of each theory. Only by eschewing an approach that seeks to dichotomize and differentiate, and instead examining the subtleties of these positions, can we understand what the theories have in common, as well as what truly differentiates them.

Among the reasons for a focus on differences is that it facilitates categorization of theorists into a neat classificatory system. One influential categorization is that proposed by Pepper [1942]. His view that theories can be divided into four ideal types of paradigms, or 'world views,' has had a marked impact on the field [Altman and Rogoff, 1987; Kuhn, 1978; Mueller and Cooper, 1986; Overton, 1984; Overton and Reese, 1973; Reese and Overton, 1970; Valsiner and Winegar, 1992]. Each theory considered here has been classified as reflecting a different world view—social-learning theory into the 'mechanistic' paradigm, Piaget into the 'organismic' paradigm, and Vygotsky into the 'contextualist' paradigm, with each paradigm regarded as incompatible with the others.

Categorizations of this sort are useful, not least because world views incorporate different root metaphors and assumptions that theories, to a greater or lesser extent, illustrate. However, a disadvantage is that similarities across theories may be disguised and intellectual linkages ignored. For example, social-learning theory is described as dealing with observable external behavior and events, with little attention paid to Bandura's discussion of the internal processes that underlie modeling (self-efficacy or information-processing capacities, for example) or to the role Bandura gives to culture [1989b]. The problem is complicated by the fact that theories themselves develop, often in light of critical reactions to earlier formulations and changing intellectual contexts. In Bandura's case, this has meant that parts of his theory, originally placed into the mechanistic camp [Kuhn, 1978], more recently have been described as illustrating organismic [Altman and Rogoff, 1987] or contextualist [Zimmerman, 1983] world views.

Interpreters of Piagetian theory barely mention social interaction and its impact on development and instead emphasize the theory's 'biological flavor' [Brainerd, 1978; Flavell, 1963]. Little attention has been paid to those aspects of Piaget's writings that deal with children's active involvement in their social world, although as Furth [1969] has noted, Piaget's interest in biological foundations of development by no means precludes a concern with the role of the social world.

Because Vygotsky emphasized social factors in development, interpreters have tended to ignore his discussions of the profound impact of maturational factors on development (factors that set limits within which social interaction may be effective), or his statements regarding imitation; for example, '. . . imitation is the source of instruction's influence on development. . . . Instruction is possible only where there is potential for imitation' [Vygotsky, 1987, pp. 210–211].

Our claim, then, is that most attention is paid to aspects of theories that differentiate them from one another, and that similarities in perspective almost by definition cannot exist, since the underlying paradigms, or world views, are held to be essentially incompatible. A number of researchers have attempted to draw on perspectives representing several world views [Mueller and Cooper, 1986] or viewed different parts of a theory as reflecting different camps [Altman and Rogoff, 1987]. For the most part, however, scholars have tended to agree with Pepper's dictum that 'eclecticism is confusing' [Pepper, 1942, p. 104], and to the extent that integration has been attempted, it has been at the expense of redefining the contextualist view as falling within organicism or, according to Overton [1984], forcing a compromise between the organismic and mechanistic world views by stripping from the latter its basic assumptions.

INTELLECTUAL ROOTS OF THE THREE THEORIES

A Russian, a Swiss, and a North American might be expected to inhabit entirely different intellectual worlds, but this is not the case. Although there are significant differences between the theoretical positions of Vygotsky, Piaget, and Bandura, there are also important similarities that should not cause great surprise. The three theoretical perspectives share certain intellectual foundations. The development of each occurred in contexts that were in part shaped by the work of the others. Moreover, the theorists share a basic aim—to understand development. It thus makes sense first to examine the three theories in the context of the intellectual traditions in which they developed.

Vygotsky was well aware of contemporary intellectual developments in both Europe and North America and often cited European and American philosophers and psychologists [Kozulin, 1990; Rosa and Montero, 1990]. Many of Vygotsky's intellectual debts are less easy to trace now than when his work was first published; in the current Russian editions of his collected works, many passages originally attributed to others have now had the quotations marks removed [Valsiner, per. commun., 1991]. Among those Vygotsky cited, however, he explicitly acknowledged the debt he owed to Janet for ideas regarding the social nature of development [Van der Veer and Valsiner, 1988]. Vygotsky also referred often to Piaget, critically when Piaget appeared to downplay social influences on development [Vygotsky, 1988], approvingly at other times: 'In part . . . Piaget demonstrates . . . the huge role played by social factors in the development of the structure and functions of child thought' [Vygotsky, 1984, p. 86].

Piaget's works also contain many references to the views and research of his intellectual contemporaries and predecessors, not only in Europe but also North America. Not surprisingly, some of those Piaget cites approvingly (notably Janet, Claparede, and Baldwin) were also well known to Vygotsky. The publication of Vygotsky's work in English [Vygotsky, 1962] also received critical attention from Piaget [1962a; Piaget and Inhelder, 1969]. Moreover, Piaget shared with Vygotsky certain philosophical roots. For example, Piaget transformed a Kantian-inspired view of epistemology into one essentially dialectical in nature, probably under the inspiration of Hegel [Wartofsky, 1983]. Vygotsky's path to dialectics also started from Hegel; although it took a different route, via Marx and Engels. Piaget and Vygotsky clearly shared the belief that development constitutes a dialectical process [Wartofsky, 1983; Wozniak, 1975, 1987; Youniss, 1978].

Bandura's intellectual roots are not as clearly intertwined with those of Vygotsky and Piaget. However, both Bandura and Vygotsky were highly critical of simple stimulus-response models derived from behaviorism and mechanistic materialism. Both recognized the crucial impact of mediating factors—primarily cognitive (mental representations and information-processing abilities) for Bandura, and cultural symbols (language, tools, and institutions) for Vygotsky. Bandura briefly discussed Piaget's work on cognitive development, although he criticized Piaget's emphasis on the child's activity with the physical and logico-mathematical world and his perceived disregard of the impact of the social world [Bandura, 1986]. In part, Bandura's work developed in opposition to (and thus was influenced by) Piaget's view of cognitive development. However, in common with both Piaget and Vygotsky, Bandura believes that children do not passively imitate models in their social world, but are cognitively active in this process.

Similarities of perspective and shared intellectual backgrounds provide somewhat indirect evidence of compatible thinking. A more specific instance of intellectual influence is that provided by Baldwin [Cairns, 1992]. Vygotsky approvingly cited Baldwin [Valsiner and Van der Veer, 1988] for stressing the role of social factors in development. For example, Baldwin declared that the task of genetic psychology was to 'specify those forms of social interaction which enable individuals to develop' [Baldwin, 1913; quoted in Mugny and Carugati, 1989, p. 3]. He also employed the notion of sociogenesis ('social heredity') to describe how a child internalizes relevant influences from the social world as personality and understanding develop [Baldwin, 1895/1906]. Vygotsky's argument that interpersonal processes are transformed into intrapersonal characteristics mirrored Baldwin's (1895/1906) view: '[Imitation] enables me to pass from my experience of what you are, to an interpretation of what I am; and then from this fuller sense of what I am, back to a fuller knowledge of what you are' [p. 323].

Piaget's descriptions of the 'circular reactions' that occur in the sensorimotor stage are explicitly related to Baldwin's earlier work, and the very concepts of assimilation, accommodation, and equilibrium are all to be found in Baldwin's [1895/1906] writings. Piaget [1975/1985] argued explicitly, toward the end of his life, that 'as J.M. Baldwin saw quite clearly, the formation of the self is connected to early interpersonal relationships and especially to imitation' [p. 76].

Bandura does not cite Baldwin directly, but the latter clearly articulated the importance of social models for the developing child's behavioral functioning. Rosenthal and Zimmerman [1978] draw explicit connections between Bandura's emphasis on modeling influences and Baldwin's descriptions of the process of imitation. For example. Baldwin [1895/1906] wrote:

> It is not only likely—it is inevitable—that he [the child] makes up his personality, under limitations of heredity, by imitation out of the 'copy' set in the actions, temper, emotions, of the persons who build around him the social enclosure of his childhood [p. 340].

Both Baldwin and Bandura concentrated great effort on the explanation of the central processes that, as they develop, mediate and transform simple perceptions of imitated influence.

The intellectual worlds inhabited by Vygotsky, Piaget, and Bandura were thus not entirely separate from one another. Nonetheless, local social, intellectual, and historical contexts in which the theories developed also deserve consideration. Vygotsky developed his views in the context of building a psychology appropriate to the new Soviet state, one that was explicitly Marxist in orientation. As Kozulin [1990] points out, Vygotsky's Marxism was neither narrowly doctrinaire nor based on a 'mechanistic materialist' base of simple stimulus-response propositions. Nevertheless, dialectical materialist Marxist philosophy was without doubt an influence of major importance to Vygotsky [Blanck, 1990; Lee, 1985; Rosa and Montero, 1990; Scribner, 1985; Wertsch, 1985].

Piaget's and Bandura's theories also developed in the context of dissatisfaction with the simple stimulus-response mechanisms of learning theory. Although he did not ignore social factors, Piaget's intent was to explain how children come to know their world in the course of their own actions on it. He clearly did not regard them as "blank slates" waiting to be written on by those around them, as the following passage reflects:

> In the common view—the content of intelligence comes from outside, and the coordinations that organize it are only the consequences of language and symbolic instruments.

> But this passive interpretation of the act of knowledge is in fact con-
> tradicted at all levels of development [Piaget 1970/1983, pp. 103–104].

Bandura's theory also developed in opposition to the views expressed by contemporary learning theorists, although, unlike Piaget, Bandura was more interested in building on this base than developing an entirely different theoretical structure. His reformulation of traditional learning theory is profound, arguing for bidirectional reciprocal determinism incorporating within a 'triadic' model individual characteristics (such as beliefs, goals, expectations, and rule-making abilities), as well as the individual's behavior and the social environment [Bandura, 1989a, b]. This model is far removed from one based on simple unidirectional stimulus-response connections. Rather than de-emphasizing social factors, as Piaget did, Bandura sought to incorporate them into a radically modified version of learning theory.

COMMONALITIES IN CONCEPTUALIZING THE ROLE OF SOCIAL FACTORS

The theories of Vygotsky, Piaget, and Bandura thus developed in intellectual contexts that were shared in some ways, although they differed in others. Resulting similarities in theoretical perspectives include the presupposition that the social world plays a major role in children's cognitive growth. Piaget paid less explicit attention to social factors than did Vygotsky or Bandura, and Vygotsky was more concerned than the others with the interrelations of macro- and micro-social influences. Yet all three treated social influences partly at the level of cultural and historical context (macro factors) and partly at the level of interpersonal (micro) interactions.

Vygotsky

Vygotsky was clearest regarding the links between social factors of a cultural and historical nature and those of an interpersonal nature. Institution, tools, and symbol systems are the products of human beings, developed in various ways by different cultures over historical time. Vygotsky [1983] described the complex dynamics of historical and cultural development as follows:

> Culture creates special forms of behavior, changes the functioning of mind, constructs new levels in the developing system of human behavior . . . In the process of historical development, a social being changes the means and methods of his behavior, transforms natural inclinations and functions, develops and creates new, specifically cultural, forms of behavior [pp. 29–30].

From the Vygotskian perspective, interpersonal interactions can only be understood with reference to these historical and cultural forms. For example, the nature and processes of interaction between an adult and a child in a school setting cannot be fully understood without reference to the meaning imparted by that historically and culturally organized context (school), to the tools of learning, and to the meaning that the interaction itself has for the participants. Thus, social and cultural institutions, technologies, and tools channel the nature and focus of interpersonal interactions, which in turn mediate the development of children's higher mental functions (such as thinking, reasoning, problem-solving, mediated memory, and language).

According to Vygotsky's [1981] 'general genetic law of cultural development,' 'Any function in the child's cultural development appears twice, or on two planes. First it appears on the social plane, and then on the psychological plane' [p. 63]. Vygotsky argued that rather than deriving explanations of psychological activity from the individual's characteristics, the unit of analysis should be the individual engaged in social activity. Learning from others more competent in culturally appropriate skills or technologies is a prime example. Criticizing Piaget's contemporary position that children's development must precede learning, Vygotsky [1978] argued that 'learning is a necessary and universal aspect of the process of developing culturally organized, specifically human psychological functions . . . [T]he development process lags behind the learning process' [p. 90].

However, Vygotsky also believed that alongside the social-cultural-historical influences on development was a 'natural line' corresponding to purely biological changes:

> Within a general process of development, two qualitatively different lines of development, differing in origin, can be distinguished: the elementary processes, which are of biological origin, on the one hand, and the higher psychological functions, of sociocultural origin, on the other . . . The history of the development of the higher psychological functions is impossible without a study of their prehistory, their biological roots, and their organic disposition [Vygotsky, 1978, p. 46].

Vygotsky believed the development of speech to be paramount in the development of higher mental processes, but he also considered the use of tools other than language to be important both in phylogenetic and ontogenetic development. Vygotsky's discussion of grasping, for example, illustrates how mother-infant interaction helps the child to understand the signification of gesture well before the child is capable of language use. Thus, Vygotsky [1978], describing children's development in the first year of life, argued that 'the child's system of activity is determined at each specific stage both by the child's degree of organic development and by his or her degree of mastery in the use of tools' [p. 21].

The 'natural' line of 'organic development' (maturation) does not simply disappear when the mediated or 'cultural' line appears:

A normal child's socialization is usually fused with the processes of his maturation. Both lines of development—natural and cultural—coincide and merge one into the other. Both series of changes converge, mutually penetrating each other to form, in essence, a single series of formative sociobiological influences on the personality [Vygotsky, 1983, p. 22].

Elsewhere Vygotsky [1978] argued:

The zone of proximal development defines those functions that have not yet matured but are in the process of maturation, functions that will mature tomorrow but are currently in an embryonic state. These functions could be termed the 'buds' or 'flowers' of development rather than the 'fruits' of development [p. 86].

The influence of the social world is thus restricted to bounds that are set by the child's previous developmental course and by limits that are defined partly by the child's present development state and what can be achieved in collaboration: 'Instruction is only useful when it moves ahead of development. When it does, it impels or wakens a whole series of functions that are in a stage of maturation lying in the zone of proximal development' [Vygotsky, 1987, p. 212]. Instruction or assistance clearly has an upward bound that is determined by the child's potential at that time and by the nature of the collaboration:

We said that in collaboration the child can always do more than he can independently. We must add the stipulation that he cannot do infinitely more. What collaboration contributes to the child's performance is restricted to limits which are determined by the state of his development and his intellectual potential [Vygotsky, 1987, p. 209].

The zone of proximal development is thus the difference between what a child can accomplish independently and what he or she can achieve in conjunction with another, more competent person. The zone is not some clearcut space that exists independently of the process of joint activity itself, however. Rather, it is created in the course of social interaction:

We propose that an essential feature of learning is that it creates the zone of proximal development; that is, learning awakens a variety of developmental processes that are able to operate only when the child is interacting with people in his environment and in collaboration with his peers [Vygotsky, 1978, p. 90].

Vygotsky did not focus on peer collaboration, however, concentrating for the most part on adult guidance of development. This focus is hardly surprising, as adults are typically more skilled at the task or problem and more easily able to provide assistance appropriate to the child's current level of thinking [Ellis and Rogoff, 1982, 1986; Gauvain and Rogoff, 1989; Radziszewska and Rogoff, 1988].

Vygotsky's approach has been termed 'co-constructionist' [Tudge et al., 1991; Valsiner, 1987] to capture the mutual and interwoven links he drew between individual and social factors. Vygotsky was adamant that the only way to guard against reductionism of the individual to the social or the social to the individual was to use a unit of analysis that encapsulated both. Word meaning was one such unit, he argued [Vygotsky, 1987]; others, used by his followers have included 'tool-mediated action' and 'goal-directed action' [Leont'ev, 1981; Wertsch, 1985, 1991; Wertsch and Sammarco, 1985; Tulviste, 1991; Zinchenko, 1985]. Meaning, tools, and goals all necessarily relate the individual and the social world of which the individual is a part, for they are all formed in a sociocultural context. Understanding the use of tools (psychological or physical) is jointly constructed by the developing child and by the culture in which the child is developing, with the assistance of those who are already more competent in the use of those tools and in culturally appropriate goals [Tudge et al., 1991]. These units of analysis therefore integrate the micro-social contexts of interaction with the broader social, cultural, and historical contexts that encompass them.

Piaget

One oft-mentioned difference between Piaget and Vygotsky is that Piaget began with the individual child who progressively becomes social, whereas for Vygotsky the child is social from the start [Tudge and Rogoff, 1989]. In fact, the Piagetian infant is in some senses maximally social, making no distinction between self and outside world. Piaget's interest in the social world was primarily with social influence at the micro-level, or interpersonal contact. Piaget noted this influence from 3 or 4 months of age, when infants begin to imitate the gestures of adults who have just imitated them—a 'prefiguration of representation' [Piaget and Inhelder 1966/1969, p. 55]. Piaget and Inhelder [1966/1969] cited Escalona approvingly:

> Contact with persons . . . becomes more and more important, heralding a transition from contagion to communication (Escalona). Even before the formation of a self complementary to and interacting with others we witness the elaboration of a whole system of exchanges through imitation and the reading of general signs [p. 24].

Indeed, for Piaget the very concept of accommodation is inherently linked to imitation from the first year of life. Before the end of the senso-rimotor stage, a social model may act as a source of imitation even when it is no longer present. This 'deferred imitation' is considered the product of new representational abilities [Piaget, 1962b].

Piaget also described situations in which moral development and the development of rule-based play occur within the framework of peer social interaction and cooperation [Piaget 1932/1965]. Interaction between peers can be seen as both a cause and a consequence of the slow decline in child-hood egocentrism that occurs between the ages of 3 and 7 [Piaget, 1923/1959]. Social factors of an interpersonal nature play an even larger role in children's development once children are able to take another's per-spective into account [Piaget, 1945/1977], and peer social relations take on a key role in adolescence. Indeed, 'the organization of formal structures must depend upon the social milieu as well . . . A particular social envi-ronment remains indispensable for the realization of [the possibilities ac-corded by the maturation of the nervous system]' [Inhelder and Piaget, 1955/1958, p. 337].

Piaget did not solely concern himself with social factors of an inter-personal nature, however. He argued, for example, that moral judgments are influenced by interactions with both peers and adults (the latter providing the 'morality of constraint'—of obeying a rule out of respect for adult au-thority, as well as by the historically formed nature of social institutions. Piaget distinguished 'primitive' from 'modern' societies at least in part by the former's requirement for absolute compliance of children to adult de-mands [1932/1965]. Piaget [1970/1983] also accepted that different cultural practices (such as the presence or absence of formal schooling) can prevent adolescents from reaching formal operational thinking, as well as retard the rate at which children pass through earlier stages of development. Similarly, he believed that historical changes within a culture, such as the introduc-tion of more 'modern' approaches to schooling, are likely to affect the na-ture of adult-child and child-child interpersonal relations [Piaget, 1970].

Of the three theorists, only Piaget argued that peer interaction is both qualitatively different from and superior to adult-child interaction in facili-tating cognitive growth. Under conditions of unequal power, a child may well accept the adult's view but is unlikely to undergo the cognitive re-structuring necessary for cognitive development [Piaget, 1945/1977, 1948/1959]. By comparison, when a peer has a different perspective, the equal power relations allow for argument and subsequent development:

> Criticism is born of discussion, and discussion is only possible among equals: cooperation alone will therefore accomplish what intellectual con-straint [unquestioning belief in the adult's greater knowledge] failed to bring about [Piaget, 1932/1965, p. 409].

Piaget thus believed that the development of rule-based play and per-spective-taking both occur in interaction with peers rather than adults.

In his early work, Piaget [1923/1959] argued that children below the age of 7 are unlikely to benefit from social interaction, given the egocentric nature of preoperational thought. Subsequently, however, in the third edition of *The Language and Thought of the Child*, Piaget modified that view, stating that even during the preoperational stage, children can engage in the sort of discussion likely to lead to development. During this period, the child 'fluctuates between two poles, the monologue—individual or collective—and discussion or genuine exchange of ideas' [Piaget, 1948/1959, p. 258]. The ability to engage in discussion and argument helps children move beyond the preoperational stage.

Piaget accepted that adults aid children's development, acting as 'the source of educational and verbal transmissions of cultural elements in the cognitive sense' [Piaget and Inhelder, 1966/1969, p. 116]. Moreover, Piaget [1928/1977] believed that teacher-child interaction was useful 'to the extent that the intelligent teacher [is able] to efface him or herself, to become an equal and not a superior, to discuss and to examine, rather than to agree and constrain morally . . .' [p. 231]. Nevertheless, Piaget emphasized the importance of peer, rather than adult-child, interaction.

It is thus clear that Piaget believed that social factors have a major role to play in development, both at the interpersonal and historical-cultural levels. He made this belief apparent as early as 1928: 'Social life is a necessary condition for the development of logic. We thus believe that social life transforms the individual's very nature' [Piaget, 1928/1977, p. 239]. Toward the end of his life, he returned to the same theme, declaring that 'the most remarkable aspect of the way in which human knowledge is built up . . . is that it has a collective as well as an individual nature' [Piaget, 1967/1971, p. 359].

Bandura

Social influences, not surprisingly, play a large role in a theory originally labeled 'social learning.' However, Bandura does not posit unidirectional influences of social factors. His basic theoretical construct of 'triadic reciprocal determinism' treats social factors as influencing and being influenced by personal and behavioral determinants:

> Personal and environmental factors do not function as independent deter-minants; rather, they determine each other. People create, alter, and destroy environments. The changes they produce in environmental conditions, in turn, affect their behavior and the nature of future life [Bandura, 1986, p. 23].

Bandura views the social determinants of development as occurring by means of observation:

Fortunately, most human behavior is learned by observation through modeling. By observing others, one forms rules of behavior, and on future occasions this coded information serves as a guide for action . . . The models who figure prominently in children's lives . . . serve as indispensable sources of knowledge that contribute to what and how children think about different matters [Bandura, 1986, pp. 47, 486].

However, Bandura has also enumerated the various mediating cognitive capabilities that help determine the observer's subsequent development and action. He has increasingly emphasized cognition, with mental representations and information-processing abilities viewed as mediating links between stimulus and response. As early as 1971, Bandura wrote: 'in social learning theory observers function as active agents who transform, classify, and organize modeling stimuli into easily remembered schemes rather than as quiescent cameras or tape recorders that simply store isomorphic representations of modeled events' [p. 21]. The emphasis on cognition is reflected, perhaps belatedly, in a new terminology—'social cognitive' theory [Bandura, 1986], replacing 'social learning' theory [Bandura, 1977]. Other mediating factors besides cognition that Bandura considers critical include biology and maturation. 'Physical structure and sensory and neural systems affect behavior and impose constraints on capabilities' [1989b, p. 3].

Thus, Bandura and his followers have argued that social influences can only operate within the constraints imposed by the 'hard wiring' of the psychological system at its current level of maturation [Bandura, 1989b; Rosenthal and Zimmerman, 1978; Zimmerman, 1983]. Bandura also believes that the consequences of the observer's own behavior affect learning and motivation for future action. Bandura's most recent emphasis on the importance of personal self-efficacy as a determinant of behavior also signals a shift toward heightened consideration of individual factors in social-interactive contexts [Bandura, 1989a; Wood and Bandura, 1989].

Bandura also recognizes the impact of the broader sociocultural context on development. For example, in discussing the development of psychosocial functioning, Bandura [1989b] argues that 'diversity in social practices produces substantial individual differences in the capabilities that are cultivated and those that remain underdeveloped' [Bandura, 1989b, p. 1]. Similarly, Bandura [1986] argues with regard to the development of sex roles, 'A comprehensive theory of how roles get linked to gender must extend well beyond gender conception to a social analysis of how institutional structures and sanctions shape gender roles' [p. 98]. Elsewhere, he states, 'Proximal social influences of parents, teachers, and peers, as well as distal social and symbolic influences from mass media and cultural institutions all serve to promote gender development' [Bussey and Bandura, 1992, p. 1237].

Bandura believes that peers can be useful models: 'Peers serve several important efficacy functions. Those who are most experienced and competent provide models of efficacious styles of thinking and behavior. A vast amount of social learning occurs among peers' [Bandura, 1989b, p. 45]. However, unlike Piaget but in common with Vygotsky, Bandura does not believe that peer interaction is necessarily more effective than child-adult interaction, arguing that facilitation of cognitive development depends primarily on the model's greater competence and perceived qualities [1986, 1989b]. Whether the model is a peer or an adult is therefore less important for Bandura than is the attitude of the child toward the model, the way in which the model is treated (whether rewarded for his or her behavior), and the personal characteristics of the model.

MANIFESTATIONS OF THE THEORIES IN RESEARCH

We have argued that there are more similarities in the theories of Vygotsky, Piaget, and Bandura than are apparent from the superficial contrasts and differences between them that are often drawn. One reason, it was suggested, is a tendency on the part of interpreters to try to place theorists into easily differentiable categories. A second reason, on which we concentrate in this section, is that empirical research and the theory on which it is based do not necessarily mesh. In particular, the ways in which these theories have been operationalized in research does not, in many instances live up to the complexity afforded by the theories themselves. This fact is perhaps not surprising, given that few pieces of empirical research are intended to test more than a few hypotheses derived from the theory on which the research is based. Nevertheless, in undertaking research, proponents of the theoretical positions examined here have rather consistently stressed particular aspects of the theories, aspects that serve to emphasize dissimilarities between them.

Research in the Tradition of Vygotsky

Vygotsky himself [1978] argued that there should be a close interrelation between theory and methodology:

> In general, any fundamentally new approach to a scientific problem inevitably leads to new methods of investigation and analysis. The invention of new methods that are adequate to the new ways in which problems are posed requires far more than a simple modification of previously accepted methods [p. 58].

For the most part, scholars working in the Vygotskian tradition have focused their attention on children in collaboration with adults [Cole, 1985; Edwards and Mercer, 1987; Newman et al., 1989; Tharp and Gallimore, 1988; Valsiner, 1984, 1987; Wertsch, 1979; Wertsch and Hickman, 1987;

Wertsch et al., 1984; Wertsch and Sammarco, 1985]. A distinguishing characteristic of this research is the fact that at least as much attention is paid to the processes of interaction as to the consequences of that interaction. This emphasis is exemplified in the approach taken by Wertsch and his colleagues examining mother-child interaction in the course of solving model-copying problems or by Valsiner's [1984, 1987] study of the 'co-construction' of culturally appropriate mealtime behavior. Wertsch [Wertsch, 1985; Wertsch and Hickmann, 1987; Wertsch et al., 1984; Wertsch and Sammarco, 1985] argues that the immediate results of the collaboration (the problem solution) are less important than the ways in which mothers and their children arrive at a solution. These ways vary as a function of sociocultural factors, such as whether or not the mothers have the goal of error-free solution [Wertsch et al., 1984], and the extent of direct or indirect assistance they provide [Wertsch and Sammarco, 1985].

Other Vygotskian scholars have focused on processes of interaction in one type of sociocultural institution—school [Edwards and Mercer, 1987; Newman et al,, 1989; Tharp and Gallimore, 1988]. They have described how shared understanding is constructed in the course of joint activity and communication between teachers (those more competent at certain culturally valued tools and skills) and students. As Wertsch [1991] convincingly shows, one of those tools is the mode of discourse valued in school.

Although the Vygotskian scholars have focused their attention on adult-child interaction, there has also been some interest in peer interaction [Forman, 1987, 192; Forman and Cazden, 1985; Forman and McPhail, in press; Gauvain and Rogoff, 1989; Kol'tsova, 1978; Kol'tsova and Martin, 1985; Martin, 1985; Radziszewska and Rogoff, 1988; Rubtsov, 1981, 1991; Rubtsov and Guzman, 1984–1985; Tudge, 1990, in press]. Forman in particular has fulfilled the Vygotskian requirement of focusing on the 'history' of behavior (i.e. examining development over time) by following her dyads across repeated sessions, describing how 9- and 13-year-olds attain joint understanding in the course of collaboration [Forman, 1992; Forman and Cazden, 1985; Forman and McPhail, in press]. Forman has also situated her findings in a macro-social context by examining the presuppositions of interaction within a school context.

Tudge [1990, in press] has argued that full understanding of the effects of peer collaboration on cognitive development can only be gained by focusing on the collaborative processes themselves, and that therefore the most appropriate unit of analysis is the dyad, rather than the individual. His findings indicated that shared understanding attained in the course of interaction was critical in bringing about cognitive change, but that children could be led to regress as well as progress as a consequence of such collaboration. As Bandura might argue, a partner's competence may be a necessary, but not sufficient, condition in assisting development. Accurate perception of the partner's greater competence may be critical. Perhaps for this reason, Vygotskian researchers who have contrasted peer and adult-child collaboration have found that children paired with an adult subsequently improved more than those paired with a same-age or slightly older child [Ellis and Rogoff, 1982, 1986; Radziszewska and Rogoff, 1988; Rogoff and Gauvain, 1986].

These studies demonstrate that joint understanding, or intersubjectivity, is arrived at in the course of interaction. They imply that such understanding is crucial for cognitive development. The adult-child literature also illustrates that successful joint completion of a task may occur prior to the child's being able to complete it alone, thus reversing the view, derived from traditional cognitive psychology and from social cognitive theory, that competence must precede performance. Furthermore, it demonstrates the Vygotskian concept that development first occurs between people and only subsequently is internalized or appropriated by the individual.

However, there are limitations to much of the Vygotskian-inspired research. A number of scholars have called attention to the fact that much of it has focused solely on the effects of interaction at the interpersonal level, with insufficient attention paid to the interrelations between interpersonal and sociocultural levels [Cole, 1985; Luria, 1976; Tulviste, 1991; Wertsch, 1985, 1991; Wertsch et al., 1991; Zinchenko, 1985]. Moreover, Vygotskian research has been insufficiently concerned with the way in which maturation (the 'natural' line of development) relates to the interpersonal and sociocultural processes that are the typical foci, despite the fact that this interface is of major theoretical concern.

Research in the Tradition of Piaget

Despite the fact that Piaget acknowledged the importance of social factors in development, he did not view them as central enough to set himself or his coworkers the task of exploring their significance. Researchers in the Piagetian tradition have focused on the individual as the unit of analysis and examined the child's solitary attempts to make sense of the physical, logical, or mathematical world. Work by Piaget himself on the role of social interaction is sparse and confined to a period early in his career [Piaget, 1932/1965, 1923/1959]. It has been left to others to take seriously Piaget's writings about the impact of the social world on development [Bearison, in press; Furth, 1987; Youniss, 1983]. Scholars working in the Piagetian tradition have taken as their starting point Piaget's views of the importance of discussion between peers who bring different perspectives to the task. They have undertaken to show that this type of discussion—termed 'cognitive conflict' or 'sociocognitive conflict'—is highly beneficial in promoting cognitive development [Ames and Murray, 1982; Doise et al., 1975, 1976; Doise and Mugny, 1984; Perret-Clermont, 1980; Perret-Clermont and Schubauer-Leoni, 1981].

The task most commonly used to illustrate the effectiveness of cognitive conflict has been conservation. Children are pretested individually to establish their status as conservers or nonconservers and then brought together in pairs or triads. To ensure socio-cognitive conflict (stemming from a difference in perspectives), only one of the partners is a conserver. The children are asked to reach a joint conservation decision—for example, whether there still are equal numbers of objects in two rows after those in one row have been spread further apart. Subsequently, individual posttests are conducted, to assess whether nonconservers have learned to conserve. The outcome, rather than the process of interaction, has typically been the focus, and the unit of analysis is the individual, rather than the dyad.

Results of this experimental procedure have been impressive. After reviewing a variety of such studies, Murray [1982, 1983] concluded that between 80 and 94% of nonconservers attained conservation after been paired with a conserving peer. Reasons offered by new conservers typically are not simple imitations of those given by their conserving partners [Botvin and Murray, 1975; Perret-Clermont, 1980]. Murray and his colleagues [Ames and Murray, 1982; Murray, 1982, 1983] hold that the mechanism fostering development is the cognitive conflict generated by the initial difference in perspectives. Other Piagetian scholars have argued that 'opposition of divergent cognitive responses' is important but that cognitive development still requires 'social coordination of points of view' if it is to be successful [Mugny et al., 1984, pp. 127–128], and that mutual collaboration is more effective than conflict per se [Bearison et al., 1986; Glachan and Light, 1982; Light and Perret-Clermont, 1989].

Piaget-inspired research on the effects of peer interaction has focused almost exclusively on social factors at the micro level. Even Piagetian cross-cultural researchers have been primarily concerned with the extent of support for Piaget's theories in different cultures [Dasen and Heron, 1981; Newman et al., 1983]. However, a few researchers have examined interpersonal influences in cultural context. Mackie [1980, 1983] studied the effects of peer interaction among children of European and Pacific Island descent in New Zealand. She argued that 'more attention needs to be paid to [macro] social variables mediating the effect of social interaction on cognitive development' [1983, p. 148], after finding that her Polynesian participants were less likely than Europeans to engage actively in interaction. Tudge [1989] examined social interaction in a mathematical balance beam task among children from the USA and Soviet Union, but found no evidence that growing up in a supposedly more collectively oriented culture affected the nature or results of interaction. Focusing on subcultural differences, Perret-Clermont [1980] examined patterns of social interaction in conservation tasks among children of different social classes, and similarly found little to differential them.

Some scholars working within a Piagetian framework have become concerned with the processes, in addition to the consequences, of interaction [Bearison, in press; Bell and Grossen, 1989; Light and Perret-Clermont, 1989; Perret-Clermont and Brossard, 1985; Perret-Clermont et al., 1991]. The focus of these studies is more on collaboration than on conflict, and the concept of intersubjectivity (shared understanding) is invoked as the mechanism relating the interactional processes to the cognitive consequences of the interaction. Perret-Clermont et al. [1991] have argued, in fact, that the unit of analysis should not be the individual at all, but rather the interacting partners. It is interesting to note that they have supported these arguments with reference as much to Vygotsky as to Piaget.

In summary, despite the wealth of Piagetian-inspired research, very few Piagetian scholars have focused on the effects of social interaction on children's development. Those who have done so have been concerned almost exclusively with interpersonal interaction, with little attention paid to influences at the sociocultural level. Even Piagetian scholars interested in cross-cultural issues rarely have been concerned with the ways in which cultural phenomena are expressed at the interpersonal level. Moreover, Piagetian researchers interested in the relations between social interaction and development have focused more on the consequences than the processes of interaction; those who are exceptions to this rule are as likely to invoke Vygotsky as Piaget when considering process variables.

Research in the Tradition of Bandura

Similar shortcomings in conducting research that does justice to the complexity of the theory are visible in much of the research addressed to Bandura's theory. Of the three theorists, Bandura has developed the most experimentally rigorous empirical research program. Insistence on experimental control has perhaps limited the scope of such research, relative to the bidirectional and contextualizing nature of the theory. From early in his career, Bandura's stated object was to combine real-life situation with strict experimental control in order

> to reproduce as closely as possible the social stimuli and responses that occur in real life situations concerning which the experimenter wishes to make causal statements. However, this does not imply that laboratory experiments should be designed to reproduce real life in toto; if they were, the experimenter would necessarily relinquish the crucial scientific strategy of manipulating one variable while holding others constant, and thereby forfeiting the possibility of establishing precise cause-effect relationships [Bandura and Walters, 1963, p. 46].

Because of the concern with experimental control, and the difficulty of experimentally controlling the influences of macro-social and internal developmental factors, social cognitive researchers in Bandura's tradition have focused largely on aspects of the models and the conditions said to underlie imitation of the model, with less attention given to children's 'internal' development (Bandura's emphasis on personal self-efficacy being a notable exception). Moreover, only recently has much attention been paid to social factors at the macro-level [Bandura, 1990; Bussey and Bandura, 1992].

Most social cognitive researchers influenced by Bandura have explored the ways in which models (typically adults) affect the behaviors of observers (typically children) in an experimental setting. In general, the findings support the contention that modeling has a clear impact on development. Keller and Carlson [1974] showed that 3- and 5-year-olds were capable of learning appropriate social behavior after observing a film of slightly older children modeling such behavior. Similarly, Birch [1980] demonstrated clear changes in children's food preferences based on the influence of same-age peers. Others have found clear modeling effects in the areas of language acquisition [Hood and Bloom, 1979] and moral judgment [Leon, 1984]. Zimmerman and his colleagues [Rosenthal and Zimmerman, 1972; Zimmerman, 1983; Zimmerman and Lanaro, 1974] have studied social influences on the attainment of conservation, arguing that the critical mechanism is not cognitive conflict, as the Piagetians proposed, but rather a type of rule learning in which the less advanced nonconserver models the position of a more advanced partner. However, perceived social power or efficacy appears to mediate the model's influence [Bandura et al., 1967; Davidson and Smithy, 1982], and therefore the most effective models tend to be adults.

Research on social interaction inspired by Bandura's theory has thus most often examined social phenomena in terms of effects on observers' behavior, demonstrating changes brought about by exposure to particular social models. However, some work has dealt with the effects of being a model [Toner et al., 1978]. Responsibility for being a model of self-restrained behavior resulted in higher levels of restraint, compared to levels in children not given this responsibility. Yet, in both cases (of models and observers), although Bandura [1986] discusses the 'two-way influence process' involved in observational learning, experimenters have limited themselves to analyzing results based on the individual as the unit of analysis, rather than focusing on the mutual interplay of interacting partners, an approach that might lend itself more effectively to the study of bidirectionality of effects.

DIFFERENCES IN CONCEPTUALIZING THE RELATION OF SOCIAL AND INDIVIDUAL FACTORS

We have argued that the three theorists considered are more similar than one might expect based on much of what is written about them. Each theorist takes account of social factors, both at the interpersonal and cultural levels, and each believes that individuals play an active role in their own development, and that maturation plays a critical role. However, the fact that research stemming from these theoretical positions devotes unequal attention to these factors supports the prevailing view that the theories are quite different.

Nonetheless, some genuine differences remain among these theories, differences not attributable solely to the emphases accorded by the theories' interpreters. Social influences on development were not as central to Piaget [Forman and Kraker, 1985; Piaget, 1970; Tudge and Rogoff, 1989], as they were to Bandura and Vygotsky. Moreover, Bandura's conceptualization of the nature of the relation between social and individual is critically different from that of Vygotsky (with Piaget closer to the latter than the former).

A useful distinction has been suggested by Valsiner and Winegar [1992] between 'contextualizing' and 'contextual' approaches. Contextualizing approaches view the social world as an important context in which development occurs; if one changes the context, development is likely to be altered. Nonetheless, individual and context are conceptually distinguished, and one can focus on the effects of the context on a child, or on the effects of a child on his or her context. Contextual approaches, in contrast, make no such distinction, essentially blurring the boundaries between individuals and the contexts in which they are situated.

Vygotsky's theory is the clearest example of a contextual theory. Individual development cannot be conceived outside a social world, and that social world is simultaneously interpersonal, cultural, and historical. In other words, from a Vygotskian perspective one cannot consider social interaction between peers or between adults and children without understanding the historically formed cultural context within which that interaction takes place. Children's cognitive development is thus not the product simply of biological maturation, nor of interaction between them and others in their environment (which is the level at which both Piaget and Bandura deal primarily with social factors), but is intricately related to history and culture [Tulviste, 1991]. This relationship is clearly not unidirectional, for cultures develop as a result of human action and interaction. Cole [1985] could thus describe interactions within a child's zone of proximal development as being the place 'where culture and cognition create each other.'

At the interpersonal level as well, Vygotsky's theory most explicitly builds upon a transactional view of development—the view that the influence of interacting partners cannot, either in principle or in reality, be separated [Altman and Rogoff, 1987; Sameroff, 1975]. Scholars working in a Vygotskian framework have consistently argued that social influences are not somehow 'outside' the individual, ready to be internalized by the child [Newman et al., 1989; Rogoff, 1990; Shotter, 1989, in press; Tudge, 1992; Tudge et al., 1991; Valsiner, 1987; Wertsch, 1985, 1991; Wertsch and Bivens, in press]. Rather, both partners change in the course of interaction. New understanding, gained through collaboration, is a product of the child's original understanding, the partner's different understanding, the child's difficulties with the task and the ways they are expressed in the course of the interaction, the partner's responses to those difficulties, and so on. Since this process evolves over time, and each person's responses depend on what the other has previously done or said, the outcome is one that cannot be attributed to either one or the other. The unit of analysis accordingly extends beyond the individual.

Although Piaget focuses· on social factors far less than either Bandura or Vygotsky, he argued that interaction between social partners should be considered in the same way as a child's interactions with the physical world: 'The social relations equilibrated in cooperation . . . [are] exactly like all the logical operations exercised by the individual on the external world' [Piaget, 1945/1977, p. 159]. Equilibration, occurring as a result of interactions between a child and the environment (whether physical or social), is such that the child never simply internalizes some aspect of that environment. Piaget [1945/1977] argued that as a result of engaging in discussion, interlocutors may arrive at a new, equilibrated level of understanding that is related to what both individuals brought to the discussion. In true dialectical fashion, the resulting changes in both children are not explicable in terms of the separate influences of either, but in the mutual interplay of influence. Similar arguments have been made by Bearison [in press], Light and Perret-Clermont [1989], and Youniss [1983].

In this regard, Piaget's theory approaches the status of a contextual theory. However, the vast bulk of the research that Piaget conducted devoted no attention to social factors, even to the extent of his not considering the influence of his questioning on the thinking of his own children. The same is true of Piaget-inspired scholars who have conducted research on the effects of social interaction. They have almost always conceived of the effects as unidirectional and only rarely examined interactional processes, in order to assess mutual or transactional influences.

In Bandura's theory, context is ever-present, particularly the immediate context (agents in the social world who are potentially available as models) but also the broader societal context. Bandura argues that the relation between individual and context is reciprocal, rather than unidirectional, and stresses the active nature of children, who seek out models on the basis of their preexisting attitudes and interests as well as their current developmental status [Bandura, 1986]. Nevertheless, scholars conducting research from Bandura's social cognitive perspective appear primarily interested in the impact of the external social world on the developing child, and thus most often view the influence of a model as if it were conceptually separate from the observer. Indeed, the model need not be physically present, except in videotaped form or on television. The interacting elements, therefore, are viewed as independent, with the child needing to internalize what is 'out there' in the environment. The reciprocal processes of which Bandura writes are not a focus of research in this tradition.

SUMMARY AND CONCLUSIONS

The purpose of this article has been to examine the theoretical positions of Vygotsky, Piaget, and Bandura with respect to the relations between social factors and cognitive development. Because of a predilection for categorization on the part of interpreters and because empirical research tends to be more narrowly focused than the theory on which it is based, an impression has been fostered that these theoretical positions are highly dissimilar. However, the three theorists did not work (and do not continue to work, in Bandura's case) in intellectual isolation. Each theory developed in a shared intellectual environment, in a context shaped by the work of either one or both of the others, and with a shared goal of making sense of the nature of development. As a result, the theories in fact have much in common.

We conclude, however, that although commonalities exist, important distinctions remain. Although each theorist accepts that the social world (considered both at the macro- and micro-levels) plays a role in individual development, only Vygotsky argues that development must be understood in terms of the interpenetration of social factors, of both a historical/ cultural and an interpersonal kind, and the child's individual development. Both Piaget and Bandura argue that environment-organism influences are bidirectional as the unit of analysis, arguing that an individual's development can only be understood by knowing how the individual has processed what has been internalized (Bandura) or comes to make sense of his or her own activity on the outside world (Piaget). In Vygotsky's theory, the process of collaborating with another person, more competent in the skills, tools, and technologies of the culture, is the way in which greater understanding is reached. This greater understanding is not something that is outside the child and has to be taken inside; rather, it is created in the very process of interaction—an initially joint product in which the child has a part, based on his or her original understanding and degree of involvement. Vygotsky's unit of analysis therefore must go beyond the individual actor.

PART IV:
COMPARISON OF THEORIES

STRAUSS ARTICLE

Choose three of the theories discussed by Strauss and compare and contrast them with respect to the following issues: a) source of motivation; b) source of knowledge; c) relationship between learning and development. Refer to the text, the Strauss article, and class discussion when formulating your answer.

_____

_____

_____

_____

_____

_____

_____

TUDGE/WINTERHOFF ARTICLE

Briefly discuss differences and similarities among the three theorists' views of the relation between the social world and cognitive development.

_____

_____

_____

_____

_____

_____

_____

PART V

INTELLIGENCE TESTING, STANDARDIZED TESTING AND ASSESSMENT: THE LABELING GAME

THE LABELED CHILD

by Karen Morrow Durica
Durica teaches at Carl Sandburg Elementary School
Little, Colorado, USA

I pray for the labeled child;
That child who is gifted and talented.
No longer can she be lazy and idle
Or a daydreamer.
So much more is expected
Of those as gifted and talented as she.

I pray for the labeled child;
That child who is learning disabled.
No longer will the world expect brilliance
No longer will someone tell him to reach for the stars
Because that is where greatness will be found.

I pray for the labeled child;
That child who is dyslexic.
Reading—oh, the joy of reading!
Will always be hard for her to find.
No matter that she can recite—no sing—
Mary Had A Little Lamb,
She won't be able to read it,
At least not without difficulty.
She will learn that all her friends
Who laugh and cry and wonder about books
Can do so because they are not dyslexic.

I pray for the labeled child;
That child who is A.D.D.
An unorganized bubble of hyperactivity.
No longer will someone teach him to cope in a world

That values compliance.
No longer will someone say "You can do this;
Oh, it may be hard, but it is within you to do this."
A dose of medicine now replaces the need for that inner effort
And eliminates the possible victory.

I pray for the labeled child;
That child who is emotionally handicapped.
That child who rebels
Because she should rebel.
The child who acts out
Because there is nowhere else
For the hurt and anxiety and fear to go.
The child who is diagnosed "sick."
When perhaps her actions are the one true sign of sanity
In the demented world in which she is forced to live.

I pray for the child of no label.
In a system which marks so many special,
This child neither shines nor demands.
For this child life has been neither harsh nor generous.
This is the one who "makes" the teacher's day
Because there are so many children who need real attention.

I pray most for all for some magic day
When the tests, the labels, and the names
Will disappear—will be forgotten.
When each child who enters a classroom
Will be an apprentice of learning.
When each classroom will be a safe place
To discover—on your own—
What will be the struggles of your life,
And the victories.
When the feeble and the bright,
The gregarious and the shy
Will all find their place
In the great adventure of education.
When the only label that will be attached to anyone is

LEARNER.

Reading Teacher, 1995, 503.

PIAGET, IQ, AND THE NATURE-NURTURE CONTROVERSY

by H. G. Furth
Catholic University of America, Washington, D.C.

Abstract. Piaget's concepts of experience and subject-object interaction are clarified. Species-specific developmental experiences that are common to all people are distinguished from particular learned experiences on which individual differences are based. Four basic assumptions of IQ tests—age constancy, scholastic validity, standard environmental and performance sufficiency—are examined and found alien to Piaget's theory. In conclusion, heredity is not a concept that can be statistically separated from environment and thus from Piaget's standpoint the nature-nurture controversy is devoid of meaning.

Piaget's theory of intellectual development is frequently interpreted as being an interactionist and maturational stage theory. This interpretation can be defended but requires an understanding of the words 'interaction' and 'maturation' rather different from their traditional use. One speaks of two factors interacting when these two factors have a clearly defined existence and contribute in differing proportion to the existence of a third factor. In this manner the traditional nature-nurture question is approached. Statistics are used to arrive at a numerical estimate of the relative importance of either innate or environmental factors on intellectual development.

One may legitimately ask what stand Piaget's theory could take on this question. From his insistence on the internal regulatory mechanisms of development it would be easy to conclude that his theory attributes an overriding role to innate and hereditary conditions. Similarly, when the word maturation is applied to a theory of development, the stress is on the innate side of the supposed contributing factors. Piaget's conception of developmental stages could then be readily seen in the light of an internal physiological mechanism to which environmental contributions are almost incidental.

It is the purpose of this paper to show first that the suggested interpretations of Piaget's theory are quite inadequate and misleading. After these preliminary considerations we shall concern ourselves with Piaget's position vis-a'-vis three basic questions in the nature-nurture controversy, namely, individual differences, standard tests, and heredity.

EXPERIENCE AND INTERACTION IN
PIAGET'S THEORY

First, one cannot in Piaget's view neatly separate organisms and environment as two preexisting entities the interaction of which would lead to the development of human intelligence. Second, the stages of which Piaget speaks are not physiological mechanisms but mechanisms of human behavior. The condition for their appearance is not, or is not merely, the maturation of physiological organs but primarily human behavior in a human environment. The repetition of the words human in the preceding phrase is to underline the type of behavior and environment that is required and the common bond that links these two notions. In other words, not just any existence or activity leads to stage characteristic development but activities that are species-specific in a biological sense, that is in our case, activities to which evolution has adapted the human person and his environment.

In line with Piaget's thinking human behavior in all its varieties can be considered from two angles. First, as representative of common human capacities of knowing and, second, as representative of particular skills and individually varying contingencies. For instance, an infant who can walk purposefully from one place to another in his immediate neighborhood demonstrates at the same time the common sensorimotor mechanism of 'knowing to walk' and the particular knowing of his immediate whereabouts. Depending on one's interest, one can focus on the particular learning aspect of this achievement in which case the particular contingencies of the environment play a crucial role, or one can focus on the common species-specific aspect of walking behavior in which case one ignores the particular and individualistic components and considers only the common components of the environment, e.g., gravity, stable physical objects, visual and factual cues, etc.

Take as another example of a more theoretical behavior children's comprehension of combinatorial properties. A child may have blocks of three colors in front of him and make pairs or triplets of blocks of different colors. To understand a sequence of two or three different items is easy enough for a three- or four-year-old. To learn to name colors or to identify some other items that could be arranged in a sequence, say, a spoon, a fork, and a knife, is also an easy achievement. These identifications presuppose of course among other things particular contingencies to which the individual child was exposed. But it takes the further experience of a number of years until the child comprehends combinational ordering in a systematic manner, e.g., blue blue, blue yellow, blue red, yellow blue, yellow yellow, etc. This ordering is not a thing which the child can find in his environment; on the contrary, it is what Piaget calls a reflective feedback from the child's own actions on the environment. The experience of ordering which the child has—actively doing the ordering himself or observing it in another person's doing—can be described from two viewpoints. Either as a physical or simple experience mainly responsible for particular learning as exemplified above, or as logical-mathematical experience that leads in the typical seven- to nine-year-old child to a basic understanding of sequential properties. Consequently, Piaget would propose that experience with the environment is indeed needed for the acquisition of combinatorial thinking, but the crucial factor is the developmental—Piaget calls it logical-mathematical—aspects of the experience that is a reflective feedback from the child's own activities and not the physical aspect of the experience that focuses on the physical properties of the environment.

These examples illustrate that the preconditions of developmental stages are much more than either maturation of physiological tissue—even though it may be a necessary factor—or becoming acquainted with information that only the physical or social environment can supply; although both of these factors are obviously necessary. In Piaget's theory the critical variable is developmental experience with its attendant reflective feedback. This is the immediate causal factor of human intelligence and is as common and species-specific as any other biological characteristic of human persons.

These three factors—physiological maturation, learning of particular environment information and developmental experience—are not separately existing processes or behaviors. Rather they are three interrelated aspects of one concrete reality, namely, the growing child in his cognitive activity. Just as cognition is a partial aspect of the child's total functioning which includes motivational and dynamic aspects, similarly intelligence (or preforms of intelligence) according to Piaget is a partial aspect that enters into all cognitive activities at all stages of development.

Take the words subjective and objective in relation to organism and environment. For traditional positivistic philosophy there is no doubt how the four words should be paired: objective goes with the environment and subjective with organism. The objective is the facts of which the 'real' world is made, whereas the subjective is the contribution of the individual who has not yet learned the objective facts. Development in this view is a learning of these facts and a decrease of subjectivity comes about in direct proportion to the intake of objectivity.

Piaget, however, points out two meanings of the word subjective. One meaning links the word to what is individualistic in behavior, in an idiosyncratic and deforming sense that contrasts with the eventually necessary perspective of adult logic; the other meaning is almost the opposite, namely that component of the person that contributes to the construction of the aforementioned perspective. This component is nothing else but human intelligence conceived as the biological common basis that makes men thinking human beings. Thus Piaget studies in intelligence what is common or species-specific to man. Objectivity, far from being found in the outside world, is the product of this common subjective contribution in contact with the common environment. A child fails in objective thinking, not because he has not learned enough objective facts from outside, but because he has not yet constructed powerful enough mechanisms of thinking by means of which he can have a socially common measure and criterion of objectivity. For Piaget, objectivity is not present at the beginning of intellectual development in the form of environmental specifications but at the end of the development in the form of internal subject-produced criteria of objectivity.

The biologically common environment is but the counterpart of the common subjective in all human beings. Indeed, biology has never been able to separate the two poles of organism and environment since one is adapted to the other through evolution. These two poles are not independent entities the interaction of which produced intelligence. Rather they should be considered as mutually related in such a way that as one changes the other changes. In the case of human development, the common environment, in and on which the subject acts, is to be conceived as dependent on the mechanisms of thinking; these the subject continually constructs in the course of and as a consequence of acting. In a similar vein one can assert that behavior and the underlying mechanisms of behaving and thinking are dependent on the common environment to which human beings are biologically adapted.

Consequently this position cannot be called maturationist or interactionist in the traditional sense. The fact of behavioral experience within a human environment as an obligatory component in individual development is contrary to the usual notion of maturation as opposed to personal experience. The mutual dependence and reciprocal construction of the subject as knower and the environment as objectively known is inconsistent with the usual meaning of the interaction of two presumably given factors.

INDIVIDUAL DIFFERENCES

With this as background we turn to three basic problems closely related to the nature-nurture controversy. First there is the question of individual differences. Piaget's theory apparently does not take into account the differences but rather focuses on what is common and biologically characteristic in the functioning of human intelligence. He takes seriously the proposition that one has first to understand the basic nature of a phenomenon before studying its range of variations. Piaget's investigations are not unlike those of ethologists who seek to discover species-specific characteristics of behavior about certain animals. These investigators know full well that innumerable pre- or postnatal conditions can alter certain typical behavior patterns but, nonetheless, no scholar would deny that there are behavior patterns as characteristic of a species as physiological or anatomical features.

The place for individual differences in Piaget's theory was indicated above with the distinction between two aspects of experience and two aspects of environments. Developmental experience with its reflective feedback and the common environment are critical for the development of the general human capacity for knowing, i.e. intelligence. Particular physical experiences and particular environments plus, one may add, particular skills or deficiencies in instrumental modalities (e.g., so-called creative talent in special domains or sensorial deficiencies) are aspects of knowing that are susceptible to wide individual differences. These differences are then manifested in the learning of practical or symbolic skills. Moreover, since these two aspects of knowing cannot be dissociated, the distinction although theoretically clear and necessary is not one that can be externally manipulated or observed. It is, in the final analysis, a question of perspective: In any behavior we can focus on one or the other aspect. Piaget has coined the distinction between operative and figurative knowing where operative refers to the action and transforming aspect of knowing and figurative to the configurational and static aspect of knowing. One can then link up the phrase 'operative learning' with the basic common development of intelligence from birth to adulthood. This operative development provides the framework of behavioral and thinking mechanisms which make possible the learning of particular figurative content. Thus, while Piaget has concentrated his interest on what is common in human intelligence, there is ample opportunity in his theoretical setting to look for individual differences.

ASSUMPTIONS OF IQ TESTS

The second question addresses if not the core of the nature-nurture controversy, at least its indispensable tool, namely, the intelligence test. How is the intelligence of Piaget's theory related to the intelligence of IQ tests? Piaget's answer is unambiguous: There is only a weak or superficial relation; essentially IQ intelligence and what Piaget calls operative intelligence, are two different things. One can put the situation more mildly by saying that Piaget's theory and intelligence tests look at the same phenomenon, but look at them from two different perspectives. This difference is no accidental historical coincidence but rather the outcome of a purposeful divergence from common scientific tradition. If Piaget's theory owes a historical debt to the psychological and scientific atmosphere before him, this is only as natural for his as for any theory. But it is remarkable that Binet's influence for German and English psychology has been almost uniquely identified with his methodology for measuring intelligence; whereas in Piaget's case Binet's theoretical and experimental work remained preponderant. The ironic result was that Piaget's psychological career in fact started in the laboratory of Binet's collaborator Simon on research connected with standardization of some verbal test items. But Piaget found himself much more interested in the thinking mechanisms underlying right and wrong answers of children than simply tabulating the frequency of different kinds of responses.

Four assumptions are commonly accepted by all types of standardized IQ tests and all of them would be severely questioned by Piaget. I call them here the assumptions of (1) age constancy, (2) scholastic validity, (3) standard environment, and (4) performance sufficiency. Assumptions 1 and 2 are prerequisite for the statistical treatment of IQ scores. Assumption 1 identifies chronological speed of achievement with greater intelligence and assumption 2 accepts scholastic success as a valid criterion for IQ test scores. Piaget admits and documents a much greater age variability than would be acceptable for measurement purposes. His own observations have shown Piaget that, e.g., responses characteristic of the most advanced stage in physical thinking can be found in one child of 6 years and another child of 15 years [Piaget, 1969, p. 202]. In all his work one encounters data attesting to a large span of years in which stage-typical responses were observed. Thus, for the drawing of a tube that somersaults from the edge of the table to the floor Piaget and Inhelder [1971, p. 127] report 25% correct anticipations at 4 years up to 70% correct at 8 years; on the correct intersection of two classes [Inhelder and Piaget, 1969, p. 178] the percentages rises from 15 at ages 5–6 to 82 at ages 9–10. Not only that, Piaget [1969, p. 205] observes without surprise that the same child thinks at a higher substage in connection with the concept of life and at a lower substage with the related concept of consciousness.

Nowhere does Piaget pretend that stages of thinking reached in one domain will necessarily be found in the thinking of the same person in another domain. Nor does he consider stages as linked to an absolute chronological age; when Piaget mentions ages for purposes of illustration he speaks at the same time of the observed range of variations and the possibility that in a different environment and with different schooling some other age range may be discovered. Stages for Piaget mean nothing else than a lawful and logically consistent succession of one stage necessarily before another as children grow up into adults. However, even though operative stages are lawfully ordered and constitute common human acquisitions, they have a personal history of slow and gradual preparation, elaboration and final stability.

There is ample evidence that all healthy persons in all societies and ranks of life reach the stage of concrete operation. A like assertion cannot be made with equal confidence for formal thinking. Piaget is rightly cautious on this point. The closer a person is to adulthood the more likely is it that individual and particularly also sociocultural preferences and opportunities have a decisive influence on the content and manner in which a person's intelligence is used. Piaget [1972] suggests that some type of formal thinking is likely to be observed in all cultures where adults are seriously engaged in a speciality of their concern (e.g., building of ships, administration of law). We all know, moreover, that in some domains we ourselves apply a higher level of thinking than in others and in this respect great individual differences even within a homogeneous subgroup of society are the rule rather than the exception.

The reader may by now be rightly impressed by the ample indications for individual variations in a theory which he perhaps suspected to be a rigid, internally controlled clockwork. But then, he may ask, of what use is Piaget's theory if the intelligence he speaks of does not proceed in a statistically standardized fashion? Perhaps this is not the place to expose the inadequacy of the scientific perspective which underlies this kind of question. Instead I would like to present Piaget's reply to the usefulness of learning machines [Piaget, 1970, p.78], and apply it to IQ tests. If IQ tests are found to be highly correlated with and, therefore, predictive of scholastic success, this merely shows something about the present aim and character of the schools; he would say further that schools have indeed much to do with the things that IQ tests sample, but they have not much to do with creative and challenging thinking. Consider how absurd it would be if a physical activities teacher who spent day after day in appropriate and challenging activities would require some outside expert to evaluate a child's potential on a one-shot basis. Apart from the isolated case where medical advice is needed for an exceptional condition, would you not wonder what this teacher had been doing with the child all along? If educators are eager to have IQ scores on a child, one can only conclude that ordinary classroom activities do not give them good opportunities to evaluate the child's intelligence. In short, IQ tests are valid indicators of scholastic performance to a degree to which operative evaluation in Piaget's sense could never lay claim. But this fact may turn to the theoretical and practical advantage of Piaget's theory if IQ-measured intelligence is thereby proven to be similar in character to scholastic achievement tests; such similarity would be undesirable for an evaluation of operative intelligence. I close this paragraph on scholastic validity by reminding the reader of the origin of intelligence tests: Binet devised his tests as an instrument of selection of retarded children for public education. Are schools meant to select and adapt children to the school, or should the school adapt itself to the psychological development of the child? If the teaching profession and society at large is ready to choose the second alternative, Piaget's theory may turn out to be of immense practical utility [Furth, 1970].

The assumption of a relatively homogeneous environment is implicit in the concept of any standard measure that claims to represent a person's potential as distinct from his achievement. The ideal of a culture-free intelligence test keeps constantly coming up and represents the counterpart of this homogeneous environment idea. In this respect the IQ test tradition finds itself in a curious situation. In the early part of its history the hereditary character of IQ was almost universally accepted. Consequently the fact of differing environments did not create any serious problems. But with the gradual emergence of an associationistic stimulus-response model in which every human behavior was said to be explainable in terms of similar learning processes due to the environmental stimuli, the difference between intelligence and learned achievement became theoretically indefensible. Investigators discovered with surprise the modifiability of IQ [e.g., Skeels, 1966]. Naturally, what is learned can be forgotten or, if greater incentives are provided, can be learned better. To bolster an impossible theoretical posture one must have recourse to a presumed standard environment. In fact in studies where mean IQ differences are used to claim the intellectual superiority or inferiority of certain groups of people, control of environmental conditions is now a routinely accepted methodological precaution.

However, on what grounds can one assume that environmental factors—whatever their nature—are normally distributed? Do parental love and acceptance, emotional and economic stability of the family, to mention just some universally recognized important factors, come along a continuum that fits the standard curve? If one begins to question the quantitative continuity and considers that a certain quantitative diminution brings about easily recognizable qualitative changes (e.g., poverty, parental neglect), the whole statistical interpretation of environmental comparability and of interactive factors become suspect. In short, the theory underlying the measurement of IQ makes presumptions about the environment that are not confirmed by empirical evidence.

Interestingly, Piaget's biological theory does have a solid basis for the common human aspect of the environment; this is the counterpart of the common operative aspect of development which all human beings share. But it was shown above that these aspects have no separate existence from individual contingencies. The common human environment may adequately explain the common human aspects of intellectual development, but it cannot become the basis for a normally distributed range of individual performances.

This leads to the last point relative to IQ measures, namely the assumption that performance provides reasonable evidence for intelligence. Piaget and his associates have consistently rejected this assumption. Their position follows logically from the conceptual distinctions between a particular overt performance and the underlying mechanism or operative capacity. As Inhelder [1966] puts it: 'To determine that a subject is capable of solving such and such a problem is one thing, while to understand how he manages to do so is quite another' (p.300). Inhelder has been the person in Geneva most closely associated with what can be called a Piagetian equivalent of an IQ test, ever since she published in 1943 a first application of Piaget's tasks to the diagnosis of mental retardation [Inhelder, 1968].

Inhelder's observations highlight in a profound manner the differences between the IQ approach and the operative assessment. Whereas the IQ approach uses more or less arbitrary cut-off points at 75 or at 50 and is open to administrative and social abuses of which we now are only too painfully aware, Inhelder interprets the character of the retarded intelligence in terms of Piaget's theory as follows. Mildly retarded persons are those whose thinking remains closed at the concrete stage; they show no indication of being open toward the formal stage. Severely retarded persons are those who do not reach the stage of concrete operations. Briefly, Inhelder's diagnosis is based on an operative assessment by means of clinical interview; it includes a qualitative explanation of retardation motivated in terms of its own theory. In distinction, the quantitative indicant of an age-dependent intelligence quotient by itself reveals nothing about the character of the thinking deficiency.

Significantly, this early success in describing mental retardation within Piaget's framework has not been matched by a comparable success in substituting his operative tasks for the more common uses of IQ tests. For over 20 years attempts at meaningful standardization of Piaget's tasks have been undertaken, notably in Geneva, in North America and in other parts of the world. Both from a theoretical and empirical angle I am surprised that Genevans regard with equanimity recurrent efforts to construct what is sometimes called a superior type of IQ test. This test would be based on standardized age norms for the acquisition of certain Piagetian tasks and stages. Perhaps this is partly due to Piaget's disinclination to make any firm statements about the adequacy or inadequacy of how his theory is being interpreted and applied. He does not consider himself the founder of a 'school' that has to monitor its followers.

But it is surely instructive to note the difference between the meaning of the word intelligence when applied to the description of developmental stages or to the diagnosis of certain deficiencies and the different meaning when applied to interindividual differences. For the first purpose Piaget's theory is eminently applicable and has produced potentially exciting results in investigation of retarded, aphasic, psychotic and senile persons. The theory has also shown its fruitfulness in describing the intellectual development of persons deprived of usual channels of experience, namely, blind and deaf children. For the second purpose of differential psychology Piaget's theory itself seems to indicate, as I attempted to demonstrate in earlier sections, that individual differences cannot fall under a general norm. When one encounters significant time lags in performance, Piaget thinks, one can explain them, but only after the event: 'It is not possible to have a general theory of these resistances' [Green et al., 1971, p.11].

Piaget's principal contribution is his elaboration of the mechanism of knowledge; these mechanisms are the basis of any intelligent performance and any specific learning. To attempt to measure the amount of this common intelligence is like measuring life or health. When something is substantially wrong with one's physical health, medical experts can probably diagnose a deficiency or a disfunction. But the vast bulk of the population could not possibly be placed along a cumulative continuum. Society is quite satisfied if the medical practitioner after a thorough check-up pronounces a patient in good health. If nothing more exact suffices with physiologic mechanisms which are precise in functioning and much more readily observable why should one expect a greater exactness with psychological mechanisms that function in order to open the human organism to the limitless inventions of the human spirit? During a 1969 conference on measurement and Piagetian theory, Piaget insisted that the main problem of development is to establish the method of construction of true novelties. The novelties invented by the individual, Piaget says [Green et al., 1971 p.212], 'do not stem simply from the potentialities of the human race as a whole—we cannot yet even imagine to what heights human invention will lead—', but they also come about through individual initiative and individual or interindividual activities.

It is, therefore, a mistake to assume that performance even on Piaget's tasks can be taken as a direct reflection of specific stage dependent thinking mechanisms. This implies among other things that operative tasks have to be adapted to different sociocultural contexts. These settings have a powerful influence not merely on the particular content to which operative mechanisms are applied but also on the manner in which these mechanisms are used. Piaget's associate Bovet [1970] reported that Algerian children seemed at first strikingly successful in conservation of matter in contrast to conservation of length. Additional probes made clear that this was an unstable pseudoconservation. Such apparent discrepancies from Western performance patterns were interpreted as due to differing day-to-day activities and cultural experiences.

To conclude this section on IQ tests I would interpret Piaget's position as incomparable with any individual score that purports to show the innate potential, the general learning ability or whatever other descriptions are used to distinguish IQ from achievement measures. There remains the final question as to how Piaget envisages the relation of what he calls intelligence to heredity.

INTELLIGENCE AND HEREDITY

For Piaget, intelligence is not a content but a mechanism of individual construction; we can, therefore, understand that he is not merely opposed to a consideration of intelligence as caused by mechanisms of learning of environmental information. He is likewise opposed to the view that attributes the source of intelligence to heredity transmission of genetic information: 'If, biologically speaking, learning and heredity and its content are excluded, there remains this fundamental reality . . . which constitutes the necessary preliminary condition for every kind of learning and even for heredity itself: namely, the organizing faction with its absolute continuity a function which is not transmitted but is continuous, conserving itself from transmission to transmission' [Piaget, 1971, p. 332]. Anatomical features, physiological functioning and certain forms of instinctual behavior can be said to be tied to structures transmitted by heredity. But the extraordinary constructive plasticity and the generality and eventual necessity of human intelligence cannot in Piaget's theory derive merely from organically-tied hereditary structures. When Piaget proposes that the structures of intelligence have their source in the genetically evolving and individually developing knowledge that reflects on its own equilibrated functioning, the question whether heredity or learning is more important in human intelligence loses all of its meaning. In this sense Piaget's biological theory is both revolutionary and liberating. One can only hope that its widespread popularity today is not merely a reaction to the abuses to which the IQ tradition has led—of which the nature-nurture controversy is a prime example—but that Piaget's theory can become the occasion for a more humanly relevant, that is, biologically grounded, perspective on intelligence and the human person.

WHAT GOOD IS THIS THING CALLED INTELLIGENCE AND WHY BOTHER TO MEASURE IT?

by Asa G. Hilliard
Georgia State University

This article contains a review of issues and documentation concerning the possibility of "measuring" the intelligence of students. The construct validity of "intelligence," the role of cultural context as a modifier of the meaning of test results, and the lack of meaningful predictive validity of IQ tests are discussed. A discussion of the utility of the intelligence construct and IQ measures, and their relationship to the design of beneficial pedagogy follows. Based on reviews of empirical evidence, it is concluded that the measurement of intelligence as practical, at present, makes no contribution to the design of instruction that is beneficial to students, as far as academic achievement is concerned. The main effects of the present popular intelligence measures are found to be negative.

Our ultimate message is a strikingly simple one. The purpose of the entire process—from referral for assessment to eventual placement in special education—is to improve instruction for children. The focus on educational benefits for children became our unifying theme, cutting across disciplinary boundaries and sharply divergent points of view.

> These two things—the validity of assessment and the quality of instruction—are the subject of this report. Valid assessment, in our view, is marked by its relevance to and usefulness for instruction. (Holtzman, 1982, pp. x, xi)

While academic failures are often attributed to characteristics of learners, current achievement also reflects the opportunities available to learn in school. If such opportunities have been lacking or if the quality of instruction offered varies across subgroups of the school-age population, then school failure and subsequent E.M.R. referral and placement may represent a lack of exposure to quality instruction for disadvantaged or minority children. (Heller, Holtzman, & Messick, 1982, p. 15)

> The IQ test's claim to validity rests heavily on its predictive power. We find that prediction alone, however, is insufficient evidence of the test's educational utility. What is needed is evidence that children with scores in the E.M.R. range learn more effectively in a special program or placement. As argued in more detail in Chapter 4, we doubt that such evidence exists, although we are not prepared as a panel to advocate the discontinuation of IQ tests, we feel that the burden of justification lies with its proponents to show that in particular cases the tests have been used in a manner that contributes to the effectiveness of instruction for the children in question. (Heller et al., 1982, p. 61)

I must state at the outset that I come to the discussion of the utility of "intelligence" testing and the utility of the intelligence construct from the point of view of an educational psychologist interested in the improvement of education. I recognize that there can be many reasons for interest in "measuring" whatever is possible to be measured, perhaps just for its own sake.

Of course, the question of the utility of mental measurement can easily be divorced from the question of whether intelligence can be measured simply for the sake of doing it. It is also clear that, in a free society, scientists ought to be able to pursue any interesting question for which they can find support, or which they can do on their own, so long as they do not harm. So research to determine if such a thing as intelligence exists and, if it does, what its nature is, is likely to continue, and I have no quarrel with that.

However, major concerns arise when psychometricians and others move beyond inquiries about human intellect to the application of their science to the area of human problem solving. It is at this point that we must be concerned about the validity of connections between mental measurement and success in problem solving in teaching and learning.

For many reasons, some of them obvious, the primary focus of my critique is on the use of mental measurement in education. Using IQ tests for predicting recidivism in the criminal justice system, studying the impact of nutrition on cognitive development, and other such interests will continue to preoccupy those involved in mental measurement. Of course, any use of mental measurement should be justified on the basis of its contribution to improving the human condition.

By looking at education, certain principles can be illuminated, some of which can be applied to many other areas of use of mental measurement.

THE ILLUSION OF MEASUREMENT:
THE QUALITY OF THE DATABASE

Although it is not my intention here to go into detail about the nature of the phenomenon: intelligence, how it is organized, and what it does, I cannot help but make a couple of passing observations. I do this to indicate my strong belief that psychological scientists have not yet measured intelligence, and that whatever the results of IQ testing are, they should not be treated as if they validate a scientific description of intelligence.

Some years ago, I recall having a conversation with Jerrold Zacharias and Judith Schwartz at MIT. The conversation was about mental measurement. I will never forget the expression of disdain that Zacharias had for the efforts of psychologists who attempt to measure intelligence. He insisted that the word measurement in science had a very precise meaning and that the instruments and qualification procedures of IQ psychometrics could not meet the scientific criteria that would allow us to say that they were indeed measuring devises.

His criticism was not about cultural bias, fairness, or other popular points; he raised the specific point about the nature of the phenomenon being measured and, in particular, whether an interval scale for quantification could be constructed to measure the phenomenon. Of course, if an interval scale cannot be constructed, then measurement does not occur.

> The main defect in both sides, or either side, of this argument is that the protagonist pays so little attention to the quality of the data base. They revert to saying that the data are not very good, but let's use them anyway because they are all we have.
>
> The worst error in the whole business lies in attempting to put people, of whatever age or station, into a single, ordered line of "intelligence" or "achievement" like numbers along a measuring tape: eighty-six comes after eighty-five and before ninety-three. Everyone knows that people are complex—talented in some ways, clumsy in others; educated in some ways, ignorant in others; calm, careful, persistent, and patient in some ways; impulsive, careless, or lazy in others. Not only are these characteristics different in different people, they also vary in any one person from time to time. To further complicate the problem there is variety in the types of descriptions, the traits tall, handsome, and rich are not along the same sets of scales as affectionate, impetuous, or bossy.
>
> As an old professional measurer (by virtue of being an experimental physicist), I can say categorically that it makes no sense to try to represent a multi-dimensional space with an array of numbers ranged along one line. This does not mean it's impossible to cook up a scheme that tries to do it; it's just that the scheme won't make any sense. It is possible to strike an average of a column of figures in a telephone directory, but one would never try to dial it. Telephone numbers at least represent some kind

of idea; they are all addressed like codes for the central office to respond to . . . Implicit in the process of averaging is the process of adding. To obtain an average, first add a number of quantitative measures, then divide by however many there are. This [all very simple] provided the quantities can be added, but for the most part with disparate subjects, they cannot be. (Zacharias, 1977, pp. 69, 70)

One of the interesting things to me is that these types of issues seldom if ever receive serious attention in published work in psychometrics. Rather, the professional conversation is usually confined to safe ground, that is, to the mathematics of statistical procedures or to the formal properties of a research design. But Zacharias and others raise the fundamental issue about the nature and quality of the data purportedly being measured. Psychometric "science" assumes but does not demonstrate the quality of the database that is being processed.

As with the case of Zacharias, opinions of linguists such as Roger Shuy (1977) get little or no response from the psychometric community. Yet he, like Zacharias, deals scientifically with the fundamentals of the nature of the phenomenon being measured, the quality of the database. In his classic article, Shuy makes the point, the profound point, that the most important part of language is its deep structure or deep meaning, its functional semantics. Its surface structure, that is, its phonology and vocabulary, can be quantified very easily. However, Shuy argues that the part that interests the psychologist most, the semantics, are from the point of view of a linguist, least susceptible to measurement by traditional tests.

I suspect that the views of the physicist and the linguist are too hot to handle for the psychometrists who attempt to measure the mind. I am unaware of any recognition of these difficulties in the applied mental measurement literature. I might add that it is in precisely these two areas of concern that we find the source of what some refer to as cultural bias in the IQ test. But it is really a validity problem, not mainly a bias or fairness problem.

In 1989, a summit conference was held on the construct of intelligence and its measurement in Melbourne, Australia. A set of selected papers from that conference was published in 1991 (Rowe, 1991). Helga Rowe was principal research officer for the Australian Council for Educational Research. To the best of my knowledge, this was the most recent summit to attempt to make a state-of-the-art statement about the measurement of intelligence. Psychologists from 14 countries were represented at the seminar, and the conference was used as a satellite conference preceding the 24th International Congress of Psychology, which took place in Sydney, Australia.

Several important points appear in the conference papers. First, the importance of context in mental measurement was recognized:

Erickson's (1984) overview of research from an anthropological view shows, for example, that mental abilities (including language and mathematical abilities) that were once thought to be relatively or even totally (as presumed by classical learning theory and Piagetan developmental theory) independent of context, are much more sensitive to context than traditionally thought. Cognitive process such as reasoning and understanding develop in the context of personal use and purpose. The demand characteristics of a learning task can be changed by altering the context within which it is presented. (Rowe, 1991, p.6)

This fundamental matter of context makes measurement matters messy. It raises the number of variables to be considered exponentially. To recognize context is to complicate the task of the psychometrist astronomically. It is time for measurement scientists to stop sweeping such difficulties under the rug. Rowe (1991) goes on:

As pointed out by Erickson (1984), differences in performance as described earlier, cannot be explained merely in relation to abstract versus concrete thinking, as has been quite generally assumed. Rather, the differences in performance are very much related to differences in problem definition by self and others. When a person has made the problem of his own, i.e., when he/she has formulated a task or question, he/she goes through a series of cognitive processes including decision-making points, each involving personal abilities, knowledge, and skills, as well as the process of social interaction that do not come into play when, for example, he/she is engaged in completing a worksheet or doing an IQ test. It is not just that learning tests are often "out of context" as Erickson . . . notes, but they are in a context in which the power relationships and processes of social interaction are such that the student has no influence on problem formulation and the tasks offer no context of personal use and purpose.

A full appreciation of the role of context, personal purpose and use, and of process of social interaction would fundamentally reshape our conceptualizations of and approaches to assessment, as well as to teaching and learning. (p.7)

Like the measurement perspective of the physicist Zacharias and the linguistic perspectives of the linguist Shuy, this issue of context raises another point that psychometric scientists have yet to address. The points are not trivial, but the responses to them have been, if we look at applied mental measurement in education today.

A second interesting point that came out of the Melbourne conference was that psychologists have no common definition of or theory of intelligence.

Although scientific psychologists have been studying intelligence for a century, they do not seem to have come closer to a widely acceptable, consistent general theory of intelligence. On the contrary, they offer an array of limited, although usually sophisticated subtheories, addressing specific issues, with little concern for integration with other views. (Richele, 1991)

Finally, the Melbourne seminar on intelligence revealed several places where researchers failed to find the expected correlation between IQ and achievement in complex problem solving.

As can be seen in table 13.1, the overall results failed to fulfill the expectations of a close positive relationship of intelligence test scores and performance scores derived from system control. The reported correlation coefficients are remarkably low; in most cases they are close to zero. Few coefficients reach values of .4–.5. Only in four studies . . . can correlation coefficients of this size be found. Thus the reported results from these studies do not support the general assumption that intelligence tests are good predictors of an individual's performance when operating a complex system . . . In addition, most studies agree with respect to the interpretation of the results in two important ways. One, it is argued that the tasks (i.e., simulated systems) have higher ecological validity and are closer to reality than problem situations, such as intelligence tests' items, or the Tower of Hanoi . . . which have traditionally been studied by cognitive psychologists. Two, the low correlation coefficients allow us to infer that intelligence test scores cannot be regarded as valid predictors for problem solving and decision making in complex, real-life environments. (Kluwe, Misiak & Haider, 1991, pp. 228, 232)

Once again, these are not trivial issues, but the response to them has been trivial if we look at common practice in the schools.

To summarize, there are several nontrivial, interrelated, and overlapping measurement issues and problems that bear on the construct validity and the measurement validity of intelligence.

1. The poor quality of the database.
2. The inability to construct an interval scale.
3. Performing addition on unlike quantities.
4. The loss of meaning from the responses of clients due to ignoring the context of responses which give them meaning.
5. The failure to consider the sciences of cultural linguistics (Hoover, Politzer & Taylor, 1991; Smith, 1978, 1979) and cultural anthropology (Cole, Gay, Glick, Sharp, et al., 1971; Hall, 1977; Helms, 1992) and

their meaning for the psychometric use of language as a measurement medium.

To fail to deal aggressively with these issues is to reduce the measurement of intelligence activities to little more than a meaningless ritual.

APPLYING INTELLIGENCE AND ITS MEASUREMENT IN SCHOOLS

When it comes to the schools, the debate over the technical and scientific issues in mental measurement are of peripheral interest. However, when mental measurement is applied in the schools, then the value of that activity for school improvement must be examined. It can be seen from the quotations at the beginning of this article, quotations that come from the National Academy of Science panel report on placing children in special education, that the school use of tests calls for tests that assist in the design of instruction that results in benefits to students. By linking the activities in mental measurement to school treatment strategies and by linking both of those to student outcomes, and in particular beneficial outcomes, the traditional task and goal of mental measurement must be transformed. Initially, traditionally, and presently in the United States, the goal of mental measurement was and is merely ranking and classification to predict achievement (Hilliard, 1990).

So the matter of requiring that professional activity be beneficial to students is the most important conceptual or paradigmatic change in American education as far as the use of intellectual assessment is concerned.

By requiring the benefits criterion, a whole new range of research studies is called for: true validity studies, instructional validity studies. How can validity studies that ignore variation in school treatment, failing to control for it, be considered scientifically valid (Kozol, 1991)? If mental measurement, on the other hand, is to be used for diagnosis and remediation, how can validity be determined in ignorance of the reliability, validity, and quality control of the instructional practices, regular and "special"? Do children benefit from the uses of psychological services, especially the measurement of IQ? At the same time, do children benefit from special teaching services that are dictated by the results of tests? Are the services to which students are sentenced special pedagogically? The answers to each of these questions seem to be a resounding "no" (Glass, 1983; Hehir & Latus, 1993; Heller et al., 1982; Skyrtic, 1991). In other words, the record on instructional benefits to students as a consequence of the use of mental measurement is abysmal.

Two points have not yet been considered in looking at the benefits question. First, we find that when good teaching is offered to children, many of whom fall into traditionally low-performing categories, their "intellectual disabilities" appear to disappear (Backler & Eakin, 1993; Edmonds, 1979; Sizemore, 1988). In other words, there are children in schools whose grades and IQ test scores have been low, traditionally, who live in impoverished and even violent neighborhoods with all the things that are supposed to make learning difficult, but who are some of the highest academic performers in their school districts or even in their states. Perhaps IQ predicts the quality of school treatment that children are likely to receive.

If a school such as the Vann school in Pittsburgh, the Madison school in Pittsburgh, or the Martinez school in Dallas is serving a population of students that would be expected to fall in the lower academic achievement quartile, but their actual performances places them in the highest academic quartile, then the IQ correlation is a failure; IQ did not predict such achievement. Yet we find precisely that in many cases. But we really only need to find it in one case to show that the IQ tests predict future achievement if teaching service quality is not equalized as a part of the context within which children operate. Mental measurement and intelligence theorists have yet to do the types of validity studies to prove or disprove this. A rare exception may be found (Fuller, 1977).

Second, we must ask the question, is mental measurement in the schools a prerequisite to the production of successful achievement with children? I have been seeking out high-performing schools and teachers for the better part of three decades now. One of the things that is striking to me is that in excellent schools there are almost no cases where the use of IQ or other means of making estimates of the mental capacities of students is an important part of the considerations for the design of instruction in these excellent schools, nor does IQ inform instructional design for successful teachers! The highest performing educators work without the IQ net! Conversely, IQ teachers and IQ schools have nothing to brag about.

It ought to be clear to virtually anyone who looks at this problem that the current IQ ritual is irrelevant to the design of powerful, successful instruction for students, or that if mental measurement or assessment is to become useful in the school experience, then a paradigm shift is needed.

Fortunately, such a paradigm shift has already occurred among many psychologists and educators who are attempting to apply the work of cognitive change psychologists (Dent, 1991; Feuerstein, 1979, 1980; Feuerstein, Klein & Tannenbaum, 1991; Hehir & Latus, 1993; Hilliard, 1987a, 1987b; M.R. Jensen, 1992; Lidz, 1991).

To summarize, at the moment, psychology has yet to demonstrate its ability to measure the capacity of any children, let alone the capacity of children who are situated in different cultural and low socioeconomic contexts, using the medium of a standard language and cultural material in a set of pluralistic cultural contexts. Second, psychometrics cannot be developed by quantifying things that are not quantifiable. Third, IQ psychometry cannot validate the treatment categories to which mental measurement sentences schoolchildren, for example, the "educable mentally retarded" category and the "learning disabilities" category. Moreover, even if it could, educators have no unique, validated differentiated pedagogy for such categories. Fourth, there is a large database on effective schools that make no reference whatsoever to the mental measurement of intelligence, and there is a smaller database on highly effective schools, also without mental measurements. Therefore, the mental measurement of intelligence is no way a prerequisite for present success in school. No body of data shows that any use of traditional IQ or mental measurement is tied to valid teaching and learning. Therefore, IQ measurement is a professionally meaningless ritual, a ritual with unnecessarily harmful consequences, that shapes professional thought and action in a negative way, causing professionals to overlook successful strategies and approaches in education. It is a ritual that shapes student self-image in a negative way.

THE CONSEQUENCES OF
INVALID THEORY AND PRACTICE

It is almost scandalous that professionals in psychology today who serve the children of all the people have bought into the IQ myth. Unhappily, Arthur Jenson (1969, 1980) is not alone among psychologists, for example, who believe in the genetic inferiority of people of African descent when compared to Europeans. Snyderman and Rothman (1990) report on their survey of psychologists and researchers, many of whom are diplomates in their respective professional associations, such as some of the members of the American Psychological Association:

> In this case, a plurality of experts (forty-five percent) and a majority of respondents, believe that black-white IQ difference to be the product of both genetic and environmental variation, compared to only fifteen percent who feel the difference is entirely due to environmental variation. Twenty-four percent of experts do not believe there are sufficient data to support any reasonable opinion, and fourteen percent did not respond to the question. Eight of the experts (one percent) indicated a belief in an entirely genetic determination. That a majority of experts who respond to this question believe genetic determinants to be important in the black-white IQ difference is remarkable in light of the overwhelming negative reaction from both of the academic and public spheres that met Jensen's statement of the same hypothesis. Either expert opinion has changed dramatically since 1969, or the psychological and educational communities are not making their opinions known to the general public. (pp. 128–129)

Clearly, there is a need to explore the impact of such beliefs on the helping behavior of professionals, which parallel very closely the beliefs of the general public (Duke, 1991). A well-documented, clear history of gross abuse exists here (Gould, 1981; Guthrie, 1976; Kamin, 1974). Where we can see that there is no database to support the idea that mental measurement is helpful, such opinions raise the question of whether mental measurement is harmful. That is the question to which serious attention of researchers must be turned. The only justification for using IQ routinely, or for employing a system dependent on IQ, is that clear and substantial benefits (academic achievement benefits) accrue to students. It is not a good argument to say that IQ testing helps to get resources, when neither the IQ test nor the help that the resources bring are beneficial.

The poverty of psychometric science is revealed when we note that there is no scientific definition of the variable "race" (Fairchild, 1991; Montagu, 1974; Yee, 1983). There is no scientific accounting for the intervening variable of school "treatment." There is no scientific accounting for linguistic and cultural diversity in the design of measuring instruments (Helms, 1992). But psychometricians are supremely confident of their measurement and of the predictive validity of their instruments.

THE PROMISE OF INTELLIGENCE THINKING

Research in mental measurement can continue. Research in the utility of mental measurement can continue. But what good is intelligence if it does not help us to change instruction? Like thousands of others, I am deeply impressed with some of the advances in the study of the human mind and how it works. I am impressed with Jean Piaget, Milton Budoff, Robert Sternberg, Reuven Feuerstein, and Mogens Jensen (1992). I am impressed with the work of Howard Gardner (1983). They and others have given us a language that clarifies the working of the human mind, that highlights its dynamism, its growth as an open system, and the variety of ways in which the human mind can express itself, sometimes referred to as "multiple intelligences." But all of these advances in thinking will come to naught if the fundamental paradigm that brought us here is not revised.

I see people take the work of psychologists like Feuerstein, whose interest is in cognitive functions and structures, and instead of looking at the power of the approach to produce changes in learners, become interested in how to score the assessment system and how to compare students to each other in a system that does not have ranking as its goal. I am interested too in the treatment of Gardner's (1983) work, where many people who come to it with the old paradigm bring with them an interest in scoring multiple intelligences so that individuals may be ranked in multiple ways rather than one, losing, in my opinion, the potential of the construct change. Gardner's construct change enlarges the vision of educators about the variety in intellectual processes. It implies the need to address a broader range of curriculum goals. But the construct change is not accompanied by a paradigm shift. We may wind up with seven ways to hurt children rather than one. The essence of the paradigm shift is that we view the human intelligence as modifiable, as growing. That is just as true of the "seven intelligences" as it is of the one (Suzuki, 1984). Sorting people into the new categories and ranking them within the categories will be as meaningless pedagogically as using one dimensional intelligence. On the other hand, the multiple intelligence map opens up the mind of the teachers to targets for mediation, to enhance potential and to enrich curriculum.

I want to make it clear that I do not oppose research and the attempts to define intelligence and to measure it systematically. What I do oppose is acting as if those tasks have already been completed. I do not oppose attempting to use what is learned from the study of how the human mind functions to improve the education process. What I do oppose is acting as if nonpedagogically trained psychologists and noninstructionally related mental measurement devices have a meaningful and beneficial application to the design of effective instruction for students. I believe that the inertia in traditional practice prevents psychologists from putting their best foot forward.

I have often said that there is another paradigm for conceptualizing and assessing mental functions, a paradigm which has already been shown to be useful in improving the instructional process. This means that there is a meaningful function for psychologists in the educational process, a function which includes assessment, if not measurement, at this time, but a function which requires a fundamental change in the role of psychologists. In fact, to be prepared to perform a meaningful assessment, psychologists must become master teachers (Feuerstein, 1980; M.R. Jensen, 1992). It is through the application of teaching, of somewhat known validity, that learners can be provoked to reveal patterns of thinking and learning that can be used to construct educational dialogue that can result in cognitive, affective, and content benefits for students.

I am willing to leave the door open; perhaps the future will yield a traditional test or assessment of intelligence and a consensus on the construct to benefit students. Should the benefits be clear and unmistakable, I shall be the first to embrace such an approach. However, my experience as a teacher, and my understanding of the goals of psychometrics, leave me pessimistic about these possibilities, the fundamental issue being whether the mind is fixed and limited or modifiable and susceptible to growth through nurturing. Depending on our beliefs on this issue and our beliefs about the efficacy of instruction, we embark on one of two paradigmatic paths that diverge at an ever-growing rate.

Models of mental functioning, such as those proposed by the cognitive modifiability psychologists and by the multiple intelligence psychologists, are useful because they answer the question of how to measure intelligence, but by conceiving of intelligence in the way that they do, they imply a pedagogical map that has vast implications for teacher training, assessment approaches, and approaches to the evaluation of achievement outcomes. For example, Gardner's (1983) map of multiple intelligences is less interesting to me as a device for classifying people among the intelligences than it is to establish the rich domain of human functioning toward which educational facilitation can be directed for all learners.

I believe that we have been stuck in the old paradigm because of politics, not because of professionalism. The activity of psychologists in ranking and classifying ethnic populations, who are deemed "racial" populations, is a blot on the history of the profession, with a stain that clouds professional perception even to the present day. Psychology is, or ought to be, a healing discipline; if not, then not only does the construct of intelligence and the measurement of intelligence become irrelevant, but psychology itself perhaps ought not exist. Happily, the model of what we could become and what we ought to become already exists. The kind of intelligence in the healing paradigm may someday be fully articulated and, yes, even measured.

Certainly, we want to assess the mind in valid and appropriate ways and to use the information from that assessment to create a better life for the people. But the beneficial aspects will not come about automatically, and until such time as they do come about, why bother to apply what we know about intelligence? Just stay in the laboratory until there is something beneficial to offer.

IS THE BELL CURVE A RINGER?

by David G. Wangler
University of Alberta

In reading, thinking, or writing about *The Bell Curve* (Herrnstein & Murray, 1994) it is important, perhaps critical, to note that the book is not primarily about race or what the authors call ethnic differences (p. 271). The first sentence of the preface to the book states "this book is about differences in intellectual capacity among people and groups and what those differences mean for America's future." The book itself excluding the appendixes is 527 pages long. Roughly 70 pages (269–340) are devoted exclusively to the relationship between race and IQ. About 14% of the actual text considers the relationship between IQ levels and racial/ethnic background. Despite the fact that 86% of the book considers IQ primarily in reference to class, it is the three chapters out of a total of 22 that deal with the IQ-race relationship that has received the most attention from critics on both the right and the left.

There are large problems with the racial ethnic comparisons that Herrnstein and Murray make in the chapter that compares ethnic differences in cognitive ability. Herrnstein and Murray compare blacks and whites, but they note that they categorize people on the basis of "whatever they prefer to be called" (p. 271). These comparisons suggest that there are distinct racial groups and that these groups differ on many variables including IQ. It is obvious that a black person looks different than a white person, but is there a pure black or a pure white group? Are we comparing somewhat, largely, or completely black people with white individuals who are qualified in a similar manner. If yes, how do we label or categorize someone who is half white and half black? A recent book, *The History and Geography of Human Genes* by geneticists Cavalli-Sforza, Menozzi, and Piazza (1993), suggests that after we get by surface traits such as skin color or hair texture there are very few significant differences among human groups. They note, as have many others including Murray and Herrnstein, that there is much greater variation within groups than there is between groups in terms of differences. Their conclusion is that at the level of genes, the very idea of race is lacking in significance. Now if at the genetic level we are remarkably similar, how can Murray and Herrnstein argue for genetically based differences in IQ? If Cavalli-Sforza et al. are correct, and there is much support for their position in modern anthropological and demographic studies, then the idea that there are substantial genetic differences between races is either suspect or false. How can one compare IQ scores according to a category that does not exist?

Herrnstein and Murray are aware of this problem and even cite Gould's observation that:

> We now know that our usual metaphor of superficiality—skin deep—is literally accurate. Say it five times before breakfast tomorrow; more important, understand it as the center of a network of implication: "human equality [i.e., equality among the races is a contingent fact of history]." (p. 296)

The authors of *The Bell Curve* try to get around this problem by writing "but some ethnic (racial) groups nonetheless differ genetically for sure, otherwise, they would not have differing skin color or hair textures or muscle mass. They also differ intellectually on the average" (p. 297). But we are still faced with the problem of which ethnic/racial category to put someone in who looks black but whose genes are 50% white. To complicate matters further, Europeans, who are the primary representatives of the white group in *The Bell Curve*, are believed to be a hybrid group made up of 65% Asian and 35% African genes. Thus the designated white group in this book is anything but white.

The word racist has been used extensively to describe both the book, the three chapters dealing with racial differences, and the authors themselves. It is probably not beneficial or helpful to label people we disagree with as being racists or rednecks or bleeding heart liberals or limousine socialists. It is indeed possible that the people who present positions that are contrary to or in direct opposition to our own may not only have something to say but may possess aspects of the truth that we have overlooked or ignored. In listening to and considering their positions we may well strengthen or understand our own position better. This was eloquently said by John Stuart Mill (Cohen, 1961) in his "Essay on Liberty" wherein he wrote that:

> The peculiar evil of silencing the expression of an opinion is, that it is robbing the human race; posterity as well as the existing generation; those who dissent from the opinion, still more than those who hold it. If the opinion is right, they are deprived of the opportunity of exchanging error for truth: if wrong, they lose, what is almost as great a benefit, the clearer perception and livelier impression of truth, produced by its collision with error. (p. 205)

Mills goes on to suggest that stifling an opinion is evil even if it is false.

> First: the opinion which it is attempted to suppress by authority may possibly be true. Those who desire to suppress it, of course deny its truth; but they are not infallible. They have no authority to decide the question for all mankind, and exclude every other person from the means of judging. To refuse a hearing to an opinion, because they are sure that it is false, is to assume that their certainty is the same thing as absolute certainty. All silencing of discussion is an assumption of infallibility. Its condemnation may be allowed to rest on this common argument, not the worse for being common. (p. 205)

The Bell Curve presents many ideas that are contrary to majority opinion and especially to mainstream social science perspectives. It is a book that should be carefully read, debated, and discussed. Its evidence should be extensively analyzed and weighed and, if and where possible, complemented or refuted. The authors should not be regarded as Neo-Nazis (Rosen & Lane, 1994 p. 14) as one critic labeled them, nor should their work be seen as sleazy and an intellectual mess, as Ryan (1994, p. 11) suggests. Any attempt to deal with controversial social or individual problems has to be done in a candid, forthright manner that is devoid of namecalling or mudslinging. This has been the exception rather than the norm in the numerous reactions to this book. What is desperately needed if we are to overcome our own ignorance and achieve some modicum of truth (notice the small t) is contrary evidence of a rational, empirical, or logical nature. Perhaps any discussion of class or racial differences in reference to IQ or any other variable like race or class should be guided by Pascal's observation that "we know too little to be dogmatic and too much to be skeptical."

With this in mind it is necessary to consider the significance or value of a book like *The Bell Curve*. The book contains a wealth of information on a number of different topics. It is difficult not to be impressed by the range of ideas and information presented and by the large number of graphs, charts, and illustrations used to clarify and condense the material presented. If you are into statistics, charts, graphs, as a way of concisely presenting data and results, then this book is for you.

On the general and primary theme of the relation of intelligence to social status and social pathology, *The Bell Curve* clearly demonstrates that being in the bottom one or two deciles of the IQ range of the population is often associated with high levels of social pathology. To quote the authors, "We have tried to point out what a small segment of the population accounts for such a large proportion of those problems" (p. 549). The problems referred to in the quote are things like illegitimacy: "The knowledge that 95 percent of poor teenage women who have babies are also below average in intelligence should prompt skepticism about strategies that rely on abstract and far sighted calculations of self interest" (p. 387). Poverty is also noted: "The high rates of poverty that affect certain segments of the white population are determined more by intelligence than by socioeconomic background" (p. 141).

The authors acknowledge that the level of education one achieves is related to social class, but then note that "if cognitive ability is high, socioeconomic disadvantage is no longer a significant barrier to getting a college degree" (p. 154).

In terms of race, intelligence, and the level of education, *The Bell Curve* points out that for those possessing the 103 average IQ of all high school graduates, the chance of completing high school went up if one was black or Latino:

> Consider, for example, graduation from high school. As of 1990, 84 percent of whites in the NLSY had gotten a high school diploma, compared to only 73 percent of blacks and 65 percent of Latinos, echoing national statistics. But these percentages are based on everybody, at all levels of intelligence. What were the odds that a black or Latino with an IQ of 103—the average IQ of all high school graduates—completed high school? The answer is that a youngster from either minority group had a higher probability of graduating from high school than a white, if all of them had IQs of 103: The odds were 93 percent and 91 percent for blacks and Latinos respectively, compared to 89 percent for whites (p. 319).

In opposition to many sociologists, Herrnstein and Murray see almost all the variables noted above as relating to or emanating from intelligence. Their position is that low intelligence is an important factor in where the individual finds himself or herself in the social class structure of the United States. To use their terms, "we want to consider poverty and educational level and illegitimacy and many other social indices and pathologies as an effect rather than a cause—in social science terminology as a dependent not an independent variable" (p. 129–130).

The extensive discussion of intelligence and its relationship to the presence or absence of financial, occupational, or educational success leads to one of the most controversial issues in *The Bell Curve*. If it is intelligence rather than class or race that is most influential in determining one's job, socioeconomic status, or general success in life, then the question of the source of IQ looms large. This is the reason for so much of the volatile and heated controversy that surrounds this book and its general theme.

First a note of clarification. The authors of *The Bell Curve* are not arguing that IQ is primarily genetic and therefore minimally or not at all vulnerable to modification. They state clearly and without equivocation:

> If the reader is now convinced that either the genetic or environmental explanation has won out to the exclusion of the other, we have not done a

sufficiently good job of presenting one side or the other. It seems highly likely to us that both genes and the environment have something to do with racial differences. What might the mix be? We are resolutely agnostic on that issue; as far as we can determine, the evidence does not yet justify an estimate (p. 311).

To add to this, a box on page 410 describes the significant influence of the environment on human development and intelligence. It uses the example of a feral child and concludes with this sentence: "If the ordinary human environment is so essential for bestowing human intelligence, we should be able to create an extraordinary environment to raise it further." The authors observe that the relationship of IQ to intelligence is not well understood.

> Even so, the instability of test scores across generations should caution against taking the current ethnic differences as etched in stone. There are things we do not yet understand about the relation between IQ and intelligence, which may be relevant for comparisons not just across times but also across cultures and races (p. 309).

But the potential optimism present in this part of the book is dashed in other sections when the authors state: "An individual's realized intelligence, no matter whether realized through genes or the environment, is not very malleable" (p. 314); "For many people there is nothing they can learn that will repay the cost of teaching" (p. 520).

Could the situation be that bad? Are the options so limited in number and extent that some groups of individuals should be written off? Are there any successful programs anywhere or is the only possible conclusion that:

> Taken together, the story of attempts to raise intelligence is one of high hopes, flamboyant claims and disappointing results. For the foreseeable future, the problems of low cognitive ability are not going to be solved by outside intervention to make children smarter (p. 389).

Two points need to be made here. One is that it may be time to back off, cut a little slack, or direct a little "benign neglect" to the significance and value of IQ numbers and instead look for concrete, specific ways of helping students who are disadvantaged, from whatever source, to simply do better in schools. (*The Bell Curve* is a substantial and informative book, but is it possible it is too concerned with IQ scores? If one had a choice between having a higher IQ score or doing well in school, which would most people choose?) There are programs that are effective, in some cases highly effective, in helping the disadvantaged to do well in school. Following is a description of a school in the middle of the Chicago ghetto. It is full of black and generally poor children whose academic performance, if *The Bell Curve* is correct, should be at the lowest levels.

As the patience of whites for other whites wears thin, the black inner city will simultaneously be getting worse rather than better. Various scholars, led by William Julius Wilson, have described the out migration of the ablest blacks that has left the inner city without its former leaders and role models. Given a mean black IQ of about 85 and the link between socio-economic status and IQ in ethnic populations, the implication is that the black inner city has a population with a mean IQ somewhere in the low 80s at best, with a correspondingly small tail in the above-average range (p. 522).

Somehow, this school that has a very clear, highly disciplined, and structured program with very high expectations of its students has "achieved honors as an academic institution above the national norms in all disciplines."

In the Chicago ghetto today the only institutions with a record of consistently getting people out of the underclass are the parochial schools. They pay their teachers much less than what public-school teachers are paid but they can screen their applicants, their principals can hire and fire, and they can and do impose many rules on both the students and their parents. (Ghetto public "magnet" schools that are allowed to screen are also successful.) Father George Clements, the pastor of the Holy Angels Catholic Church, describes the regimen at its elementary school this way: "We have achieved honors as an academic institution above the national norm in all disciplines. We bear down hard on basics. Hard work, sacrifice, dedication. A twelve-month school year. An eight-hour day. You can't leave the campus. Total silence in the lunchroom and throughout the building. Expulsion for graffiti. Very heavy emphasis on moral pride. The parents must come every month and pick up the report card and talk to the teacher, or we kick the kid out. They must come to the PTA every month. They must sign every night's homework in every subject. They must come to Mass on Sundays. They must take a required course on the Catholic faith. The kids wear uniforms, which are required to be clean, pressed, no holes. We have a waiting list of over a thousand, and the more we bear down, the longer the list gets (Lehman, 1986, p. 69).

But Holy Angels is not the only Catholic school in the US that appears to be effective in educating those at the lower levels of American society. James Coleman, the American sociologist compared the effectiveness of public and parochial schools in the US. He found that it is useful to note that Catholic elementary schools in the US get no public funding, pay their teachers much less than public school teachers get paid, generally have little or no technical support, and spend about half to one third less on each of their students than their public counterparts. Despite all this, they do a much better job of educating their students, many of whom come from the lower echelons of American society than the public schools do.

In their book *Public and Private Schools*, Coleman and Hoffer (1987) compared Catholic and public schools over a three-year span. They found that poorly funded and equipped Catholic schools did a much better job of educating their students than the public schools did. In that three-year span, the Catholic school students gained almost one full grade equivalent in verbal and mathematical abilities.

A third example that is even more dramatic than the previous two may help. On page 444 of *The Bell Curve* this observation appears:

> Our proposal will sound, and is, elitist, but only in the sense that, after exposing students to the best the world's intellectual heritage has to offer and challenging them to achieve whatever level of excellence they are capable of, just a minority of students has the potential to become "an educated person" as we are using the term. It is not within everyone's ability to understand the world's intellectual heritage at the same level, any more than everyone who enters college can expect to be a theoretical physicist by trying hard enough. At every stage of learning, some people reach their limits. This is not a controversial statement when it applies to the highest levels of learning. Readers who kept taking mathematics as long as they could stand it know that at some point they hit the wall, and studying hard was no longer enough.

But the film *Stand and Deliver* may be instructive. It describes the teaching approach, work ethic, and perhaps most importantly the high expectations of Jaime Escalante for his lower-class Latino students. By dint of hard work, perseverance, diligence, discipline, and a profound commitment to their academic development, Escalante taught his students enough advanced math so that they could pass the Educational Testing Services (ETS) calculus exam. As the film makes clear (and as actually happened) the representatives of ETS did not believe that lower-class Latino high school students could learn math and especially calculus. Like Herrnstein and Murray, they assumed that you can't get blood (i.e., passing grades on an ETS calculus exam) out of stone (i.e., lower-class Latino students). At the end of the film, there is an indication that more and more lower-class Chicano students from that school took and passed the calculus exam. In an interview, Edward Olmos, who played the part of Escalante in the movie, noted that of the original 18 students who took and passed the calculus exam, 17 went to and finished college. Perhaps Mill was correct when he suggested that "one should always aim high and when you achieve that you won't achieve only that."

It is recognized that none of these examples has control groups or is capable of statistical analysis, and they are certainly not very empirical in their data or results. But could that not be positive? They give a sense of what is possible, not what is measurable.

These effective programs demonstrate that the problems that characterize North American education today are not going to be resolved, or perhaps even diminished, by *The Bell Curve* or any book like it. Perhaps Tyrell's (Schumacher, 1973) distinction of convergent and divergent type problems will be helpful. Most serious human problems and especially those associated with education are not of the convergent variety. A convergent problem is one that is open to logical, mathematical, or purely rational solutions. Math problems and many scientific questions are of this nature. Divergent problems are those that emanate from and are expressive of human relationships in all their myriad possibilities in human communities. These difficult issues are seldom open to resolution by mathematical or logical procedures. *The Bell Curve* presents all its findings in a convergent mathematical format. Social science data like those found in *The Bell Curve* can provide useful information, but are usually not complete or clear enough to indicate clear and specific solutions. In opposition to this, divergent problems generally express issues for which there are no quick or easy or uniform answers. They encourage or demand that we go beyond what we clearly understand into realms where individual or social values are the determining factors.

Convergent problems are much easier to deal with than divergent ones. They often have distinct, clear answers and are readily and effectively expressed through charts, graphs, numbers, and various statistical or mathematical techniques. *The Bell Curve* presents its material as if the question of IQ and its relationship to class or race or social pathology were simply a matter of numbers and charts and lines on graphs. But there are distinct and highly significant social norms involved in how we value, express, and respond to variables like cognitive ability or intelligence. We may need a book that analyzes these social values as much as we need a book like *The Bell Curve* that seems to avoid them. Our most significant and complex social problems and especially the numerous problems associated with the process of education are not going to be resolved or even approached by a recipe-like process of putting in two egg charts, a tablespoon of statistical analyses, and then sifting in three graphs in hope that an or the "answer" will be discovered after 45 minutes in the social oven. If we begin to value the statistical findings, graphs, and charts that constitute so much of *The Bell Curve* over the individual students in our schools or citizens in our cities then any chance of accurately envisioning, much less solving, our social problems may be lost. Keyes (1975) said this cogently in his novel *Flowers for Algernon*:

> "Don't misunderstand me," I said. "Intelligence is one of the greatest human gifts. But all too often a search for knowledge drives out the search for love. This is something else I've discovered for myself very recently. I present it to you as a hypothesis: Intelligence without the ability to give and receive affection leads to mental and moral breakdown, to neurosis, and possibly even psychosis. And I say that the mind absorbed in and in-

volved in itself as a self centered end and to the exclusion of human relationships can only lead to violence and pain." (pp. 173–174)

The Bell Curve is a useful, perhaps necessary, book, but it has to be seen and understood in reference to the values of North American society. To view it outside that framework could not be just invalid, but harmful.

COGNITIVE ASSESSMENT OF CLASSROOM LEARNING

by Robert C. Calfee
Stanford University

The key words of the title are a challenge. A plausible alternative, for instance, might be classroom assessment of cognitive learning. The issues would remain the same: (a) authentic rather than superficial evaluation of student achievement, (b) high-level learning rather than low-level training for students, and (c) professional teachers rather than civil service managers of instruction. The aim of this article is to explore the relations among these three domains, with particular emphasis on applications in urban settings serving students at risk for academic failure. My main point is that cognitive assessment by the classroom teacher is essential to foster the achievement of the cognitive and metacognitive student learning called for in national reports. In other words, higher standards for students will require higher levels of instructional support by teachers.

Conditions in U.S. schools have changed rapidly during the past several decades. At the turn of the century, when teachers held greater authority over classroom instruction and assessment, and when education was a scarce and selective resource, student assessment depended on actual performance of academic tasks, and students had to show their work and explain their thinking. Assessment was authentic, learning was cognitive, and teachers were professionals. To be sure, most students, especially those from disadvantaged backgrounds, were denied these benefits because educations emphasized identification and selection rather than opportunity to learn.

Today's rhetoric emphasizes high standards, high-level "cognitive" learning, teacher autonomy, and accountability. Sound the alarm—the nation's well-being depends on improving schools! Although schools may be doing as well as ever in some respects (Bracey, 1993), the game has changed. Tomorrow's graduates face demands quite unlike those of previous generations. Schools are asked to promote high levels of achievement for all students, and the education of inner-city students is the test bed for significant enhancement of American education. Standardized test scores, the primary indicator of educational achievement, suggest that urban education is holding its own despite draconian difficulties (Mullis, 1991). The major thesis of this article is that authentic assessment of cognitive achievement outcomes requires informed teacher judgment. Accomplishing this task calls for a fundamental change in the teacher's assessment role, but the outcome will be more trustworthy measures of student achievement. In addition, assessment reform along those lines has the potential of serving as a policy lever for improving education in urban settings.

First, I will sketch the progression in assessment concepts from early times through midcentury behaviorism and on to today's metacognition. Then I will discuss parallel changes in assessment policies and practices, including recent developments for teachers and policymakers. Additional support for the argument can be found in other recent articles (Calfee, 1992a, in press; Calfee & Hiebert, 1991a, 1991b; Hiebert & Calfee, 1992).

THE CHANGING FACE OF LEARNING AND SCHOOLING

Turn-of-the-century education in America reflected an elitist style of life. With the Industrial Revolution, the need for a more capable workforce, and the arrival in the cities of multitudinous immigrants, behaviorism provided an ideal conceptualization for handling a difficult administrative problem (Calfee, in press); schooling was redefined as specific objectives, individualized instruction, and the teacher as manager. Intervening research illuminated the strengths and limits of this approach; a highly specified program is effective when the objectives are predetermined and the main task is practice for skill mastery. If the goal is to prepare youngsters for a thinking society, however, then the model of school as a training institute needs to be supplanted by the vision of an inquiring community, where critical reasoning, the ability to analyze and explain, and adaptable decision making are the norms for students and for teachers.

Behaviorism also meshed well with the multiple-choice paradigm employed in most standardized tests, and it is understandable that a cheap, efficient, and scientific strategy would be favored by midcentury school administrators. However, behaviorism came under increasing challenge as a theoretical position, and in the 1970's, cognitive psychology emerged as the dominant paradigm (Calfee, 1981). The computer metaphor legitimized investigations of human thought and language, reaching a peak in the 1980's, when this rudimentary image began to change:

> The human memory seems to be not at all like a storeroom, a library, or a computer core memory, but rather presents a picture of a complex, dynamic system . . . In fact, human memory does not, in a literal sense, store anything; it simply changes as a function of experience. (Estes, 1980, p.68)

In the 1990's, cognitive psychology emphasizes the structure of knowledge more than the processing of information, reflection as much as thinking, the situation as well as the stimulus, and the social setting along with the individual. Long-term memory is now center stage, emphasizing categories of knowledge, the interplay of language and thought, strategic and dynamic "knowing" and "doing" and a new appreciation of the concept of metacognition. Computers cannot really "reflect," computer thought is not linked to action as in human beings, and so the computer metaphor led scholars to overlook the constructivist aspects of cognition.

Stimulus and response have taken on new meanings during these paradigm shifts. Stimulus as situated context (Brown, Collins & Duguid, 1989) encompasses the entire array of circumstances that affect the individual; the individual remains the focus for the cognitive psychologist, but with a new appreciation that the individual cannot be genuinely understood outside of the context. On the response side of the equation, response as performance (Bennet & Ward, 1993) calls for a broader examination of the individual's total reaction to a situation. Specifiable behaviors are still part of the equation, but the cognitivist is also likely to record qualitative facets of performance and to ask questions such as "What are you doing and why are you doing it?" Transfer has reappeared in new garb. The conditions of original learning and the context of a novel situation are critical determinants of whether transfer takes the high road or the low road (Salomon & Perkins, 1989).

These changes in conceptions of learning and thinking have been paralleled by changes in the rhetoric of schooling (e.g., Resnick, 1987); unfortunately, practice has been largely unaffected by the rhetoric. Following the demands for "minimum competency" in the 1970's, *A Nation at Risk* (National Commission on Excellence in Education, 1983) moved that agenda toward "high-level thinking." Small-scale studies have demonstrated the benefits of cognitive approaches; indeed, a metanalysis by Wang, Haertel, and Walberg (1984) reveals that metacognitive and cognitive factors outweigh all other factors in school learning, including family background, except for classroom management. According to this review, the social and motivational domains have less impact on student learning, and institutional policies are at the bottom of the list in their effects on student learning.

Rhetoric and reality are seldom the same, of course. Today's teaching force and the academics preparing tomorrow's teachers are imbued with the concepts of the behaviorist era. Textbooks and tests continue to drive students toward the achievement of specific objectives by presentation, practice, reinforcement, and testing. Behaviorist practices remain the dominant influence in schools serving students in urban settings (McGill-Franzen, 1993); the prevailing assumption is that these students may respond to training, but that they are incapable of reflective thought. Moreover, their teachers are most likely to find themselves in situations where creativity (for teachers as well as students) is a luxury beyond reach. The task of the school in these situations is to promulgate the basic skills. Higher standards and portfolios may dominate the national agenda for schools, but the inner cities continue to struggle with basic skills and multiple-choice tests.

THE CHANGING FACE OF ASSESSMENT

In earlier times, assessment of student achievement was the teacher's responsibility. The process was not perfect, and the policymakers of that time worried about bias, reliability, and validity—issues that remain high on today's agenda (Linn, Baker & Dunbar, 1991). Students were often underrated because of race or sex. Grades reflected conformity more than achievement. With the appearance a half century ago of the technology of standardized tests, experts pronounced these problems resolved. The goal of effective and efficient measurements of educational achievement had been attained; subjective teacher judgment was a thing of the past. During the "managerial" revolution of 1920–1960, externally mandated standardized test results became the authority for judging educational outcomes. Learning was identified with specific behaviors, which were in turn linked to standardized objectives, frequently as multiple-choice or short-answer items. The machinery of standardized tests became entrenched, affecting the allocation of time and the design of materials. In reading and mathematics (the primary domains of elementary and middle-grade schooling), worksheets and end-of-unit tests dominated daily exercises with behavioral objectives. Curriculum, instruction, and assessment had all become standardized.

During the past several years, a call had arisen for authentic assessment, for exhibitions, portfolios, and performances (Valencia & Calfee, 1991). Authentic assessments represent a fundamental shift in the way that educators think about the outcomes of schooling. Several features distinguish this movement:

* Production is more important than recognition; students must demonstrate that they can actually do something, rather than simply picking the "right" answer.
* Projects are more important than items, an emphasis on depth over breadth, on validity over reliability.
* Informed judgment is more important than mechanized scoring. The teacher replaces the Scantron (a mechanical device frequently employed by teachers to score locally developed multiple-choice tests) as the central character in the assessment process.

Although similar in some ways to earlier forms of teacher-based assessment, the new methods are marked by several distinctive features. Assessment in this model is integrative. Student projects yield a wealth of information about reading and writing, as well as research skills. The portrait extends over a broad reach of the elementary curriculum, formal (literacy, literature, social studies, art) and informal (initiative, cooperation, persistence). This assessment model emphasizes high-level competence. From the teacher's perspective, the critical achievements are "top-down": the capacity to wrestle with the overall structure of a discourse, an awareness of audience, a sense of thematic coherence. It also focuses on meta-language, the capacity to "show your work" and explain your reasoning; the right answer with the wrong reasoning does not count.

Assessment in this model is situated. All students may produce final products of exceptional quality, and so it is virtually impossible to grade on the basis of differential performance. However, students vary in the amount of support and encouragement they need during the project, in their approach to the task, in their ability to sustain the effort, and in their willingness to assist and to seek out assistance.

Finally, assessment is guided by development standards. A teacher's notes may be synoptic, readable only by other professionals. Nevertheless, his or her guideposts are as clearly articulated as a scope-and-sequence chart. His or her assessments are not numeric but they refer to growth and to relative strengths and weaknesses.

This brief sketch covers the key concepts in a movement that is having substantial impact on many of the nation's schools and teachers (Calfee & Perfumo, 1993). The foundations of the movement are inherently sociocognitive, and the potential for enhancing the quality of schooling is substantial. On the other hand, authentic assessment, whatever its status and merits, is far more commonplace in well-to-do suburban schools, whereas urban schools are, in general, still entrenched in the behavioral-objectives paradigm. The prevailing pattern for students identified as at risk is a less rich, slower paced, and less demanding curriculum (Allington, 1989; McGill-Franzen, 1993). Decisions about individual students are moderated by teacher expectations and capabilities. Teachers who expect less of their students are more likely to water down the curriculum, and the students' literacy achievements suffer correspondingly (Ashton & Webb, 1986). Curriculum, instruction, and assessment for these students are grounded in behavioral concepts passed down from central authorities through administrators to teachers; federal and state funds for students eligible for support under ESEA (Elementary and Secondary Education Act) Chapter 1 (aid for dependent children) and special education still call for monitoring by standardized assessment. To be sure, efforts are under way as this article is written to change this state of affairs (USOE [U.S. Office of Education], 1993), but the legacy of the past is unlikely to fade quickly.

IMPLICATIONS FOR TEACHERS AND POLICYMAKERS

The concept of cognitive assessment of cognitive achievements carries substantial entailments for everyone involved in urban schooling. For teachers, the significant issues include locus of control, professional efficacy, and the notion of assessment as applied research. Locus of control is captured by the contrast between externally and internally mandated assessment policies. Administrative pressures for accountability by principals, school boards, state superintendents and governors, and federal agencies have led to the development and implementation of externally mandated assessment systems that address certain problems in certain ways:

* Origins: Development and validation of assessment methods by a central agency responsible to a top-level policymaker.
* Methods: Adherence to standardized procedures and routinized administration; professional judgment is neither needed nor allowed.
* Outcomes: Cost-effective (i.e., cheap) methods yielding simple numbers that either pass or fail a set criterion.

Advocates of internally mandated assessment have challenged each of these facets of external policy control by proposing quite different approaches:

* Origins: Developmental and validation of methods by a professional community of teachers directly responsible to themselves and their clientele.
* Methods: Reliance on procedures springing from a shared understanding of curriculum and instruction, procedures that are adapted according to situational context.
* Outcomes: Case-effective (i.e., expensive) methods requiring informed judgment and yielding complex "portraits."

Internal assessment is clearly more compatible with cognitive schooling, whereas external assessment fits the behavioral model. Depending on conditions and resources, either of these end points (and the many combinations between them) may make sense. If the aim of an educational system is to select an elite for special advancement and if assessment costs are to be minimized, then standardized approaches are appropriate, When educational needs are substantial and resources scanty, when professionals are scarce and yes-no decisions are needed, standardized routines have an advantage. However, if one views the inner cities as a resource for human potential (Howe, 1990), then it seems critical to return to teachers the responsibility and authority for informed assessment.

What elements provide a technical core for teachers, for those who deal daily with young children and adolescents? Three themes seem central to this core: (a) a metacognitive curriculum and instruction; (b) sensitivity to student diversity; and (c) collegiality exemplified by the "school as a community of inquiry" (Calfee, 1992b). The notion of the teacher as a practical researcher cuts across these elements and places assessment at the center of the enterprise. The inquiring teacher views teaching as an experimental activity, requiring generations of hypotheses, variations in conditions, collection of data, and interpretation of findings. Like other researchers, the inquiring teacher operates publicly, through activities that can be described objectively and that others in the educational community can understand and replicate.

Hiebert and I (Calfee & Hiebert, 1991a, 1991b; Hiebert & Calfee, 1992; also Meichenbaum, Burland, Gruson & Cameron, 1985), in our discussions of assessment as applied research, emphasize three tasks: planning, collecting data, and interpretation. The ultimate aim of assessment activities in this model is guiding instruction to ensure that all students achieve a high level of achievement. Assessment at the classroom level has both summative and formative elements. That is, the teacher must keep in mind the ultimate goals for the year, but equally important are the day-to-day and even moment-to-moment events. Success on a given task is not simply a sign of mastery but must be joined to larger curricular goals. Momentary failure challenges the teacher to consider changes in the situation that reveal the causes of a problem and to guide the student toward success.

Continual reflection on students' performance is the pivotal property of cognitive assessment that sets it apart from behavioral assessment, and it is for this reason that we speak of this approach as applied research. As such, it demands an inquiring mind. The metaphor carries several significant implications. For instance, what a researcher does and how he or she does it are important, but even more critical is the why. In some areas of science, theory provides a basis, but research is often driven by hunches, hypotheses, and concepts. The activity cannot be mindless. Science is driven by the need to understand. Tyler (1991) distinguished assessment that is defined by surface activities rather than underlying constructs; "Principles [constructs] can be generalized since they have been developed by observations of a variety of practices that revealed similarities among the diversities" (p.4). When viewed as research, a principled assessment outcome is generalizable across a range of variables: time, situations, clients, instruments, and observers.

Research also depends on explicitness. The scientist may work alone; however, for a finding to be accepted, it must be communicated, explained, and survive public review and criticism. A canon of science is replication; the work must be described clearly enough so that others can follow it.

The classroom teacher is in a unique position to apply the experimental method. When the connection between assessment and instruction is close, then initial observation leads to intervention, followed by the next round of observation. In this situation, the purpose of assessment is not only to determine student performance but equally to guide the teacher's instructional decision.

The cognitive assessment model carries a cost, of course. The tasks require technical expertise that goes beyond the capabilities of many of today's teachers. The conceptual base is complex, requiring appreciation of cognitive strategies for curriculum and instruction, as well as assessment strategies. Unfortunately, most of today's teachers received their preservice training a decade ago or more, and the evidence suggests that this preparation was often brief and unrelated to classroom assessment or instructional practice (Hiebert & Calfee, 1989; Stiggins & Conklin, in press). Surveys of portfolio programs often turn up haphazard collections of student work and poorly constructed performance-based assessments (Wiggins, 1991). Teachers understandably feel ill-equipped to handle the challenge of portfolio assessment (Calfee & Perfumo, 1993). Although they have the potential to meet the portfolio challenge, they will need well-designed and adequately supported staff development to acquire skill and confidence. Without skill, classroom assessment is likely to be misguided and invalid. Without confidence, it simply will not happen.

One response to this state of affairs is to return to external authorities for guidance, but this answer begs the question. A cognitive curriculum cannot be dictated from on high, given the diversity of students in today's classrooms and the goal of equity. The school system that seeks to realize the potential of every student, whether for reasons of equity or economics, must invest in preparing teachers to carry out assessments that incorporate informed professional judgment. If, rather than viewing the urban classroom as a battlefield staffed by paraprofessionals, we envision a community of inquiring professionals, then a substantial task lies before us, especially in urban settings, in promoting the professional competence and self-esteem of classroom teachers.

Turning now to the role of policymakers, the challenge of instituting a cognitive curriculum is daunting, especially when the spotlight is placed on urban schools. Perhaps the most fundamental challenge is to ensure validity and accountability while respecting local empowerment in the midst of diversity in students and circumstances. Linn et al. (1991) suggest three policy criteria for evaluating alternative assessments:

1. Are the consequences for schooling an improvement over present practice? Do teachers respond to the innovations with broader, more meaningful, and fairer instruction?
2. Is the content of the assessment an improvement over present practices? Is it of high quality, cognitively complex, and related to students' background and the tasks they will encounter in life after school?
3. How do innovative assessment methods match up against criteria for current tests: reliability, validity, cost, and efficiency?

Relatively few proponents of cognitive assessment have addressed the issue of reliability: consistency in student work over judges and tasks, and generalizability across contexts. Interrater reliability depends on shared understanding to interpret and evaluate the contents of the portfolio and, ultimately, the person it represents. The evidence from writing assessments shows that complex achievements are amenable to reliable evaluation if judges are knowledgeable and carefully trained. Research suggests that consistency is readily attained over competent raters (teachers) but is more difficult to achieve over tasks and contexts (cf. Baker, O'Neil & Linn, 1993; Shavelson, Baxter, Pine, Goldman & Smith, 1991). Variability in tasks and contexts is expected in portfolios, further complicating the reliability issue.

Validity issues require serious consideration of the proposals offered by Messick (1989), Cronbach (1988), and Shepard (1993), among others, defining validity by constructs rather than computer printouts. Portfolio approaches promise validity, but technical support for this claim is another matter. Face validity (does the test resemble what it claims to assess?) is assumed in authentic assessment, but it is often activity based rather than conceptually grounded. Consequential validity (does the test lead to appropriate action?; Messick, 1989) is presumably enhanced when assessment is embedded directly in classroom activities and decisions, but the substance of these activities and decisions is critical. Construct validity is the greatest challenge for any assessment; the potential of alternative methods, including portfolios, depends on strengthening the linkages to curriculum and instruction and on developing effective techniques for analysis, interpretation, and reporting. The technical foundations for establishing reliability and validity are well established in the work of ethnographers and case study methodologists, and the techniques are likely to be more user-friendly for classroom teachers than existing testing technologies. Moreover, we have working models in California's *Program Quality Review* process (California State Department of Education, 1993), among others; unfortunately, these models generally have less impact on public opinion than do standardized test reports.

Finally, fairness for students and teachers is problematic whenever validity is suspect. We begin with the assumption that all students possess the potential to achieve high levels of intellectual and academic performance (Calfee & Curley, in press; Calfee & Nelson-Barber, 1991). When a student performs poorly on a test, then the question is the degree to which the data are a valid indicator of student potential. Large-scale standardized tests of behavioral objectives gather the same information under the same circumstances from all students. One can easily demonstrate the limitations of tests under these conditions (Hill, in press). Authentic assessments—portfolios and performance assessments—have advantages and limitations and are by no means a surety that all students will have an opportunity to demonstrates their full potential. Standardized tests came into being to assure that teachers (and administrators) did not introduce bias and subjectivity ("halo" effects) in judging student achievements. The cognitive assessments being proposed today may reinstitute earlier prejudices unless steps are taken to ensure that teachers employ the best knowledge and practice available—and that knowledge base is far more substantial today than at the turn of the century.

Realizing the potential of this knowledge, however, requires the transformation of today's teaching force from behaviorism to metacognition, from workers who do as they are told to professionals capable of reflective and collegial problem solving. As Sarason (1990) put it, "Whatever factors, variables, and ambience are conductive of the growth, development, and self-regard of a school's staff are precisely those that are crucial for obtaining the same consequences for students in a classroom" (p.152). For our inner cities, this transformation will require a significant investment in "opportunity to learn" for teachers.

INTELLECTUAL ASSESSMENT TIPS

by Ronald L. Taylor
Professor of Special Education, Florida Atlantic University

Although classroom teachers are not directly involved in the administration of individual intelligence tests, they are frequently in a position to interpret the results of those instruments. Put in the proper perspective, intelligence test results can provide some useful information to facilitate educational decision making. More often than not, however, such data are used only for classification purposes and are either ignored or misinterpreted in educational use.

In addition to an overall IQ, most intelligence tests also yield an "intellectual profile" based on the student's performance on a variety of cognitive tasks (usually referred to as subtests). Both the IQ and the associated profile can be useful for the classroom teacher. There are, however, several myths and cautions that must be addressed before those uses can be put into the proper perspective.

MYTH #1: IQs are constant and change very little for an individual during the school years.

In fact, IQs can change quite significantly for an individual for a variety of reasons. We should not assume that once we know a student's IQ, we really know the child's intellectual ability. Educational, environmental, and behavioral factors as well as differences in test-taking behavior can all affect the score.

MYTH #2: An IQ is a measure of a child's intellectual potential.

In fact, an IQ is more an indicator of a student's intellectual performance than intellectual potential. One should not assume that a child with a low IQ will not be able to learn. Such a statement would be true only if all children have had the same learning exposure and opportunity. Clearly, those children with limited opportunities will be at a disadvantage on an intelligence test. A better method of determining intellectual potential is to determine how efficiently and effectively a person learns new tasks. Many IQ tests do include measures of this "fluid" intelligence.

MYTH #3: A "scattered profile" is an indication of a learning disability.

In fact, the "average person" has a considerable amount of scatter (relative strengths and weaknesses) in the intellectual profile. Difference between the Verbal and Performance IQ on the popular WISC-R is at least 15 points for approximately 25% of the population (Kaufman, 1979). In one large study, the average VIQ/PIQ difference was almost 11 points (Taylor, Ziegler, & Partenio, 1984). Such differences are often cited as being "clinically significant." Similar findings have been reported when looking at specific subtest profiles as well (Kaufman, 1979; Taylor, Partenio, & Ziegler, 1983).

CAUTION #1: There are a number of factors that can affect scores on an intelligence test other than the student's intellectual ability.

Factors such as motivation, anxiety, test wiseness, and health/emotional state of the student can affect the scores. In addition, differences in administration, examiner bias, rapport, and cultural/language differences between the student and examiner could affect the results (Taylor, 1989).

CAUTION #2: The reliability of subtest scores is generally lower than the reliability of the overall IQ.

This very important point must be considered when interpreting the cognitive profile. Care must be taken not to overinterpret the results.

USE #1: A student's IQ is a generally good predictor of academic achievement.

A number of studies indicate that IQ, particularly verbal IQ, correlates in the moderate range with achievement test scores (e.g., Reschly & Reschly, 1979). It should be kept in mind, however, that both the IQ and the achievement scores might change over time (see MYTH #1).

USE #2: A student's profile of intellectual strengths and weaknesses can be helpful to determine areas for further assessment.

The role of assessment information for the teacher should be to provide suggestions regarding what and how to teach. Arguably, results from intelligence tests do not provide this type of information. Writing IEPs from intelligence test data alone is clearly inappropriate. IQ results can, however, indicate other areas that might need "probing," particularly related to instructional strategies. Are there indications of verbal problems, inattention, poor memory skills? These areas could be further evaluated using educational materials incorporated into a classroom setting. One suggestion is to familiarize yourself with the task demands of the various subtests—look beyond subtest names.

SUMMARY STATEMENTS

1. Use IQ as a general indicator of a student's intellectual performance at a given time.
2. Do not use profile analyses to "diagnose" a problem. Do use a profile analysis informally to determine general strengths and weaknesses and to determine areas for further informal evaluation.
3. Do not overinterpret any IQ data, assume that they measure intellectual potential, or assume that they will never change.

ADD: ACRONYM FOR ANY
DYSFUNCTION OR DIFFICULTY

Gay Goodman and Mary Jo Poillion
University of Houston

The purpose of this article is to review the professional literature related to the identification of causes and characteristics of attention deficit disorder (ADD) in school-age learners. Forty-eight articles and books written by leading authors in the field were synthesized to determine the extent of agreement regarding the characteristics and causes of this frequently used label. A total of 69 characteristics and 38 causes were cited, evidencing no clear-cut pattern for identifying the condition and little agreement for what causes ADD. Implications for current practices of diagnosis and treatment as well as future research directions are discussed.

In the past decade, the term attention deficit disorder (ADD) has surfaced with increasing frequency in education circles. Through the years, the term has been expanded to include children who were previously referred to as hyperactive or minimally brain damaged. Numerous terms have been used to categorize these children (Houlihan & Van Houten, 1989), including attention deficit disorder with hyperactivity, minimal brain dysfunction, and hyperkinetic reaction to childhood. At present, the term preferred by the American Psychiatric Association (APA) (1987) is attention deficit-hyperactivity disorder (ADHD). Often the labels referring to ADD children are used interchangeably to describe a learner who is evidencing school problems of one sort or another. More recently, the ADD acronyms have filtered into the medical genre of lay persons. There has even been some discussion in favor of creating a new special education category or handicapping condition for children who are diagnosed as having ADD. A recent issue of *The Special Educator* (Kahn, 1989) summarized a California court case in which a local school district was found to be in violation of Section 504 of Public Law 93-112 (1973), the Vocational Rehabilitation Act (*Federal Reg-*

ister, 1977). The Office of Civil Rights found the district liable for providing special education services to a child who was labeled ADHD despite the fact that this handicapping condition is not covered under Public Law 94-142, the Education for All Handicapped Children Act of 1975 (*Federal Register*, 1977).

It is generally assumed that children diagnosed as having ADD evidence a common set of characteristics that emanate from a common etiology, or at least one of several etiologies. As such, the ADD terminology is also assumed to offer those who use it the advantages of other types of labels applied in the fields of education and psychology. Some of these include providing concerned parties an ability to relate the diagnosis to specific treatment, providing professionals an abbreviated means of communicating, delineating clear and appropriate methods for classifying child behavior, establishing criteria for interpreting and assessing research findings, and promoting specific programs for certain special interest groups (Heward & Orlansky, 1986).

For a nomenclature (or labeling) system to be effective, however, the common characteristics attributed to the system must be known and agreed upon by all who use the system. The purpose of this article is to review the literature related to ADD to determine if a commonly agreed upon set of characteristics exists that can be observed in children so labeled. If so, what are these characteristics? Can the manifestation of these characteristics be measured with the degree of specificity needed to justify creating special education diagnoses and placements? Are they sufficiently reliable and valid to warrant the design of instructional interventions for the children who are the recipients of ADHD as a diagnostic label?

METHOD

EVOLUTION OF ADD LABEL

An historical examination of the Diagnostic and Statistical Manual of Mental Disorders (DSM) published by APA (1952, 1968, 1980, 1987) indicates that there has been a rapid evolution in the terminology used to label children who are commonly referred to as having ADD. This category was not included in the original version of the DSM (1952). The only diagnostic classification for these children in that edition was called organic brain syndromes. In the next edition, DSM-II (APA, 1968), the terminology was changed to include the category of hyperkinetic reaction to childhood and adolescence. In the DSM-III (APA, 1980), the diagnostic category was changed once again. It is in this edition that the attention deficit disorder terminology first appears. The categories included are attention deficit disorder with hyperactivity, attention deficit disorder without hyperactivity, and attention deficit disorder-residual. The latter category is reserved for youngsters who were previously diagnosed as hyperactive but who have outgrown the characteristics warranting the label. In the DSM-III-Revised (APA, 1987), the three categories delineated in the previous edition are consolidated and labeled attention deficit-hyperactivity disorder. The 1987 edition cites 14 characteristics, of which the child must manifest any eight to receive the diagnosis.

Thus, the nomenclature used to describe ADD has undergone many changes in its brief history. The trend in these changes is clear. The field has shifted from a very narrow, medically based category to a much broader more inclusive, and more subjective category. It is understandable, then, that more children are eligible for receiving a label that has less meaning. In part, this could be because the characteristics for ADD have been subjectively defined by a committee rather than having been developed on the basis of empirical evidence (Cantwell, 1987).

PARAMETERS OF THE LITERATURE REVIEW

Citations in the professional literature addressing attention deficit disorder began to appear in the 1970's. Since then, hundreds of journal articles have focused on the topic. We conducted a thorough exploration of this literature to locate citations that describe the causes and characteristics of ADD. We began with computer searches of sources provided by the Council for Exceptional Children's ERIC Clearinghouse on Handicapped and Gifted Children and the Silver Platter Psychological Abstracts (PsychLit) (1989 editions). Attention deficit disorder, hyperactivity, causes, and characteristics were key terms that narrowed the search to 131 ERIC abstracts and 57 PsychLit abstracts. Additionally, we contacted the ADHD Association of Texas Resource Service to ensure the inclusion of materials available to parents or lay persons. Persons responding on behalf of this service contributed 23 books and articles on identification issues.

In total, 211 documents were screened to determine whether they presented a list of characteristics or causes of ADD. All citations that met this requirement were included. Also included were empirical studies attempting to isolate causes and characteristics of ADD. The literature search indicated that no single author or group of authors has contributed more than two or three publications to the topic of either ADD characteristics or its causes. As a result, no one has emerged as a clear leader in the field. In all, 53 authors contributed to the 45 books and journal articles included in the review. Although date of publication was not prescribed as a limiting variable in the review, with two exceptions, the information found was published or presented subsequent to the 1980 introduction of the ADD categories in the DSM-III.

Because the identification of causes and characteristics could conceivably vary according to professional orientation, an effort was made to ensure the representation of various disciplines. Literature was reviewed in the medical (Crook & Stevens, 1987; Silver, 1984), psychological (Hunsucker, 1988; Ingersoll, 1988; Prior, Sanson, Freethy, & Geffen, 1985), psychiatric (Rutter, 1989; Wender, 1987), and educational (Cruickshank, 1985; Martin & Martin, 1984; Schworm & Birnbaum, 1989) disciplines.

The topical diversity of the 211 publications warranted a categorical approach to screening. Literature selected for inclusion specifically identified causes and/or characteristics as a basis for defining the disorder (Bohline, 1985; D. J. Cohen, Caparulo, & Shaywitz, 1981; Kiger, 1984; Trites & Laprade, 1983), promoted particular etiologies (David, Hoffman, Sverd, & Clark, 1977; Klein, 1988), addressed conceptual issues (Houlihan & Van Houten, 1989; Rutter, 1989), critiqued assessment procedures (Bacon, 1982; Breen & Barkley, 1983; Gordon & McClure, 1983; Lufi & Cohen, 1985; McGee et al., 1985; Ownby, 1983), differentiated types or degrees of ADD (Brown, 1984; N. J. Cohen & Minde, 1983; Douglas, 1988; Prior et al., 1985), or compared the behavior of children diagnosed with ADD with that of nonhandicapped children or those with other disabilities (Cunningham & Siegel, 1987; Dykman, Ackerman, & Holcomb, 1984; Holborrow & Berry, 1986; Kuehne, Kehle, & McMahon, 1987; Rapport, Tucker, DuPaul, Merlo, & Stoner, 1986).

A final criterion used in selecting articles for this review was the audience for whom the literature was targeted. Of particular interest was whether the characteristics and causes described for practitioners (i.e., parents, teachers, physicians, and psychologists) directly involved in the identification and treatment of children diagnosed with ADD were similar to those defined by researchers for research purposes. We reviewed 32 articles and books published for psychologists, psychiatrists, physicians, and university faculty involved in researching ADD issues, along with 13 sources published for parent education and lay reference.

RESULTS

ADD CHARACTERISTICS

NUMBER OF CHARACTERISTICS

Examination of all the sources of information on the characteristics of ADD indicated that a vast number were cited by the authors reviewed. The characteristics cited were very diverse and often subjective in nature. In general, authors showed lack of agreement regarding ADD characteristics, and, at times, characteristics mentioned by different authors were contradictory. Regarding the first of these facts, a vast number of characteristics are attributed to children with ADD. In the 39 sources reviewed, 69 characteristics were cited as descriptive of learners with ADD. These characteristics are displayed by author and date of publication in Table 1. It appears that professionals and authors in this field have elaborated considerably on the characteristics that have been listed in the DSM editions since ADD has been included as a category. The variance in the number of characteristics cited by the authors reviewed averages eight, but ranges from two (Douglas, 1988; Kirby & Grimley, 1986; Silver, 1984) or three (Cunningham & Siegel, 1987; Kiger, 1984; Lufi & Cohen, 1985; McGee et al., 1985; Prior et al., 1985) to 25 (Hunsucker, 1988). Writings that include the most characteristics were prepared for parents and other lay persons. These include the writings of both Hunsucker (1988) and Wender (1987) who include 25 and 24 characteristics, respectively. This proliferation of characteristics would seem to make it easier for parents to locate descriptors for their children's behavior, regardless of whether the true source of difficulty is an attention deficit disorder.

The pattern emerging in the evolution of ADD is similar to that experienced by the profession with regard to children labeled as having minimal brain damage (MBD) or minimal brain injury (MBI). This label emerged as a medically based, organic syndrome. Ultimately, a government task force generated a list of 99 characteristics considered symptomatic of this condition. It was largely because of this proliferation of symptoms and a vagueness of the definition that the same task force recommended abandoning the term in 1966 (Coles, 1987). Nearly 25 years later, a similar pattern is emerging with respect to ADD.

DIVERSITY OF CHARACTERISTICS

A second concern evident from a review of the literature relates to diversity in the nature of characteristics attributed to these learners. Types of characteristics cited in the original list seemed to have evolved from a broad range of domains. To provide an organizational schema for reviewing these characteristics, each characteristic was assigned a categorical domain to determine if any clear pattern of characteristics might emerge.

The procedure for organizing characteristics by domain was conducted in three phases. First, a panel of three educational diagnosticians was convened. The panel was asked to generate and define a list of domains to which the 69 ADD characteristics could be assigned. This resulted in the identification of eight domains. In the second phase, five psychologists and psychiatrists were asked to assign independently each of the 69 characteristics to the most appropriate domain. Responses were then tabulated, and degree of interrater agreement was calculated. If 80% (four out of five) of the raters agreed on the appropriate domain, a permanent assignment of the characteristic was made. Characteristics were submitted to each panel member a total of three times. Ultimately, 80% of the panel reached agreement on the assignment of 56 out of 69 characteristics. During the final categorization phase, four additional diagnosticians were called together as a group to assign the remaining 13 characteristics.

Results of this procedure to assign characteristics to domains are displayed in Table 1. It shows the characteristics organized by eight broadly defined domains. In addition to the usual attributes in the attentional and activity domains, numerous authors included a wide range of characteristics in the domains of temperament, and in the general area of impulse control. These characteristics include everything from lying and immaturity to using poor judgment. One author (Rutter, 1989) even cites a demographic variable—small family size—as being a characteristic of children with ADD.

LACK OF AGREEMENT OF CHARACTERISTICS

A third and related concern is the lack of agreement among authorities as to what these characteristics are. Table 2 presents the characteristics attributed to children with ADD in order of the frequency with which they were cited by the various authors.

It is noteworthy that there is no single characteristic that all authors agree is exhibited by children with ADD. In fact, no characteristic is cited by more than 80% of the authors, and only four of the 69 characteristics are listed by more than 50%. At the other extreme, there are 19 characteristics proposed by only one author. Of the 69 characteristics, 59 were put forth by less than 20% of the authors. Although most of authorities agree that the differential diagnosis of ADD requires the manifestation of only some characteristics, questions concerning the validity of the diagnosis are raised by the fact that children could be labeled ADD without evidencing any of the same symptoms or characteristics.

SUBJECTIVITY OF CHARACTERISTICS

A fourth concern is the subjective nature of many of the variables cited as being characteristic of ADD learners. Such characteristics as "loses materials" (APA, 1987; Hunsucker, 1988; Ingersoll, 1988), "is disorganized" (APA, 1980; Bacon, 1982; Crook & Stevens, 1987; Hunsucker, 1988; Jordan, 1988; Scott, 1987), "excessive talking" (APA, 1987; Hunsucker, 1988; Ingersoll, 1988; Schworm & Birnbaum, 1989), and "stubbornness" (Ingersoll, 1988; Wender, 1987) are relative terms. Their significance varies with the observer's perception and value system and with the degree to which the characteristic is manifested. Significance can also be confounded by the age and developmental level of the child. Appropriate behavior for a 4-year old may be interpreted as pathological behavior for a 9-year old. The DSM-III-R listed its criteria in descending order of discriminating power and prefaced it with the directive, "Consider a criterion met only if the behavior is considerably more frequent than that of most people of the same mental age." (p.52) The guide "considerably more frequent," however, is subjective and provisions for a standardized measurement are lacking. Related to the subjective nature of many of these characteristics are their "nonobservable" quality. Terms such as "poor foresight and planning" (Kuehne, et al., 1987), "emotional problems" (Bohline,

TABLE I
CHARACTERISTICS OF ATTENTION DEFICIT DISORDER BY DOMAIN

Domain	Characteristic	FEINGOLD '74	DSM.III '80	BARKLEY '81	BACON '82	D.COHN, ETL '81	NJ HEALTH '82	TXMHMR '82	BREEN/BRKLY '83	N.COHEN/MINDE '83	GILLBERG/ERT AL '83
A	Constantly beginning tasks		X		X						
A	Daydreams										
A	Difficulty following directions		X		X						
A	Difficulty following rules			X							
A	Disorganized		X		X						
A	Dissociation										
A	Distractible	X	X	X	X	X					X
A	Extremely organized										
A	Forgetfulness										
A	Inefficient attent.										
A	Loses materials										
A	Perseverates										
A	Poor concentration		X		X			X			
A	Short attention span	X	X		X	X	X	X	X		
A	Short term memory										
C	Academic difficulty										
C	Cognitive immaturity										
C	Creative										
C	Fig.bckgrnd pathl'gy										
C	Intelligent										
C	Lower mean IQ										
C	No significant acad. difficulty										
C	Perceptual deficits										X
C	Poor audit.proc's'ng										
C	Poor reader				X						
C	Underachiever				X						
C	Vis.-motor diffic.										
D	From small families		X		X						
H	Climbs excessively		X								
H	Dsn't remain in seat		X								
H	Excessive talking										
H	Fidgets w/hands/feet		X								
H	Has diffic. playing quietly										
H	Hyperactive	X	X	X	X	X	X		X		X
H	Movement in sleep		X		X						

TABLE I (continued)

Domain	Characteristic	GORDON/MCLURE '83	OWNBY '83	TRITES/LAPRADE '83	DYKMAN ET AL '84	KIRBY/GRIMM '84	MARTIN/MARTIN '84	MARTIN '84	SILVER '84	BOLINE '85	CRUICKSHANK '85
A	Constantly beginning tasks							X			
A	Daydreams										
A	Difficulty following directions										
A	Difficulty following rules				X						
A	Disorganized										X
A	Dissociation										
A	Distractible		X	X	X			X	X		X
A	Extremely organized										
A	Forgetfulness							X			
A	Inefficient attent.										
A	Loses materials										
A	Perseverates				X			X			
A	Poor concentration			X				X		X	
A	Short attention span	X	X	X	X	X	X	X		X	X
A	Short term memory							X			
C	Academic difficulty							X			
C	Cognitive immaturity									X	
C	Creative										
C	Fig.bckgrnd pathl'gy										X
C	Intelligent										
C	Lower mean IQ										
C	No significant acad. difficulty										
C	Perceptual deficits										
C	Poor audit.proc's'ng										X
C	Poor reader										
C	Underachiever										
C	Vis.-motor diffic.							X			
D	From small families										
H	Climbs excessively										
H	Dsn't remain in seat										
H	Excessive talking										
H	Fidgets w/hands/feet										
H	Has diffic. playing quietly										
H	Hyperactive	X	X	X							X
H	Movement in sleep										

TABLE I (continued)

Domain	Characteristic	LUFI & COHEN '85	MCGEE ET AL '85	PRIOR ET AL '85	BROWN/ WYNNE '84	HOLBOROW/ BERRY '86	RAPPORT/ ETAL '86	CROOK/ STEVENS '87	CUNNINGHAM/ SIEGEL '87	DSM-III (R) '87	KUEHNE ET AL '87
A	Constantly beginning tasks									X	
A	Daydreams										
A	Difficulty following directions										
A	Difficulty following rules										
A	Disorganized							X			
A	Dissociation										
A	Distractible					X		X		X	
A	Extremely organized										
A	Forgetfulness										
A	Inefficient attent.										
A	Loses materials									X	
A	Perseverates										
A	Poor concentration		X						X		
A	Short attention span	X			X	X	X	X		X	X
A	Short term memory										
C	Academic difficulty										
C	Cognitive immaturity										
C	Creative										
C	Fig.bckgrnd pathl'gy										
C	Intelligent										
C	Lower mean IQ										
C	No significant acad. difficulty										X
C	Perceptual deficits										
C	Poor audit.proc's'ng										
C	Poor reader										
C	Underachiever										
C	Vis.-motor diffic.										
D	From small families										
H	Climbs excessively										
H	Dsn't remain in seat									X	
H	Excessive talking									X	
H	Fidgets w/hands/fee									X	
H	Has diffic. playing quietly									X	
H	Hyperactive	X	X		X	X		X			X
H	Movement in sleep										

TABLE I (continued)

Domain	Characteristic	SCOTT '87	WENDER '87	DOUGLAS '87	HUNSUCKER '88	INGERSOLL '88	JORDAN '88	RUTTER '89	SCHWORM/BIRNBAUM '89	SZATMARI/ETAL '89
A	Constantly beginning tasks	X								
A	Daydreams				X					
A	Difficulty following directions	X			X					
A	Difficulty following rules					X				
A	Disorganized	X			X		X			
A	Dissociation									
A	Distractible	X	X		X	X	X			X
A	Extremely organized				X					
A	Forgetfulness									
A	Inefficient attent.									
A	Loses materials				X	X				
A	Perseverates									
A	Poor concentration	X								
A	Short attention span	X	X	X	X		X		X	X
A	Short term memory				X		X			
C	Academic difficulty		X		X			X		
C	Cognitive immaturity									
C	Creative				X					
C	Fig.bckgrnd pathl'gy									
C	Intelligent				X			X		
C	Lower mean IQ									
C	No significant acad. difficulty									
C	Perceptual deficits									
C	Poor audit.proc's'ng		X		X					
C	Poor reader									
C	Underachiever									
C	Vis.-motor diffic.		X							
D	From small families							X		
H	Climbs excessively	X	X							
H	Dsn't remain in seat									
H	Excessive talking				X	X		X		
H	Fidgets w/hands/feet		X							
H	Has diffic. playing quietly									X
H	Hyperactive	X	X		X	X	X	X	X	X
H	Movement in sleep	X								

TABLE I
CHARACTERISTICS OF ATTENTION DEFICIT DISORDER BY DOMAIN

Domain	Characteristic	FEINGOLD '74	DSM. II '80	BARKLEY '81	BACON '82	D. COHEN, ET AL '81	NJ HEALTH '82	TXMHMR '82	BREN/BRKLY '83	N. COHEN/MINDE '83	GILBERG/T AL '83
I	Accident prone										
I	Blurts answers to ?'s		X								
I	Can't delay gratfctn										
I	Doesn't wait turn		X	X	X						
I	Engages in risky physical play										
I	Fails to follow through		X	X	X						
I	Greater suprvsn need		X	X	X						
I	Impulsive		X	X	X	X	X				
I	Interrupts others										
I	Poor foresight and planning										
I	Poor judgment										
P	Early sympton onset		X		X	X					
P	Immaturity								X		
P	Poor bladder control										
P	Poor muscle coord.	X				X					X
P	Six-month delay						X				
P	Language delay										
S	Demands attention										
S	Emotional problems								X		
S	Greater degree of questioning adults										
S	Insists on having own way										
S	Lack of compliance										
S	Lies easily										
S	Low frustration										
S	Low self-esteem								X		
S	Poor conduct			X							X
S	Poor social skills								X		
S	Short friendships										
T	Aggressive										
T	Irritable					X					
T	Meek; dosn't spk out										
T	Negative attitude			X							
T	Seems Depressed								X		
T	Stubborn										

TABLE I (continued)

Column header (vertical author/year labels):

```
                    G        T    D         K    M
                    O        R    Y         I    A              C
                    R        I    K         R    R              R
                    D        T    M         B    T              U
                    O        E    A         Y/   I              I
                    N/       S/   N         G    N/       B     C
                    M        L              R    M    S   O     K
D                   C    O   A    E    K    I    A    I   H     S
o                   L    W   P    T    I    M    R    L   L     H
m                   U    N   R    T    I    R    T    L   I     A
a                   R    B   A    A    G    L    I    V   I     N
i                   E    Y   DE   L    E    E    Y    E   N     E     K
n Characteristic    '83  '83 '83  '84  '84  '84  '84  '84 '85   '85
```

Domain	Characteristic	'83	'83	'83	'84	'84	'84	'84	'84	'85	'85
I	Accident prone										
I	Blurts answers to ?'s										
I	Can't delay gratfctn	X									
I	Doesn't wait turn										
I	Engages in risky physical play				X						
I	Fails to follow through		X	X	X				X		
I	Greater suprvsn need										
I	Impulsive	X	X	X	X	X	X	X	X		
I	Interrupts others										
I	Poor foresight and planning										
I	Poor judgment										
P	Early sympton onset										
P	Immaturity										
P	Poor bladder control										
P	Poor muscle coord.							X			X
P	Six-month delay										
P	Language delay										
S	Demands attention							X			
S	Emotional problems								X		
S	Greater degree of questioning adults										
S	Insists on having own way										
S	Lack of compliance										
S	Lies easily							X			
S	Low frustration							X			
S	Low self-esteem							X			
S	Poor conduct								X		
S	Poor social skills										
S	Short friendships							X			
T	Aggressive										
T	Irritable							X			
T	Meek; doesn't spk out										
T	Negative attitude										
T	Seems Depressed										
T	Stubborn									X	

TABLE I (continued)

Domain	Characteristic	LUFI & COHEN '85	MCGEE ET AL '85	PRIOR ET AL '85	BROWN/ GWYNNE '84	HOLBORT/ BERRY '86	RAPPORT ET AL '86	CROOK/ STEVENS '87	CUNNINGHAM/ SIEGEL '87	DSM-III(R) '87	KUEHN ET AL '87
I	Accident prone										
I	Blurts answers to ?'s										
I	Can't delay gratfctn					X				X	
I	Doesn't wait turn						X				
I	Engages in risky physical play									X	
I	Fails to follow through					X		X		X	
I	Greater suprvsn need						X				
I	Impulsive	X		X		X	X	X			X
I	Interrupts others									X	
I	Poor foresight and planning										X
I	Poor judgment										
P	Early sympton onset									X	
P	Immaturity										
P	Poor bladder control										
P	Poor muscle coord.					X					
P	Six-month delay										
P	Language delay										
S	Demands attention					X				X	
S	Emotional problems										
S	Greater degree of questioning adults			X		X					
S	Insists on having own way										
S	Lack of compliance										
S	Lies easily										
S	Low frustration					X	X				
S	Low self-esteem										
S	Poor conduct			X							
S	Poor social skills								X		
S	Short friendships										
T	Aggressive		X		X						
T	Irritable										
T	Meek; dosn't spk out										
T	Negative attitude										
T	Seems Depressed										
T	Stubborn										

TABLE I (continued)

Domain	Characteristic	SCOTT '87	WENDER '87	DOUGLAS '87	HUNSUCKER '88	INGERSOLL '88	JORDAN '88	ROUTER '89	SCHWORM/BIRNBAUM '89	SZATMARI/ETAL '89
I	Accident prone		X						X	
I	Blurts answers to ?'s									
I	Can't delay gratfctn			X					X	
I	Doesn't wait turn	X			X					X
I	Engages in risky physical play		X		X	X				
I	Fails to follow through	X	X		X	X	X		X	
I	Greater suprvsn need	X	X		X	X				
I	Impulsive	X		X	X		X	X		
I	Interrupts others									
I	Poor foresight and planning									
I	Poor judgment				X					
P	Early sympton onset	X	X		X			X		
P	Immaturity		X				X			
P	Poor bladder control		X							
P	Poor muscle coord.		X					X	X	
P	Six-month delay						X			
P	Language delay							X		
S	Demands attention		X		X	X				
S	Emotional problems						X			
S	Greater degree of questioning adults									
S	Insists on having own way						X			
S	Lack of compliance			X						
S	Lies easily									
S	Low frustration									X
S	Low self-esteem	X								
S	Poor conduct		X		X	X	X	X	X	
S	Poor social skills									
S	Short friendships									
T	Aggressive									
T	Irritable									
T	Meek; doesn't spk out				X					
T	Negative attitude					X				
T	Seems Depressed				X					
T	Stubborn		X		X					

A-Attentional   C=Cognitive/Academic   D-Demographic   H=Hypractve
I=Impulsive   P=Physical/Devlpmntl   S=Soc/Emotional   T=Tmperment

TABLE 2

CHARACTERISTICS OF ATTENTION DEFICIT DISORDER BY FREQUENCY CITED

Domain	Characteristics of ADD	Count	% of Total
A	Short attention span	32	82.05%
H	Hyperactive	29	74.36%
I	Impulsive	28	71.79%
A	Distractable	20	51.28%
I	Fails to follow through	15	38.46%
P	Poor muscle coordination	10	25.64%
S	Poor conduct	09	23.08%
A	Poor concentration	09	23.08%
P	Early onset of symptoms	09	23.08%
I	Greater need of supervision	08	20.51%
I	Doesn't wait turn	07	17.95%
A	Disorganized	06	15.38%
A	Difficulty following directions	05	12.82%
A	Constantly beginning task	05	12.82%
I	Engages in risky play	05	12.82%
S	Demands attention	05	12.82%
H	Climbs on things excessively	04	10.26%
H	Excessive talking	04	10.26%
H	Fidgets with hands/feet	04	10.26%
I	Can't delay gratification	04	10.26%
S	Low frustration level	04	10.26%
C	Academic difficulty	03	7.69%
A	Loses material	03	7.69%
C	Poor auditory processing	03	7.69%
A	Short-term memory	03	7.69%
H	Movements during sleep	03	7.69%
A	Difficulty following rules	03	7.69%
P	Immaturity	03	7.69%
S	Lack of compliance	03	7.69%
S	Poor social skills	03	7.69%
T	Aggressive	03	7.69%
S	Emotional problems	03	7.69%
S	Low self-esteem	03	7.69%
T	Seems depressed	03	7.69%
A	Daydreams	02	5.13%
A	Inefficient attention	02	5.13%C
C	Cognitive immaturity	02	5.13%
C	Visual-motor difficulty	02	5.13%
I	Accident prone	02	5.13%
H	Doesn't remain in seat	02	5.13%
A	Perseverates	02	5.13%
I	Blurts out answers to questions	02	5.13%
S	Lies easily	02	5.13%
I	Poor foresight and planning	02	5.13%
S	Greater degree questning adults	02	5.13%
S	Short-lived friendships	02	5.13%
T	Irritable	02	5.13%
T	Negative attitude	02	5.13%

TABLE 2 (continued)

CHARACTERISTICS OF ATTENTION DEFICIT DISORDER BY FREQUENCY CITED

Domain	Characteristics of ADD	Count	% of Total
T	Stubborn	02	5.13%
P	>Six-month delay	02	5.13%
A	Dissociation	01	2.56%
A	Extremely organized	01	2.56%
C	Figure-background pathology	01	2.56%
A	Forgetfulness	01	2.56%
C	No signfcnt acad. difficulty	01	2.56%
C	Perceptual deficits	01	2.56%
C	Poor reader	01	2.56%
C	Underachiever	01	2.56%
C	Creative	01	2.56%
C	Intelligent	01	2.56%
P	Language Delay	01	2.56%
C	Lower mean IQ	01	2.56%
D	Comes from small families	01	2.56%
P	Poor bladder control	01	2.56%
I	Interrupts others	01	2.56%
I	Poor judgment	01	2.56%
H	Has difficulty playing quietly	01	2.56%
S	Insistent on having own way	01	2.56%
T	Meek; doesn't speak out	01	2.56%

A-Attentional   C=Cognitive/Academic   D-Demographic   H=Hypractve
I=Impulsive   P=Physical/Devlpmntl   S=Soc/Emotional   T=Tmperment

1985; Breen & Barkley, 1983; Jordan, 1988; Wender, 1987), "forgetfulness" (Martin & Martin, 1984), and "accident proneness" (Rutter, 1989) are non-observable constructs and must be inferred from other behaviors or behavior patterns, which are not delineated by the authors.

Although some authors, such as Rutter (1989), stress the importance of assessing the degree of the ADD characteristic in context, this procedure relies on subjectivity in the differential diagnostic process. The subjectivity of these factors will affect reliability in a negative way.

CONTRADICTORY CHARACTERISTICS

A final concern is that more than 10% of the characteristics appear to contradict each other. For example, Cohen et al., (1981) cited "under-achievement" as a trait of children with ADD, whereas Kuehne et al., (1987) reported that these children have no significant academic difficulties. Hunsucker (1988) cited "normal intelligence" (p. 11) as an ADD characteristic, whereas Rutter (1989) described this population as having a "below average mean IQ" (p.7). Finally, four sources (APA, 1987; Hunsucker, 1988; Ingersoll, 1988; Schworm & Birnbaum, 1989) cited "excessive talking" as an identifying characteristic; however, Hunsucker (1988) argued that children with ADD can also be characterized by "meekness" and the "inability to speak out."

COMPARISONS OF CHILDREN WITH AND WITHOUT ADD

The authors whose works are summarized in Tables 1 and 2 have presented largely clinical descriptions that attempt to identify a range of characteristics associated with ADD. Some of these authors, as well as others, have all tried to verify specific ADD characteristics through empirical comparisons of children with ADD with other groups of children.

For example, Ackerman, Dykman, and Oglesby (1983) studied males and females in four comparison groups. These groups were labeled

(a) hyperactive
(b) reading disabled
(c) hyperactive and reading disabled, and
(d) attention disordered.

Significant gender differences were found in the areas of intelligence, achievement, personality, and cognitive styles. On average, the girls had lower IQs than the boys on the Wechsler Intelligence Scale for Children-Revised. The boys had higher reading-spelling scores and, with the exception of the nonhyperactive reading disabled students, higher arithmetic scores than the girls. The girls rated themselves less tolerant of intense stimuli but more tolerant of patient waiting. The boys rated themselves higher on self-control and willpower. Parents rated the boys more assertive-aggressive than the girls. In a measure of cognitive style, both genders had identical color-naming speeds, yet the boys' speeds were correlated with age, whereas the girls were not.

Ackerman, et al., concluded that because boys are more aggressive and sensation seeking, their behaviors are identified more often as being hyperactive than behaviors of girls. Other than gender differences, however, few differences were found for children in each comparison group. These results seem to indicate that, for at least the variables under consideration in this study, the characteristics of the child with ADD, or hyperactivity, cannot be distinguished from other youngsters with reading disabilities.

Similar conclusions can be drawn based on a study conducted by Copeland and Weissbrod (1983), who administered a series of tests to compare the cognitive styles of learning disabled (LD) children with hyperactivity and without hyperactivity, and non-learning disabled children without hyperactivity. On all but one task, the children with LD (whether or not hyperactive) used less mature strategies than the children who were nonhyperactive and non-learning disabled. Significant cognitive differences were not found between children with learning disabilities and those who were hyperactive and learning disabled. This indicates that, in general, the addition of a hyperactivity label to learning disabled children's problems cannot be reliably determined on the basis of their performance of the tasks under consideration.

Other research efforts have focused on characterizing an attention deficit by defining specific forms of attention, then observing the performance differences between children who are and are not hyperactive. According to Brown and Wynne (1984), young children who are hyperactive differ significantly from their peers who are not hyperactive in all areas of attention. Hyperactive adolescents appear to improve their ability to come to attention and to focus on salience, but remain significantly behind their nonhyperactive peers in sustaining attention and impulse control.

Other studies have produced either differing or contradictory results. Chee, Logan, Schachar, Lindsay, and Wachsmuth (1989) conducted two experiments to determine differences in the ability to sustain attention among three groups: boys with ADHD, boys with conduct disorders, and boys who served as normal controls. The poor performance of hyperactive children evidenced in Chee et. al.'s first experiment was not repeated in the second experiment. Results of the second study indicated that the waning of attention was apparent in all groups, and that the poor performance of the boys with ADHD suggested the possibility of practice as a variable.

In a study comparing hyperactive and normal children, Prior et al. (1985) found that the hyperactive group was not more distractible than the control group. They did not misfocus their attention to a greater extent than did the control group, and they sustained attention over a relatively long and concentrated task. In a more recent study, van der Meere, van Baal, and Sergeant (1989) compared the attention abilities of hyperactive and learning disabled children. They found that the hyperactive group did not show divided attention disturbance, but appeared to be delayed in their motor decision process.

Viewed collectively, these studies provide contradictory and confusing results. The ADD-type child was not shown to have significantly different characteristics from children with other handicapping conditions. The contradictory results contributed by studies examining attentional factors are particularly important because short attention span is the most frequently reported characteristic of the child with ADD. Yet, two studies indicate no significant difference between the children with ADD and the normal controls in terms of sustaining attention.

In a recent review of the literature involving children who are hyperactive, Houlihan and Van Houten (1989) highlighted the disagreement in defining the characteristics of these children. They stressed the need for researchers to isolate primary and secondary effects of this disorder. To date, researchers have not done so. It is unlikely, however, that such a ranking of primary and secondary effects would resolve validity issues until greater agreement exists among authorities concerning the causes of ADD, as well as what characteristics these children evidence and how a differential diagnosis can be reliably made.

CAUSES OF ADD

Presumed causes of ADD have generated almost as much professional interest as efforts to characterize the disorder. In fact, our review revealed 25 authors who have posited etiological factors. Their findings are summarized in Table 3. Even though fewer authors have addressed causative factors than characteristics, many of the same trends emerge.

NUMBER OF CAUSES

First, as with ADD characteristics, an extensive number of causes have been postulated to explain why ADD children evidence undesirable behavioral, social, and learning characteristics. Thirty-eight factors were cited by the 25 sources under review. Some authors, such as Feingold (1974), have promoted a particular theory. He believed that food allergies are at fault. To date, however, little empirical support for this position has been found. Werry (1988) also ascribed to a particular theory of causation. He wrote that there is an inborn temperamental predisposition that is genetically transferred. Although no one has isolated a specific gene that contributes to ADD, there is some evidence that ADD-type behaviors tend to reoccur in families (Barkley, 1981). Also, these behaviors are considerably more prevalent among low birth weight babies (Klein, 1988). Finally, there is support for lead toxicity causing hyperactivity (David, et al., 1977). Theories of other environmental sources of toxicity causing ADD are still speculative at this stage.

DIVERSITY OF CAUSES

The causes posited to explain ADD cover several diverse categories, with no apparent pattern of agreement. The three-step procedure described above for assigning characteristics to categorical domains was repeated with the list of 38 causes. Resulting categories include organic, intellectual/developmental, psychological, environmental, and birth complication factors. There is no clear preference for any of these among the authors cited. In fact, the number of causes attributed to these categories is fairly evenly distributed, with a majority (10) falling under the organic category and the fewest (3) assigned to the birth complication category. This is interesting in light of past history. Originally, children with learning disabilities were thought to be affected primarily by either organic or sensory deficits. After the extensive empirical investigations of the 1960's, however, little supporting evidence was uncovered to substantiate either of these causative factors. Subsequently, the diagnostic labels previously used to identify many of these children have been eliminated, while the organic etiology theory has gained momentum. With few exceptions, causes in both categories remain largely unsupported.

TABLE 3
CHARACTERISTICS OF ATTENTION DEFICIT DISORDER BY DOMAIN

Domain	Causes	FEINGOLD '74	DAVID '80	D. COHEN, ET AL '81	NI HEALTH '82	TX MHMR '81	COPELAND & WEISBROD '82	GILLBERG ET AL '82	OBRZUT & HYND '83	DYKMAN ET AL '83	MARTIN/MARTIN '83
B	Blood Incompatibility		X								
B	Low Birth Weight		X				X				
B	Perenatal/Prenatal problems		X		X	X	X	X			
E	Allergies	X									X
E	Classroom Teacher Techniques				X						
E	Diet; food additives	X			X	X					X
E	Ill-fitting underwear										X
E	Learned Behavior										X
E	Physical Environment (hot room)										X
E	Radiation leak from TV				X						
E	Reaction to sedatives										
E	Task difficulty and situational factors										
E	Toxicity (lead, toxic waste)				X	X					
E	Vitamin deficiencies				X						
E	Worms or fleas										
I	Auditory figure-ground deficit										X
I	Educational deficits				X	X					
I	Immature language development										X
I	Tactile/kinesthetic ground deficit										X
O	Biochemistry				X						
O	Brain abnormalities							X		X	
O	Brain damage		X								X
O	Genetics			X			X	X			
O	Inborn temperamental predisposition				X	X					
O	Physiological basis										
O	Lateralization										
O	Maturation delay						X				X
O	Meningitis		X								
O	Muscular tension										X
O	Neurodevelopmental immaturity			X			X	X	X		
O	Tactile defensiveness										X
O	Underlying central defect in self-regulation			X							
P	Anxiety										
P	Conduct disorders										
P	Frustration										
P	Low self-image										X
P	Personal space needs										X
P	Psycho/Social relationships				X	X	X				

TABLE 3 (CONTINUED)
CHARACTERISTICS OF ATTENTION DEFICIT DISORDER BY DOMAIN

Domain	Causes	SILVER '84	CRUICKSHANK '85	CROOK/ STEVENS '87	DSM III(R) '87	SCOTT '87	WENDER '87	DOUGLAS '88	HUNSUCKER '88	INGERSOLL '88	JORDAN '88
B	Blood Incompatibility										
B	Low Birth Weight						X				X
B	Perenatal/Prenatal problems	X				X	X			X	
E	Allergies		X								
E	Classroom Teacher Techniques										
E	Diet; food additives		X								
E	Ill-fitting underwear										
E	Learned Behavior										
E	Physical Environment (hot room)										
E	Radiation leak from TV										
E	Reaction to sedatives										
E	Task difficulty and situational factors										
E	Toxicity (lead, toxic waste)								X		
E	Vitamin deficiencies										
E	Worms or fleas										
I	Auditory figure-ground deficit										
I	Educational deficits										
I	Immature language development										
I	Tactile/kinesthetic ground deficit										
O	Biochemistry	X					X		X		X
O	Brain abnormalities	X		X							
O	Brain damage										
O	Genetics	X				X	X		X	X	X
O	Inborn temperamental predisposition			X			X				
O	Physiological basis					X					
O	Lateralization	X									
O	Maturation delay	X									
O	Meningitis										
O	Muscular tension										
O	Neurodevelopmental immaturity			X	X						
O	Tactile defensiveness										
O	Underlying central defect in self-regulation							X			
P	Anxiety										
P	Conduct disorders										
P	Frustration										
P	Low self-image										
P	Personal space needs										
P	Psycho/Social relationships			X							

TABLE 3 (CONTINUED)

CHARACTERISTICS OF ATTENTION DEFICIT DISORDER BY DOMAIN

Domain	Causes	KLEIN '88	WERRY '88	HOULIHAN & VAN HOUTEN '89	RUTTER '89	SCHWORM & BIRNBAUM '89
B	Blood Incompatibility					
B	Low Birth Weight	X				
B	Perenatal/Prenatal problems					
E	Allergies					
E	Classroom Teacher Techniques					
E	Diet; food additives			X		
E	Ill-fitting underwear					
E	Learned Behavior			X		
E	Physical Environment (hot room)					
E	Radiation leak from TV					
E	Reaction to sedatives			X		
E	Task difficulty and situational factors					X
E	Toxicity (lead, toxic waste)			X		
E	Vitamin deficiencies					
E	Worms or fleas					
I	Auditory figure-ground deficit					
I	Educational deficits					
I	Immature language development					
I	Tactile/kinesthetic ground deficit					
O	Biochemistry					
O	Brain abnormalities				X	
O	Brain damage					
O	Genetics	X	X			
O	Inborn temperamental predisposition	X				
O	Physiological basis					
O	Lateralization					
O	Maturation delay					
O	Meningitis					
O	Muscular tension					
O	Neurodevelopmental immaturity					
O	Tactile defensiveness					
O	Underlying central defect in self-regulation					X
P	Anxiety					X
P	Conduct disorders					X
P	Frustration					
P	Low self-image					
P	Personal space needs					
P	Psycho/Social relationships					

When considering the problem of number and diversity of presumed causes, one should pay special attention to the list postulated by Martin and Martin (1984). They cited a total of 15 causes, nine of which are not mentioned by any other author on our list. These causes include situational factors such as room temperature, low self-image, and muscular tension. Resulting from this particular focus, another category of "situational environmental etiology" could be assigned for consideration. With Martin and Martin's causative factors removed from the list, however, there are still 29 causes remaining, 13 of which are suggested by only one source. Of these 13, no more than four can be attributed to the same source (Schworm & Birnbaum, 1989). A total of six other sources have contributed to the list of characteristics that are supported by only one author. Thus, even when the list is controlled for the numerous factors contributed by Martin and Martin, an extensive list of possible causes remains, and there is still little general agreement about what causes ADD.

LACK OF AGREEMENT

Only one presumed cause—genetics—is cited by almost half the authors (48%) as a cause of ADD. Only an additional two causes are cited by more than one-fourth of the authors (perinatal/prenatal problems, 36%; neurodevelopmental immaturity, 28%). More than half the causes mentioned were included in only one source.

LACK OF EMPIRICAL VALIDATION

A final problem with respect to the causes of ADD is related to the difficulty of empirically validating cause-effect relationships. Just as it is unlikely that one disorder can produce 69 largely unrelated or oppositional characteristics, it is equally unlikely that all the causes on this lengthy list are responsible for causing the same disorder. Unfortunately, there is little empirical validation for any of these theories of causation.

Most of the causes identified empirically have been based on correlational studies. One exception is the identification of lead toxicity as a potential cause of hyperactive behavior. David, et al. (1977) identified lead toxicity as a cause of hyperactive behavior by analyzing the urine samples of children diagnosed as hyperactive. The degree of exposure to lead required for the disorder is unknown, however. Also unknown is the percentage of children exposed who ultimately manifest any ADD characteristics.

CONCLUSION

Thirty-nine documents addressing hypothesized characteristics of children with attention deficit disorder were reviewed for this paper. Collectively, documents attribute 69 different characteristics to children labeled

ADD. Little agreement was found among authors regarding these characteristics. Many of the characteristics were subjective in nature and, at times, contradictory. The characteristics were also diverse in nature emanating from eight different domains. Several studies comparing the characteristics of children labeled ADD to the characteristics of other children were also reviewed. These studies have produced confusing and contradictory results. Children labeled ADD were not found to have characteristics different from those of children with other handicapping conditions. Studies examining attentional factors failed to find significant differences between children with and without ADD. In addition to documents addressing characteristics of children labeled ADD, we reviewed 25 papers that address possible causes of ADD. Authors of these works attributed the disorder to 38 possible causes. Independent reviewers assigned the characteristics to five different domains. Little agreement was found among authors regarding the numerous and diverse causes addressed, and little empirical validation was found to support any of the causes.

Because of the uncertainty of the nature of ADD, the label has limited value for the purpose of communication, planning, and decision making among educators. It does not offer professionals the advantages of other diagnostic labels. Children labeled ADD do not appear to have a commonly agreed upon set of characteristics or symptoms. Authorities in the field have discrepant views of not only who these children are, but what causes their apparent variance from the general population. In fact, from the list of potential characteristics reviewed here, it is possible that two professionals could refer to a child as having ADD, and have opposite profiles in mind. Two professionals could also observe the same child and make different diagnoses. As such, the ADD acronym offers little in the way of delineating clear and appropriate methods for classifying children's behavior. Because of these reliability and validity issues, the ADD label contributes little to the interpretation and implementation of research findings. In fact, some of these problems in determining causes and characteristics of ADD could also be responsible for the fact that little is known about educational treatments that improve the performance of these children.

IMPLICATIONS FOR RESEARCH IN ADD

Many of the reliability and validity problems discussed above have implications for research on children with ADD. If researchers cannot make valid assumptions about who merits an ADD label and are unable to measure the inclusion criteria reliably, it is impossible to generate and test hypotheses related to what causes this disorder and how to prevent or treat it. Ascertaining the reliability and validity of the constructs under consideration is, in fact, central to making any statistical inferences related to the disorder.

There are additional research-related problems. One is the difficulty obtaining a legitimate sample population of children with ADD. As the number of characteristics and symptoms has increased, it has become progressively easier for children who are increasingly diverse in characteristics to receive the ADD label. It is unlikely that they are affected by a common cause. Assessing the impact of any independent variable, whether it is to determine causation or an effective treatment, becomes difficult.

Another problem with research efforts in this area involves the tautological nature of the diagnosis of this condition. The rationale for ADD diagnoses flows from observation of symptoms, to inference of condition, then to validation of condition by observation of symptoms. The question in education is "Why does Johnny fail to pay attention, complete his work, stay in his seat, and so forth?" The answer is "Because he has an attention deficit disorder." "How do you know he has ADD?" "Because he doesn't pay attention, complete his work, stay in his seat, and so on." Tautological theories are almost impossible to validate empirically because the diagnosis depends on the symptoms, and vice versa.

The problem in researching the ADD label are reminiscent of the research problems encountered in the 1960's with the MBI and MBD labels. A proliferation of symptoms, or characteristics, was attached to the label, but no cause-effect relationship was ever established between symptoms and brain injury/dysfunction. Research efforts proved futile, and the terminology gave way to the learning disability label. The learning disability label seems to be suffering a similar fate. If a child is of normal intelligence and below grade level in school achievement, he or she can be labeled LD with any number of secondary characteristics diagnosed. Still no cause-effect relationship has been established, and few other characteristics or symptoms have been validated. As professionals have become disenchanted with the term, they are turning increasingly to ADD as an explanation of the wide variety of children's problems in school. If reliability and validity issues are not resolved for ADD, it will be impossible to study this diagnosis empirically. Without specific characteristics and causes identified for this disorder, ADD may share the same fate as MBI, MBD, and LD. As a result, the children who are identified as having this disorder will fall victim to the ineffective cycles and spirals in America's educational system.

MALE ORDER

By G. Pascal Zachary
Staff Reporter of *The Wall Street Journal*

Boys Used to Be Boys,
But Do Some Now See
Boyhood as a Malady?

Marty Wolt, a Quirky Kid, Resisted 'Sick' Tag,
Yet Pressure to Label Is Huge

The Gender-Equity Factor

FORT MYERS, Fla.—Marty Wolt's teacher at the Three Oaks Elementary School here will never forget him.

A transfer from Tampa, Marty entered third grade, a scrawny brown-haired boy with a quizzical look and a feverish imagination. He annoyed fellow students by following them, pad and pencil in hand, jotting down their every word. He overheard Carol Cebak, his teacher, tell another teacher she was pregnant and blabbed it to the whole world. He led a class strike over a math assignment, persuading 25 other kids to repeatedly shout, "No pay, no work!"

Ms. Cebak says she wasn't amused. She summoned Marty's mother to the school and told her that he probably had a mental disorder and should be medicated. If her son didn't shape up, she warned, he might end up in a special-education class. "I always thought Marty had ADD," says Ms. Cebak, referring to the most common diagnosis for childhood misbehavior, attention-deficit disorder.

Marty's mother, Beth Wolt, disagreed. Marty's "disease," in her opinion, was that he was a boy—rambunctious, bright and bored with school. Convinced that her son's eccentricities didn't make him sick, she girded for a fight.

Ms. Wolt's struggle, in fact, is being waged by many other parents

357

who, along with a growing number of educators, pose a troubling question: Is boyhood being pathologized? Have schools and other institutions become so fixated with the order and labels that what used to be considered ordinary boyhood traits are now thought of as abnormal or deviant?

Consider that the number of U.S. children classified as disabled is skyrocketing: In 1985, a record 5.4 million were so identified, nearly one-quarter more than 10 years ago. Of these disabilities, ADD is the fastest growing, with the ranks nearly doubling over the past five years. Boys, by most estimates, make up 80% to 90% of all ADD cases.

Including ADD, more than 70% of these children labeled as disabled have no clear condition such as mental retardation. Instead, they exhibit a grab bag of "learning disabilities" or "speech and language impairments." A child who ignores directions, for instance, may be diagnosed as having an "auditory processing" deficit, even though his hearing is fine.

It isn't that such diagnoses aren't often useful or real. But critics object to the phalanx of teachers, counselors, and administrators who insist on the medical diagnoses or clinical classifications when boys refuse to nap, sit still, fail to fulfill their ill-defined potential, scrap with their peers or otherwise defy authority.

In viewing these traits as disabilities, schools "have pathologized what is simply normal for boys," says Diane McGuinness, a University of South Florida psychology professor. Adds Michael Gurian, a therapist in Spokane, Wash., and the author of a book on the virtues of boys, "The country is making the argument, without often realizing it, that boyhood is defective."

What is certain is that teachers, counselors, administrators and even parents have incentives to label—or mislabel—boys who, in prior times, would just be considered overly active, eccentric, dreamy or in need of adult attention. Many teachers face crowded classrooms, and pressures by gender-equity advocates to make schools "fairer" for girls, a goal that some say inevitably has meant a crackdown on "boyish" behavior. One example: the expulsion last year of a six-year-old North Carolina boy for sexual harassment for kissing a female classmate.

Schools stress order, and boys are less likely than girls to sit still, follow directions, and think and act cogently. On top of that, parents are often too busy, or too bewildered or guilt-ridden by the insistence of school authorities that their sons are disabled, to resist these labels. Ms. Wolt and others, for example, note that it is typical for schools to use a tag-team approach: teachers, counselors, administrators, maybe even psychologists, all gathered around a parent to press a disability designation.

"What is the likelihood that any given mother or father will hold out against this horde?" asks Denis Donovan, a child psychiatrist in St. Petersburg, Fla. "It's close to zero."

Those who doubt such pressures are real should also consider this: ~gh schools don't like to talk about it, they get a $420 federal bounty for each student labeled "disabled," a bonus some think is at least partly responsible for the recent disabilities bulge. Even the U.S. Department of Education, which promotes screening through federal subsidies, concedes that practice has gone too far. "We've had a problem with overidentification," spokesman Jim Bradshaw says.

Real Problems

No one suggests that schools aren't vexed by an increase in violent or antisocial behavior, or that there aren't disturbed or disabled boys and girls who benefit from screening, counseling and medical help. Mary Ellen Byrnes, a Santa Rosa, Calif., mother, for example, initially resisted an ADD diagnosis of her son Michael, who had chronic public temper tantrums. She later relented and put her son on medication. "Now at home he is a gem," she says. Many other parents, seeing their children flounder in their studies or having problems with their peers, insist upon a disability designation in order to get special attention for them. And teachers—citing a decline in disciplinary standards among students and school rules that limit how they can mete out discipline—often see a disability diagnosis as the most effective way of getting treatment for students who prove disruptive to the rest of the class.

Moreover, labels have always been associated with boys and unruly behavior, says Bernard Cahan, an Atlanta child psychiatrist. ADD, he says, merely reflects a more scientific approach, allowing educators and parents to formulate ways to "remediate" unproductive behaviors.

Tough Judgments

Many, however, are convinced this pendulum has swung too far; that boys who often need no more than understanding or patience are being tagged with labels that could haunt them for the rest of their lives. In a growing number of states, notably Maryland, Pennsylvania and Iowa, schools have launched programs to help teachers better handle difficult children without labeling them as disabled.

The mania for labeling persists, though, spawning difficult situations for some parents. Last year, Keegan Smith, a six-year-old in Largo, Fla., received a 54-minute "timeout" after he bent a fork at lunch. The school, says his mother Amy, threatened to evaluate the boy for disabilities. Ms. Smith resisted and Keegan's own defense rang true. "I saw other kids doing it," he says. "I thought it was cool."

If cool is risky, so is daydreaming. In an Oregon town, another mother last year attended what she thought was a routine teacher's conference. Instead, she was greeted by six people, including a psychologist and the principal. They accused her son of looking out the window too much and making "limited eye contact" with others. "I was aghast, in shock," recalls the mother, who wished not to be identified. "They started using strange words. They wanted my son tested for autism!" The mother refused.

Marty's Trials

Nobody knows of this pressure and anguish more than 37-year-old Beth Wolt. Her son Marty was a handful almost from birth. At nine months, he took his crib apart. His first two years, he never slept through the night, and he developed into a nonstop talker and doer. One night, at age three, he threw all of his toys out of his bedroom window.

Those were Marty's salad days. His troubles really began in nursery school, at age four. He lasted just a week in his first school. Ms. Wolt pulled him out when his teacher, tired of listening to his chatter, threatened to shut his mouth with masking tape. Marty left a second school after a week on the heels of charges that he annoyed other kids and refused to nap.

At this point, Ms. Wolt faced her first crisis. She found a third nursery school and, rather than take any chances, quit her job as a bank teller and went to work as an aide in her son's classroom. This helped. Ms. Wolt allowed Marty to skip naps and go shopping with the school cook. In the store, he would run up and down the aisles, letting off steam.

Troubled Move

The next year, Marty went to kindergarten in Frisco, Texas, where the Wolts then lived, and things went well. But when the Wolts moved to Tampa, Fla., Marty's new teacher immediately concluded that he suffered from attention deficit disorder and insisted he take Ritalin, a drug meant to focus his attention. She vowed to make him wear a diaper in class if he didn't stop acting like a baby. She told Ms. Wolt, "I can't deal with him."

Though hurt, Ms. Wolt took the teacher's complaints seriously; after all he could drive her to distraction as well. He had a habit of waking her up in the middle of the night to share his latest tall tale. She had only stopped the practice by giving Marty a tape recorder and promising to listen to his recordings the next morning.

Fearing his expulsion from regular classes, she took him to a pediatrician, who also advised Ritalin. Ms. Wolt resisted and took her son to a neurologist in search of hard evidence of attention-deficit disorder. The neurologist subjected Marty to two tests over three months. No abnormalities were found, though psychiatrists say absence of physical abnormalities doesn't rule out the presence of ADD. Despite the results, Ms. Wolt's resolve wavered. Married not long after high school, she now wanted to go ~ollege full time. She couldn't do that while baby-sitting her son. Maybe ~perts were right. Caving in, she put Marty on Ritalin, told his teacher ~d. Within a week she noted disturbing changes. "I missed him," she says. "He wasn't there. He did everything he was supposed to do. But his personality was gone. He'd cry at the drop of a hat."

After a month, she dropped the medication, but never told Marty's teacher. Her son's problems at school eased, perhaps because his teacher thought she had a fresh start with him. By year end, his grades were A's and B's; his teacher wrote Ms. Wolt gushing notes of praise.

Resisting a Label

Marty continued to do well the next year, in second grade. Taking no chances, Ms. Wolt, holding off her education, volunteered at his school nearly everyday. Then came third grade and a blow up with Carol Cebak, Marty's pregnant teacher at Three Oaks Elementary School. When Ms. Cebak pushed a disability label, Ms. Wolt pushed back. As a compromise, the school asked its guidance counselor, Barbara Lyons, to help. She got Ms. Cebak to adjust class assignments to better hold Marty's attention and, citing his high IQ score of 132, put him in a class for advanced students one day a week.

Perhaps most importantly, Ms. Lyons met with Marty daily, rewarding him with stickers and praise. She also listened, which meant a lot to Marty, who had come to regard many adults as oddly opaque. "She heard me," he said. "I like it when somebody is listening. Who doesn't?"

Ms. Wolt did her part too. She examined herself, coming to accept complaints by her husband, Marty Sr., that she coddled Marty. Recognizing that "some of his reasoning seemed crazy," she reined him in. To settle disputes, she held mock trials during which he made his case for being treated unfairly at school or at home. Then, weighing the evidence, she would make her ruling. Usually, Marty accepted the verdict.

Feeling alone in her trials, Ms. Wolt formed a support group for parents of troubled kids at the school. Rather than resent Ms. Cebak, she gave her steady encouragement and permission to touch Marty to help get his attention. When the school year ended, she gave Ms. Cebak a T-shirt that said: "I survived Marty!"

The momentum carried over to fourth grade. Marty won school math and science awards, exchanged letters with a U.S. senator about environmental protection and even surrendered his Nintendo player when his mother thought it hurt his studies. At the end of the school year, Marty's teacher wrote him, "You've had the best school year of your life, both academically and behaviorally." Ms. Wolt felt good enough to finally start college.

More Setbacks

Then came more setbacks. In fifth grade, Marty drew complaints at school for being disruptive. Ms. Wolt responded swiftly to Marty's latest flap. She moved into his classroom for a full three weeks, sitting next to her son. "I didn't like it," he says. But he calmed down.

Marty moved to middle school for sixth grade. He struggled academically and his quirkiness dogged him. The school guidance counselor repeatedly told him that he should ask his mom for Ritalin. At first Marty shot back that the counselor was wasting his time. But, controlling his temper, he began to learn "not to listen to other people when I hear what I don't like." The next time his counselor extolled Ritalin, Marty just laughed.

Ms. Wolt was less philosophical. After a half dozen of such episodes, she burst into his office unannounced, threatening him with a lawsuit if he talked to her son again. The conversations stopped.

A small, soft-spoken woman, Ms. Wolt has a fierce gaze but is polite and hardly intimidating. Her attack on school experts surprised her and at the time she wondered if she was mistaken. Maybe her son needed more than rules and understanding. "You lay awake at night," she says, "thinking, 'My God, please let me be right.'"

Growing Up

High school finally began to bring what Ms. Wolt had hoped for: vindication. Marty seemed largely to have outgrown his disruptive boyish behavior; his conflicts with teachers all but stopped.

Now 17, and in the 11th grade, he is taking college-prep courses and has shown himself capable, despite a lapse here and there, of making good grades in courses that interest him. He writes screenplays as a hobby and works 20 hours a week at Pizza Hut. He gets himself to school on his own and, despite keeping late hours, is rarely tardy for class.

His third grade teacher, Ms. Cebak, says she still thinks "he would have adjusted better with medication." But his grade school guidance counselor, Ms. Lyons, says Marty suffered as a child from little more than a lack of self-discipline and an overactive imagination.

The adults who deal with Marty at Estrero High School side with Ms. Lyons, basing their views on how he behaves now. "I'm a real believer in not labeling students," says Fred Bose, the school's principal. "Some students have to be judged a little differently."

The last in the line of Marty's guidance counselors, Toni Rhodes, adds: "I like Marty. He's very funny. He is not afraid to stand up for his opinions."

Marty remains something of a cutup and a rebel. He knows he is different: "I try to be," he says. "Otherwise, how is someone going to know it's me?" He thinks its wrong to penalize a person for that and won't for-
ᵉ those who tried to brand him as sick. "I turned out OK," he says.

As for adults, Marty still sees, and laughs about, their follies. In one
ᵉenplays, loosely based on his own experience, a teacher stead-

fastly ignores requests for help from students, symbolizing the school's heartlessness toward those with problems. At work at Pizza Hut, he fields a call from an adult who insists on knowing the exact size of the chopped onions the restaurant uses in its sauce. Resisting a snide remark, he puts the caller on hold, for a long time. Later, his mother, watching him tossing pizza dough and wisecracking with an older dishwasher, shakes her head, amazed at how he kept his spirit. "They never crushed him," she says.

ACKNOWLEDGMENTS

Many people have more than generously assisted us along the way in the preparation of this work. We would especially like to acknowledge our colleagues at the University of Houston, Cheri Jones, Kimberly Wristers, Karen Snead, and Barbara Korth. We would also like to thank Dr. Dennis L. Morrison, of the University of Houston and San Jacinto College South for his guidance and patience throughout the preparation of this publication. A special thanks goes to Ms. Sharon Brener of the DePelchin Children's Center in Houston for her understanding and support. We would also like to thank our family members, Carol Liberman and Glenn Laird, for their love, help, and understanding. To all of these individuals we owe a great debt.

Dov Liberman and Helen M. Gore-Laird